AF832088

Selected Essays on Economic Policy

Also by G.C. Harcourt

A 'SECOND EDITION' OF *THE GENERAL THEORY* (*two volumes, edited with P.A. Riach*)

CAPITAL AND GROWTH: Selected Readings (*edited with N.F. Laing*)

CAPITALISM, SOCIALISM AND POST-KEYNESIANISM: Selected Essays of G.C. Harcourt

CONTROVERSIES IN POLITICAL ECONOMY: Selected Essays of G.C. Harcourt

ECONOMIC ACTIVITY (*with P.H. Karmel and R.H. Wallace*)

KEYNES AND HIS CONTEMPORARIES: The Sixth and Centennial Keynes Seminar held in the University of Kent at Canterbury (*editor*)

INCOME AND EMPLOYMENT IN THEORY AND PRACTICE: Essays in Memory of Athanasios Asimakopulos (*edited with Alessandro Roncaglia and Robin Rowley*)

INTERNATIONAL MONETARY PROBLEMS AND SUPPLY-SIDE ECONOMICS: Essays in Honour of Lorie Tarshis (*edited with Jon Cohen*)

ON POLITICAL ECONOMISTS AND MODERN POLITICAL ECONOMY: Selected Essays of G.C. Harcourt (*edited by Claudio Sardoni*)

POST-KEYNESIAN ESSAYS IN BIOGRAPHY: Portraits of Twentieth-Century Political Economists

READINGS IN THE CONCEPT AND MEASUREMENT OF INCOME (*edited with R.H. Parker*)

READINGS IN THE CONCEPT AND MEASUREMENT OF INCOME: Second Edition (*edited with R.H. Parker and G. Whittington*)

SOME CAMBRIDGE CONTROVERSIES IN THE THEORY OF CAPITAL

THE DYNAMICS OF THE WEALTH OF NATIONS: Growth, Distribution and Structural Change – Essays in Honour of Luigi Pasinetti (*edited with Mauro Baranzini*)

THE MICROECONOMIC FOUNDATIONS OF MACROECONOMICS (*editor*)

THEORETICAL CONTROVERSY AND SOCIAL SIGNIFICANCE: An Evaluation of the Cambridge Controversies

THE SOCIAL SCIENCE IMPERIALISTS: Selected Essays of G.C. Harcourt (*edited by Prue Kerr*)

50 YEARS A KEYNESIAN AND OTHER ESSAYS

Selected Essays on Economic Policy

G.C. Harcourt
Emeritus Reader in the History of Economic Theory
Emeritus Fellow
Jesus College, Cambridge, and
Professor Emeritus
University of Adelaide

palgrave

© G.C. Harcourt 2001
For details of original publication of papers in this book, please see pp. xiv–xvi.

All rights reserved. No reproduction, copy or transmission of this publication may be made without written permission.

No paragraph of this publication may be reproduced, copied or transmitted save with written permission or in accordance with the provisions of the Copyright, Designs and Patents Act 1988, or under the terms of any licence permitting limited copying issued by the Copyright Licensing Agency, 90 Tottenham Court Road, London W1P 0LP.

Any person who does any unauthorised act in relation to this publication may be liable to criminal prosecution and civil claims for damages.

The author has asserted his right to be identified as the author of this work in accordance with the Copyright, Designs and Patents Act 1988.

First published 2001 by
PALGRAVE
Houndmills, Basingstoke, Hampshire RG21 6XS and
175 Fifth Avenue, New York, N. Y. 10010
Companies and representatives throughout the world

PALGRAVE is the new global academic imprint of St. Martin's Press LLC Scholarly and Reference Division and Palgrave Publishers Ltd (formerly Macmillan Press Ltd).

ISBN 0–333–94632–4

This book is printed on paper suitable for recycling and made from fully managed and sustained forest sources.

A catalogue record for this book is available from the British Library.

Library of Congress Cataloging-in-Publication Data
Harcourt, G. C., 1931–
Selected essays on economic policy / G.C. Harcourt.
p. cm.
Includes bibliographical references and index.
ISBN 0–333–94632–4 (cloth)
1. Australia—Economic policy. 2. Finance, Public—Australia. 3. Economic policy. 4. Finance, Public. I. Title.

HC605 .H288 2000
338.994—dc21

00–042181

10 9 8 7 6 5 4 3 2 1
10 09 08 07 06 05 04 03 02 01

Printed and bound in Great Britain by
Antony Rowe Ltd, Chippenham, Wiltshire

Contents

Foreword

It is a real pleasure to be able to write this Foreword to Geoff Harcourt's latest selection of essays as this gives me a chance to pay tribute to a distinguished colleague who also happens to be an old and valued friend. The fact that the essays deal with a wide range of policy issues – something that has been at the centre of my own work, both academic and in various advisory capacities – makes this pleasant task also professionally rewarding.

I met Geoff in the mid-1960s when, soon after leaving university, I joined the Faculty of Economics and Politics in Cambridge. On my first morning in the Faculty there was a knock on the door. Geoff walked in, introduced himself and we chatted about what I had done (which up to that point was not much) and what I intended to do (which, in retrospect, was undoubtedly too much). With an American economist with whom I was sharing the room in the Faculty I joined him later for coffee in the Senior Common Room. We had hardly entered the Room before he started to introduce us to a number of the extraordinary assembly of economists who were teaching in Cambridge at the time. Thanks to Geoff I managed to meet over the next few days most members of the Faculty.

There was, in fact, nothing new or unusual in this. Among Geoff's many contributions to academic and social life in Cambridge has been his ability to ensure that the visitors and newcomers to the Faculty – especially those at the beginning of their career – are absorbed quickly into the community. Many of these young economists went on to become eminent both nationally and, in quite a few cases, internationally. I doubt that anyone in the University appreciates fully the important role that Geoff has played, by befriending many of them, in promoting unconsciously the goodwill and affection towards the Faculty and Cambridge in general around the world. The same applies also to many students, undergraduates and postgraduates who have flocked regularly in large numbers to his lectures or, in many cases, to ask him for help in their work and for advice in planning their career.

That is another valuable function that he has performed unofficially over the years. I cannot think of anyone who has been consulted in my time in Cambridge as much about both academic and non-academic matters as Geoff. The reason for this is not difficult to find. He belongs to that almost extinct of species: a very busy, extremely hard-working academic who always finds time to help young colleagues and students and takes genuine pleasure, and almost parental pride, in their success. The door to his room was always open. Anyone could drop in, and virtually everyone associated with the Faculty did: young and not so young, research students and some of the most distinguished economists in the world. I cannot remember a single occasion, either in the 1960s or since we both returned to Cambridge in the 1980s, when he could not find time to stop whatever he was doing and discuss my own work, or some other matter that I had come to see him about.

In retrospect, I hope that we have not wasted too much of his time. But although he and I have rarely worked in the same area of the subject I have always found these discussions stimulating. Unlike so many economists these days Geoff has an unusually wide range of interests and contacts. It is still a mystery to those of us who have known him for a long time where he manages to find all that energy to follow so closely developments in so many different fields of economics. His own publications include contributions to economic theory, history of economic theory, intellectual biography, applied economics and economic policy. As a result, he is frequently able to suggest some recent publication in one's own field that one is not aware of, or provide information about someone who is engaged in a closely related field of research.

Not surprisingly, Geoff commands both respect from his peers for his professional achievements and affection from those who know him and admire his personal qualities of kindness, generosity, genuine interest in the welfare of others, modesty and a sense of humour. This explains also why he managed to pull off something that few people would have thought possible at the time: analyse the often bad-tempered debates on capital theory within and between the two Cambridges (UK and Massachusetts) in the 1960s (G. C. Harcourt, (1972), *Some Cambridge Controversies in the Theory of Capital,* Cambridge University Press) without attracting the wrath from the warring camps! On the contrary, his efforts met with general praise.

Yet, in spite of such a successful plunge into 'high scholasticism' of a kind more appropriate to the Cambridge of the Middle Ages than to Cambridge in the closing decades of the twentieth century, Geoff cared too deeply about the economic and social consequences of the crises and stagflation of the 1970s to waste his time on obscure points of economic theory. For someone who, as he points out in the Preface to this volume, 'always regarded the *raison d'être* of our profession as helping to influence and make policy', the time had come to become more involved directly in some of the most important issues of the day.

As a result, most of his essays on economic policy – all of which are included in this volume – have been written and published since 1970. They reflect his concerns as well as his wide range of interests: economic and social consequences of inflation; unemployment and growth; some systemic issues that arise under capitalism, socialism and in a mixed economy; social limits to growth; and, appropriately in conditions of global economic interdependence, a 'modest plan' to save the world from the speculators. As someone who, rightly, believes that collective problems require collective coordination and action to solve them, his analysis and policy prescriptions are close to those of Keynes, Kalecki, Kaldor and his Australian mentor and great friend Eric Russell – the economists that he admires most. The task of economists is to help government design and pursue policies that reflect 'the general will' of the governed.

I look forward, therefore, to writing, if not the Foreword, at least a review of his next volume of essays on economic policy, dealing with some of the burning issues at the beginning of the twenty-first century.

Cambridge MIĆA PANIĆ

Preface

The present selection of essays contains virtually all my writings on policy from the earliest times to the present day. Occasional minor amendments have been made to provide consistency of book style. I was a bit shocked to find there were only 24 (out of, to date, a total of over 160 papers) for I have always regarded the *raison d'être* of our profession as helping to influence and to make policy. Of course, this may be done directly by proposing specific policies, following analysis of the issues which give rise to them; or, indirectly, through theoretical and applied work, or by examining what others, greats past and present, have done. So following this rather lame excuse, let me summarise the contents of the volume.

I start with an essay (originally published in the 1998 symposium in *Economic Issues* on the contemporary relevance of post-Keynesian economics) on the links between my evolving structures of thought about economics and the policy proposals I have made over the past 40 years or more. In Part II are four essays which set the background to my policy recommendations. In the first essay I tease out from the findings of the controversies in capital theory, their significance for policy. In the second essay I discuss the approach to theory and policy of my greatest Australian mentor and friend, the late Eric Russell, who died in 1977. I first met Eric in 1958 when I took up a lecturing post at Adelaide. He was a major influence on my thinking from then on. He remains my guide to attitudes to policy-making and the strengths and limitations of economic theory – and economists.

The next two essays contain my thinking on the links between theory, policy and politics at the end of the 1970s. The first of them is a contribution to the *Festschrift* for Wilfred Prest who was the Professor at Melbourne when I was an undergraduate in the 1950s. The second, written with Prue Kerr, sets out the background to the ideas on economic policy that I subsequently fed into the Australian Labor Party's (ALP) National Committee of Inquiry in 1978–79. The four essays make it easier to see where I come from as far as making policy is concerned.

In Part III I jump backwards to three papers that I wrote soon after I finished my PhD in 1959. They show that I had absorbed Marx's injunction 'Accumulate, accumulate, that is Moses and the prophets!' and was thinking about schemes to keep the process going! I believe that the two papers on investment allowances still make sense but that the paper with Jim Bennett on 'Taxation and Business Surplus' (1960) is a complete muddle. Jim had just returned from the other Cambridge (MIT) and our joint effort is a real hotch-potch of incompatible approaches – my fault, not Jim's, he was always consistently an MIT person. The fourth paper, written in my last year at Cambridge as a young don before I returned to Adelaide, is, I think, a good example of how useful the post-Keynesian approach can be to economic issues. It is the high-water mark of my writings as far as the use of squiggles is concerned. Yet I was soon able to reproduce the essence of its contribution in a very simple diagram which only involved a 45° line and a number of concave to the origin curves (see Harcourt, 1972: 64).

Part IV, accounting conventions and policy, contains my first-ever single-authored article. I wrote it while a research student at Cambridge and presented it to the research students seminar presided over by Piero Sraffa. It was concerned with what happened to tax payments by different companies if company incomes for tax purposes were estimated by using replacement rather than historical costs. Piero nearly stopped me and my paper dead in our tracks when, early on in the presentation, I compared aggregate depreciation allowances at historical cost in the UK with their capital consumption at replacement cost. He asked: 'why should anyone ever want to compare them?!' The other two papers spell out the implications for policy in the UK and the USSR (as it then was) of the findings of 'The Accountant in a Golden Age' (Harcourt, 1965; Sardoni, 1992). In the first essay, I tried to relate the effect of mis-measurement of 'true' profits by accountants on the acceptance of an incomes policy by both sides of the class war in the UK. I fear I emerged more on the side of capital than labour in the discussion, almost New Labour, 30 years ahead of its time. In the other paper I discuss the wrong signals, as far as the choice of technique is concerned, of the particular forms of the, then in vogue, bonus scheme for managers in the Soviet Union.

The subject matter of Part V is package Deals. Some of them relate to what I would like to have seen, had there been a power in government which I supported; others were designed within the constraints imposed by governments in power which I did not support. Thus the first two essays, and especially the second, contain policies within the latter category. In 'The Social Consequences of Inflation' I include a description of the so-called Adelaide Plan that Eric Russell, Barry Hughes, Philip Bentley and I put together in the early 1970s. The third essay in the section, 'Making Socialism in Your Own Country' was my swan song to Australia before I returned to Cambridge in 1982, just before the ALP was elected and Bob Hawke became prime minister. A little of what I proposed actually was implemented but I would not push a process of cause and effect *too* hard. The next four papers are complementary to one another: my ideas on package deals of policy in and for the 1990s. There is a considerable overlap with those suggested in previous decades – after all, Marx and Keynes would have had no trouble in interpreting the last 20 to 30 years within their frameworks of reference – but I have tried to move with the times as internationalisation of markets has spread and the dominance of industrial and commercial capital by financial capital has become much more pronounced. So much so that I generalised the Tobin tax without at the time being aware of its existence.

The last part contains general essays on policy. It starts with a suggestion for the payment of prisoners made when I was Secretary of the Howard League for Penal Reform in South Australia in the early 1960s. It shows what the application of simple economic theory may do for social policy. The next essay was inspired by Fred Hirsch's *Social Limits to Growth* (1977). I think his book and my essay have some essential ideas for those who wish to create a just and equitable society. 'University Ideals and the Market', a genuine cry from the heart for the preservation of the sorts of ideals that prevailed when I was an undergraduate in the 1950s, seems to me even more pertinent and relevant now than when it was originally written, especially in Australia. The final two essays celebrate a number of great economists and their views on policy. Alas, Colin Clark and Nicky Kaldor are dead – but not their ideas; nor are Joe Stiglitz and John Cornwall who were much influenced by Kaldor in particular, as I was too.

Personal acknowledgements

As in the companion volume to this selection, Harcourt (2001), I want to express my heartfelt thanks to Tim Farmiloe for making publication possible; Micá Panić, not only for his generous foreword but also for the many years of friendship and inspiration; Susan Cross for her great support and help in getting the manuscript ready; and last but never least, Joan for her love and understanding. I hope that, in some small way, the ideas here may help to make agreeable societies for our children and grandchildren to live and work in.

November 1999 G. C. Harcourt

References

Discussion Paper no. 6 (1979) 'Economic Issues and the Future of Australia', in Australian Political Studies Association, Australian Labor Party National Committee of Inquiry, *Discussion Papers* APSA Monograph no. 23, Flinders University of South Australia.

Harcourt, G. C. (1965) 'The Accountant in a Golden Age', *Oxford Economic Papers*, vol. 17, 66–80. Reprinted in C. Sardoni (ed.), *On Political Economists and Modern Political Economy. Selected Essays of G. C. Harcourt* (London: Routledge, 1992).

— (1972) *Some Cambridge Controversies in the Theory of Capital* (Cambridge: Cambridge University Press).

— (2001) *50 Years a Keynesian and Other Essays* (London: Palgrave).

Hirsch, F. (1977) *Social Limits to Growth* (London: Routledge & Kegan Paul).

Acknowledgements

The author and publishers wish to acknowledge with thanks the following for permission to reproduce copyright material:

The editors of *Economic Issues* for permission to reprint '"The End of a Perfect Day": "Horses for Courses" and Policy Proposals', *Economic Issues*, vol. 4, part 1, March 1999, 7–20.

University of Western Australia Press, the editor of *Revue d'Economie Politique* and Routledge for permission to reprint *Theoretical Controversy and Social Significance: An Evaluation of the Cambridge Controversies* (the 1975 Edward Shann Memorial Lecture), University of Western Australia Press, 1975.

The University of Newcastle, NSW, and Routledge for permission to reprint 'Eric Russell, 1921–77: A Great Australian Political Economist' (the 1977 Newcastle Lecture in Political Economy), Research Report no. 36, reprinted in *The Social Science Imperialists. Selected Essays. G. C. Harcourt*, edited by P. Kerr (London: Routledge & Kegan Paul, 1982), 331–45.

Melbourne University Press and Routledge for permission to reprint 'On Theories and Policies', Chapter 4 of J. P Nieuwenhuysen and P. J. Drake (eds) *Australian Economic Policy* (Melbourne: Melbourne University Press, 1977), 40–52, reprinted in *The Social Science Imperialists. Selected Essays. G. C. Harcourt*, edited by P. Kerr (London: Routledge & Kegan Paul, 1982), 315–28.

Ian Novak and Prue Kerr for permission to reprint 'The Mixed Economy', Chapter 14 in J. North and P. Weller (eds), *Labor* (Sydney: Ian Novak, 1979), 184–95.

The editor of the *Australian Journal of Agricultural Economics* and A. D. Barton for permission to reprint 'Investment Allowances for Primary Producers', *Australian Journal of Agricultural Economics*, vol. 3, December 1959, 12–18.

The editor of the *Economic Record* and J. W. Bennett for permission to reprint 'Taxation and Business Surplus', *Economic Record*, vol. 36, August 1960, 425–8.

The editor of the *Australian Accountant* for permission to reprint 'Investment and Initial Allowances as Fiscal Devices', *Australian Accountant*, September 1962, 473–7.

The editor of the *Economic Journal* for permission to reprint 'Investment-Decision Criteria, Investment Incentives and the Choice of Technique', *Economic Journal*, vol. 78, March 1968, 77–95.

Routledge for permission to reprint 'The Quantitative Effect of Basing Company Taxation on Replacement Costs', *Accounting Research*, vol. 9, January 1958, 1–16, reprinted in *The Social Science Imperialists. Selected Essays. G. C. Harcourt*, edited by P. Kerr (London: Routledge & Kegan Paul, 1982), 9–27.

The editor of *The Banker's Magazine* for permission to reprint 'Incomes Policy and the Measurement of Profits', *The Banker's Magazine*, December 1964, 361–4.

Oxford University Press for permission to reprint 'The Measurement of the Rate of Profit and the Bonus Scheme for Managers in the Soviet Union', *Oxford Economic Papers*, vol. 18, March 1966, 58–63.

The editor of the *Australian Accountant*, Wheatsheaf Books Ltd and New York University Press for permission to reprint 'The Social Consequences of Inflation', *Australian Accountant*, October 1974, 520–8, reprinted in *Controversies in Political Economy, Selected Essays of G. C. Harcourt*, edited by O. F. Hamouda (Brighton: Wheatsheaf Books Ltd., New York: New York University Press, 1986), 231–49.

The Economic Society of Australia for permission to reprint 'Policy and Responses for Australia', *Economic Papers*, no. 60, December 1978, 61–69.

The Director of the Research School of Social Sciences, Australian National University and Routledge for permission to reprint 'Making Socialism in Your Own Country' (the 1982 John Curtin Memorial Lecture, August 1982), reprinted in *On Political Economists and Modern Political Economy. Selected Essays of G. C. Harcourt*, edited by C. Sardoni (London: Routledge, 1992), 281–96.

The editor of *The Cambridge Review* for permission to reprint 'Markets, Madness and a Middle Way', *The Cambridge Review*, vol. 114, no. 2320, February 1993, 40–5.

The editor of *The Economic and Labour Relations Review* and Edward Elgar Publishing Ltd, Cheltenham, Glos, for permission to reprint 'Macroeconomic Policy for Australia in the 1990s', *The Economic and Labour Relations Review*, vol. 4, no. 2, December 1993, 167–75, reprinted in *Capitalism, Socialism and Post-Keynesianism. Selected Essays of G. C. Harcourt* (Cheltenham, Glos, Edward Elgar, 1995), 25–31.

The editor of *Economic and Political Weekly*, and Edward Elgar for permission to reprint 'Taming Speculators and Putting the World on

Course to Prosperity: A "Modest Proposal"', *Economic and Political Weekly*, vol. xxix, 17 September 1994, 2490–2, reprinted in *Capitalism, Socialism and Post-Keynesianism. Selected Essays of G. C. Harcourt* (Cheltenham, Glos, Edward Elgar, 1995), 32–38.

Oxford University Press and the editor of *The Economic and Labour Relations Review* for permission to reprint 'Economic Policy, Accumulation and Productivity', Chapter 8 in J. Michie and J. Grieve Smith (eds), *Employment and Economic Performance: Jobs, Inflation and Growth* (Oxford: Oxford University Press, 1997), 194–204. Revised version published as 'Pay Policy, Accumulation and Productivity', *The Economic and Labour Relations Review*, vol. 8, June 1977, 78–89.

The editor of the *Australian Quarterly* for permission to reprint 'The Payment of Prisoners', *Australian Quarterly*, December 1961, 86–9.

The editor of *Economic Forum*, Wheatsheaf Books and New York University Press for permission to reprint 'Notes on the Social Limits to Growth', *Economic Forum*, Summer 1981, 1–8, reprinted in *Controversies in Political Economy, Selected Essays of G. C. Harcourt*, edited by O. F. Hamouda (Brighton: Wheatsheaf Books Ltd, 1986), 273–81.

The Master and Fellows of Queen's College, Melbourne for permission to reprint 'University Ideals and the Market', the Third Halford Cook Memorial Lecture, Queen's College, University of Melbourne, May 1996, 1–11.

The editor of *Economic Analysis and Policy* for permission to reprint 'Economic Theory and Economic Policy: Two Views', *Economic Analysis and Policy*, vol. 27, September 1997, 113–30.

Macmillan and Mehdi Monadjemi for permission to reprint 'The Vital Contributions of John Cornwall to Economic Theory and Policy: A Tribute from Two Admiring Friends on the Occasion of his 70th Birthday', in M. Setterfield (ed.), *Growth, Employment and Inflation. Essays in Honour of John Cornwall* (Houndmills, Basingstoke, Hants: Macmillan, 1999), 10–23.

Part I
Introduction

1
'The End of a Perfect Day': 'Horses for Courses' and Policy Proposals*

Introduction

When you approach the end of the official stretch of your professional life, you are able to impose far more structure and meaning on what you have done than when you actually did it! So I try to present in this essay a *précis* of the relationships I have developed over the years between my political and religious beliefs, how I have learnt and done economics, and the rationale these have provided in turn for the various policy proposals I have made over the past 40 years and more. By 'horses for courses', I mean an approach which is situation-specific. That is to say, it invokes no preconceived ideas or general theory about the underlying structural relationships and their interrelationships. It is the approach of Kalecki rather than of Friedman.

Formative years

I started economics as a schoolboy in the late 1940s in Melbourne, Australia. The principal textbooks were Hubert Henderson's *Supply and Demand* (1922) and J.R. (as he then was) Hicks's *Social Framework*

*Originally published in *Economic Issues*, vol. 4, part 1, March 1999, 7–20. The title of the paper is meant to invoke Paul Robeson singing 'When you come to the end of a perfect day'. May I say how grateful I am to Peter and Paul for allowing me the opportunity to provide a swan song to the Post Keynesian Study Group, even if I seem at the moment to be having more farewells than Madame Melba? I thank but in no way implicate Stephanie Blankenburg, the editors and the participants in the conference at Stoke-on-Trent for comments on the swan song and/or a draft of the essay.

(1942). (I reckon both gave a better grounding in the concepts and approaches of economics than what often passes for economics in the A-level syllabus these days.) My undergraduate years (1950–53) were spent at the Commerce Faculty of the University of Melbourne (especially crucial were the wonderful years I spent at Queen's College), where I did a four-year honours degree. The course was noted for its enthusiastic Cambridge orientation – Marshall, Pigou, Keynes, D. H. Robertson, Kahn, the Robinsons, Sraffa, Kaldor – but it also took in, in my case anyway, a thorough grounding in the classical economists and Marx and, in the modern era, Maurice Dobb and Michal Kalecki. In addition, I read a lot of Hayek's work on knowledge and on capital theory. For mathematical economics we read Hicks's *Value and Capital* (1939), Samuelson's *Foundations* (1948) and much duopoly theory *à la* R. G. D. Allen (1938), for example. In I.O. we read Chamberlin (1933) and Triffin (1942) as well as Kaldor and the other UK contributors. The theory of the trade cycle was one of my passions; I read Schumpeter's two volumes (1939), Rostow's first book (1948) and we had lectures on Hicks's *Contribution* . . . (1950) and the criticisms of it in the review articles of Kaldor (1951) and Swan (1950). Boulding's *Economic Analysis* (1948) was our standby advanced text.

At the same time as I was imbibing all this economics fare, I was radically changing my religious and political beliefs. I moved from being a carbon copy of my parents' views – they were assimilationist agnostic Jews and right-wing in politics – to becoming a democratic Christian socialist. I reached my political stance much more quickly than my religious one, see, for example, Harcourt (1998) for an account and explanation.

The single most influential article I read as an undergraduate was Kurt Rothschild's classic, 'Price Theory and Oligopoly' (1947). In it he argued that oligopolists were as interested in secure profits as they were in maximum profits, so that Clausewitz's *Principles of War* (1943) was a more appropriate approach to the analysis of their behaviour and of oligopolistic market structures than those of either imperfect or monopolistic competition. In my fourth-year undergraduate dissertation, I tried to put Rothschild's analysis into the framework of *The General Theory* to see if it made any difference to the systemic behaviour of capitalist economies. I singled out one issue – Keynes's argument in the chapters on the consumption function that the accountants' and businesspersons' practice of 'financial prudence' – 'writing off' the book values of durable assets well before they were due for replacement

– created an additional source of contractionary bias in the economy. I conjectured whether this was indeed so when non-competitive market structures ruled the roost; I looked at the reserve policies of a sample of Australian companies during the years of the Great Depression to see whether my tentative theoretical inferences were supported by their behaviour. (The verdict was the Scottish one, 'not proven'.) This started a long-standing interest in the relationship between firms' behaviour, market structures and systemic performance.

After a detour into applied research for a Master's degree (I designed a pilot survey of income and saving in Melbourne for the Reserve Bank of Australia, to see whether it was feasible to set up an annual Australia-wide survey – it was not), in August 1955 I went, newly married to Joan Bartrop, to King's College, Cambridge (of course), to do a PhD. I worked first with Nicky Kaldor and then with Ronald Henderson. Initially, my topic was the implications for the theory of the firm and the trade cycle of secure profits being as important as maximum profits in oligopolistic firms. The dissertation ultimately became the implications of using historical-cost accounting procedures for setting prices and measuring incomes for dividend and taxation purposes in periods of inflation. I put the historical-cost pricing models of Trevor Swan, Eric Russell and Russell Mathews and John Grant into the Marxian-Kaleckian framework of Joan Robinson's *Accumulation of Capital* (1956) to derive my inferences. (At least implicitly, a post-Keynesian structure to my economics was emerging.) The inferences were tested against the NIESR data set of Profit and Loss Accounts, Balance Sheets and Funds Statements of UK quoted public companies just then emerging.

My first policy proposals were that the measurement of profits for taxation (and dividend) purposes should be on a replacement-cost rather than an historical-cost basis, as should the setting of prices by firms. Despite my socialist principles I was acting as a hired prize-fighter for the capitalists with my proposals, trying to save capitalism from itself! For good measure I also started on a long-to-continue investigation of the impact of investment allowances and other investment-incentive schemes on investment decisions and outcomes.

First Adelaide years

My first lecturing post was in Adelaide. I started in March 1958 where I had the great good fortune to have as colleagues, my close friend from

Melbourne days, Bob Wallace, and Peter Karmel (the youthful Professor), Eric Russell, and John Grant and Russell Mathews. The last two were an inspiration and help to me as I finished (indeed, in one sense, virtually started anew) my PhD dissertation. Karmel bequeathed to me his course on Outlay, the introduction to Keynesian economics for the first year, when he became the first Vice-Chancellor of the newly established Flinders University of South Australia at the beginning of the 1960s. His lectures, mine and subsequently Bob Wallace's were the basis of my first book, *Economic Activity* (1967), jointly authored with Peter and Bob. Appropriately, after an examination of the ingredients of the Keynesian system, the final chapter was on policy. It absorbed our own views on fiscal, monetary, exchange rate and incomes policies within the framework of Swan's influential and fundamental internal-external balance diagrams and analysis.

Karmel was also responsible for me writing a review article of Wilfred Salter's classic, *Productivity and Technical Change* (1960). Salter's contributions were a major influence on my thinking from then on. They were the basis of several of my papers in the 1960s and 1970s following the tragic death of Salter in 1963 at the ridiculously early age of 34. Austin Robinson said of Maynard Keynes that those whom the gods love die young but in the case of Salter (and subsequently of Eric Russell, too), this was taking things far too far.

Harold Lydall (who succeeded Karmel at Adelaide) posed for me the puzzle which subsequently gave rise to my best-known article (apart from the 1969 survey of capital theory), 'The Accountant in a Golden Age', Harcourt (1965a). He had found, using arithmetical examples, that the values of the accounting rate of profit differed significantly from the values of the economic rate of profit (represented by the internal rate of return). I posed the question: Suppose we place an accountant in a Golden Age where we know the value of the rate of profit because expectations are always fulfilled, will the accountant's tools of trade tell us what we already know? The answer, of course, is 'no'. Depending upon how the accountant calculates depreciation allowances, on the shape of the expected cash flows over the lifetimes of the assets, and on whether we are in stationary states or steadily growing ones, the accountant's answers differ, often by a wide margin, from the 'correct' answers. Franklin Fisher (1983, 1984) was subsequently to cause a great stir in the 1980s when the same results were used by him to defend IBM in an anti-trust case. So again, unwittingly, I was, at one remove, a lackey of the system.

Most of all though it was Eric Russell who became my mentor (and dear friend). He had already made his mark with a classic paper, co-authored with James Meade (Meade and Russell, 1957).[1] Meade and Russell is still the starting point for understanding how the Australian economy works, in particular, how the distributive shares between the farmers, the industrialists and the wage-earners are determined, see Harcourt (1977a; 1982) for a full account of the genesis and contents of the paper. Eric was to use this framework in his evidence on behalf of the wage-earners before the Arbitration Commission in the 1950s and in his seminal work on an incomes policy for Australia in the 1960s. He and Salter (they had cooperated in presenting evidence for the wage-carners) were way ahead of their time in advocating the setting of nominal income increases according to the rates of increase of effective productivity *plus* prices, so that equity and efficiency could both be achieved.

This crucial policy recommendation has as foundations both Eric's Kaleckian-type understanding of how the Australian economy works and the Salterian analysis of how such a rule may move the economy into a high productivity growth scenario. If the rule is combined with a full employment policy, we may attain a sustainable situation, in the sense that because wage-earners (and others) receive agreeable rises in real incomes, full employment without too much inflation may be achieved for indefinite periods. In my most recent writings on policy, Harcourt (1997a), I have returned to these themes in order to show how the dilemma associated with the political economy of *getting* to full employment, on the one hand, and *staying* there, on the other, first posed by Kalecki in 1943 in his remarkable paper 'Political Aspects of Full Employment' (reprinted in Kalecki (1971), has some chance of being resolved.

As I mentioned above, Kaldor was my first supervisor. Soon after I started lecturing at Adelaide, I decided to give a course of lectures to intending honours students on Kaldor's postwar contributions to the theory of distribution and growth. Like many others, I was puzzled by his assumption that, at least in the long period, full employment was the natural state of a growing capitalist economy. (Paul Samuelson was to tease him as Jean-Baptiste Kaldor; I would like similarly to tease those, far too many, modern economists who still accept the proposition.) With my interest in pricing policies and their link to systemic behaviour, it was natural for me to ask what pricing policies implicitly underlay Kaldor's 'Keynesian' macro theory of distribution, especially so, when, in his 1957 *Economic Journal* paper, he stated that the mechanism worked in the short period as well as in the long period (and he still maintained the assumption of full employment. In some papers he tried to show that full employment was an outcome rather than an assumption but he never could produce a coherent account of why, and after 15 years or so he quietly dropped his insistence on it.)

In Harcourt (1963), I showed that the most unusual pricing policies were implied and that they differed as between the consumption goods sector and the investment goods sector. While this was a negative conclusion, I thought the way forward was not to abandon his 'Keynesian' theory of distribution (it was, of course, in a more acceptable form, Kalecki's theory too) but his untenable assumption of full employment in the short period and the long period. It was hearing (they were never published as such) Solow's 1963 Marshall Lectures on two mythical creatures, one called 'Joan', the other, 'Nicky', that spurred me on to write a positive contribution. This incorporated the Kalecki–Kaldor distribution mechanism, my own work on pricing policies, Salter's work on the choice of technique, and the insights I had gained from *The Accumulation of Capital* and succeeding literature, and Sraffa's classic, *Production of Commodities by Means of Commodities* (1960). I wrote the first draft of the paper (Harcourt, 1965b) in the Autumn of 1963 when I was on leave from Adelaide in Cambridge. I was greatly helped by comments from John Cornwall in particular and it has remained the starting point for much of my work ever since.

A young don at Cambridge

In October 1964 I started a University Lectureship in the Faculty of Economics and Politics at Cambridge and a Fellowship at Trinity Hall. Drawing on the foundations of the previous six years in Adelaide, I wrote a string of papers around these and other themes. Going on around me were the debates on capital theory between the two Cambridges – Joan Robinson asked me to sit in on her exchanges with Ken Arrow and Bob Solow in 1963–64 when they were spending a year's leave at Cambridge. It was an awe-inspiring experience, more noted, I fear, for heat than light. Vincent Massaro and I were also writing a review article of Sraffa's book, consulting with Piero himself while we did it. Joe Stiglitz was in Cambridge as a graduate student from MIT and Hahn and Matthews were writing Hahn and Matthews (1964). The capital-reversing and reswitching results also started to appear with Levhari's *Quarterly Journal of Economics* article (1965) bringing things to a head (Samuelson's 1962 surrogate production function paper already had Pierangelo Garegnani and Luigi Pasinetti buzzing, also Joan Robinson.) I was an intensely puzzled onlooker for though I had taken a great interest in capital and growth theory when an undergraduate, in *The Accumulation of Capital* when a graduate student, and in Kaldor's distribution and growth theory when a young lecturer, I was certainly not anywhere near on top of the issues, nor able to keep up with the pace at which thrust and counter-thrust were occurring around me.

But as well as writing theoretical papers, I also wrote on policy, even going so far as to apply the results of 'The Accountant in a Golden Age' to an analysis and critique of the unintended effects of the bonus scheme for managers in the Soviet Union on the choice of techniques in planned economies (Harcourt, 1966).

As far as capitalism was concerned, my ideas were focused by the request from Aubrey Silberston to write a paper on the choice of technique in the East and the West for a conference in Nice on plan and markets. 20 or so bourgeois economists lived it up in decadent splendour with a similar number from the USSR and Eastern European countries. This led me to use a characteristic post-Keynesian approach to analysis. I compared the investment–output and investment–labour ratios which would be chosen in otherwise identical situations, according to whether businesspeople were assumed to use rules derived from the axiomatic approach to theory associated with the assumptions of profit-maximisation and cost-minimisation, or behaved as they said they did and used a 'rule of thumb' such as the pay-off period criterion (POPC), or the accounting rate of profit, or, in the case of socialist managers, some variant of the recoupment period criterion. I showed that with orders of magnitude likely to be met in the real world, POPC resulted in a more investment-intensive, less labour-intensive technique being chosen than resulted from the use of any other investment-decision rule.

I then combined this analysis with an examination of various investment-incentive schemes – accelerated depreciation, investment allowances, cash grants – to see what effect these had on the techniques chosen and whether the latter accorded with the stated intentions of the policy–makers who introduced the schemes, see Harcourt (1968; 1982). I understand this work resulted in a file on me in the UK Treasury in the late 1960s, one which was soon to be matched by the file the spooks were to keep on me for my anti-Vietnam-war activities in Australia.

Direct action and capital theory

Now a sea-change occurred in my politics and economics. We returned to Adelaide at the beginning of 1967. I was already scandalised by Australia's role in the Vietnam war and determined to do something about it. The outcome was 5½ years of direct action averaging 2½ days a week on anti-war activities in South Australia. While I had been from the early 1950s a member of the Australian Labor Party (ALP), in the late 1950s, early 1960s, President of the local sub-branch, and also active in penal reform though the Howard League, I had always gone through the 'usual' channels. Now I became committed to direct action with the usual provisos, especially that you followed the same rules of argument with opponents as you would in academic arguments and that you were willing to respect your opponents even though you disliked their arguments.

The most important intellectual influences on me articulating my new position on direct action and involvement were Noam Chomsky's essay 'The Responsibility of Intellectuals' (1967) and Hugh Stretton's *The Political Sciences* (1969); the practical influences were the day-to-day experiences of helping to organise a protest movement. My economic analysis changed as well; my personality intruded more into my writing, and, as I no longer accepted that ideology and analysis could be separated, I made the former explicit in my teaching and writings, especially by the end of the 1960s.

As to direct action, I thought it justified if the cause itself was fundamental and all other avenues had been tried seriously and found wanting. Of course, 'favoured nation treatment' could not be claimed for those taking direct action, especially University Professors with Tenure, though fairness of treatment by police and courts alike when the law was broken could be. That is to say, the legal consequences of breaking the law had to be accepted but the person involved did not have to accept being bashed up by police, or false accusations – set-ups

– such as happened then, especially in the early days of the antiwar protests when the protesters were a small and much reviled minority whose views were generally unacceptable to the population at large.

As for economics, in 1968 Mark Perlman asked me to write the survey article on capital theory for the newly formed *Journal of Economic Literature* (for the full story, see Harcourt, 1999). This forced me to get inside the debates that I had witnessed raging around me in Cambridge and resulted not only in the 1969 survey article but also in my 1972 book and its sequels, especially Harcourt (1975, 1976). The latest of these is only six pages long, Harcourt (1994a, 1995). Though the arguments are pitched at a high level of abstraction (as befits doctrinal and conceptual arguments), I tried not to lose sight of the implications for policy, see, for example, Harcourt (1975).

Life at the sharp end

As inflation started to emerge and then accelerate in the 1970s, I turned my attention to policy-making concerning its control. I was one of the earliest to argue for indexation in the Australian context (this practice had been followed for many years in Australia through our centralised wage-fixing institutions, but had been abandoned for several years prior to the outbreak of inflation). Together with Eric Russell, Barry Hughes and Phillip Bentley, I formulated in August 1974 a package deal of proposals which came to be called the Adelaide Plan. An integral part of the proposals was a variant of indexation, one which stressed proportionality, at least up to quite high income levels, rather than flat-rate adjustments to most incomes. We proposed that the scheme be commenced in the early months of the first quarter of 1975 with the line held, more or less, on money-wages in the meantime. (This was to allow the recent very large increases in money-wages and those already in the pipeline to feed through into prices by the end of 1974.)

Whatever the equity merits of the flat-rate versions in the then situation of badly ruptured relativities, the effects of introducing such a scheme could be disastrous as an anti-inflation measure. Since the situation was extraordinarily serious – unchecked, rates of inflation of the order of 30 per cent per annum or more could have emerged by the end of 1974 – equity (and efficiency) considerations had to take back seats for the time being.

Allied with the indexation scheme were proposals that company profits and the prices of companies' products be controlled through the tax system. We suggested that (with obvious exceptions for new companies, or those that recently made losses) profits be such as to not exceed the average of the net profit to sales ratio of (say) the previous three years. Any excess would be taxed away completely, that is, we proposed a 100 per cent excess profits tax. Also any money-wage increases (measured per hour and including the value of fringe benefits and other factors that add directly to costs) in excess of those allowed by indexation and a mild (say 3 per cent per annum) adjustment for relativities were not to be allowable as a cost for tax purposes; their consequent inclusion in taxable profits would bear a 100 per cent tax rate also. In this way profit margins per unit would be controlled (larger profits could still be made by selling larger volumes) and there would also be a considerable incentive for businesspeople not to acquiesce in wage payments in excess of the norms established for the emergency period, that is, sweetheart agreements would be out. The accounting profession in their capacity as auditors would be a vital link in this scheme of things. For they would have to certify that the net profit to sales ratios and wage payments had not exceeded the allowable limits.

The 3 per cent per annum increase allowed for relativities was necessary both because of gross departures from established norms in recent leap-frog movements in money-wages and also to make sure that trade union officials have worthwhile jobs – indexation by itself is tantamount to voting them out of a job, something neither they nor their union members would wear. With really badly out-of-line relativities, the adjustments might have to take a number of years. The self-employed would be subject to a similar system of excess income control, by using the personal income tax system. Promotions, and so on, could be handled by a version of Keynes's deferred pay system whereby excess income over the average increase indicated by indexation plus (mild) adjustments for relativities would be deferred for (say) two years, a modest rate of interest being paid on these amounts in the meantime.

By itself, indexation would only serve to stabilise the rate of increase of prices, not to bring it down. To bring it down we must look for 'dampeners' in the cost of living index in the form of reduced food prices (at the farm gate), increases in productivity (here the threat of a recession was a real worry as productivity tends to fall with the onset of a recession) and State and Australian Government behaviour with regard to charges, direct and indirect taxes. Thus, it was vital that the Australian Government put the State Governments in such financial positions that they would not have to raise charges or introduce State taxes; indirect and direct tax cuts would also be desirable, if the macroeconomic situation warranted it. Here the recession might be a blessing in disguise, as far as the cost-push elements of inflation are concerned, for tax cuts would be needed for demand management purposes. Given very favourable circumstances, we estimated that inflation rates *could* be down to single figures (high ones, alas) by the first quarter of 1976.

We took the view that the present inflation, whatever its initial causes, was now predominantly wage-price and wage-wage, that is to say, it had a life of its own in terms of these elements. We therefore were opposed to measures which implied a sharp rise in unemployment which was sustained for a considerable period of time, because they are inhumane and inappropriate. We felt that some package deal such as ours, the strands of which were not original but borrowed freely, could have secured wide community consensus and, conceivably, just might have worked. The alternatives were a move towards hyper-inflation (prices rising at 50 per cent per annum or more), with all its attendant and undesirable political and social consequences and anxieties, including, as an outside chance, the destruction of our democratic institutions themselves; or a wholesale and widespread freeze of wages and prices; or the deliberate creation of unemployment, in order to shock the system and break through the expectations barrier. We felt that the last would have been the worst of all possible worlds, enough to create a great deal of unnecessary misery and loss of employment and output, not enough to have a significant effect on money-wage increases, unless it were to be held for an intolerably long time, certainly over a year. We stressed that we were faced with a serious inflationary situation, to which had to be added the possibility of a world-wide slump, in which the whole capitalist world was moving in unison, all parts of which were faced with inflation and tackling it by reducing demand. Prospects were bleak but we stressed that these were the alternatives before us and that our proposals, unpalatable as they may be in the short run, were relatively the least unpalatable of them all.

As well as tackling inflation we also wanted to support the efforts of Ralph Willis, who was subsequently to be an important Minister in the

Hawke and Keating ALP governments of the 1980s and 1990s but who was then a lone voice crying in the ALP wilderness.

At the end of the 1970s after the ALP had been badly beaten in the 1975 and 1977 Federal elections, I was appointed the economist on the ALP's National Committee of Inquiry into why the Party had done so poorly and how they should rethink their policies and administrative institutions in order to make a comeback. I wrote the first draft of Discussion Paper no. 6, 'Economic Issues and the Future of Australia' (1979). I drew on the post-Keynesian ideas I set out in 'On Theories and Policies' (1977b, 1982), 'The Mixed Economy' (with Prue Kerr, 1979) and the work I had done with Eric and the others on the Adelaide Plan. (Tragically, Eric died in February 1977 so that his wise counsel was missing just when it was needed more than ever.) The discussion paper was meant to be the broad background to the economic policies of the ALP government when it was returned to power in 1983 – only very indirectly, of course, but I like to think that the Accord between wage-earners (through the Australian Council of Trade Unions) and the government in its early years owed something to our debates and suggestion in the 1970s.

Before I left Adelaide and Australia in September 1982 to take up a post in the Faculty at Cambridge and a Fellowship at Jesus, I outlined my policy views in the 1982 John Curtin Memorial Lecture 'Making Socialism in Your Own Country' (Harcourt 1986), just before the ALP was returned to power with Bob Hawke as Prime Minister. In essence my proposals involved redistribution through the public sector as the *quid pro quo* to wage-earning groups for accepting incomes policies directed at the rate of increase of money incomes, using the traditional Australian institutions of indexation and the Arbitration Commission. Fiscal and monetary measures were to be directed towards the level of activity, the rate of growth and the post-tax distribution of income. Nationalisation of certain key industries including financial intermediaries was put back on the agenda for discussion and I sat on the fence concerning the tariff, i.e. leave it as it is and concentrate on export promotion. (The act in my professional life I most regret in retrospect is that I publicly supported, as did most other Australian economists at the time, the cut in tariffs by the Whitlam ALP government in the early 1970s.) I opted for a fixed exchange rate, with the proviso that in an economy like Australia's, a change might have to be contemplated from time to time.

Renewed burst on policy

The final thing to say is that from 1992 on I have had a burst of renewed and sustained interest in policy. The immediate stimulus was a request to give the 1992 Donald Horne Address, 'Markets, Madness and a Middle Way', in Melbourne in February 1992. It spawned further papers, one on macroeconomic policy for Australia in the 1990s (1993a; 1995), another on 'The Harcourt Plan to "Save" the World' (1993b). This subsequently become 'A "Modest Proposal" for Taming the Speculators and Putting the World on Course to Prosperity' (1994b; 1995). In 1997 I published the paper on economic policy, accumulation and productivity, Harcourt (1997a), to which I referred above and gave the Seventh Colin Clark Memorial Lecture on 'Economic Theory and Economic Policy: Two Views', Harcourt (1997d). The latter drew on a review, Harcourt (1997b), I wrote of Joe Stiglitz's 1990 Wicksell Lectures, *Whither Socialism?*, Stiglitz (1994, 1996) and a review article, Harcourt (1997c), of Kaldor's 1984 Mattioli Lectures, Kaldor (1996). In all these papers I tried to make explicit the fundamental differences made to policies advocated depending upon what particular view of the world is taken. That is to say, whether markets and entire systems are regarded as strongly equilibrating mechanisms, on the one hand, or as exhibiting cumulative causation processes (associated with Allyn Young, Myrdal and Kaldor), virtuous or vile, on the other. The former is the stance of most variants of mainstream economics, not least the Chicago economics of Friedman and Lucas. The historical backdrop is the rise of monetarism, 'the incomes policy of Karl Marx', as Balogh so rightly called it, the deregulation of financial markets and the creation of flexible labour markets. The last is a euphemism for recreating the reserve army of labour so as to have, as Samuelson (1997) now says and many of us had already said in the 1970s, a cowed labour force.

The idea of the Horne Addresses is to ask an Australian living abroad to come home to give a wide-ranging address on issues of vital importance for Australian citizens. The conjunction of events to which mine was addressed was the launching of the Republican movement in Australia and the U-turn on economic policy of the Federal ALP government that was then occurring. The background was the emerging reaction against the 'let the market rip' policies of the 1980s which characterised part of economic policy in Australia, and the crowing over, and then second thoughts about, the implications of the collapse of Communism. I never held any brief for the awful regimes of the USSR and the Eastern European economies but I did point out that the achievements of those Western industrialised capitalist economies that had gone overboard on Hayekian/Friedmanite policies from the 1970s on were not that much to write home about either. There was therefore a case to be made for middle ways – the Kaleckian approach to democratic socialism, for example, for Eastern Europe, the Keynes/Kaleckian (with modern additions) post-Keynesian blueprints for Australia and other similar countries.

I preceded my outlines of middle ways with an account of what modern (and not so modern) theory had to say about the conditions which need to be satisfied for markets to be safely left to do their thing, pointing out (as Kaldor and Stiglitz do, too) that these conditions are spectacularly *not* satisfied in the markets for labour, foreign exchange, financial assets and housing. I recognised that it was a *non sequitur* to jump to the proposition that some form of intervention and regulation would *necessarily* do better – the case for this had always to be made.

As I said above, the common theme connecting these papers was the argument that many markets and indeed economic systems themselves are characterised by cumulative causation processes. This viewpoint implies that very different policy proposals and institutions are needed than those associated with the more orthodox general equilibrium framework. Radically different attitudes would be taken towards, for example, speculators and speculation because their systemic effects would not be the benign ones identified by, for example, Milton Friedman in his well-known article on the case for flexible exchange rates (1953).[2]

The essays on macroeconomic policy relate principally to the problems of small open economies. It allowed me to ride some hobby horses, for example, that government expenditure should not principally be used for pump-priming but rather should fit in with the longer-term needs of economies, taking into account the social and political philosophy of the government in power. I also drew attention to the danger of forgetting those old-fashioned but profound lessons from the writings of Russell and Salter concerning the macroeconomic effects of incomes policies on rates of accumulation, and from Kalecki concerning the vital differences between getting to, and then sustaining, full employment. Because at the economy level capital and labour are complements, changing money incomes according to changes in the cost-of-living *and* effective productivity is not only equitable, it is also efficient. It encourages investment in profitable, productivity-enhancing industries and hastens the decline of industries whose time has not only come but gone.

In the paper on a 'modest proposal' I tried to set out the problems of the various broad regions of the world, show how they are interrelated and what particular combination of policies and institutions might serve to tackle their problems effectively and simultaneously. There is a Utopian tinge to such an exercise (though I did try to take into account the constraints imposed by present political and ideological climates). Nevertheless, unless such interrelationships and schemes are explicitly set out, it is difficult to get people of good will to think about the causes and cures of the world's ills. Next step the universe, of course.

If it were to be asked had I ever considered being an official policy advisor, the answer is 'yes' – and I decided not to be. In 1974 I was approached by Jim Cairns, who taught me at Melbourne University and who was then Deputy Prime Minister of Australia and Federal Treasurer in the Whitlam government, to see whether I would consider being either Governor of the Reserve Bank of Australia or permanent head of one section of an intended revamp of the Commonwealth Treasury. To the first request, I said 'no' immediately, adding 'You know me, Jim, I'm a real man, not a money man'. I promised to think about the second request but on reflection and, especially, after talking to Eric Russell and Peter Karmel, I said 'no' to it, too. They pointed out (and I agreed) that I had neither the appropriate temperament nor the necessary guile to withstand the inevitable machinations of very bright civil servants who would undoubtedly be resentful at having a rank outsider brought in over their heads.

Au revoir

So that is it – to date, I retire in September 1998. I intend to spend 8–9 months in Cambridge working on the project which brought me back to Cambridge in 1982 – the intellectual history of Joan Robinson and her circle. The other months I hope to spend in Australia working on policy. July will be sacred for playing cricket at Jesus.[3] Sounds idyllic?!

Notes

1. The ideas were really Eric's, as Meade acknowledged. He said that the greatest act of his then six months in Australia was when he persuaded Eric to co-author the paper with him.
2. In writing about the taming of speculators by use of carrot and stick methods, I realised the great temptation associated with authoritarian regimes. They do not have trouble with speculators because they shoot them or, at least, put them in jail.
3. Alas, I did my back in umpiring (!) in the 1999 season and so am reduced to long bike rides.

References

Allen, R. G. D. (1938) *Mathematical Analysis for Economists* (London: Macmillan).

Boulding, K. E. (1948) *Economic Analysis*, rev. ed. (New York: Harper & Brothers Publisher).

Clausewitz, C. Von (1943) *Principles of War*, Translated and edited by Hans W. Gratzke, London: John Lane (the Bodley Head).

Chamberlin, E. H. (1933) *The Theory of Monopolistic Competition, A Reorientation of the Theory of Value* (Cambridge, Mass.: Harvard University Press).

Chomsky, N. (1967) 'The Responsibility of Intellectuals', in T. Roszak (ed), *The Dissenting Academy* (New York: Pantheon Books).

Discussion Paper no. 6 (1979) 'Economic Issues and the Future of Australia', in Australian Political Studies Association, Australian Labor Party National Committee of Inquiry, *Discussion Papers*, APSA Monograph no. 23, 1979, Flinders University of South Australia.

Fisher, F. M. (1984) 'The Misuse of Accounting Rates of Profit: Reply', *American Economic Review*, vol. 74, 509–17.

— and McGowan, J. J. (1983) 'On the Misuse of Accounting Rates of Return to infer Monopoly Profits', *American Economic Review*, vol. 73, 82–97.

Friedman, M. (1953) *Essays in Positive Economics* (Chicago: Chicago University Press).

Hahn, F. H. and Matthews, R. C. O. (1964) 'The Theory of Economic Growth: A Survey', *Economic Journal*, vol. 74, 779–90.

Harcourt, G. C. (1963) 'A Critique of Mr Kaldor's Model of Income Distribution and Economic Growth', *Australian Economic Papers*, vol. 2, 20–36.

— (1965a) 'The Accountant in a Golden Age', *Oxford Economic Papers*, (NS), vol. 17, 66–80.

— (1965b) 'A Two-Sector Model of the Distribution of Income and the Level of Employment in the Short Run', *Economic Record*, vol. 41, 103–17.

— (1966) 'The Measurement of the Rate of Profit and the Bonus Scheme for Managers in the Soviet Union', *Oxford Economic Papers*, vol. 18, 58–63.

— (1968) 'Investment-Decision Criteria, Investment Incentives and the Choice of Technique', *Economic Journal*, vol. 78, 77–95.

— (1969) 'Some Cambridge Controversies in the Theory of Capital', *Journal of Economic Literature*, vol. 7, 369–405.

— (1972) *Some Cambridge Controversies in the Theory of Capital* (Cambridge: Cambridge University Press).

— (1975) *Theoretical Controversy and Social Significance: An Evaluation of the Cambridge Controversies*; Edward Shann Memorial Lecture, University of Western Australia Press.
— (1976) 'The Cambridge Controversies: Old Ways and New Horizons – or Dead End?', *Oxford Economic Papers*, (NS), vol. 28, 25–65.
— (1977a) 'Eric Russell 1921–77: A Great Australian Political Economist' (the 1977 Newcastle Lecture in Political Economy), reprinted in Harcourt (1982).
— (1977b) 'On Theories and Policies, in J. P. Nieuwenhuysen and P. J. Drake (eds), *Australian Economic Policy* (Melbourne: Melbourne University, Press).
— (1982) *The Social Science Imperialists. Selected Essays. G. C. Harcourt*, ed. P. Kerr (London: (Routledge & Kegan Paul).
— (1986) *Controversies in Political Economy: Selected Essays of G. C. Harcourt*, ed. O.F. Hamouda (Brighton: Wheatsheaf).
— (1992) 'Markets, Madness and a Middle Way', *The Second Annual Donald Horne Address*, Melbourne: Monash University. Also published in *Australian Quarterly*, vol. 64, 1–17.
— (1993a) 'Macroeconomic Policy for Australia in the 1990s', *The Economic and Labour Relations Review*, vol. 4, 167–75.
— (1993b) 'The Harcourt Plan to "Save" the World', *At the Margin*, issue 1, 2–5.
— (1994a) 'The Capital Theory Controversies', in Philip Arestis and Malcolm Sawyer (eds.), *The Elgar Companion to Radical Political Economy* (Aldershot, Hants: Edward Elgar).
— (1994b) 'Taming Speculators and Putting the World on Course to Prosperity: a "Modest Proposal"', *Economic and Political Weekly*, vol. 29, 2490–92.
— (1995) *Capitalism, Socialism and Post-Keynesianism. Selected Essays of G.C. Harcourt* (Cheltenham: Edward Elgar).
— (1997a) 'Economic Policy, Accumulation and Productivity', in Michie and Grieve Smith (1997), 194–204.
— (1997b) 'Review of Stiglitz (1994; 1996)', *Journal of Institutional and Theoretical Economics*, vol. 153, 590–91.
— (1997c) 'The Kaldor Legacy: Reviewing Nicholas Kaldor, *Causes of Growth and Stagnation in the World Economy*', *Journal of International and Comparative Economics*, vol. 5, 341–57.
— (1997d) 'Economic Theory and Economic Policy: Two Views' (The Seventh Colin Clark Memorial Lecture, 1997), *Economic Analysis and Policy*, vol. 27, 113–30.
— (1998) 'Political Economy, Politics and Religion: Intertwined and Indissoluble Passions', *The American Economist*, vol. 42, 3–18.
— (1999) '"Horses for Courses": The Making of a Post-Keynesian Economist', in Arnold Heertje (ed.), *The Makers of Modern Economics*, Vol. IV (Cheltenham, UK-Northerthem MA, USA; Edward Elgar) 32–69.
— Karmel, P. H. and Wallace, R. H. (1967) *Economic Activity* (Cambridge: Cambridge University Press).
— and Kerr, P. M. (1979) 'The Mixed Economy', in J. North and P. Weller (eds) *Labor* (Sydney: Ian Novak).
Henderson, H. D. (1922) *Supply and Demand* (London: Nisbet).
Hicks, J. R. (1939) *Value and Capital* (Oxford: Clarendon Press).

— (1942) *The Social Framework: An Introduction to Economics* (Oxford: Clarendon Press).
— (1950) *A Contribution to the Theory of the Trade Cycle* (Oxford: Clarendon Press).
Kaldor, N. (1951) 'Mr Hicks on the Trade Cycle', *Economic Journal*, vol. 61, 833–47.
— (1957) 'A Model of Economic Growth', *Economic Journal*, vol. 67, 591–624.
— (1996) *Causes of Growth and Stagnation in the World Economy* (Cambridge: Cambridge University Press).
Kalecki, M. (1943) 'Political Aspects of Full Employment', *Political Quarterly*, reprinted in Kalecki (1971), 138–45.
— (1971) *Selected Essays on the Dynamics of the Capitalist Economy 1933–1970* (Cambridge: Cambridge University Press).
Levhari, D. (1965) 'A Nonsubstitution Theorem and Switching of Techniques', *Quarterly Journal of Economics*, vol. 79, 98–105.
Meade, J. E. and Russell, E. A. (1957) 'Wage Rates, the Cost of Living and the Balance of Payments', *Economic Record*, vol. 33, 23–28.
Michie, J. and Grieve Smith, J. (eds.) (1997) *Employment and Economic Performance. Jobs, Inflation and Growth* (Oxford: Oxford University Press).
Robinson, J. (1956) *The Accumulation of Capital* (London: Macmillan).
Rostow, W. W. (1948) *The British Economy of the Nineteenth Century: Essays* (Oxford: Clarendon Press).
Rothschild, K. W. (1947) 'Price Theory and Oligopoly', *Economic Journal*, vol. 57, 299–320.
Salter, W. E. G. (1960) *Productivity and Technical Change* (Cambridge: Cambridge University Press).
Samuelson, P. A. (1948) *Foundations of Economic Analysis* (Cambridge, MA: Harvard University Press).
— (1962) 'Parable and Realism in Capital Theory: The Surrogate Production Function', *Review of Economic Studies*, vol. 29, 193–206.
— (1997) 'Wherein do the European and American Models Differ?' Address delivered at the Bank of Italy, 2 October 1997.
Schumpeter, J. A. (1939) *Business Cycles: A Theoretical and Statistical Analysis of the Capitalist Process*, 2 Vols., (New York: McGraw-Hill).
Sraffa, P. (1960) *Production of Commodities by Means of Commodities. Prelude to a Critique of Economic Theory* (Cambridge: Cambridge University Press).
Stiglitz, J. E. (1994, 1996) *Whither Socialism?* (Cambridge, MA: MIT Press).
Stretton, H. (1969) *The Political Sciences. General Principles of Selection in Social Science and History* (London: Routledge).
Swan, T. W. (1950) 'Progress Report on the Trade Cycle', *Economic Record*, vol. 26, 186–200.
Triffin, R. (1942) *Monopolistic Competition and General Equilibrium Theory* (Cambridge, MA: Harvard University Press).

Part II

Background to Policy Recommendations

2

Theoretical Controversy and Social Significance: An Evaluation of the Cambridge Controversies*

I am delighted and most honoured to be asked to give the 1975 Edward Shann Memorial Lecture, and so to be included in the first XVIII, if not the first XI. I am sure it would try your patience if I were to play a full 100 minutes. In order to justify my selection, though, I shall try to put in four effective quarters, replete with creative hand ball, strong body work, and constructive play mainly from left of centre. The accounts that I have read of Professor Shann reveal a delightful character, down to earth and intimately involved in all manner of things, from the care of his students to the important political and economic issues of his day. He certainly is a man after my own heart and I like to think that we would have got on, even if we were to differ vigorously but fairly, in a tight checking game, over the virtues of the market. I hope he would have approved of, at least in principle, my public stand on the Vietnam War; I am sure he would have approved of, my recent involvement in the public debates on anti-inflationary policy and the theoretical but related issues of the appropriate body of economic theory with which to analyse the development through time of capitalist economies.

Let me turn, then, to my main theme for tonight: the theoretical and social significance of the Cambridge controversies in capital theory, the so-called Cambridge–Cambridge debates of the last twenty-two years.

* The 1975 Edward Shann Memorial Lecture. I am especially indebted to Peter Kenyon for helpful discussions when the first draft of this lecture was being written. I am also grateful to Neil Laing, Eric Russell and Bob Wallace for their comments on a draft. As usual I thank them all but implicate none. The lecture draws heavily on material which is the basis for an article in a symposium on these issues and which is to be published in the *Revue d'Economie Politique* in 1976, see Harcourt (1977).

A sharp division between these two aspects logically cannot be made, for like trend and cycle, analysis and ideology and Samuelson and Solow, they are indissolubly mixed. Nevertheless, it is a convenient division for purposes of exposition, so I adopt it and deal first with the theoretical significance, and then with the significance, if such there be, for society. I shall survey various, very differing views of the controversies, indicating where I believe truth lies and what the ongoing implications for theory and practice both are likely to be and should be, for the two, unfortunately, have not as yet converged into one. I shall proceed by outlining what I take to be the gist of the various approaches. The debate is, of course, a continuing one but I think that we have now reached a position where some broad generalisations and evaluations may usefully be made. I shall proceed as if the principal issues and results were familiar to my listeners. (For those, however, who are either coming at them afresh or wish to refresh their memories, there are a number of convenient sources which together provide an exhaustive overview, from all points of view, of the whole controversy, which I shall include in the written version of the lecture: see Blaug (1974), Dobb (1973), Hahn (1972: 1–18, 1974, 1975b), Harcourt (1972, 1976), Kregel (1973), Ng (1974), Pasinetti (1974), Robinson (1974, 1975a, 1975b, 1975c, 1975d), Rowthorn (1974), Samuelson (1966, 1975), Solow (1975), Stiglitz (1974).)

The lecture is in two sections. First, the theoretical issues are examined and evaluated in Section I. In the second section the social significance, and especially the implications for policy, is speculated on.

I

The theoretical issues resolve themselves into two groups, the first of which relates to the questions actually being asked, the second to the appropriate methodology to be used. Endless confusion has occurred in the literature because these two underlying strands have not always been made sufficiently explicit. As to the first head, the principal questions being discussed, at least as seen by the post-Keynesian school (the leaders of which include Joan Robinson, Kahn, Kaldor and, as a guiding spirit, Piero Sraffa), are some of those with which the great classical political economists and, of course, Marx, were concerned: 'the relation between accumulation and the distribution of the net product of industry between wages and profits' (Robinson 1975e, p. 398), together with discussions of the origins of profits, their size (absolutely and as a rate) at any moment of time and over time, and the analogous aspects of wages. Solow recently (in his review, Solow (1975), of Blaug (1974) and Pasinetti (1974)) made clear his agreement with this evaluation. He discussed the orthodox view (the old-time religion that, according to Joan Robinson, is good enough for him) of how profits (interest) arise and what determines their size and rate in conditions of certainty, and when monopoly, short-run shortages and risk have been ruled out by assumption. 'The third component of profit is the routine return to capitalist firms under tranquil conditions in the absence of monopoly' (p. 277).[1] Also connected to these questions are those which concern the concepts of natural, as the classicals had it, or normal, as Marshall would say, prices, and the relations between distribution and the relative price system, where the latter is seen as the relative (natural) prices of broad classes of commodities. The distinguishing characteristics of the commodities are determined both by their ultimate uses and by the classes in society who principally are associated with those uses. These questions constitute a natural link between the works of Ricardo, Marx and Sraffa; they have received particular attention from Garegnani (1958, 1960, 1970a) and Eatwell (1974).

Though the debates have been designated as recurring within the context of capital theory, in fact four related strands of theory are involved: value theory (which is absolutely central), capital theory itself, growth theory and distribution theory. Joan Robinson, who started these particular debates with her 1953 article. 'The Production Function and the Theory of Capital' (Robinson 1953–4), was at the time searching the literature for the orthodox theories of profits and choice of technique *at the level of the economy as a whole*. She was in the process of working out the various strands of her theory of growth, her generalisation of *The General Theory*, as expressed fully in *The Accumulation of Capital* (Robinson 1956). (The latter itself was inspired by Harrod's seminal works in this area (Harrod 1939, 1948) and left-over business from the true Keynesian revolution.)

Growing out of the preoccupations discussed above but also intimately associated with them, is another set of issues which provides the link through to the second head of methodology. These relate to the post-Keynesian critique of orthodox or mainstream neoclassical analysis, especially the theory of value, production and distribution which loosely comes under the head of marginal productivity theory. There have been a number of strands of this critique, emanating principally (in these contexts) from Dobb, Joan Robinson, Kaldor, Garegnani, Pasinetti and Sraffa. The critique has concerned itself, first with the logical tenability of certain propositions thought to be associated with the traditional neoclassical approach to value and distribution, especially those theories which draw on the concepts of supply and demand as their fundamental tools. Secondly – here the link occurs – it has concerned itself with the methodological procedure of using (long-period) equilibrium comparisons in order to throw light on actual processes in capitalist economies as they evolve through actual historical time. Thus the theoretical contexts may be seen to be both classical and modern. They are classical, and especially Marxist, in that they are concerned with the 'laws of motion' of capitalist economies; that is to say, the historical processes of growth, with which are associated endogenous technical changes as a result of the internal workings and possibly contradictions of the system, and of transition from one mode of production to another, the latter an aspect honoured more by default than in practice or by profundity. They are modern because, with the exceptions of Harrod and some of the post-Keynesian school (and, recently, Sir John Hicks – see Hicks 1975), though orthodox economists have returned in the post-war period to a preoccupation with classical problems of accumulation, growth (both descriptive and optimal) and distribution, they have brought with them the tools and perspectives which were attained during their sojourn in the land of the margin (see Harris 1975). There they were preoccupied with a different set of problems, the properties – existence, uniqueness, stability – of an equilibrium state when the resources to be allocated by competitive markets are exogenous to the analysis itself. By contrast, Harrod and the post-Keynesians brought with them to the renewed interest in classical and Marxist problems, the Kaleckian–Keynesian solution of the realization problem, so that the advances in the theory of the short run of the 1930s could be integrated with the post-war developments.[2]

The neo-neoclassical economists, on the whole, have explicitly preferred to assume away the effective demand aspects. They have grafted the neoclassical analyses of allocation in situations of full employment onto their analyses of movements through 'time' due to accumulation, in which the savings dog wags the investment tail,[3] 'capital' is substituted for labour, and technical progress, whether disembodied or embodied, is usually exogenous. Initially, neoclassical growth theory was principally concerned with steady-state analysis. Very quickly, however, modifications and extensions were made as the conditions of stability were investigated outside the domain of the simple one all-purpose commodity model in which there was, in effect, perfect foresight because of the assumption of malleability of the one all-purpose commodity. The steady-state now serves merely as a reference point and as a means of flexing intellectual muscles (see Hahn, 1971; Hicks, 1975).[4] The focus of the analysis has been, to a much greater extent, on the traverse – the initial and ultimate response of the economy to a new factor, say an innovation or an autonomous change in the saving rate, the path it is likely to follow and the possibility of it finding its way, both technocratically and, more generally, by postulating the behaviour of its economic agents, to a new equilibrium position (see Samuelson 1975).

Bound up with the methodological issues is the further question as to which particular branch of neoclassical analysis is both relevant to the principal questions being asked and is under attack. I have argued elsewhere (see Harcourt 1975a, 1976) that it is the neoclassical theories which, misleadingly in my view, are dubbed 'aggregative', viz. the aggregate production function growth models and econometric studies, much of international trade and orthodox development theory, and the rate of return model at the economy level, which are both relevant and vulnerable. Those neoclassical models which are associated with (J. R.) Hick's *Value and Capital*,[5] and with the general equilibrium models of Arrow–Debreu, whatever their logical robustness (believed by Arrow and Hahn, for example, to be very great), are not designed to answer the questions at present under discussion. Rather, they are concerned with what rigorously may be said to be true of the properties of the invisible hand, another major insight and preoccupation of the classical political economists from Adam Smith on (see Arrow and Hahn, 1971; Hahn, 1973b; Arrow, 1974). The reason why it is the aggregative theories which are relevant has to do with the attempts of modern theory to tackle the classical questions, especially of the distribution of income, in the context of a class-dominated society. Perhaps it should not be necessary to stress this at the moment in an integrated capitalist world which is dominated by an inflationary crisis which is itself intimately bound up with competing class claims on national products. Admittedly, the modern scenario is much more complicated than the simple triad of landlords, capitalists and workers of the classical stage. Nevertheless, it certainly is an indispensable element of the analysis, far more relevant than an attempt to start with isolated, utility-maximising economic agents with their arbitrary initial distribution of resources, between whom power is diffused equally, which, on the whole, are the characteristics of the orthodox approach to these questions.

Yet the questions themselves have been rejected as uninteresting (Vanags, 1975: 335; Blaug, 1974: 57)[6] or ill-defined (Hahn 1974, 1975b) and the consequent preoccupation with the *meaning*, much more important than the *measurement* of capital, has been rejected as irrelevant for neoclassical analysis and results (see Bliss, 1975; Stiglitz, 1974; von Weizsäcker, 1971). We need only quote Steedman's view (in his review, Steedman (1975), of Blaug (1974)) conclusively to refute this point.

> Their [the post-Keynesian theorists'] good reason [for emphasising the heterogeneity of capital goods but not of labour] lies in the fact that different types of labour do not *need* to be aggregated and can receive different wages while, in long-run equilibrium theory, capital goods have to be aggregated, in value terms, since the [rate of profits] on their value is uniform.
>
> [p. i]

That is to say, for those who dismiss the concept of classes as too vague and woolly to be included in rigorous economic analysis and who seek for universality of principles rather than a more modest set which is tied to time and place, in which the sort of economy that the writer has in mind is explicitly specified – its institutional framework, 'rules of the game' and social relationships – the whole issue has an air of mystery and incomprehension, of being 'rather silly' and unable 'to capture the interest or imagination of economists outside the circle of immediate participants in the two Cambridges' (Vanags, 1975: 334).

All sides of the argument are agreed that there is much wrong with the state of orthodox economic theory at the moment;[7] but here the agreement ends – or almost, for it is also almost agreed that concentration on equilibrium states, as usually or traditionally defined, is one of the root causes of the trouble. Joan Robinson has been attacking what she considers to be the characteristics of the neoclassical concept of equilibrium and equilibrium analysis since at least 1953. Especially has she attacked what she considers to be a characteristic neoclassical methodology of attempting to analyse what are essentially processes occuring in time by comparisons of long-period equilibrium states, a methodology which allows 'time' to be modelled only in so far as it has the characteristics of space (see Bliss 1974).

We should note at this point an important argument by Garegnani. In his view, a belief in long-period gravitation towards natural prices has been shared by all economists up until *Value and Capital* (Hicks 1939). It is this belief that has justified the use of comparisons as an analytical device for 'studying the *permanent* effects of changes in the conditions of the economy' (Garegnani, 1975: 1). Furthermore, it is *not* this methodological procedure which is at fault but, rather, its use *in conjunction with the concepts of supply and demand*, the characteristic procedure of neoclassical economists, including Marshall, the original Austrians, Walras and Wicksell. Garegnani (1958, 1960, 1970a, 1970b, 1973, 1975) has concentrated his criticisms on both the difficulties in the concepts of the supply and demand for labour and especially 'capital', and on the need for there to be a 'well-behaved' relationship between 'capital' and the rate of profits in order that unique and stable equilibria may both exist *and* be attained.

> It is therefore apparent that this difficulty ... concerns the theory (i.e. the way in which the 'centres' of gravitation of the system are determined), and not the *method* of analysis based on such 'centres' ... no similar difficulty arises for the Classical economics who used the same method but did not determine the 'centres' of gravitation as equilibria between supply and demand.
>
> (Garegnani, 1975: 12)

Be that as it may, in place of this method, Joan Robinson has called consistently for a return to a predominantly Keynesian methodology whereby actual historical time is modelled by placing an economy down in history and letting it evolve under the influence of its own past historical experiences and present expectations of the future, in which environment there is an ever present uncertainty of the future, an uncertainty which, by its very nature, cannot be modelled by probability distributions and the like.[8]

In more formal terms, Pasinetti (1974: 43–4) has described the Keynesian method as being akin to the Ricardian one; the economic theorist has a duty to name which relationships between variables exhibit a one-way direction, 'such an overwhelming dependence in one direction (. . . such a small dependence in the opposite direction)', and which are so interrelated as to be properly treated as part of an interdependent system of simultaneous equations.

> The characteristic consequence of this methodological procedure [which also includes singling out for consideration those variables that are thought to be most important] is the emergence in Keynes, as in Ricardo, of a system of equations of the 'causal type' or . . . of the 'decomposable type', as opposed to a completely interdependent system of simultaneous equations.
>
> [p. 44]

Joan Robinson (1975e: 397–8) comments at this point:

> Since the word 'causal' always raises philosophical blood pressure [for a good example see Hahn, 1974: 36–7], the point may be put more concretely: the Keynesian system is designed to show the consequences, over the immediate and further future, of a change taking place as an event at a moment of time, while the equilibrium system can only compare the differences between two positions or two paths conceived as coexisting in time, or rather outside time.

Kalecki also used a similar method, in that he divided time into short periods, each with its own past and expectations of the future, and then let the process unravel as the happenings of one short period were passed on to be the historical or initial conditions of the next, the actual events now helping to form the expectations of the next period. Thus for Kalecki, at least in his later work, the trend and cycle were indissolubly mixed, not separable as in statistical techniques and much neoclassical growth theory.[9] (This approach is well exemplified in Asimakopulos and Burbidge (1974), a post-Keynesian analysis of tax incidence at the economy level, and in Asimakopulos (1977), an endogenous theory of investment in a Kaleckian model.)[10] Hicks, too, uses a similar methodology in *Capital and Time* in order to trace out the immediate and ultimate consequences of a change (in technical possibilities) intruding itself into an existing equilibrium position. He uses a full-employment equilibrium path as the reference point from which to measure divergences as the story unfolds (see Hicks, 1975). It is, moreover, only the early parts of the story – what Hicks calls the Early Phase – which are likely to be of relevance to an explanation of actual events in actual time.[11]

There are, of course, parallel developments in orthdox neoneoclassical theory, in that out-of-(long-period)-equilibrium processes, and studies of transient paths, are its stock in trade, as are the methods of temporary and momentary equilibria. Where the two approaches differ from one another relates especially to their modelling of economies. In one there are still, at least until very recently, isolated economic agents between whom power is diffused equally, usually price-takers *in markets which clear each instant*. In the other we have broad distinct classes classified by their differing functions in the economy and by their different spending, saving and accumulating characteristics, models which, like Ricardo's are 'highly simplified but . . . not arbitrary fanciful constructions like those of Debreu.'[12] Moreover, there is not the same dependence on temporary and/or momentary equilibria, in the sense of market-clearing *prices*, as the means of modelling *actual* processes.

The particular strands of the post-Keynesian approach which has been outlined above are on the whole neglected by its critics. They have tended rather to concentrate on the formal results, for example, those which emerged from the reswitching debates of the mid to late 1960s, the details of which I have not time to discuss tonight. Thus Hahn in one of his many attacks on those he now calls 'the reactionaries' (because he interprets them as a back-to-Ricardo movement) chooses to focus attention on Piero Sraffa's propositions (which are set out in Sraffa, 1960), usually as interpreted by Sraffa's followers. Hahn argues that the post-Keynesian school is concerned with the wrong issues and uses the wrong arguments (see Hahn, 1975a, 1975b). He criticises Sraffa's propositions for their complete lack of operational and/or empirical content (with the exception of the assumption of a uniform rate of profits, which is patently empirically false). That is to say, we have only a set of logical propositions which are of necessity true, not even in principle capable of being falsified empirically. (Presumably such an approach is alright in the theory of optimal growth but not in a prelude to a critique of economic theory.) He is willing (now) to give Sraffa and others an alpha for demonstrating that there is no *necessary* inverse relationship between the rate of profits and the (value of) capital;[13] he is not willing to draw the further inference that Sraffa's propositions were designed as a prelude to a critique of neoclassical-type answers via supply and demand concepts to the questions of accumulation, growth and distribution with which the classical political economists were concerned. Hahn regards these as non-questions for moderns. With the same breath, though, he is willing to praise modern general equilibrium theorists for having provided a rigorous (but, on the whole, negative) set of answers to another grand question which has classical origins, namely, the ability of the invisible hand in a competitive system of isolated economic agents to bring about a satisfactory disposition of economic resources (see Arrow and Hahn, 1971; Hahn, 1973b). Yet it is this sort of theory that underlies (erroneously, evidently) Friedman and Harry Johnson's apologia and propaganda for the virtues of a free market system.[14] And, just for good measure, Hahn (1975b: 362) regards everyone of Sraffa's formal propositions as consistent with and, indeed, deducible from modern general equilibrium theory.

Hahn is very conscious of the rudimentary state of the economic theory which he champions, despite its great technical difficulty. He has, in several seminal articles, discussed the unlikelihood of a growing 'capitalist' economy which contains heterogeneous capital goods (though usually no recognisable capitalists or workers) going through time in a full-employment equilibrium state. He also has been concerned with the puzzles of putting money into general equilibrium models and taking the auctioneer out, so that something akin to Keynesian involuntary unemployment may be made to appear. In passing, he has ridiculed the simple neoclassical models. And he has stressed the nature of an equilibrium as a situation which, *if it were to exist* and if the assumption of maximising behaviour were to be made – 'like Marxian Economics, orthodoxy is founded on the hypothesis of the greedy, rational, self-seeking capitalist' (Hahn, 1974: 35) – would require, as a matter of logic, that certain simple relationships, sometimes akin to textbook marginal productivity relationships, would of necessity hold. But he is most insistent in stating that the proof of existence implies neither uniqueness nor local nor global stability and that it is the latter which are of relevance to the issues discussed in the present theoretical debates.[15] Nor will he allow anything concerning determination or explanation to be drawn from the equilibrium relations. This is a point of view with which Joan Robinson would certainly agree, for it underlies her discussions of logical and historical time and the related concepts of equilibrium and causal models respectively.[16] What Hahn is reluctant to admit – he does grant that 'the neoclassical textbook' is a fair target, hastening to add that 'textbooks [and their "vulgar theories"] are not the frontier of knowledge'[17] – is that the very errors that he deplores in the post-Keynesians are more to be found in a large part of the literature that goes under the name of neoclassical economics, viz. the simple growth models, the econometric studies of the relative contributions of 'deepening' and technical progress to productivity growth over time, and much of the orthodox theory of international trade and development. That there is much at stake has been witnessed to by the recent, in the event, abortive, attempts to defend the neoclassical propositions which underlie these constructions *by means of analyses which consist of equilibrium comparisons* (see, for example, Gallaway and Shukla 1974).

Solow wishes to ride two horses at once. First, he takes a pragmatic approach to the simpler stories, the neoclassical parables which underlie the econometric work and which are only guides to empirical work, even if there is no rigorous theory necessarily to back them up even as possibilities.[18] (The outcome of the reswitching and capital-reversing debates is to show that the parables do not necessarily hold, even as the outcome of long-run equilibrium comparisons, let alone as a description of actual processes – see Harcourt, 1975a: 315–29). Evidently we are to treat them as correct until refuted by empirical findings.[19] But if the world is modelled by a predisposition to find certain relationships there, and if certain observations are to be viewed 'as if' they were the empirical counterparts of the theoretical variables of the model, it is hard to see how the facts could refute them, as opposed to providing the orders of magnitude of the coefficients in the imposed relationships (see Shaikh 1974 and Solow's reply – Solow, 1974). Secondly, Solow is a great proponent of highbrow rigorous theory which, like Hahn and Stiglitz (1974: 898–9), he argues is independent of any relationships and concepts, especially aggregate ones, against which logical objections have been established when the simpler versions of neoclassical theory are examined.

The strongest attacks in the *present* debates or, rather, those most distressing to the protagonists involved, come not from the post-Keynesians on the neo-neoclassicals, nor from the neo-neoclassicals in reply, but from the Marxist and radical enonomists' camp – and the attacks are on the post-Keynesians, not the neo-neoclassicals. (Of course, the post-Keynesians and the Marxists and their allies are united in the attacks on the neo-neoclassicals, though they stress somewhat different issues. It is their attitudes to each other which is under review here.) Two good representatives of this aspect of the controversies are Rowthorn (1974) and Roosevelt (1980) – see also Medio (1972).[20] Partly these attacks are misconceived because they fail always to distinguish between the negative aspect of the post-Keynesians' works – the critique from within, as it were, of neo-neoclassical logic – and the positive aspect whereby they try to provide an alternative approach to economic analysis, building on Marxian, Kaleckian and Keynesian underpinnings. The main thrust of the Marxists' attack relates to the (supposed) neglect of the sphere of production in post-Keynesian analysis and the (alleged) failure also to use the concept of the mode of production, whereby the spheres of production and of distribution and exchange interrelate one with another in an organic manner. This implies both a neglect of the characteristics of the mode of production, in this case, the capitalist mode, and of an analysis of the processes whereby one mode is transformed into another. It is for this reason that the post-Keynesians have been christened neo-Ricardians by Marxists – Marx, of course, made a similar criticism of Ricardo. It is also a clue to the reason why relevance in economic analysis has been defined by some radical economists in recent years as that which adds to our understanding of the inevitable transition to socialism.

Roosevelt sees the post-Keynesians (as represented principally by Sraffa and Robinson and Eatwell (1973)) as falling into the same trap as J. S. Mill whereby the laws of production are universal, technical, physical matters, but the laws of distribution reflect existing institutions and social relationships and are subject to fundamental changes, as well as varying as between one society and another and being, in the main, independent of production. He criticizes at length what he takes to be a neglect of discussion of production as a set of social relationships as opposed to physical and technical ones. He objects to the undue concentration on the distribution of the surplus as opposed to discussions of how it is created, what determines its size and the organic relationship that exists between its production and distribution through the social relationships involved, which he takes to be the principal characteristic of the capitalist mode of production. Both Rowthorn and Roosevelt are critical of the neglect of feedback relationships between the two spheres. They argue that such relationships are a characteristic of Marxian analysis but are, in their view, conspicuous by their absence in post-Keynesian analysis, especially that branch which emanates from and/or is inspired by Sraffa's work.

In contrast to Rowthorn and Roosevelt, Eatwell (1974) virogorusly defends the Sraffian strands, regarding them as constituting important advances in *Marxian* analysis, especially in regard to the form of the problem of the link between 'values' and 'prices of production', i.e. the transformation problem. The latter is not seen primarily as a problem concerned with relative prices, of the link between commodities exchanging at their Marxian or labour values and commodities exchanging at their prices of production. Rather it is seen as the link between surplus value, a social phenomenon that is a function of the social relations in the capitalist mode of production, and profits, as seen on the surface in the sphere of distribution and exchange, as a component of the prices of production. That is to say, it is concerned primarily with the origin of profits in the essence of the capitalist mode of production, instead of with the deviations of the prices of production from Marxian values, a secondary consideration.[21] This link Sraffa provides with his Standard system and Standard commodity (see Sraffa, 1960: chs IV–VI). With these constructions Sraffa is able to demonstrate by his wage-rate – rate-of-profits relation that, although the wage, rate of profits and relative prices of the Standard and actual systems are identical (see Sraffa, 1960: 23), yet in the Standard system the wage, rate of profits relation and the wage, surplus value relation exist, as it were, *prior to and independently of the relative prices*, i.e. the prices of production.[22] 'Sraffa's Standard commodity therefore possesses all the characteristics which Marx sought in the 'average commodity' which was to be the key to his solution of the transformation problem' (Eatwell, 1974: 302).[23]

Though Eatwell criticizes Medio (1972) as well as Rowthorn in his defence of Sraffa, it does appear that Medio and Eatwell agree at least on general issues. Medio's criticism of Sraffa relates to details rather than to his general approach. Thus, Medio objects to Sraffa's assumption that the wage is paid out of surplus rather than advanced and therefore part of the firms' capitals, as in the classical and Marxian tradition. Sraffa adopted his procedure, not without misgivings (see Sraffa, 1960: 9–10), because it had the convenient byproduct that the relationship between the wage (measured in terms of the Standard commodity) and the rate of profits was a very simple straight-line one.[24] Medio feels that this simplification is bought at too high a price in that it obscures the Marxian insight, whereby the wage is measured in terms of labour time, so that the working day splits conveniently into the workman working, first, for himself and then for the capitalist (surplus value). Moreover, Medio argues, in the Sraffian scheme the wage is purely a distributive phenomenon, instead of being integrated into the social and technical relationships associated with the production of output and, more importantly in this context, the surplus. Marx's macroeconomic foundations of microeconomics are thus not sufficiently emphasized in Sraffa's formulation.[25] Sraffa is well aware of this criticism for he argues (Sraffa, 1960: 10) that while his treatment of the wage formally implies that wage goods are non-basics, yet their essentially basic characteristic will show up in the formation of relative prices and profits in other ways.

We may conclude that while the Marxists and radicals legitimately may take issue on the *details* of the post-Keynesians' analysis, their general criticism that there is a neglect of the concept of the mode of production, of social relationships and of the importance of the sphere of production is not really well-founded. Marx was well known for his method of concentrating on one aspect of a large interrelated problem and putting the other aspects theoretically in cold storage, while, at the same time, stressing the importance of their interrelationships and overlaps in a complete analysis. Presumably a charitable view would allow the post-Keynesians a similar dispensation.

II

We now consider the social significance of the controversies. The theoretical issues provide a convenient launching pad. A major result that has emerged is the view of both sides that time must be modelled seriously and that analysis of processes in an uncertain environment is the most pressing problem yet to be tackled, or, at least, tackled satisfactorily. Where the protagonists differ is over the 'vision' of the economy that will go into the model to be used. Thus Hahn (1975b:

363) tells us that there is 'no Millsian complacence [in] the current mainstream theoretical literature' and that '[t]here have been important development in the modelling of information, sequence economies, uncertainty, coalitions and power. Results most damaging to neoclassical theory have recently been proved by Debreu, Sonnenschein and Mas-Collel.' Nevertheless, as Hahn himself made clear in his inaugural lecture (Hahn 1973a), he still wishes to have equilibrium – albeit in a considerably modified neoclassical sense – as a central concept and Walrasian economic agents interacting in Walrasian markets, but now, of course, without the auctioneer and recontracting, but using money, as the principal actors. Bliss, too, while properly aware of the limited advances which further concentration on steady-state analysis will bring, none the less wishes to take over to his studies of 'capital theory in the short run', a framework similar to that of Hahn. Thus he intends to use a *temporary equilibrium* analysis 'in which current markets and a restricted set of forward markets are clearing' (Bliss, 1974: 3).

The use of these approaches means that no radical changes in 'vision' are involved. Capitalism is still seen as advancing through 'a process of "deepening the structure of capital"', in which the savings decisions of atomistic individuals', as expressed in their intertemporal choices between goods today and goods tomorrow, are the driving forces of the system. 'The capitalist firm is seen merely as an intermediary between the individuals as suppliers of factors and the individuals as *rentiers* consuming their lifetime income' (Harris, 1975: 329). Consumption is the be-all and end-all of economic life, accumulation by contrast is an incidental feature, a means merely to an end. Growth in the labour force and technical advances are exogenous to the system. Crises and cycles are aberrations on a process of smooth development (though something supposedly akin to Keynesian involuntary unemployment may be deduced in some versions of these models (see, for example, Malinvaud and Younès, 1975). 'There is no identifiable class of workers displaced from property in the means of production who must depend entirely on employment in capitalistic production ... for their economic survival. It is therefore difficult to see what real historical phenomena ... this system of thought is intended to explain' (Harris, 1975: 330).[26] As Pasinetti (1974) has pointed out, Keynes was modelling an industrial society. This is a tradition which his immediate followers and their pupils have followed. By contrast,

> much of the pre-Keynesian economic thought [which is the base on which both the Bastard Keynesians and the 'new' interpreters of Keynes–Clower and Leijonhuivud – have built] does not ... refer to an industrial society, but to a more primitive ... society, in which resources (... given) are being offered and at the same time represent the purchasing power of the single individuals ... [P]ushed to the extreme, the concepts are shaped into a 'model of pure exchange' expressed precisely by a system of simultaneous equations (supply ... and demand functions) from which prices emerge as the solutions. (p. 47).

This gives rise to the 'misleading impression ... that all the problems of our time would disappear if only the [so-called Keynesian] 'rigidities' were to be eliminated ... as if [they] were the cause and not ... one of the ... inherent consequences of the industrial society in which we live' (p. 48).

By contrast, the positive contributions of the post-Keynesians are intended specifically to deal with the neglected elements which have their base in historical fact and industrial societies. Some members of the school are open to the criticism that they tend to analyse the trend independently of the cycle (e.g. Kaldor's stylized facts do not include the cycle though this has not always been true of his approach). Nevertheless, they have been attempting to provide the ingredients for a theory of growth which is '*a theory of the expanded reproduction of the capitalist mode of production on a world scale*' (Harris 1975, p. 331). When their approach is integrated with Marxian analysis, so that we return to the boundaries of our subject, as 'more generously drawn by the classical pioneers' (Dobb, 1973: 11), we will have a more suitable and richer framework for the analysis of historical developments, past and future. Lest this be mistaken for a plea for economists to be techniques Luddites, it should be said that there is no suggestion that we are to scrap modern methods of technical analysis. Rather, they are to be used at the appropriate places in this different context in order to fine up and enrich the resulting analyses. (A good example of such an application is the analytical sections of Harris's paper (1975: 331–6). I also have in mind the valuable works of Braverman (1974) and Marglin (1971), both of which throw considerable light on the detailed conditions of work, technical advances and saving in the sphere of production, aspects virtually neglected by the neo-neoclassicals and only lightly touched upon by the post-Keynesians.)

There are important social and policy implications of the two contrasting approaches. In a sense, it may not be too fanciful to argue that we are now at a position in time which is equivalent to, or at least has strong similarities with that prior to the publication of *The General Theory*. Then, it will be remembered, both practical men and many economists were advocating pump-priming measures for raising the capitalist world from its slump, but the authoritative theory which would explain exactly *why* there was the sustained slump *and* how these measures could remove it still awaited to be written and accepted.[27] Two branches of orthodoxy dominate the discussion and implementation of policy in the capitalist world: one actually (the Bastard Keynesians), one, on the whole, potentially (the Monetarist school). (Nixon at one stage gave the latter a slight run for its money and recent United Kingdom (Conservative) and Australian (Labor) administrations have flirted with some aspects of the Monetarist recommendations.) The Bastard Keynesians are in the process, which is probably very far along, of being discredited in many capitalist countries, because of the conjunction of high rates of inflation *and* unemployment. An extreme and old fashioned form of orthodoxy is bidding to take its place. 'Once again it is alleged that the private market economy can and will, without aid from government policy, steer itself to full employment equilibrium' (Tobin, 1975: 196). This is, of course, Friedman's Monetarism with its stress on the need to get markets, especially labour markets, functioning efficiently and competitively, and to remove as much as possible the discretionary role of government as well as its absorption of the community's resources. (An even more extreme view is that of Hayek (1975) and his followers, the present von Mises revivalists, who are suspicious even of Friedman and who strangely, even incongruously, want a system of free markets (again especially labour markets) and fixed exchange rates for the capitalist world as a whole.) With this go also their attempts to show that the Keynesian revolution was but an aberration – and an abortive one at that – on the mainstream of the development of liberal economic thought from Adam Smith on.

There are attempts to replace tendencies to deficiencies or excesses in the level of effective demand with the concept of the 'natural' rate of unemployment, a concept which draws on an underlying Walrasian equilibrium in competive markets in which the relative price system is the key method of allocation, and inflation is a monetary phenomenon superimposed on the workings of the real sector. '"[E]quilibrium" often allows for any steady rate of deflation or inflation, not just zero' (Tobin, 1975: 196). In a parallel movement, the Keynesian concept of involuntary unemployment is also being replaced, or whittled away to insignificance, by the job search literature in which is employed the belated discovery that an atomistic competitor in an uncertain world could have some direct responsibility for setting prices which themselves may well not be equilibrium ones.

There are also in places glimpses of and attempts to create consensus policies embodying genuine *money* income restraints and what Joan Robinson has called 'a real social contract which would satisfy the reasonable demands of the workers for more control over their own work, more security against redundancy, better social services and so forth.' This recognises a point which Keynes (and Kalecki) clearly foresaw: that prolonged near full employment would imply inflation unless there were changing attitudes and methods of *money*-wage bargaining. The post-Keynesian critique of the marginal productivity theory of distribution, together with Sidney Weintraub's work, are especially relevant at this point. These efforts tend to be timid and unsustained, to lack confidence because the authoritative theoretical backing, though by no means completely awaiting to be written, certainly does still await wide acceptance. It should also be said that amongst many of those who are attempting to provide it, there is much more ambivalence about (and/or outright hostility to) the desirability of either propping up or salvaging the capitalist mode of production than was the case when Keynes was writing *The General Theory*. It is at this juncture that the post-Keynesian contributions, both methodologically and analytically, most relevantly fit into the current policy and social situations. The above scenario is one of the themes of Joan Robinson's Richard T. Ely lecture 'The Second Crisis of Economic Theory' (Robinson, 1972). These very fundamental and practical implications are thus an important offshoot of the seemingly esoteric theoretical exchanges of the Cambridge controversies in the theory of capital.

NOTES

1. Solow (1975: 277) argues that the real dispute concerns size rather than origin, but I think that this is wishful thinking. For Solow finds his clues to size in the modern versions of Fisherian theory, 'the preferences of investors and savers ... the alternative forms of wealth available to them',

while the post-Keynesian theory has its roots in the Marxian concepts of exploitation and surplus value allied with the Keynesian–Kaleckian solutions of the realization problem, i.e. 'mainly [in] the investment decisions of profit-seeking firms, not ... the intentions to save of thrifty householders' (Robinson, 1975e: 397).

2. 'Keynes' theory of effective demand, which has remained so impervious to reconciliation with marginal economic theory, raises almost no problem when directly inserted into the earlier discussions of the Classical economists. Similarly ... the post-Keynesian theories of economic growth and income distribution, which have required so many artificial assumptions in the efforts to reconcile them with marginal productivity theory, encounter almost no difficulty when directly grafted on to Classical economic dynamics' (Pasinetti, 1974: ix).
3. 'Keynes's intellectual revolution was to shift economists from thinking normally in terms of a model of reality in which a dog called *savings* wagged his tail labelled *investment* to thinking in terms of a model in which a dog called *investment* wagged his tail labelled *savings*' (Meade, 1975: 82, emphasis in original).
4. Similarly, in the initial stages, post-Keynesian theory was preoccupied with Golden Age analysis, as a preliminary flexing of muscles prior to tackling the much harder problems of actual growth processes.
5. Hicks has recently reminded us, as a result of my denseness, that the 'non-neoclassic' John Hicks of *A Theory of Economic History* and *Capital and Time* is J. R's uncle, with which nephew he is not all *that* well-pleased (see Hicks, 1975: 365).
6. 'The great mystery of the modern theory of distribution is, actually, why anyone regards the share of wages and profits in total income as an interesting problem. It has after all little practical relevance.' To this view, happily *and* relevantly, may be contrasted Alice Rivlin's recent 'political prediction' (in her 1975 Richard T. Ely lecture, Rivlin 1975) 'that income shares ... are going to become a major focus of policy debate in the next few years' (1).
7. '[T]he present orthodoxy is in serious need of revision and perhaps of revolution ... the theory of dis-equilibrium is in considerable disarray as is the theory of intertemporal allocation in the face of uncertainty' (Hahn, 1974; 37).
8. 'The Keynesian method is to describe a set of relationships (intended to correspond to what are believed to be the revelant features of the economic system) and to trace the effects in the immediate and further future of a change taking place as an event at a moment of time' (Robinson, 1975: 92).
9. 'In fact, the long-run trend is but a slowly changing component of a chain of short-period situations; it has no independent entity' (Kalecki, 1968: 263).
10. See also Harcourt (1965) for an early example.
11. 'Convergence to equilibrium' has been shown to be dubious ... also unimportant. Even at the best, it will take a long time; and in most applications before that time has elapsed, something else ... will surely have occurred' (Hicks, 1975: 366).

12. Robinson (1975: 92). Hahn thinks Marx would have been scornful of the post-Keynesians – those who Hahn calls 'reactionaries' – because they define class by the orders of magnitude of their savings propensities. 'The reactionaries take differences in the propensity to save as their characterisation of class – how Marx would have scoffed!' (Hahn 1975a: 92). That may be – certainly his present-day followers are rather scornful – though not for this reason (see below). But how much more scornful Marx would have been of Hahn's own peculiarly sophisticated brand of Vulgar Economy.
13. 'The neo-Ricardians, by means of the neoclassical theory of the choice of technique, have established that capital aggregation is theoretically unsound. Fine. Let us give them an alpha for this.' [Hahn, 1975b: 363).
14. It is at this point that Garegnani's (nearly) unique stance is significant. For, as we saw above, he wishes both to defend a well-established methodology *and* to deduce the disquieting conclusion that when it is allied with the neoclassical emphasis on supply and demand, insuperable logical difficulties associated principally with the treatment of 'capital' prevent the approach from providing a viable theory of accumulation and distribution. 'Thus, after following in the footsteps of traditional theory and attempting an analysis of distribution in terms of "demand" and "supply", we are forced to the conclusion that a change, however small, in the "supply" or "demand" conditions of labour or capital (saving) may result in drastic changes of *r* and *w* ... would even force us to admit that *r* may fall to zero or rise to its maximum ..., without bringing to equality the quantities supplied and demanded of the two factors ... no such instability ... ever ... observed ... in order to explain distribution, ... must rely on forces other than "supply" and "demand"' (Garegnani, 1970a: 426). The response of those more favourably disposed towards traditional neoclassical theory (and its modern offshoots) has been either to evade the conclusions (Friedman, Johnson), or to change the questions, or the methodology, or both. Garegnani's lesson from the Cambridge controversies is thus a head-on confrontation, a full frontal attack, *even in terms of the long-period comparisons*.
15. 'The abstract equilibrium tells us what value the unknowns must have if there is to be equilibrium; it does not tell us anything of any economic process which establishes such values' (Hahn, 1974: 36, n. 4).
16. 'There is much to be learned from *a priori* comparisons of equilibrium positions, but they must be kept in their logical place ... cannot be applied to actual situations ... In a model depicting equilibrium positions there is no causation. It consists of a closed circle of simultaneous equations ... At any moment in logical time, the past is determined just as much as the future. In an historical model, causal relations have to be specified. Today is a break in time between an unknown future and an irrevocable past ... Movement can only be forward' (Robinson, 1962: 25–6).
17. Hahn (1975b: 363).
18. For a list of the parables, see Harcourt (1975a: 316).

19. 'The mainstream replies that this is only a crude simplification made for the purpose of applying the theory to real numbers, and so is to be judged pragmatically and not by the standards of rigorous analysis' (Solow, 1975: 277).
20. Roosevelt (1975: n. 2) acknowledges the important influence of Medio and Rowthorn's work on his own.
21. The exchanges between Samuelson (1974a, 1974b) and Baumol (1974a, 1974b) on the transformation problem also centre on these basic distinctions.
22. This, incidentally, gives a rigorous meaning to the classical view that 'distribution precedes value' (Harcourt, 1975b: 342), which Hahn (1975b: 361) finds not merely mistaken but also incomprehensible.
23. Meek (1967: 175–8) made a similar point many years ago in his classic review article of Sraffa's book (originally published simultaneously in the June and spring 1961 issues of the *Scottish Journal of Political Economy* and *Science and Society*, respectively). It was, however, obscured by his exposition in which he treated the transformation problem as being directed more towards an explanation of the deviations of the 'prices of production' from 'values'. Massaro and myself (1964: 453–4), in arguing that Sraffa had rehabilitated the labour theory of value, also pitched it in these terms rather than in the more correct terms, from the point of view of an interpretation of Marx, of the fundamental explanation of the origin of profits, themselves a surface phenomenon.
24. On Sraffa's analysis when the wage is advanced see Roncaglia (1974).
25. 'The theory of *value* performs [an] important function within the Marxian analysis of capitalism. It links Marx's 'macroeconomic model', which shows the mechanism of the system setting some basic relationships between a limited number of variables, with his 'microeconomic model' of interindustry competitive relationships' (Medio, 1972: 330).
26. Harris's paper has greatly influenced the views I have taken in the present section.
27. With hindsight, Harry Johnson (1975) is now arguing that *The General Theory* is yet another example of unnecessary English originality. He feels, moreover, that its effects are pernicious, for it drew on the unique United Kingdom experience – a special case that was nevertheless easily explainable in orthodox terms – as the basis for an unnecessary and incorrect general theory of how capitalism works.

References

Arrow, K. J. (1974) 'General Economic Equilibrium: Purpose, Analytic Techniques, Collective Choice', *American Economic Review*, vol. lxiv, 253–72.

— and F. H. Hahn (1971) *General Competitive Analysis* (San Francisco: Holden-Day; Edinburgh: Oliver & Boyd).

Asimakopulos, A. (1977) 'Profits and Investment: A Kaleckian Approach', in G. C. Harcourt (ed) *The Microeconomic Foundations of Macrosconomics* (London Macmillian), 328–42.

— and J. B. Burbidge (1974) 'The Short-Period Incidence of Taxation', *Economic Journal*, vol. 84, 267–88.
Baumol, W. J. (1974a) 'The Transformation of Values: What Marx "really" Meant (an Interpretation)', *Journal of Economic Literature*, vol. xii, 51–62.
— (1974b) 'Comment', *Journal of Economic Literature*, vol. xii, 74–5.
Blaug, M. (1974) *The Cambridge Revolution: Success or Failure? A Critical Analysis of Cambridge Theories of Value and Distribution* (London: Institute of Economic Affairs).
Bliss, C. J. (1974) 'Capital Theory in the Short-run', Buffalo, mimeographed.
— (1975) *Capital Theory and the Distribution of Income* (Amsterdam. Oxford: North-Holland; New York: American Elsevier).
Braverman, H. (1974), *Labor and Monopoly Capital. The Degradation of Work in the Twentieth Century* (New York: Monthly Review Press).
Dobb, M. H. (1973) *Theories of Value and Distribution since Adam Smith. Ideology and Economic Theory* (Cambridge: Cambridge University Press).
Eatwell, J. L. (1974) 'Controversies in the Theory of Surplus Value: Old and new', *Science and Society*, vol. xxxviii, 281–303.
Gallaway, L. and V. Shukla (1974) 'The Neoclassical Production Function', *American Economic Review*, vol. lxiv, 348–58.
Garegnani, P. (1958) A Problem in the Theory of Distribution from Ricardo to Wicksell. Unpublished Ph.D. dissertation, Cambridge.
— (1960) *Il Capitale nelle Teorie della Distribuzione* (Publicazioni della Facolta di Economia e Commercio dell' Università di Roma, XII) (Milano: Dott. A. Guiffrè Editore).
— (1970a) 'Heterogeneous Capital, the Production Function and the Theory of Distribution', *Review of Economic Studies*, vol. xxxvii (3), 407–36.
— (1970b) 'A reply', *Review of Economic Studies*, vol. xxxvii (3), 439.
— (1973) 'Summary of the Final Discussion' in J. A. Mirrlees and N. H. Stern (eds.), *Models of Economic Growth* (London: Macmillan), 365.
— (1975) 'Comment on Samuelson', Buffalo, mimeographed.
Hahn, F. H. (1971) 'Introduction' in F. H. Hahn (ed.), *Readings in the Theory of Growth* (London: Macmillan), vii–xv.
— (1972) *The Share of Wages in the National Income. An Enquiry into the Theory of Distribution* (London: Weidenfeld and Nicolson).
— (1973a) *On the Notion of Equilibrium in Economics: An Inaugural Lecture* (Cambridge: Cambridge University Press).
— (1973b) 'The Winter of our Discontent', *Economica*, vol. xl, 322–30.
— (1974) 'Back to Square One', *Cambridge Review*, vol. 96, 34–7.
— (1975a) 'Comment', *Cambridge Review*, vol. 96, 92.
— (1975b) 'Revival of Political Economy: the Wrong Issues and the Wrong Argument', *Economic Record*, vol. 51, 360–64.
Harcourt, G. C. (1965) 'A Two-sector Model of the Distribution of Income and the Level of Employment in the Short Run', *Economic Record*, vol. xli, 103–17.
— (1972) *Some Cambridge Controversies in the Theory of Capital* (Cambridge: Cambridge University Press).

— (1975a) 'The Cambridge Controversies: the Afterglow' in M. Parkin and A. R. Nobay (eds.), *Contemporary Issues in Economics* (Manchester: Manchester University Press), 305–34.
— (1975b) 'Decline and Rise: the Revival of (Classical) Political Economy', *Economic Record*, vol. 51, 339–56.
— (1976) 'The Cambridge Controversies: Old Ways and New Horizons – or Dead End?', *Oxford Economic Papers*, vol. xxviii 25–65.
— (1977) 'The Theoretical and Social Significance of the Cambridge Controversies, in Theory of Capital: An Evaluation', *Revue d' Economie Politique*, vol. 87, 351–75.
— and V. G. Massaro (1964) 'Mr. Sraffa's Production of Commodities', *Economic Record*, vol. xl, 442–54.
Harris, D. J. (1975) 'The Theory of Economic Growth: A Critique and Reformulation', *American Economic Review* vol. lxv, 329–37.
Harrod, R. F. (1939) 'An Essay in Dynamic Theory', *Economic Journal*, vol. xlix, 14–33.
— (1948) *Towards a Dynamic Economics: Some Recent Developments of Economic Theory and their Application to Policy* (London: Macmillan).
Hayek, F. A. (1975) *Full Employment at Any Price*? (London: Institute of Economic Affairs).
Hicks, J. R. (1939) *Value and Capital. An Inquiry into Some Fundamental Principles of Economic Theory* (Oxford: Clarendon Press).
Hicks, John (1965) *Capital and Growth* (Oxford: Clarendon Press).
— (1969) *A Theory of Economic History* (Oxford: Clarendon Press).
— (1973) *Capital and Time. A Neo-Austrian Theory* (Oxford: Clarendon Press).
— (1975) 'Revival of Political Economy: The Old and The New', *Economic Record*, vol. 51, 365–67.
Johnson, H. G. (1975) 'Keynes and British Economics' in M. Keynes (ed.) *Essays on John Maynard Keynes* (Cambridge: Cambridge University Press). 108–22.
Kalecki, M. (1968) 'Trend and Business Cycles Reconsidered', *Economic Journal*, vol. xxviii, 263–76.
Kregel, J. A. (1973) *The Reconstruction of Political Economy. An Introduction to Post-Keynesian Economics* (London: Macmillan).
Malinvaud, E. and Y. Younès (1977) 'Some New Concepts for the Microeconomic Foundations of Macroeconomics' in G. C. Harcourt (ed.), *The Microeconomic Foundations of Macroeconomics* (London: Macmillan). 62–85.
Marglin, S. A. (1971) 'What do Bosses do? The Origins and Functions of Hierarchy in Capitalist Production', Cambridge, Mass., mimeographed.
Meade, J. E. (1975) 'The Keynesian Revolution' in M. Keynes (ed.), *Essays on John Maynard Keynes* (Cambridge: Cambridge University Press), 82–8.
Medio, A. (1972) 'Profits and Surplus-value: Appearance and Reality in Capitalist Production' in E. K. Hunt and J. G. Schwartz (eds.), *A Critique of Economic Theory. Selected Readings* (London: Penguin Books Ltd.).
Meek, R. L. (1967) *Economics and Ideology and other Essays. Studies in the Development of Economic Thought* (London: Chapman and Hall).

Ng, Y. K. (1974) 'The Neoclassical and the Neo-Marxist-Keynesian Theories of Income Distribution: a Non-Cambridge Contribution to the Cambridge Controversy in Capital Theory', *Australian Economic Papers*, vol. 13, 124–32.
Pasinetti, L. L. (1962) 'Rate of Profit and Income Distribution in Relation to the Rate of Economic Growth', *Review of Economic Studies*, vol. xxxiv, 267–79.
— (1974) *Growth and Income Distribution. Essays in Economic Theory* (Cambridge: Cambridge University Press).
Rivlin, A. M. (1975) 'Income Distribution–Can Economists Help?' (Richard T. Ely Lecture, 1975) *American Economic Review*, vol. lxv, 1–15.
Robinson, Joan (1953–4) 'The Production Function and the Theory of Capital', *Review of Economic Studies*, vol. xxi, 81–106.
— (1956) *The Accumulation of Capital* (London: Macmillan).
— (1962) *Essays in the Theory of Economic Growth* (London: Macmillan)
— (1972) 'The Second Crisis of Economic Theory' (Richard T. Ely Lecture, 1972), *American Economic Review*, vol. lxii, 1–10.
— (1974) *History versus Equilibrium* (London: Thames Polytechnic).
— (1975a) 'The Unimportance of Reswitching', *Quarterly Journal of Economics*, vol. lxxxix, 32–9.
— (1975b) 'Reswitching: Reply', *Quarterly Journal of Economics*, vol. lxxxix, 53–5.
— (1975c) 'Introduction 1974. Reflections and Reminiscences' in *Collected Economic Papers*, vol. ii (Oxford: Basil Blackwell, 2nd ed.), vol. iii–xii.
— (1975d) 'Introduction 1974. Comments and Explanations' in *Collected Economic Papers*, vol. iii (Oxford: Basil Blackwell, 2nd ed.) iii–xiv.
— (1975e) 'Review of L. L. Pasinetti, *Growth and Income Distribution. Essays in Economic Theory*, 1974', *Economic Journal*, vol. 85, 397–9.
— (1975f) 'Letter to Editor', *Cambridge Review*, 96, 91–2.
— and J. L. Eatwell (1978) *An Introduction to Modern Economics* (London: McGraw-Hill).
Roncaglia, A. (1974) 'Labour-power, Subsistence Wage and the Rate of Wages', *Australian Economic Papers*, vol. 13, 133–43.
Roosevelt, F. (1980) 'Cambridge Economics as Commodity Fetishism' in E. J. Nell (ed.), *Growth, Profits and Property: Essays in the Revival of Political Economy* (Cambridge: Cambridge University Press) 276–302.
Rowthorn, R. E. (1974) 'Neo-classicism, neo-Ricardianism and Marxism', *New Left Review*, No. 86, 63–87.
Samuelson, P. A. (1966) 'A Summing up', *Quarterly Journal of Economics*, vol. lxxx, 568–83.
— (1974a) 'Insight and Detour in the Theory of Exploitation: a Reply to Baumol', *Journal of Economic Literature*, vol. xii, 62–70.
— (1974b) 'Rejoinder: Merlin Unclothed, a Final Word', *Journal of Economic Literature*, vol. xii, 75–7.
— (1975) 'Steady-state and Transient Relations: a Reply on Reswitching', *Quarterly Journal of Economics*, vol. lxxxix, 40–7.
Shaikh, A.. (1974) 'Laws of Production and Laws of Algebra: the Humbug Production Function', *Review of Economics and Statistics*, vol. lvi, 115–20.
Solow, R. M. (1974) 'Laws of Production and Laws of Algebra: the Humbug Production Function: A Comment', *Review of Economics and Statistics*, vol. lvi, 121.

— (1975) 'Cambridge and the Real World', *Times Literary Supplement,* (14.3.75), 277–8.

Sraffa, P. (1960) *Production of Commodities by Means of Commodities. Prelude to a Critique of Economic Theory* (Cambridge: Cambridge University Press).

Steedman, I. (1975) 'Critique of the Critic', *Times Higher Educational Supplement* (31.1.75), i.

Stiglitz, J. E. (1974) 'The Cambridge-Cambridge Controversy in the Theory of Capital: A View from New Haven: A Review Article', *Journal of Political Economy*, vol. lxxxii, 893–903.

Tobin, J. (1975) 'Keynesian Models of Recession and Depression', *American Economic Review*, vol. lxv, 195–202.

Vanags, A. H. (1975) 'Discussion' in M. Parkin and A. R. Nobay (eds.), *Contemporary Issues in Economics* (Manchester: Manchester University Press), 334–6.

Weizsäcker, C. C. von (1971) 'Ende Einer Wachstumstheorie? Zu Hajo, Rieses Missverstandnissen über die "Neoklassiche" Theorie', *Kyklos*, vol. xxiv, 97–101.

3

Eric Russell, 1921–77: A Great Australian Political Economist*

I

I am greatly honoured to be asked to give the 1977 Newcastle Lecture in Political Economy. Last year Professor Youngson kicked off the series with a fine evaluation of the contributions of the first great political economist, Adam Smith.[1] This year I want to discuss the contributions of Eric Russell to Australian political economy. This is a sad and a proud task; sad, because Eric was my friend and my mentor. I valued his good opinion more than anyone else's, as did all his friends – and now he is gone, dying suddenly on 26 February this year. It is a proud task, because it was a unique privilege to have known and worked with Eric and now, I hope, to contribute towards ensuring that his achievements live on. But I would not wish this to be a solemn occasion. Eric was the wittiest and happiest of men, enthusiastic and alive, loving and loveable, properly angry when he had to be, but polite, courteous, modest, a great man at a party, a superb sportsman, and I'd like some of that atmosphere to be here as we look at his work.

II

Eric was born in 1921. His father was a stationmaster in the Victorian Railways, so that the young Russells (there were four children) moved

* The 1977 Newcastle Lecture in Political Economy. Originally published as Research Report or Occasional Paper no. 36, University of Newcastle, Australia, 1977. I have been greatly helped in preparing the lecture by the research assistance of Anne Madden.

round a lot in Victorian country areas. Nevertheless, his secondary schooling was in Melbourne – Eric was a product of the vintage years of Melbourne High School – and he went on to the University of Melbourne during the war years, obtaining first-class honours in Arts and Economics. History, philosophy, economics, theatre and literature were his intellectual loves. An early important influence on him was the late George Paul, the Cambridge philosopher who was then at Melbourne. After the war, Eric went to King's, Cambridge, where he read for Part II of the Economics Tripos and obtained a first in the company of Frank Davidson, Harry Johnson, Robin Marris, I. G. Patel and Aubrey Silberston. He was supervised by Gerald Shove and Richard Kahn, he saw the great Keynes in action once (when, I understand, Keynes rather went after Joan Robinson). Eric was also one of the small chosen band that attended Wittgenstein's lectures at Cambridge. Returning to Australia, he taught at Melbourne, Sydney and the University of New England (it was New England University College then) before coming to Adelaide in 1952 to join his old friend and contemporary, Peter Karmel.[2] Eric stayed there for the rest of his life, except for three spells of study leave at Oxford (1960), and the London School of Economics (LSE) (1967 and 1976). He was promoted to Reader in 1958, appointed to the newly created second Chair of Economics in 1964 and became Chairman in 1966. This is not the place to assess his achievements as Chairman and University of Adelaide man generally. Suffice it to say here that they were splendid. What I want to do today is to speak of Eric Russell, the political economist.

Why do I describe Eric as a political economist? He certainly was *not* that comfortable with *some* aspects of the political economy movement in Australia today, especially those elements that tend to be dogmatic and strident in tone. Yet he *was* a political economist in the best sense of the word – he was always conscious of the political and institutional settings of any economic problem and he was interested in economics only in so far as it bore directly or indirectly on policy issues. In all the major policy issues of the postwar period Eric's was always one of the first and wisest voices (despite the fact that he published very little[3]) – and his analysis of a problem was *never* confined to what the orthodox would regard as the *economics* of it. That is to say, it was not confined to those factors which could be contained under the umbrella of maximisation or minimisation under constraints. No, as the late Maurice Dobb has it,[4] like the classical pioneers, Eric was prepared to draw more generous boundaries in order to include whatever factors from whatever 'discipline' as long as they were relevant to, and illuminating of, the problem in hand. (He was very strict about the responsibility attached to those who offered advice and he himself was extremely careful and cautious, always shaping out and making explicit where framework and fact ended and judgement, values and ideology entered in policy matters, or where they could not be unentwined.)

As a result, Eric's economics was a splendid blend of many traditions. His historical perspective always made him conscious of those sustained and fundamental forces stressed by the classical political economists, especially by Ricardo, as well as of dynamic historical processes, the different strengths of which served to differentiate both economies and epochs one from another. From the classicals and Marx, he took note of social relationships, of classes and their clashes, of contradictions and either their exacerbation or their elimination by endogenous economic processes, for Eric had a healthy respect, given the appropriate circumstances, for the survival power of the body economic and politic. From the orthodox, he took a thorough knowledge of substitution possibilities, especially over longer periods of time – he put the energy crisis into perspective as a result, while at the same time recognising it, increasingly so in recent years, as a most serious and dangerous problem. He also took from them the relevance and usefulness of supply and demand analysis in the discussions of devaluation, fixed versus floating exchange rates, and similar problems. From Keynes and Keynes's followers he took the basic insight that capitalism was a production system in which money, and financial institutions generally, played an indispensable role. Finally, from this same Keynesian tradition, together with his own instinctive sympathies and understanding, economics was to Eric, I believe, a moral science in which a sense of relevance and moral purpose was always central and to which he brought a willingness to use intuition and judgement as well as the more conventional methods of economic analysis, to acknowledge that a changing universe was its proper subject.[5]

III

I wish now to illustrate these general points by considering in some detail Eric's contributions in three areas, between which, however, there are unifying threads and strands. The first is Eric's seminal paper (written jointly with James Meade) which was published in the *Economic Record* in April 1957.[6] This paper sets out Eric's basic views on *how* the Australian economy works, what the social relationships and relevant institutions are, how the domestic price level is formed and how Australia as a small open economy responds to external happenings. This paper represents the 'vision' which Eric took with him into all his discussions of Australian economic problems. He amended and updated it through the years but, nevertheless, it represents the foundations of his thinking. It is a fascinating story as to how the paper came to be written and I have been able to reconstruct some of it from the evidence provided in his papers, in which is included his correspondence with James Meade. (The latter, incidentally, is a model of civilised and honest communication and response.)

The Meade–Russell paper sets the scene for perhaps his most important contribution: his work on an Australian wages and, latterly, incomes policy, especially his submission of evidence to the Arbitration Commission in 1959,[7] his important paper in *Australian Economic Papers* in 1965,[8] which was capped off by a talk which he gave to the South Australian teachers of economics in 1971[9] and his version of the Adelaide Plan which was delivered as a public lecture in Unley Town Hall in 1974.

The final illustration is Eric's Presidential address to Section 24 of ANZAAS (Australian and New Zealand Association for the Advancement of Science) in 1972, 'Foreign Investment Policy – What Role for the Economist?'. Ostensibly it was on the debates about foreign investment in Australia and on what an economist might be expected to contribute to the arguments. It gave Eric an opportunity to set out his views on methodology, the value of economic theory and the use of empirical evidence.

IV[10]

The Meade–Russell paper had its origin in Trevor Swan's then unpublished but already famous Swan diagram of external and internal balance, with its zones of economic unhappiness and ambiguous signals as to which instruments to use in order to hit what targets. Swan's analysis initially derived from Meade's great works on international economic policy[11] which in those days were, rightly, everybody's bible (despite Harry Johnson's savage review of Vol. I, 'The Taxonomic Approach to Economic Policy'[12]). Nevertheless, Eric sensed that in the form which Meade originally gave to his models and which Swan adopted, they belonged to, as Eric said, 'another world'; that they were in certain important respects inapplicable as models which purported to catch the crucial features of the Australian economy. Eric therefore prepared for a staff–student seminar in 1953 some notes in which he wrote down what he considered to be the critical characteristics of the Australian economy for the sorts of puzzles that were then demanding the full attention of Australian policy-makers and academic economists alike. (The immediate puzzle was the great wool boom of the early 1950s which was associated with the extraordinary demands for raw materials for stockpiling which accompanied the Korean War.) These notes formed the background to Eric's teaching of honours students in subsequent years. When Meade (who was spending six months at the Australian National University) came to Adelaide, he and Eric talked about these issues. Meade was so impressed by Eric's approach that when he returned to Canberra he wrote a paper which included orthodox models, such as he himself was accustomed to use, which gave formal content to Eric's ideas and which brought forth Eric's results. (In the opening footnote to this first draft, Meade writes: 'The analysis in this note was prompted by a discussion with Mr. E. Russell ... who suggested most of the ideas to me, though I do not want to hold him responsible for the conclusions which I have drawn from them'.) In a letter to Eric (6 September 56) which accompanied the note, Meade mentions that Dick Downing would like to publish the note in the *Economic Record*. Meade, like Barkus, was willing but had one reason for hesitation:

> With my usual inability to distinguish between my own and other people's ideas, I think that it is quite possible that every idea in the note is yours; [moreover, if Eric had in preparation a paper on the same subject] I would not want to go ahead with my note.

He asked for Eric's views on this and any comments on the analysis itself. In a letter of 8 September 56 (addressed from the LSE), Meade writes:

> ...another though has occurred to me. It would give me great pleasure if you would be willing to sign something on the lines which I sent you jointly with me.

Eric responded with a very full letter, only a draft of which remains in his files.[13] Eric ended by saying that he would like to add his name to Meade's on the paper – 'your offer is a most generous one' – but should not as it stands. He suggested three possible courses of action:

1. Meade to publish his note as it was, with Eric following on in a later issue of the *Record*, 'setting out ... the judgements involved in the policy recommendations.'
2. '[W]hat I would like the best'. 'In a joint article list, without deciding the issue, what factors would have to be taken into account in making a policy judgement. That is, present the article as a theoretical analysis, clarifying the Australian dilemma and giving a plausible framework in which economists and policy makers can make qualitative and political judgements.' (This particular approach to advice Eric always scrupulously followed himself. As he said in his ANZAAS Presidential address, '[if] there are no simple truths ... suitable for painting on a banner, it is proper to point this out ... a fault to pretend otherwise. If to do so is academic, so much the better for academic studies' (p. 1).)
3. Add a footnote to Meade's paper to the effect that certain estimates were still a matter of judgement.

Meade responded immediately (15 November 56) with a revised note 'which simply omits all policy arguments', as he 'would very much like to turn the note into a joint note ... because ... it is clear from your notes of 1953, that the basic idea is yours rather than mine'. This became the Meade–Russell paper as published; it 'includ[ed] only what [they] both wish[ed] to say – a neutral model with all policy implications suppressed' (E.A.R. to R.I.D., 26 November 56)[14]. Eric added:

> Something like it should have been put in the *Record* in 1952–3. A more interesting example for analysis in 1956 would be to work out the implications of an exchange rate variation on reduction in money wage rates relative to prices. The model would be the same ... the questions would have a less old-fashioned look

especially today!

Why did not Eric publish his ideas earlier on and on his own? What were the essential characteristics of the Australian economy, as he saw them, which made him feel that the Swan–Meade keys were to open doors to 'another world' and that he did not want to accept the policy implications of the first draft of Meade–Russell? There were two 'general reasons' why Eric had not published before. First, Swan had not published his paper(s), the ideas of which were nevertheless very influential in getting the Arbitration Commission to 'set a wage which would contribute to "internal balance" by setting an appropriate relationship between Australian and world prices'. They also underlined the abandonment in 1953 of the automatic cost-of-living adjustment.

> The economic rationale was in Swan's papers. . . . Secondly, to do the trick properly would require that [the analysis] be related in a strict way to traditional theory. Ad hoc models in a crude arithmetic (not . . . accompanied by a tight mathematical analysis) cannot budge an accepted theoretical system.

'[Therefore]', Eric wrote to Meade,

> your article from my point of view is doubly excellent. It sets out a relevant model of the Australian economy and it is related to your own previous work . . . very important that you should have done it.

The features of the Australian economy which Eric identified in his 1953 notes and which Meade incorporated, albeit in a Meadean neo-classical form, in the Meade–Russell paper are, first, the ratio of exports to national income is very high; secondly, Australian exports (at the time) were predominantly agricultural and pastoral so that they had a very low elasticity of supply in the short run. (Eric made a qualification about metals and also added that this was true more in aggregate rather than necessarily so for any one commodity.) The implications were that with fluctuations in world incomes, there were wide fluctuations in export prices. (Thus, one of the favourite exercises given to first-year Adelaide students in macroeconomics is to get them to work out the multiplier consequences of a change in the *value* of exports as opposed to a change in their *volume*. The latter is the more usual exercise in that students usually are given an exercise which is based on the model which was first developed by Joan Robinson in 1937 when she 'opened' the model of the *General Theory*, having in mind no doubt an exporter of manufactures such as the United Kingdom.[15]) Thirdly, there is a tendency for the *home* price of commodities that are exportable ('exportables') to move in sympathy with the prices of exports. (Eric added the qualification that home prices schemes, such as were prevalent in the 1950s and earlier, may weaken the link in the short run. Nevertheless, there is constant pressure on such schemes because of the need to keep some balance between the controlled and uncontrolled prices.) These characteristics, taken together, imply balance of payments problems, a tendency to induced income fluctuations and a tendency for the distribution of incomes as between rural and urban areas to fluctuate widely.

Next, we take account of the link between the consumer price index (then the *C* series) and the facts that a high proportion of wages and salaries are adjusted for variations in it, that from time to time there are adjustments to the 'real' basic wage, and that there is a '[r]emarkably strong tradition of pricing in the domestic market ... by [a] constant percentage mark-up on wage and material costs'.

It is these features taken together which cause special difficulties for policy-makers to achieve widely acclaimed objectives – high levels of employment without inflation (no excess demand), relative stability of general prices, equity in income distribution between wages and gross profits, between urban and rural incomes, balance of payments equilibrium, and the use of the price mechanism in the allocation of resources between primary and other production and between home production, exports and import replacement. 'In fact these demands on policy makers are mutually inconsistent'.

The particular problem which Meade analysed was the process that is set in train by a rise in demand for the exports of a small country that exports mainly primary products, the wage-earners of which country consume a basket in which the prices of 'exportables' and imports figure prominently and whose money-wages are linked either formally or informally to a cost-of-living index. The analysis is done in neoclassical terms – relative factor intensities determine marginal products which in turn help to determine real income shares – rather than in terms of Eric's model. The latter, in effect, incorporated the Kaleckian version of the main propositions of *The General Theory*, allied with Kalecki's microeconomic foundations, especially in manufacturing industry, and macro theory of distribution, suitably modified to take into account the Australian class structure, history and institutions, together with a realistic assessment of what the traditional workings of market mechanisms could and could not be expected to achieve.[16] In any event, the story that emerges from both approaches is the now only too familiar one of the rise in export demand (or a devaluation) ultimately making the balance of payments weaker because of the consequent reaction of money-wages and prices to the income distribution initially implied, and the consequent changes in the demand for imports and, these days, the reactions of speculators with respect to the capital account.

V

We now move to the debate about wages policy in the 1960s. This was already in Eric's mind when he was corresponding with Meade. He had been asked to give evidence, or at least advice, about the South Australian living wage and he took as the background, his views on how the Australian price level adjusted in order to bring about a distribution of income that was 'livable with'. Moreover, in the 1950s he worked extraordinarily hard for the wage-earners' cause, especially in advising Bob Hawke on the content of his ACTU (Australian Council of Trade Unions) briefs. In 1959 Eric prepared a theoretical paper (he was one of the first Australian academic economists ever to go into the witness box on behalf of the trade unions) and the late Wilf Salter prepared the empirical estimates of productivity. Eric believed that at a minimum, the wage-earning sectors of Australian society were entitled to share in *effective* productivity gains and therefore that effective productivity based on longer run underlying trends and ignoring temporary fluctuations was the appropriate concept which the Commission should have in mind in determining the capacity of the economy to pay wages. Eric's was a significant intellectual contribution in that the argument about wages was never the same again, at least not until very recently!

His views on effective productivity and the Commission were at the forefront of his thinking when he returned to the question of a wages policy for Australia in his 1965 *Australian Economic Papers* article.[17] The Commission had '[e]xplicitly in the basic wage cases of 1961 and 1964 and the margins case of 1963 ... followed the principle of adjusting *real* wages for productivity' (p. 1). By contrast, a number of economists – Eric lists Hancock, Karmel, Downing, Isaac, Cockburn and Whitehead – had been urging the Commission 'to set award wages in such a way that average money earnings increase at the same rate as the average productivity of the work force' (p. 1). By the 1965 judgement their combined influences, both directly and through employers' counsel, had been successful. '[T]he majority judgement ... rejected the principles of the 1961 basic wage judgement; explicitly denied that price increases gave grounds for increasing minimum wages ... [and] returned to the principle – without – content, that the wage should be the highest that the economy has capacity to pay' (pp. 1–2). Eric's paper explores 'in the Australian context' the implications of adjusting money-wages for productivity. His objective was to provide a rationale for the Commission's past reluctance to accept the economists' advice, and to project some of the difficulties that may follow from the 1965 policy being adopted.

The first aspect that is discussed is the mechanism by which the economists' rule is said to achieve price stability. Two essential links are concentrated on, that between awards and earnings, that between costs and prices. Only if these are invariably stable relationships which can be depended upon will the Commission's decisions do the trick, so that the choice of a lower rate of increase of award rates 'will have no "real" economic consequences other than those that might flow from worsened industrial relations' (p. 3). As to the second strand of the argument, Eric seemingly foregoes one of the major strands of his own (earlier) argument, viz., the constant mark-up hypothesis which underlies the argument for the stability of the aggregate gross profit margin in manufacturing industry. I say, seemingly, for he made the simplifying assumption of a constant mark-up, I suspect, first, because it was the *simplest* most plausible assumption for catching the characteristics of the manufacturing sector, and, secondly, because using it allowed the model builder to bring out in stark relief the role of the prices of exportables and imports *vis-à-vis* the achievement of *domestic* price stability. Moreover, he added, it is wrong, in searching for a rule for price stability, to generalise the characteristics of manufacturing industry where there are grounds for expecting stable margins (though Eric notes the exceptions, too) to other administered prices such as medical services, rent, power and transport services.

The Meade–Russell model is most in evidence in section IV of the 1965 paper where Eric analyses the implications of a productivity only rule for a 'trading nation', and also of some variants of it, for example, the domestic productivity *plus* export prices rule, which received some support from Hancock and Karmel, and which is equivalent to the effective productivity *plus* internal prices rule – '[i]n the timeless world of algebra' but not as practical policies where they are 'wildly at odds'. The first rule would entail tying money-wages to the most volatile component in the Australian price structure whereas the latter 'damps the adjustment process', an essential ingredient for any practical policy (p. 18).

In the paper, Eric attempted to work out the effects on prices, money- and real wages and the distribution of income of following the productivity rule. (The essential function of adjusting money-wages for prices as well as productivity with a fixed exchange rate is to raise the internal price level in step with world prices, thereby averting a redistribution of incomes towards the export sector; it 'might also be a first approximation to an appropriate balance-of-payments adjustment' (p. 19).) Unfortunately, in the article he made a statistical error in the calculations. (He deflated Australian costs by home production instead of by the volume of goods available in Australia.) Donald Whitehead[18] picked up the error and, correcting for it, argued that Eric had been hoist with his own petard, especially as Eric had argued that in this 'area ... numbers are the essence of the problem' (p. 15). Donald certainly was correct, as far as this particular strand of Eric's argument was concerned.[19] Despite this, the overall soundness of his arguments remain intact. The Commission serves both a useful and a realistic function if it arranges that money-wages rise in such a way that the Australian price level keeps in step with prices in the 'relevant' overseas markets. In this way, the authority of the Commission is not eroded, and when overseas events *do* demand some departure from the rule because of a disequilibrium in the balance of payments, the Commission *then* is in a position to make its decisions consistent with those of government policies as a whole. The relevance of Eric's judgement, written twelve years ago, has recently been re-affirmed by the main thesis of Deputy President Isaac's 1977 Giblin Memorial Lecture.[20]

Thus, to Eric, wages policy was as much a political as an economic problem. Indeed, as Peter Karmel has written,[21] '... the notion that there were unique solutions derived from economics angered him'.

This same insight is shown in Eric's contribution – a major one – to the 1974 so-called Adelaide Plan. Then, on a platform provided by the Liberal Movement in the Unley Town Hall (a rather incongruous speaking format for an old 'Leftie'), Eric stressed the need to find consensus, to reach people's sense of fair play, to show that sacrifices are both necessary – that the problems were serious and real – and would be shared, before the problem of inflation could be brought under control – and, most important, unemployment avoided. Hence the various ingredients involved – indexation of money-wages in return for restraint on *over* indexation payments, taxes on excess profits and/or on those who paid excess increases in wages (sweetheart agreements), the possibility of making greater profits by increasing efficiency or selling more output. There was, moreover, always his desire to work through the institutions that already existed, to appeal to the sociological and historical background which people understood and with which they were comfortable. There was also the attempt to use the carrot and stick technique in order to induce and cajole the actual decision-makers to take the directions desired, rather than to use administrative fiat. Finally, there was the overlay of pragmatism and common sense allied with humility, modest aims and a modest assessment of the likelihood of success in a complex area.

VI

Eric's agnosticism and modesty, both about his own analysis (where it was unnecessary) and about what economic analysis may be expected to achieve (where it was) were displayed in the areas just discussed, and, perhaps most clearly and at their best, in his Presidential address to ANZAAS in 1972. The paper was published in posthumously in *Australian Economic Papers*, vol. 17, December 1978, 193–206. He took as his subject, 'Foreign Investment Policy – What Role for the Economist?'. He felt that an economist might 'disentangle some of the elements in the public debate ... identify those matters of theory and fact where ... an economist [might] speak with some special authority' (p. 193). He mentioned in passing the reaction to the Treasury paper, *Overseas Investment in Australia*, published just after his own topic had been 'embedded in the ANZAAS brochures', that '[i]t was "academic" ... offered no conclusions for policy', on which he offered the comments that I have already quoted.

Eric chose three areas in order to illustrate how economic theory and assumptions are used in making decisions:

1. The balance-of-payments costs for the home country of foreign investment.
2. Whether foreign investment will add to the net real income of residents of the borrowing country.
3. Whether the price offered by foreigners and accepted for Australian assets is a proper price.

The focus was on 'what evidence [economists] offer or *can* offer about the realism and the relevance of the . . . models they use' (p. 194). In the discussions under the first head in which Eric criticised both the Treasury and the Vernon Committee discussions of this point, it is made clear that the essential judgement relates to whether or not the free market solution is always the most efficient, least painful one. Thus the Treasury, in declaring that there is little or no *special* balance-of-payments cost of foreign investment,

> argues that if the exchange rate is at the right level . . . domestic policies . . . well managed . . . the relation between prices and incomes in Australia and overseas will ensure that the balance of payments and the resources of the economy will adjust to the investment of foreign funds . . . the remittance of foreign earnings . . . will be achieved with 'ease'.
>
> (pp. 197–8)

Eric comments: 'The basic confidence of the Treasury Paper is in the efficacy and speed of working of the market mechanism' – quick response and adjustment from eager and alert businessmen, mobile and self-interested labour, ample responsive supplies of the required skills and investment funds, quick adaption of existing land and capacity to new market opportunities.

> To believe the contrary, . . . that the response of business is sluggish . . . that the process of change [is] resisted by ignorance and defensive, conventional responses, is not 'an assumption' [but] a different claim about the way the economy works in fact.
>
> (p. 198)

'The Vernon Report, for example (and the enormous tradition that it reflects) finds the market a weak instrument for securing coherent, overall objectives' (p. 198).

How, asks Eric, are we to judge between these views?

> Just because economists construct ... explore the implications of models that highlight price/output relationships, it does not follow that economists *must* or *can* with authority judge, that the Australian economy will, in fact, adapt quickly ... painlessly to small changes in relative prices. Whether theories mirror the world will not be determined by an appeal to the theories.
>
> (p. 199)

The free market advice is not based on special studies of particular countries – it is 'an all-purpose advice' which allows the economist to 'start talking as he gets off the plane' (p. 199). Or, sometimes, it is a second best: 'From Adam Smith to Harry Johnson the pro-market view has relied both on confidence in the beneficence of the invisible hand and doubts about the quality of the state apparatus' (p. 199).

In discussing additions to the net real income of residents, Eric proceeds by assuming away any transitional or adjustment problems associated with foreign investment occurring (such as had been the essence of the matters discussed under the previous head). He argues that:

> ...of necessity, the enquiry must be deductive, must appeal to general theoretical reasoning ... [for] [w]hat *is* at issue is how well based are the theoretical models and how do we judge this when we use them to make policy prescriptions.
>
> (p. 200)

At the centre of this particular argument is the neoclassical proposition that profits on a unit of capital are a measure of the increase in output that the increase in capital brings about, i.e. it depends upon the validity of the marginal productivity theory of distribution. Eric then launched into an attack on the theory and its applications that does Joan Robinson proud. The upshot of the discussion is nevertheless that 'the answer is not to be arrived at by a closer examination of the theory but ... by a judgement about the way that markets and market pressures, in fact, work' (p. 201). 'Economic theory does not tell us that competition is the case. It explores the implications of *assuming* that competition is the case' (p. 201). Again the crucial point is the need to form a view about the way the world actually works.

Finally, we come to a passage which illustrates the acuteness of Eric's mind and, especially, his critical powers.[22] In talking about the prices paid by foreigners for Australian assets during the investment process, Eric speculated about the *nature* of the prices so paid and the possibility that some of the pressure for controls on foreign investment might spring from a belief that prices arrived at in the market might be less than the 'true worth' of the assets. He added:

> The economist's paradigm market case is Wicksteed's thrifty housewife who moves among the familiar market stalls, comparing the lettuce and the cabbages, noting their well-displayed prices and at last selecting her basket of greens. After watching her, it would indeed be strange to wonder, 'but did she really prefer the goods that she in fact bought?' No, in this case, with *all* the evidence fresh and crisp before her, what she does *is* what she prefers. But we slip over to other cases where doubt is proper [and] [t]he slide from 'He does so-and-so' to 'He prefers so-and-so' to 'so-and-so is *to be* preferred', [though it may be] almost instantaneous, [is also misleadingly treacherous.] The essence of the matter is, of course, the information that is available to the parties.
>
> (p. 203)

Eric was sceptical about Meade's judgement that the market is 'the most efficient and rapid calculating machine yet devised for the solution of ... complicated economic riddles'.[23] But he was also sceptical of uncritical and empty platitudes about replacing the market by planning, and he was sympathetic towards 'economists [who] tend to favour an eclectic set of policies that largely continue the practice of the past', in the present situation, for example:

> ...an admixture of interventions in international transactions, monetary and fiscal policy changes, ad hoc attempts to restrain the rate of change of money wages through arbitration tribunals, from time to time changes in the exchange rate, some compromise about

> the objective of price stability ... untidy, discretionary, changing as the world monetary system changes.
>
> (p. 206)

He ended the paper by saying 'that one's view of the way the world works will tend to cohere with one's values and political judgements' (p. 206).

VII

Eric's own values were admirable and his political judgements, sound. Because of his own superb mind, he sometimes saw more issues, interconnections and subtleties in situations than ordinary mortals would have been capable of, so that he sensed conspiracies or saw plots which in fact were not always present. But generally and overall, he was spot on and we can only be thankful that large numbers of students, who were inspired by him and his approach, are now able to lend wise counsel in those places where decisions are made.

Eric hated injustice and under-privilege – he was at one a most dispassionate and passionate person – he valued friendship, he loved fun, good food and drink, playing squash and 'make-up' games (beach cricket and tennis), the entertainment of yer average Australian – the footy, the races – the interplay of congenial minds. His economics was always directed towards removing those obstacles in the way of others achieving such ends, if they wanted to. In the process he made the subject live marvellously for his pupils and his colleagues. As Peter Karmel said, 'it was Eric who kept facing us with the wider issues of the human condition [just as it was he who reminded] us of the limitations of our discipline'.[24]

Eric was my friend and my mentor. Much of what I think is too personal to be said in a public lecture or written in a published tribute. Nevertheless, I hope that I have managed to give you a glimpse of why he so influenced those who knew him and of why we loved him.

Notes

1. A. J. Youngson, 'Adam Smith and the Omnipresent State', Research Report or Occasional Paper no. 27, ISBN 0 7259 0247 7, Department of Economics, The University of Newcastle, November 1976.
2. Peter Karmel writes: 'In the early 1950s at Adelaide ... new professors could ... secure one or two additional posts. My turn came in 1951, and I felt

enormously flattered and happy when I discovered that Eric was prepared to come to Adelaide as senior lecturer in 1952', 'Eric Alfred Russell', *Australian Economic Papers*, vol. 16, 1977, 159.

3. See G. C. Harcourt, 'Eric Russell, 1921–77: A Memoir', *Economic Record*, vol. 53, 1977, 468–9, for an attempted explanation why.
4. M. H. Dobb, *Theories of Value and Distribution since Adam Smith* (Cambridge: Cambridge University Press, 1973).
5. V. Chick, 'Come Back Keynes', *Times Higher Educational Supplement*, 31 January 75, vol. ii.
6. J. E. Meade and E. A. Russell, 'Wage Rates, the Cost of Living and the Balance of Payments', *Economic Record*, vol. XXXIII, 1957, 23–28.
7. 1959 Basic Wage Case: Statement of Evidence by Eric Alfred Russell (mimeographed, Adelaide, 1959).
8. E. A. Russell, 'Wages Policy in Australia', *Australian Economic Papers*, vol. 4, 1965, 1–26.
9. E. A. Russell, 'Australian Incomes Policy' (mimoegraph, Adelaide, 23 April 1971).
10. This section is based upon the papers and correspondence that I have found in Eric's papers about Meade–Russell. I am indebted to James Meade for additional information and his own recollections of events.
11. J. E. Meade, *The Theory of International Economic Policy*, Vol. I, *The Balance of Payments* (Oxford: Oxford University Press, 1951), Vol. II, *Trade and Welfare* (1955).
12. H. G. Johnson, *Economic Journal*, vol. LXI, 1951, 812–32.
13. I am hoping that James Meade has the actual letter in his papers: a search of them – they are stored at the LSE – is currently being done. [It was never found, G.C.H., November 1999.]
14. In a letter to me (15 August 77), Meade comments (following his discussion of the events in the text); '[W]hen I got Eric actually to sign on the dotted line, this was regarded as the greatest achievement of my six months in Australia!'
15. Joan Robinson, *Introduction to the Theory of Employment* (London: Macmillan), 2nd edn, 1969.
16. In his Presidential address to ANZAAS, Eric repeatedly stressed the central importance of deciding whether flexibility or rigidity characterises the production and exchange spheres of the economy concerned when choosing between particular views and their associated implied or explicity recommended policies; see below, 59–61.
17. This paper was originally given at ANZAAS in Hobart in August 1965.
18. 'Professor Russell on Wages Policy: A Comment', *Australian Economic Papers*, vol. 5, 1966, 224–9.
19. Eric never published a reply to Donald but I have found in his papers drafts of a reply in which, while he concedes the immediate point, he nevertheless re-asserts the fundamental soundness of his approach and views.
20. J. E. Isaac, 'Wage Determination and Economic Policy', ANZAAS, Melbourne, 1 September 1977.

21. P. H. Karmel, 'Eric Alfred Russell', *op. cit.*, 160.
22. In Peter Karmel's tribute in *Australian Economic Papers* to Eric, his classmate at the University of Melbourne and subsequently close colleague and friend at Adelaide, we read: 'Eric was the widest read of the group and acknowledged as having the most critical mind' (159).
23. J. E. Meade, 'The Price Mechanism and the Australian Balance of Payments', *Economic Record*, vol. 32, 1956; 243.
24. P. H. Karmel, 'Eric Alfred Russell', *op. cit.*, 160.

4
On Theories and Policies*

There are at least three schools of thought which may be said to underlie current debates on policy, two of which, though they start from different theoretical premises, nevertheless largely inform our present (late 1976 but pre-devaluation) policy stances.[1] They also reflect the philosophy of the leaders of the present government, in so far as they could be said to have a coherent and consistent philosophy. The third school departs from the former two both in theoretical analysis and policy prescription. The three schools are, respectively, the monetarists (which have their greatest though by no means exclusive influence in the Reserve Bank); the Bastard Keynesians (which by and large is the stance of the treasury though there are also aspects of it in the often eclectic approach of the Reserve Bank economists, just as there are some monetarist elements in treasury thinking); and the Post-Keynesians. The Post-Keynesian school is the group of theorists who draw directly on the work of Keynes himself. The most influential members include Joan Robinson and Richard Kahn (that is to say, the people who actually worked with Keynes after he had published the *Treatise on Money* and when he was writing *The General Theory*), and their followers and contemporaries, for example, Nicholas Kaldor. The other major influences are Michal Kalecki, and

* Originally published in J. P. N. Nieuwenhuysen and P. J. Drake (eds), *Australian Economic Policy* (Melbourne: Melbourne University Press, 1977), 40–52. Comments on a draft of this chapter were made by John Burbridge, Jon Cohen, Ronald Henderson, Mervyn Lewis, Ian McLean, and the editors; however, they must be completely absolved from responsibility for *any* views expressed here.

Marx and the classical political economists, especially as the latter have been interpreted through Piero Sraffa's and Maurice Dobb's edition of and writings on Ricardo, and through Sraffa's own original works, most importantly, the *Production of Commodities*.[2] These are, of course, broad judgements, which try to discern major stances and trends, and to identify dominant themes. Clearly neither Reserve Bank nor treasury officials are homogeneous or abstract labour power.

The Friedman view

Milton Friedman's monetarist philosophy, which has a great influence on aspects of the Reserve Bank's approach, has its ideological roots in Smithian liberalism. It involves a policy of non-intervention, except for the creation and/or preservation of competitive institutions and relatively simple rules for the monetary authorities to follow, together with a much more modest role for the public sector than is the case at the moment. Its theoretical basis also lies in one aspect of the Smithian vision (another aspect leads to Marx and the Post-Keynesians), that of the efficacy and efficiency of the invisible hand, as achieved through the market-clearing properties of freely fluctuating prices in individual markets. The line goes through Walrasian general equilibrium rather than through Marshall, which is more the tradition of the second school in Australia, especially Melbourne – of the Prest era anyway – though not, of course, in the United States. Friedman's life work may be seen from one aspect as a concerted effort to pick off, decade by decade, the principal props of Keynes's system – the rival consumption functions; the relative impact of money versus investment on overall activity and prices; the liquidity preference theory of interest versus Friedman's capital theory; monetary versus fiscal policy; the relative importance of balance sheets *vis-à-vis* income and expenditure accounts; and so on. He wishes to reveal the so-called Keynesian revolution as an abortive aberration in the mainstream of economic theory and, incidentally, make the world safe for free men. (Harry Johnson has been the most prolific, indeed obsessive, expositor of this view. For obvious reasons, Friedman has been more muted, not least because, as Patinkin has argued and Friedman has conceded, Friedman's 'restatement' of the Quantity Theory has Keynesian innovations and attitudes in it.)

The practical implications of Friedman's views include an attack on detailed, and often variable, government intervention on fiscal matters, especially the irresponsibility and dishonesty of taxation through inflation in order to move resources into the public sector, a commitment to simple but sustained monetary rules, and encouragement of attempts to create flexible competitive institutions so that the real world may be made to work as if it were a Walrasian system. The latter is especially true of the attitude to labour markets, where a dislike of minimum wage regulations goes hand in hand with humanitarian plus efficiency support for comprehensive retraining and relocating schemes, coupled with the advocacy of the need for great increases in information flows. Allied with these views and the monetarist's version of the quantity theory of money is the central importance that is given to the role of expectations, especially wage-earners and businessmen's expectations about the future course of prices in relation to their money-wage receipts or payments. In particular, Friedman (and Hayek) believe that an economy, left to itself, could find its way to that level of employment where individual labour and product markets clear at the appropriate prices (the natural rate of unemployment), a process that is being continuously frustrated by misguided attempts to run the economy below the natural rate, so creating accelerating inflation. Consequently, practical policy implications must involve intermittent spells of unemployment. The object of this is to create a new climate of more moderate expectations about prices and wages so that the 'correct' relative wage and price structures may be perceived, undistorted by the overall inflationary veil. Furthermore, from such situations, the economy's markets may grope for the 'correct' relative price structure from above the natural rate, as it were, without perpetrating new bouts of accelerating inflation. Hence we have had Reserve Bank support for the treasury's short-sharp-shock thesis (which seems to have been maintained for rather a long time now), its opposition to 'excessive' public sector spending and deficit, its belief in the primacy of curing inflation, and its lukewarm attitudes to the wage indexation experiment. (A Friedmanite variant would be, of course, indexation of everything so that the relative price system would always be revealed, regardless of the overall absolute rate of inflation. Hayek, by contrast, wants a return to a regime of fixed exchange rates in order to impose strict monetary disciplines on governments – or, failing that, have them give up altogether issuing money unless they are shown to be responsible in their behaviour. Otherwise, more acceptable counterfeiters are to take over.) It should be noted that the theoretical underpinnings of the monetarist position – do but leave well alone and all will be well – are not supported by the findings of the modern mathematical work on general equilibrium theory, in particular, the ability of a competitive capitalist economy to grope successfully to an equilibrium, an equilibrium, moreover, which even if it exists, may not be either unique or locally or globally stable.[3] The monetarists' answer is, of course, that the proof of the pudding is in the eating and that their relatively simple, causal models *are* supported by *their* abundant empirical findings.

The Bastard Keynesians

The Bastard Keynesians share a similar micro-economic foundation to that of the monetarists – markets which behave as if they were Walrasian competitive ones – but part company with them on the ability of a capitalist economy left to itself to find its way, even sluggishly, to a full employment equilibrium. That is to say, they accept, correctly in my view, that Keynes's revolutionary contribution was to demonstrate the possibility of underemployment rest states, through the development of the theory of effective demand, as Kregel recently has reminded us.[4] Hence they see a role for government intervention of a macro-economic nature, such as treasury has long been accustomed to do. The Hicks–Hansen *IS–LM* analysis is their main tool of analysis. It is unKeynesian without quotes;[5] nevertheless Keynes himself in *The General Theory* is not entirely free of blame for the micro-economic foundations, though they are Marshallian not Walrasian.[6] Thus Joan Robinson has described Keynes's and the true Keynesian approach, as exemplified in chapter 21 of *The General Theory*, as follows:

> We [the 'British Keynesians'] started from the concept of the Marshallian short-period situation, in which fixed plant, business organisation and the training of labour are all given, and can be more or less utilised according to the level of effective demand. A short-period supply curve relating the level of money prices to the level of activity (at given money-wage rates) led straight from Marshall to [*The*] *General Theory*.[7]

Whether we use the Marshallian micro model of Keynes or the Walrasian micro model of the Bastard Keynesians, we have an underlying rationale for the control of both unemployment and inflation centrally to rest in the hands of the treasury through fiscal policy (aided, no doubt, by consultations with their junior partners at the Reserve Bank). The emphasis, though, is on control of the levels of real demands, so that as the product markets work themselves out, derived demands for labour show up in job vacancies plus relative wage movements. These imply, overall, a level of money-wages which, given the (short-run) level of productivity, is consistent with reasonable price stability, especially in relation to rates of increase of prices among our trading rivals.

There is, moreover, an element of Keynes's closed economy model in the argument that a cut in real wages is the only way effectively to raise employment, i.e. that a lower real wage is needed in order that the economy may move down the aggregate marginal product of labour curve towards the intersection of the demand and supply curves for labour (which signifies full employment in the labour market). This is, of course, a position which is not achievable automatically by the unaided workings of the capitalist system when there is a failure of effective demand. (In an open economy the lower real wages will also affect imports and exports.)

The micro-economic aspects of the above analysis imply that it is the product wage (the money wage deflated by the price of the products which businessmen sell) which is – in the model – the relevant one for the real wage, marginal product comparison by the profit-maximizing, cost-minimizing businesspeople. It is not, in the model, the real wage as seen by the wage-earners (i.e. their money wages deflated by an index of the prices of the commodities which they habitually consume). Yet the call in Australia in 1976 for a cut in real wages, which are said to be too high, has consistently been based on the latter, which is inappropriate even in terms of the theoretical model which props up the analysis. The appropriate calculations which are needed to see whether in fact wages are too high (we would still need to ask, relative to what) would be figures for the export sector wage, the import-competing sector wage, the non-traded goods sector wage, and so on. To my knowledge, these calculations have never been done, or at least, made public. In any event, it would be necessary also to take into account the feedback repercussions on aggregate demand of the means whereby the cuts were brought into effect, an old-fashioned maxim of Keynes which rather seems to have been forgotten in recent discussions.

Supposing such a cut in real wages to have been secured without adverse consequences on planned spending then, the argument goes, there would be the added advantages of (1) allowing the bulk of Australian exports to sell at prices which, though set abroad, nevertheless would promise profits at home, (2) reducing our demand for imported goods at any given level of activity, and (3) raising profits' share in output to a level which, at least indirectly, would encourage a rise in the level of planned investment expenditure. There is no place here for either union power or indexation – hence the unswerving hostility to the latter, and the advocacy by the treasury of the short-sharp-shock thesis (and now the sustained variant) in order to blunt the former. The above theoretical underpinnings thus have the advantage of keeping economic power firmly in the treasury's hands (despite the creation in 1976 of a separate Department of Finance), so adding weight to a natural human tendency to hold on to what has been achieved already and to ward off interlopers. The severity, indeed savagery, of its practical implications for many Australian citizens reflect in part the isolation of the decision-makers in Canberra from the human aspects of their decisions. It also reflects the contempt which practical men of affairs in the treasury (and industry) have for academic criticism and developments. These are considered to be airy-fairy stuff of no practical importance – except, of course, as Frank Davidson once remarked, for those theories of the three years or so when the decision-makers themselves were undergraduates. Then, just for once, theory magically provided the necessary structures of thought which the decision-makers have retained for ever after. (This phenomenon is not confined to decision-makers.)

Post-Keynesianism

Post-Keynesianism, as mentioned, has its roots in Keynes, Kalecki, Sraffa, Marx and the classical political economists. In recent years some have tended to take the Kaleckian rather than the road that Keynes either had taken or may have meant to take – this is especially true of Joan Robinson and her closest followers. It *is* the appropriate road for analysing the present Australian situation, for a number of reasons. First, its micro-economic foundations are to be preferred as being more relevant and realistic. In the Kaleckian framework, an explicit role is given to the administered price sector, usually identified with manufacturing. The typical firm is pictured as having a reverse L-shaped marginal (equals average variable) cost curve, implying a physical limit to production at any moment of time, with actual levels of production usually below this limit. A distinction is made between direct (factory floor) labour and indirect labour (the managing director, supervisory staff and Mrs Mops who will be there as long as the firm does not close down, and so regardless of short-run fluctuations in production).[8] This has the important implication, that as output levels are raised in the short run, overall labour productivity rises, so that it is possible to obtain a shift to profits without there being any change in prices or the size of the mark-up on average variable costs (at normal levels of output) and the costs themselves (the mode of pricing which is taken to be characteristic of this section of industry). The shift to profits has important consequences for the level of private investment expenditure. The other sectors of the economy are viewed as more conventionally competitive, with Marshallian-type demand and supply forces interacting to set prices in markets which are characterized by price-taking by the individuals in them. (Hicks has dubbed these distinctions as fixprice and flexprice respectively.) A theory of the size of the mark-up completes the story – in Kalecki's models, the degree of monopoly, in more recent developments, a link between investment expenditure plans and the resulting finance required is invoked in order to determine its size within the constraints imposed by the extent of the competitive nature of the industry, the level of activity and so on.

Secondly, within the framework, a macro theory of distribution emerges at the same time as a theory of the short-run level of activity. This is especially relevant for today's problems because it focuses directly on the inflationary consequences of inconsistent income distribution demands which are a prominent feature of the present (and past) inflationary puzzles. Thirdly, the framework is explicitly one of political economy, reflecting Kalecki's Marxist background and also Keynes's view that theory was valuable only in so far as it threw light on current problems and contributed in detail to the formation of policy. It involved, moreover, an explicit recognition of what Kalecki called the political trade cycle and the class struggle over distributive shares. He recognised very early on (as did Joan Robinson and Richard Kahn) that sustained full employment was an open-ended invitation to inflationary pressures through rises in the (efficiency) money-wage rate so that periodic interruptions of it would be needed in order 'to discipline the workers'. (The interruptions also would need to be timed *vis-à-vis* election dates.) Stability of the money wage was the clue to the stability of the whole system. Since Kalecki – and the Post-Keynesians – regard the periodic bouts of unemployment as savage and uncivilised, they, very early on again, sought alternative ways of influencing the overall level of the money-wage and, thus, given the underlying micro foundations, the overall price level: hence Joan Robinson's remark, initially in the mid 1930s, that incomes policy was her middle name.

A further desirable property of the Kaleckian version of the central propositions of *The General Theory* is that it is set in a model of cyclical growth, a model of motion, the happenings of one short period influencing the behaviour of the next. '... the long-run trend is but a slowly changing component of a chain of short-period situations; it has no independent entity'.[9] Furthermore, the model is explicitly set in a class context where the producing, spending and saving behaviour of broad sociological groups are differentiated and explained. (In Australia, one immediately thinks of exporters, manufacturers and wage-earners as a preliminary broad classification.) Moreover, the process of development over time is seen as a reproducing and expanding one (not necessarily steadily, of course) in which profit-making and capital accumulation are ends in themselves, not means to the end of maximizing the satisfactions of individuals through the patterns of their lifetime consumption. Again Kalecki is to be preferred to Keynes, in that Keynes has individual psychological underpinnings to his aggregate consumption function so that saving is discussed in terms of individuals' choices between the present and the future, rather than as a function of what particular classes are meant to do and are able to do, which is a characteristic of Kalecki's approach, and which, in my view, is the more relevant and realistic model of the process of accumulation in capitalist economies.

The above views have fundamental implications for the attitudes which will be taken to economic policy in general, especially when allocation over time is no longer seen to be the necessary product of an efficient price system. (Thus it could be argued that the recent clash over the company taxation portions of the *Mathews Committee Report* may be explained in terms of two very different 'visions' of how society may be though of as working. One view is Chicago, the other is Keynesian–Marxist in spirit.) Of course, it must be pointed out that the Post-Keynesian model as a method of theory nevertheless can encompass a wide range of political attitudes and ideologies – from Keynes plus compassion through Crosland socialism and Wedgwood Benn-ery to a Marxist restructuring of the whole society. Hence, it has also been criticised as principally a closed economy model, so that when open economy puzzles have been considered, there has tended to be a rather *ad hoc* advocacy of specific controls.

Keynes has often been criticised for making the money-wage level exogenous to his system, for examining the implications of changes in money-wages but not asking first how they came about and whether there was endogenous process involved in it all. There is some merit in the criticism, as far as Keynes himself is concerned, though it could be said in his defence that an assumption of relative constancy made more sense as a practical starting point when he was writing *The General Theory* than it would in the postwar world. Moreover, there is an endogenous story told in Book Five of *The General Theory,* though it is never spelt out very fully or far,[10] and the question of sustained full employment and the money-wage was not discussed. Nevertheless, as Paul Davidson and Sidney Weintraub have documented in detail, Keynes was fundamentally correct in seeing the central importance of efficiency wage stability for the stability of the system as a whole and his immediate followers–Kahn and Joan Robinson, for example – have carried on the analysis of the implications of this fundamental insight in very great detail indeed.[11] In recent years they have been joined by Hicks[12] and Phelps Brown, who see an important part of the postwar inflationary problem as founded in sociological and historical learning patterns, allied with deeply ingrained notions of 'flair' wages (which include a notion of a 'fair' rate of increase). This implies that long-established relativities are hallowed, and any major rupturings produce havoc. Phelps Brown has also stressed even more what he believes to be the inflationary consequences of what he sees as the shift in the balance of power to unions.[13]

One advantage that Keynes had over Kalecki in the development of the Post-Keynesian tradition was that Keynes was first and foremost a monetary economist, so that *The General Theory* was a major modification of Keynes's intended *magnum opus,* the *Treatise on Money*. Much of the latter's monetary analysis was still regarded by Keynes as relevant, to be taken as given as a background to *The General Theory*. Hyman Minsky has made this the central theme of his interpretation of *The General Theory,*[14] as has Paul Davidson in *Money and the Real World*.[15] Minsky shows that the rich balance sheet analysis of firms and households of the *Treatise on Money*, together with the new developments of *The General Theory*, imply that the main model of *The General Theory* is a theory of the (real and monetary) cyclical development of the economy. The cycles arise from the implications of disappointed expectations concerning cash flows, the accompanying distorted balance sheet patterns relative to income and expenditure accounts, themselves the products of changing states of confidence and expectations, and the reactions of firms and households to them and to their effects on the markets for financial assets. This is not to say that Kalecki ignored monetary factors. The principle of increasing risk is still a relevant part of the story and his two-sided link between profits and investment, whereby the former are both the inducement for and the means to enable, directly and indirectly, the financing of investment, are the basic ingredients of the Post-Keynesian theory of investment. The Minsky–Davidson–Keynes –Kalecki strands together may be seen as constituting the outline of a plausible alternative story to that of the monetarists (and to that of Tobin) in trade cycle analysis and the role of monetary policy.

Finally, Kalecki's approach to the theory of investment is preferable to Keynes's, for it explicitly deals with plans, construction and final implementation, explicitly taking account of the time lapses between them. As we have seen, this allows the economic process to be modelled as the happenings of one short period growing out of another. Kalecki was prepared to be more cavalier than Keynes in his treatment of time. Keynes in the end thought it best to give up trying to handle time processes in analytical detail (even though he had done this successfully in the *Treatise on Money*). He settled instead for the theory of effective demand, the possibility of underemployment equilibria (rest states), ignoring in order to make this central point (and also because he believed it was not possible to find a 'determinate time unit'), lags, processes and feedback phenomena, especially amongst expectations.

Policy approaches

With the above as background let us finally turn to a discussion of policy approaches, both of recent years and for the future. In general the events of recent years, especially the behaviour of the Liberal – Country Party coalition when in opposition and its method of coming to power, culminating in the governor-general's actions of 11 November 1975, make very poor the chances of conservative governments in Australia being able successfully to implement policies which would be consistent with Post-Keynesian analysis, even if they wished to, which clearly they do not. Moreover, the experiences of the Whitlam government while in office also make for scepticism about the chances of a social democratic government implementing successfully a 'Keynes plus compassion' policy such as that attempted by Labor. This reflects not only Labor's inexperience and, at times, incompetence, silliness and lack of resolution, and the extraordinarily difficult general problems faced by the Labor administration, but, more importantly, fundamental and deep-seated power sources in the political and economic structure of Australian capitalism. These together imposed constraints which virtually ruled out the Labor government's ability to act in certain ways. The constraints are set by both domestic and overseas business interests, by the power struggles and differing ideologies within the Labor and trade union movements themselves, by what the federal and state public services themselves will tolerate, and by the privately controlled media, all of which militate against fundamental changes in the public-private sector split, or major redistributions of wealth and income.[16] The 'animal spirits' of Australian business are so susceptible to policies which it feels to be against its own interests (whether its perceptions are right or not is another matter) and its ability to act by reducing investment spending is so effective, as to make the room for manoeuvre by a Whitlam-type government extremely limited indeed. The practical alternative, therefore, may be a reversion to a Lewis-type policy[17] whereby private consumer spending leads in both recovery and in sustained growth (in the latter accompanied by private investment spending), aided by a restructured tax system, with the public sector taking an increasingly modest role in the provision of goods and services.

Another alternative approach whereby the socialist nettle, such as is outlined in Stuart Holland's *The Socialist Challenge*,[18] suitably modified for Australian conditions, is grasped, seems far from being an election winner, or at least as being perceived as such by those who make policy and political decisions in the ALP. It seems unlikely then that there is yet another alternative, that of creating in Australia consensus policies embodying genuine *money* income restraints and what Joan Robinson has called 'a real social contract which would satisfy the reasonable demands of the workers for more control over their own work, more security against redundancy, better social services and so forth'.[19]

But, if this alternative were possible, what forms would it take? As far as maintaining a high level of employment and a satisfactory rate of growth is concerned (its composition will need attention, too, but that is another story for the moment), the single most important institutional change required in Australia is the creation of effective machinery with which to ensure that, by and large, we obtain the level and rate of change of prices which is acceptable, largely independently of measures designed to affect the level of employment and the rate of economic growth and its composition. Post-Keynesian theory suggests that there is a wide range of the level of activity over which money-wages and prices may be regarded as independent of the level of activity, at least for quite substantial periods of time. It is this proposition that needs to be exploited. Of course, we already have gone rather haltingly and reluctantly towards establishing such a set of institutions, with the introduction of pre-tax and now post-tax indexation procedures. These constitute in effect a form of incomes policy which is historically and sociologically suited to the Australian industrial environment. Indexation is understood and by and large trusted by our wage-earning groups, and present attempts by the government and its advisers to smash it seem tragically ill-advised. As argued elsewhere,[20] it is the major reform that can remove the overriding anxiety of each wage-earning group in a period of inflation, namely that its absolute real income may be eroded. In its absence, each group of necessity pitched its money-wage demands towards the upper limit of what was considered to be feasible, and employers individually were inclined to acquiesce, with the result that the overall outcome was to give an intolerably high level and rate of increase of overall money-wages and therefore prices. This led inevitably to savage fiscal and monetary policies designed to bring the rates down, policies that proved ineffectual in their aims and disastrous and tragic in their byproducts. It was a weakness of the initial arguments for indexation that, in so far as they were concerned with tackling inflation, they were coupled with egalitarian considerations. Thus flat rate adjustments other than at the bottom end of the scale were advocated in order to narrow differentials. Another major weakness, given the inflation rates that had been experienced and which were to come, was not immediately to couple pre-tax indexation with post-tax indexation.

Of course, indexation by itself is not a panacea. It needs to be coupled with a relativities *plus* productivity element, that is to say, a wages fund over and above that already spoken for by the indexation procedure proper. Its size would be determined by considerations such as whether the economy is in a transition state, as far as the creation of new institutions is concerned, or whether it has reached its new ongoing path, with the institutions securely established. The fund would allow ruptured relativities to be restored (not necessarily in one fell swoop), for relativities to change if seemingly irresistable forces suggest that this is desirable, and for all groups to receive money-wage increases which allow them to absorb their share of any general rise in prosperity that is implied by the underlying trend in national productivity, if and when the latter is resumed. (The danger is that the recent inflationary experience together with plateau and/or partial indexation procedures may have so ruptured previously long-established norms that, now, no concensus may be established as to what *is* the structure which ought to be restored. Moreover, there may no longer be that measure of good will with which to allow a new pattern either to be agreed upon or arrived at. Even if productivity growth *is* zero, it may well be necessary to have a fund with which to tackle the inherited stock of ruptured relativities over a transition phase. Of course, a successful attack on inflation itself should allow productivity to start growing again.) What must be appreciated is that the same *real* gains may be realised by employed persons through a myriad of money-wage and price combinations, but only a small range of them is consistent with the other aims of high employment, reasonable growth and remaining competitive in comparison with our main overseas rivals. The quid pro quo for the *money*-wage constraint involved would be the provision of goods and services through the public sector which is beneficial in particular to the wage-earning sectors and their children. Such, of course, was the rationale of much of Labor's programme. This means that by wage-earners foregoing unduly inflationary pressures on money-wage levels and, indeed, at times being prepared to make some sacrifice in the rate of increase of their real take-home pay, the government in return would be in a position to ensure jobs and redistribute resources in a more egalitarian manner, while at the same time maintaining activity at a level which ensures that adequate investment is undertaken, and profits received, by the private sector.

Finally, governments must put forward explicitly coherent and integrated policies, the framework and broad targets of which are fully explained to all relevant sectors. Then, they must show a determination to stick to them regardless of the inevitable flak from the various interested groups who may be adversely affected, at least in the short run and sometimes permanently. Inflexibility, of course, must not be made the only virtue. There should be minor detailed alternatives and some room for manoeuvre. Nevertheless, resolution and defined objectives, of which all are made aware, are definitely needed and have been conspicuously absent in the policies of governments of recent years.

Notes

1. Mervyn Lewis has pointed out that there is a fourth school which may be dubbed 'structuralist' and which considers macro policy from an essentially orthodox micro basis. Members include F. H. Gruen, R. G. Gregory and the I.A.C. economists. Although their influence on policy may have been considerable, it is not discussed in this essay.
2. P. Sraffa, *Production of Commodities by Means of Commodities: Prelude to a Critique of Economic Theory* (Cambridge: Cambridge University Press, 1960).
3. See, for example, F. H. Hahn, 'The Winter of Our Discontent', *Economica*, vol. xl, 1973, 322–30.
4. See J. A. Kregel, 'Economic Methodology in the Face of Uncertainty; The Modelling Methods of Keynes and the Post-Keynesians', *Economic Journal*, vol. 86, 1976. 209–25.
5. The best short account of why, is the Appendix to Donald Moggridge's Fontana Modern Masters biography of *Keynes* (London, Fontana/Collins, 1976). The basic reason is the non-independence of the *LM* and *IS* curves. They interrelate through the medium of interrelated and changeable expectations, so that movements of one (or along one), unless very marginal, inevitably imply movements, not always predictable, of the other. 'If both curves shift, there is no clear prediction possible ... as to what the final outcome will be' (166).
6. Three years later, in his *Economic Journal* comment on Dunlop's and Tarshis's findings on real and money-wages over the cycle, Keynes changed his position and enunciated what must be one of the earliest statements of the normal cost-pricing hypothesis that now is characteristic of the microeconomic foundations of Post-Keynesian theory: see *The Collected Writings of John Maynard Keynes. The General Theory of Employment, Interest and Money*, vol. VII (Macmillan, London, 1973), appendix 3, 406–12. No doubt it was all in Marshall anyway.
7. Joan Robinson, 'Review of A. Leijonhufvud, *On Keynesian Economics and the Economics of Keynes*, 1968', *Economic Journal*, vol. 79, 1969, 582. Putting the two strands, Hicks–Hansen and Marshall, together, the model may be set

out in terms of two simple diagrams which allow the price level to be introduced explicitly: see G. C. Harcourt, 'A Post-Keynesian Development of the "Keynesian" Model', in Edward J. Nell (ed.), *Growth, Profit and Property: Essays in the Revival of Political Economy* (Cambridge University Press, New York, 1980), 151–64.

8. Of this group, cleaners are probably the most vulnerable in situations of sustained unemployment.
9. M. Kalecki, 'Trend and business cycles reconsidered', *Economic Journal*, vol. 78, 1968, 263.
10. This was in keeping with Keynes's method in his book, as he wrote to Hicks (see Moggridge, *Keynes*, 92), of not 'pursuing anything very far, [his] object being to press home as forcibly as possible certain fundamental opinions – and no more'.
11. In particular, I would refer readers to Kahn's masterly paper, 'On Re-reading Keynes' (The British Academy Keynes Lecture, 1974) *Proceedings of the British Academy*) vol. lx, Oxford: Oxford University Press, 1974, 1–33. Kahn's analysis of the roles of money and money-wages in Keynes's own thought and in the Post-Keynesian tradition is absolutely authoritative. Incidentally, he outlines a package deal which in essentials corresponds to the analysis and policies most favoured in this paper, see, especially, 30–2.
12. John Hicks, *The Crisis in Keynesian Economics*, The 1974 Yrjö Jahnsson lectures (Basil Blackwell, Oxford), Lecture 3; 'What is wrong with Monetarism', *Lloyds Bank Review*, no. 118 (October 1975), 1–13.
13. Henry Phelps Brown, *Collective Bargaining Reconsidered* (Stamp Memorial Lecture, London 1971), vol. 12–13; 'A non-monetarist view of the pay explosion', *Three Banks Review*, no. 105 (March 1975), 3–24.
14. Hyman P. Minsky, *John Maynard Keynes* (Columbia University Press, New York, 1975).
15. Macmillan, London, 1972.
16. There are other ratchet-type effects which put (some) constraints on *cuts* in expenditure, e.g. the education lobby, and structural changes, e.g. the protectionist lobby.
17. M. K. Lewis, 'Why aren't taxes cut?' *Australian Financial Review*, October 19 and 20, 1976.
18. Quartet Books, London, 1975.
19. Press release of public lecture in Adelaide, April 1975. Joan Robinson was clearly pessimistic about the chances of such a policy actually coming about; nor was her heart in it anyway, for she would prefer to see society restructured on much more radical lines. However, James Meade and his happy band of intelligent radicals seem much more confident of success, as indeed we all might be, if only our worlds were exclusively inhabited by civilized, humane and enlightened James Meades, and we had as much confidence as he has in the Bastard Keynesian aspects of his analysis: see James E. Meade, *The Intelligent Radical's Guide to Economic Policy. The Mixed Economy* (Allen and Unwin, London, 1975).
20. G. C. Harcourt, 'The social consequences of inflation', *Australian Accountant*, vol. 44, 1974, 520–8.

5
The Mixed Economy*

with Prue Kerr

All ideological camps of the Australian Labor Party (ALP) are reconciled, some more happily than others, to the fact that in the foreseeable future an ALP government will be operating within the context of a mixed economy, that is to say, an economy in which the public sector plays a central role in determining the overall level of activity and the composition of national output. This reconciliation raises problems both for the extent and nature of this public sector intervention and for short-run and longer-run policies appropriate to the major economic problems of Australia. These are problems manifest in some form in most developed capitalist countries.

The former problem refers to the differing views on what constitutes a 'mixed economy'. These views range from seeing the role of government as one of managing or administering capitalism in such a way that its operation is more stable, to the role of effecting a smooth transition to a predominantly socialist economy which implies that not only are there transfers in economic decision-making out of the private sector but also that there is a social transformation as well. It is the argument of this chapter that an economy dominated by private ownership of the means of production will be subject to considerable fluctuations in the level of activity and employment; furthermore, that the implications of the decisions of the owners of the means of production bear no necessary correspondence with the interests of the rest of the community, and that in general, full employment and stable growth are exceptional circumstances. This view of the cyclical nature

* Originally published in J. North and P. Weller (eds), *Labor* (Sydney: Ian Nowak, 1979), 184–95.

of capitalism, as distinct from the views that it is either inherently stable or that it contains a long-run tendency to self-destruction, has dominated post-war economic policy in most capitalist countries. The gradually increasing degree of government intervention has created an awareness of the probable permanence of the public sector as a third entity in economic relations and, indeed, an expectation by both owners of capital and those who work for capital (directly and indirectly) that governments will actively participate in economic affairs to ensure stability. This government intervention has been aimed predominantly at manipulating aggregate demand. Governments have directly supplemented aggregate demand by their own spending and, through the respending of incomes thus created, stimulated further effective demand. Governments have also acted to mobilize that part of the surplus that would otherwise have been idle through income redistribution schemes and they have directly subsidised spending especially on investment goods.

By aiming their policies at maintaining aggregate demand at high and stable levels, governments enable corporations to make investment decisions with a greater degree of certainty, and to build plant to a scale appropriate to their expected production requirements and to operate it at a level of capacity utilisation that is optimal in the sense that it has some spare capacity to accommodate temporary increases in output. Thus fluctuations in the level of effective demand can be met by expanded output without necessarily increasing unit costs and therefore increasing prices. By maintaining the level of effective demand at high and stable levels, the level of employment is similarly secured.

The identification of the mixed economy with the welfare state points to a complementary activity by governments, the intervention on the supply side of the production process, both in providing a social wage, through welfare policies and in providing, directly, aspects of the production process which are too costly for private capital or, indirectly, through tax concessions and subsidies.

The initial question, then, of the extent of government intervention becomes more specifically one of the extent to which the government should intervene to provide the conditions conducive to private investment. O'Connor[1] has shown for the US that there is a limit to this kind of intervention which becomes apparent in a fiscal crisis – the conflict imposed on a government which chooses to administer and support capitalism and consequently finds that, on the one hand, such support requires a growing number of outlays, both for welfare and for corporate capital directly, while on the other hand its sources of revenue are constrained by static or shrinking tax bases.

The conclusion to be drawn from an analysis which demonstrates that an economy reliant on private investment will be subject to fluctuations is, then, that the role of the government in a mixed economy is not a question of the degree but of the nature of this intervention. For example, greater government control over the use of profits, traditionally exercised through fiscal policy, could avoid a fiscal crisis by being exercised through direct government participation in the production of this surplus, that is to say, by the direct involvement of the government in the production and marketing of goods in profitable industries.

Before expanding the argument which leads to this conclusion, the specific problems with which an Australian government has to deal will be outlined. The major puzzles include the control of inflationary pressures and the defeat of unemployment in a small, open economy. An immediate contributory factor to both of these problems has been the problem of inefficiency associated with the small size of both firms and markets in much of Australia's manufacturing industry: this inefficiency is related also to the level and spread of protection that has been offered to Australian manufacturing in the postwar period. In attempting to restructure industry in Australia, to stimulate output so that unit costs and therefore prices in these industries can be reduced and employment increased, an Australian government must accept as given an exchange rate and then selectively develop those industries which, with retooling, could operate at a cost level that is internationally competitive without requiring the level of real (private and social) wages in Australia to be reduced.

The crisis in manufacturing in Australia can be understood as the outcome of a number of processes which culminated in drastic threats to profit and cash flows of the (predominantly Australian-operated) firms concerned. The major contributing factors were the gradual saturation of consumer markets, which meant that lower levels of output increased unit costs while stockpiling reduced companies' liquidity; the removal of tariff protection further reduced markets, and large wage-cost increases together with those smaller markets added to this liquidity crisis.

Minsky in his recent interpretation of the main contributions of Keynes in *The General Theory*[2] has drawn our attention to the reestablishment of the cycles that result from the intimate interplay of monetary and real factors which he takes to be Keynes's most important contribution. Inflation has added considerable impact to the basic message, for it brings with it accentuating factors associated with the pricing policies of capitalist firms and conventional accounting procedures, and their implications for balance sheet structures and liquidity positions, the composition of their assets and liabilities and the relationship of these compositions one to another.

Minsky's thesis is that investment expenditure is both generated by expected cash flows *and* generates, or at least plays a large part in generating, current cash flows. These in turn help to determine the ability of firms (and households) to cope with inherited liabilities, especially their debt structures and the accompanying payments of interest and repayment of debt. Disappointments with the level of cash flows not only tend to reduce expected profitability but also to seriously impair present ability to meet inherited commitments as well as to incur future ones. Thus these financial side-effects help to accentuate the inherent tendency for investment expenditures to fluctuate in response to movements (or expectations of these) in real factors – output, employment, replacements coming due and the like. This instability, which essentially is associated with the inescapable impact of an uncertain future on the present, means that volatile investment expenditures are a principal cause of fluctuations in output and employment in capitalist economies. Minsky's contribution – and he would say that it is really Keynes's – is to show that one phase of a regularly recurring cycle inevitably grows out of the preceding phase, the amplitudes of each particular cycle being affected by the impact of unrealized cash flows (either way) on the confidence or pessimism of corporate decision-makers.

Minsky's reaction to his analysis is first to suggest that it is in the interests of the welfare of the members of a mixed economy as a whole to move towards a less important role for private investment expenditures, that public investment expenditure should increasingly take its place, for the latter may be more appropriately controlled and need be less dependent on expected and actual cash flows. Second, because private investment expenditure still exists in a mixed economy, institutions should be created which will have as their objective controlling the financial effects of fluctuating expected and actual cash flows so that they are not translated into and magnified by fluctuations in real expenditures. Moreover, it is Minsky's contention – and this is consistent with social democrats' strategies – that much private investment expenditure is needed purely to provide the capacity with which to produce consumer goods, the demand for which is forthcoming only when jaded middle-class appetites have been titillated into wanting them by advertising. At the same time, the pressing needs of the less privileged and/or minority groups and lower-paid wage-earners are left unexpressed and unsatisfied because of the starvation of the public sector of the resources with which to supply them. If, therefore, it were possible to make a switch away from private investment expenditure then the public sector spending which replaced it would serve not only more rationally to satisfy society's needs as a whole, but it would also provide a more stable base for the maintenance of employment and the achievement of growth. Moreover, such a transfer of resources would serve also to produce the ingredients for the public sector's contribution to the provision of a social wage which is an essential part of the public sector's role in making a real social contract workable.[3] Not only would employment and growth be better served, but at the same time the quid pro quo for relative money-wage stability and a moderate rise in the real *private* wage of wage-earners could be provided through the public sector. A major problem then would be of providing conditions of reasonably confident expectations of satisfactory future profits so that the demand for resources to be used by the private sector can be sustained. The policy requirements with regard to this sector, then, must be directed to establishing institutions that encourage its continued accumulation and yet which are politically realistic institutions for Australia.

Appropriate institutions would be those which reduced uncertainty about the profitability of private investment projects, and one major contribution to this uncertainty in the recent past has been future costs. Institutions already exist in Australia which influence the levels and changes in the levels of costs and prices, some more effectively than others. It can be argued then that the historical and sociological antecedents exist in Australia which make it politically viable for wage indexation before and after tax to be an integral part of any ALP policy with regard to prices and incomes. Its use in conjunction with Arbitration Commission procedures as the base on which agreements about the structure of relativities and overindexation payments can be erected offers the possibility of achieving the sort of money-wage constraint and therefore domestic price level which will allow Australia to maintain a cost level such that, given its exchange rate, it can compete internationally in selected industries: a competitive cost level in the sense that it is consistent with the high level of activity and employment and the standard of living to which Australian wage-earners have become accustomed, and which is consistent with external balance.[4]

To the criticism that indexation procedures prolong (or may do so, in the absence of 'dampeners' in the system) an approach to a rate of increase of money-wages and prices which fulfils the above criterion, the answer is first, that foreign reserves and additional borrowing may be used to see through the transition – after all that is one of their *raisons d'être*. Moreover, it is better in terms of economic stability to use our reserves and loans for this purpose than to frequently adjust the exchange rate or maintain a floating exchange rate. Because of the links through the domestic prices of 'exportables' and 'importables' to the Australian wage-earners' cost of living, the latter measures carry the danger of cumulative devaluations and continuously accelerating inflation.

That is not to say that in certain circumstances and as a once-and-for-all measure as opposed to a continuing one, wage-earners may at some stage be asked to accept less than full indexation when external events imply a permanent change in the real income of the country as a whole. The way to implement this for the wage-earning group would most naturally occur through the indexation procedures. Such an approach was implied for several years in the Commission's own procedures whereby it adopted a rule of effective productivity *plus* prices as a guide to the money-wage increases it awarded[5] and it seems also to be a strand of the August 1977 judgment by the full court. It certainly has much to commend it as part of an overall anti-inflationary package in the Australian context, as well as fitting in with the strategy of a social democratic government developing a mixed economy, of providing a growing social wage in return for some constraints by the wage-earning groups themselves. The contribution of private capital is implicit in the growing social wage as this latter implies a redistribution of the surplus, a proportion of which (large at the initial stages of transition) is private profits generated by private investment. A growing social wage entails a redistribution of the surplus from production away from its point of production to the workforce and its dependents as a group, where this redistribution is not reliant on the market for its final allocation between uses and/or users.

An important proviso is that the wage-earning groups be persuaded that the devaluation is justified in terms of a considered policy move which is part of a strategy to bring Australian manufacturing back to a competitive position as described above. This is as opposed to a devaluation being the means solely of redistributing incomes to other sections of the community as it has done recently in favour of the rural and mining sectors.

Asking the wage-earning groups as a whole to accept the trade-off of a higher social wage for a lower private wage has as its counterpart the private sector accepting the increasing intervention of the state sector in the production of marketed goods and services out of which it too generates and realises a surplus or profit. A higher social wage cannot be achieved without the government producing its own surplus because of the constraint of a fiscal crisis mentioned earlier, which arises from the limit to the tax base and to increases in taxes (not to mention that in effect wage-earners typically end up paying the tax for their own social wage, which is *not* the aim of the policy of a social-democratic government).

The combination of a fixed exchange rate and institutions to monitor price and money-wage levels would, together, reduce uncertainty both for wage-earners about their real future incomes and for the remaining private sector about future costs. A fixed exchange rate would also reduce the likelihood of speculative capital flows in and out of Australia which in the past have had a destabilising effect on employment and the level of activity. If private sector spending is stabilised and the public sector can generate the necessary surplus, a healthy level of growth can be maintained and thus employment can also be stabilised.

Having talked about the need to select those manufacturing industries which can be competitive in the sense described, given the exchange rate, a more detailed look at this sector is required. As mentioned early in the chapter, the pending demise of Australian manufacturing has been the most obvious of the immediate causes (and manifestations) of unemployment and inflation. The proximate nature of its inefficiency and the removal of the accompanying high and often arbitrary levels of protection coupled with odd bouts of import quotas, which perpetuated its inefficiency while maintaining high levels of employment in manufacturing, mean that if employment is to be dependent on this sector important structural changes need to be engineered.

Several alternative scenarios can be posed from within the existing social framework. As far as the ALP and especially the trade union wing of the ALP is concerned, there is deep-seated opposition to tariff cuts. This exists for the very good reason that with the present exchange rate, the levels of costs and productivity growth which reflect the often outdated technology and/or the small scale of output in relation to capacity, and existing institutional channels for retraining and relocating wage-earners, there is no hope of providing employment opportunities at anywhere near the rate that would be needed to absorb those who will become unemployed if the IAC (Industry Assistance Commission) efficiency-is-all approach is followed. Thus while the efficiency that would undoubtedly result in those firms and industries which survived the long haul of tariff reform would provide rising real incomes *for those who were in employment* – they would also benefit from the full involvement as Australian consumers in the international division of labour through imports – this would be small comfort for the substantial numbers who would continue to remain in the reserve army of the structurally unemployed. Especially would this be so if the community continued in its present barbarous and uncivilised attitude to those who are unemployed, ably spurred on and indeed led by the Fraser government to distract voters from its economic mismanagement. Thus the seemingly obstinate hostility to the enlightened recommendations of innumerable IAC reports is based on the sort of horse-sense that prevails in a well-organised and intelligent wage-earning sector but which is lacking in those whose blinkers lead them to look to efficiency – one of whose criteria is not employment opportunities created – as a sole determinant, and whose own jobs tend to be the secure and comfortable ones of a tenured public service (or an academic department).

The other scenario from within the current social context is deliberately to accept the inescapable trade-off between efficiency and employment. This involves resurrecting a level of protection which secures the level of employment for the manufacturing sector consistent with what the primary and tertiary sectors can otherwise provide. The corollaries of this are that many firms which do not operate efficiently for their level of output (and industries which are not efficient in terms of competitiveness with imports) will survive, and that economies of scale will not be achieved. These two factors mean that prices in manufacturing will stay comparatively high *vis-à-vis* those of Australia's international competitors, thus keeping the real value of money-wages low and making these money-wages high relative to productivity. It also means that growth in productivity and in real incomes will be sluggish or non-existent. This return to a high-protection era results in the kind of situation with which the United Kingdom and New Zealand are already coming to grips. It is a situation associated with levels of absolute income that are adequate and it also could be coupled with redistributive schemes which alleviate to some extent the lot of those on the low end of the income scale. Faced with a clear choice between efficiency and employment there seems little doubt that the bulk of the electorate would choose employment. A problem with such a choice is that it would inflate the costs of other sectors, in particular of the rural sector; money-wage costs would be high relative to productivity in agriculture due to the inflated cost of wage goods imposed by tariff protection and the imported capital equipment of the agricultural sector would be higher priced due to the tariffs. Thus the profitability of this sector would suffer as it would effectively subsidise manufacturing. If it were to make a contribution to export earnings then ironically it too might require subsidising. Should mineral export earnings put pressure on the exchange rate the situation for both manufacturing and rural sectors would be exacerbated and even higher levels of protection would be required.

These two scenarios are, however, based on the same analytical framework as that adopted by the IAC, that is, they rely on market forces as the determinants of the (potential) outcomes. If the mixed economy is to have social significance as well as economic implications then these are not the only possible solutions. Before turning to the possibilities where market forces (and whatever degree of interference is considered necessary to modify their effects) are secondary, it is interesting to consider the alternatives which apparently are deducible from the IAC analysis. The first of these relies for its conclusion on the rationale that without tariff protection the free market eventually will resolve the problem of which industries should survive for Australia, their survival to be based on their efficiency; the free market will allow consumers' preferences together with unrestricted resource and commodity flows to determine the most efficient allocation of resources in response to market price signals. However, as Ajit Singh has argued,[6] if the economy is in disequilibrium in terms of its international competitiveness and its balance of payments, the trade and payments position of that economy can affect its growth and its manufacturing development through its impact on the level and structure of demand on investment. The level of demand will be affected if there is such a persistent pressure on the balance of payments that governments cannot counter low effective demand when the demand for exports falls. The impact on the structure of demand will especially affect manufacturing since it is characterised typically by economies of scale so that as demand for its output falls, costs and therefore prices will rise making it even less competitive, thus pushing it out of the market, and this will be so regardless of the initial competitiveness of the industry. Investment is vulnerable on three accounts. Investment decisions will be affected by the above-mentioned influence on aggregate demand of a persistently adverse foreign trade position; investment will be reduced if foreign competition reduces profitability; and if the reduced profitability is low relative to that in other countries, investment funds may flow out of the economy to countries enjoying faster growth rates and higher profitability. In an economy in disequilibrium these factors can interact in a cumulative and circular chain of causation tending to perpetuate and worsen the disequilibrium. If trade continues on the same terms, then the manufacturing sectors will suffer: if there are flexible exchange rates, the recovery in those industries which may be competitive if able to operate at levels which exploit economies of scale will still depend on expectations and confidence of investors.

To argue the alternative scenario, that erection of tariff barriers will protect the manufacturing sector as a whole, is to deny that Australia's position as an open economy is a part of an international economy in which world production and market conditions are constantly changing, so that there exists constant pressure on Australia to respond by adjusting domestic production and/or marketing policies. If such adjustments involve progressively increasing protection to try and maintain domestic production conditions, this is merely exacerbating the conditions for further strains in the future. The characteristics of an international economy are important if the appropriate strategy for a mixed economy is to be developed. It must be understood that capitalism has developed beyond the freely-competitive phase, and beyond the monopolistic-competitive phase at the national level, to a phase of monopoly capitalism dominated by internationally-operating corporations. This has two important implications. That the dominant mode of production is international capitalism means that the national economy is dependent on the decisions of private corporations whose interests do not necessarily coincide with those of the national economy. Furthermore, the decisions are made by corporations acting at an international level which, therefore, have no incentive to coordinate their decisions with the strategy of the national government (although they manipulate the reverse cooperation) and which therefore can frustrate individual national governments' policies and entire strategies. For example, the multinational character of a corporation enables it to shift funds from one country to another, thus being able to ignore a credit policy that a government may be trying to implement, thereby frustrating the aim of such a credit policy. This contradiction between national government and international capitalism leads to the conclusion that a trade policy which is purely protectionist cannot be effective even in terms of protecting employment for too long, as with accumulating pressure on the balance of trade created by such a policy a multinational corporation can shift production to another base. And a highly protectionist policy also creates an allied strain on international relations with trading rivals and partners as demand for their exports stays low on account of both the high tariff and the low real income growth.

The argument is now full circle. Both in the short run and continuing, there will be an inflationary and an employment problem with which Australia as a predominantly capitalist economy will have to cope. If a government is to resolve these problems then the mixed economy must be one in which traditional government activity in fiscal and monetary policies is seen as only a part of a changed role for a public sector, and appropriate institutions to reduce the dependence of the economy on private investment decisions must be designed. The employment problem is partly structural, as explained above, and also made more apparent by the workforce itself expanding as married women return to work in increasing numbers. But the cyclical nature of unemployment resulting from an economy reliant on private investment decisions has been made worse by government measures through fiscal and monetary policies, because of the Bastard Keynesian and Keynesian *cum* Monetarist diagnosis of recent inflationary troubles followed by the resulting policy propositions.[7] These reflect the firm belief that high levels of unemployment are necessary in order to influence expectations, and also that higher levels of unemployment are here to stay due to structural factors which are associated with the tendency for a rightward shift in the Unemployment-Vacancies curve. The failure explicitly to recognise the interrelatedness of the unemployment, inflation and international character of production and marketing has led to a great deal of inconsistent ad hocery in economic policy-making by governments of both major political parties (although the Fraser government strategy was consistent and probably, in their terms, successful).

In opposition to the above view on how to run a mixed economy, post-Keynesian analysis has demonstrated that an open economy which relies on private capital's decisions is inherently unstable and tends to both inflation and unemployment. Counter-cyclical policies aimed at administering capitalism and protectionist policies aimed at isolating manufacturing from competition with the rest of the world will eventually be ineffective. Thus the government's intervention in a mixed economy must be of a changed nature. It needs to create institutions that can encourage the level of private investment it considers desirable while engaging in the production of a surplus through its own activities so that it can fulfill its redistributive goals and provide a social wage without having to create ever-increasing deficits. (The recent spate of deficit-size fetishism has placed serious constraints on the use of monetary and fiscal policy. So brainwashed are we that a rising deficit is the harbinger of future inflation, that the rise in interest rates that now accompanies the rise in the deficit if it is financed by new bond issues virtually ensures that crowding-out occurs of our own making.) Government will also need to redirect resources as part of an overall restructuring plan, to enable those areas of manufacturing which it is considered could become efficient in terms of utilising economies of scale and being competitive internationally, given the exchange rate consistent with rural and mineral exports, to develop. Being competitive internationally would entail new investment in more modern technology, which would increase productivity and allow growth of real incomes. With the inevitability of an expanding mineral sector, manufacturing associated with mineral refinement could provide necessary new opportunities. However, incentive schemes which rely on private capital's response are attempts to make the 'market' allocate resources in a way it would otherwise not do. It is probably more 'efficient' for the public sector to take the initiative directly in these new pursuits. Implicit in all this is the development of an incomes policy. The adoption of institutions such as incomes policies reflects the conclusion that capitalist production bears no necessary relation to the productive service rendered. State intervention must therefore be of a different nature than merely organising capital more efficiently. Its intervention needs to be of the Holland type[8] whereby major private firms are taken into public ownership and investment expenditure decisions in those firms are made from that position.

An incomes policy can combine with both fiscal and monetary policy and be consistent with the rate of growth expected as resources are reallocated and restructuring takes place. It can also maintain consistency between the level of activity and employment and the social wage being provided, in conjunction with the exchange rate.[9] In the Australian case, as we have argued elsewhere,[10] the appropriate Australian institutions are pre- and post-tax indexation coupled with a relativities wages fund to allow flexibility and opportunity for trade-union actions, especially by their leaders, as well as faith in the procedures of the Arbitration commissioners by the wage-earning groups. That the Arbitration Commission sees itself as playing such a role is implicit in the judgment of the full bench in August 1977, with its rebuke to the Fraser government in general and to the treasurer in particular, both for their analysis and for their attack on the Commission as an institution. Of course, it is easy to sympathise with both viewpoints; it is frustrating for the Commonwealth government not to be able completely to have its way over wages and prices. Nevertheless, while an ALP government also would like to have such controls, it may well hesitate about acquiring them if only because it would be fearful of the use that could be made of such powers by a government less sympathetic to the interests of wage-earners and especially trade unionists. The second-best solution probably is therefore vigorously to defend the independence of the Arbitration Commission.

The successful maintenance of a private capital sector will depend on whether Australian business and overseas investors will be prepared to work within such a framework, or whether their income and capital withdrawals will be such as to put pressure on our balance of payments and exchange rate so as to make this approach impossible. Especially will this be so if it also means they are unwilling to take up even the much smaller amount of private investment expenditure that is envisaged for them. Their reluctance should be reduced by the greater certainty with which future expectations could be held, since the economy's costs would be more stable and its level of output and employment would also be more stable. The taking over of private firms by the state was indeed hinted at by Keynes,[11] in the generalisation that investment may need to be socialised if the capitalist mode of production is to continue at all: what we have argued is that the economy would be a part of a more civilised society if the capitalist mode of production and the ruling ideas on which it exercises control become secondary to a more socialised mode of production.

Notes

1. J. O'Connor, *The Fiscal Crisis of the State* (New York: St Martin's Press, 1973).
2. H. P. Minsky, *John Maynard Keynes* (New York: Columbia University Press, 1975). For an excellent summary of his main thesis see Minsky, 'The Financial Instability Hypothesis: An interpretation of Keynes and an Alternative to "Standard Theory"', *Challenge*, March/April 1977.
3. Joan Robinson has put it this way: '[A] real social contract . . . would satisfy the reasonable demands of the workers for more control over their own work, more security against redundancy, better social services and so forth' (press release of her public lecture in Adelaide, April 1975). Joan Robinson was pessimistic about the chances of such a policy actually coming about; nor was her heart in it anyway, for she would prefer to see society restructured on much more radical lines.
4. These are discussed in greater detail in G. C. Harcourt, 'The Social Consequences of Inflation', *Australian Accountant*, vol. 44, no. 9, 1974 chapter 13 this volume; and G. C. Harcourt, 'On Theories and Policies', in J. Nieuweuhuysen and P. Drake (eds), *Essays on Australian Economic Theory* (Melbourne: Melbourne University Press, 1976). Chapter 4, this volume.
5. See E. A. Russell, 'A Wages Policy for Australia', *Australian Economic Papers*, vol. 4, nos 1 and 2, 1965, 1–26.
6. Ajit Singh, 'UK Industry and the World Economy: A Case of Deindustrialisation?', *Cambridge Journal of Economics*, vol. 1, no. 2, 1977, 113–36.
7. For full account of this thesis see Harcourt, 'On Theories and Policies', Chapter 4, this volume.
8. S. Holland, *The Socialist Challenge* (London: Quartet Books, 1975).

9. The case for this approach in the UK may be found in F. Cripps, 'The Money Supply, Wages and Inflation', *Cambridge Journal of Economics*, vol. 1, no. 1, 1977, 101–112.
10. See Harcourt, 'The Social Consequences of Inflation', Chapter 13 this volume; Harcourt, 'On Theories and Policies', Chapter 4 this volume; and Harcourt, 'Theoretical Controversy and Social Significance' (1975 Edward Snann Memorial Lecture in Economics, University of Western Australia), Perth, 1975, Chapter 2 this volume.
11. 'I expect to see the state, which is in a position to calculate the marginal efficiency of capital-goods on long views and on the basis of general social advantage, taking an even greater responsibility for directly organizing investment', J. M. Keynes, *The General Theory of Employment, Interest and Money* (London: Macmillan, 1936), 164.

Part III

Taxation Reform and Investment Incentives

6
Investment Allowances for Primary Producers*

with A. D. Barton

The purpose of this article is to show that the scheme of investment allowances outlined below would be preferable to the present system of special depreciation allowances as a means of encouraging investment by primary producers, especially investment by low-income farmers. The need for increased primary production for balance-of-payments reasons is assumed and increased investment is the major means of bringing this about.[1] The main determinant of the ability of farmers to invest is the excess of their disposable incomes over the costs of maintaining a required standard of life.[2] The effectiveness of the above schemes depends largely upon the extent to which they increase these surpluses. The empirical studies to date suggest that special depreciation allowances have not been very effective in encouraging investment in primary production, especially by low-income farmers.[3] Furthermore, it appears that low-income farmers are not always aware of the existence of special depreciation allowances.[4] Their effectiveness is even further reduced by this ignorance.

The article is in four sections. Section I contains a description of special depreciation allowances and of the proposed scheme of investment allowances. In the remaining sections the impact of both schemes on investment is analysed for different situations, and the relative merits of the two schemes are assessed.

* Originally published in the *Australian Journal of Agricultural Economics*, vol. 3, 1959, 12–18. The writers are indebted to the members of the Departments of Economics and Commerce, University of Adelaide, for their criticisms of this article. The responsibility for the views expressed is, of course, that of the writers.

I

Special depreciation allowances

Special depreciation allowances for primary producers were introduced in July 1951. They entitled primary producers to depreciate for tax purposes their assets[5] acquired since this date at 20 per cent per annum of prime cost.

Investment allowances

Under the proposed investment allowances scheme, depreciation rates would be based on the effective working lives of assets, and taxable incomes would be calculated in the normal way. Income tax would be assessed on the basis of these taxable incomes. Actual tax payable would be these assessments *less* a fixed proportion of the costs of investments carried out during the year. This investment allowance rate would be fixed by Parliament. For example, if the rate were fixed at 10 per cent a farmer with a taxable income of £5000 would be liable (at 1958–59 rates) for £1700 in tax. If he had bought a tractor for £1000 during the year, he would receive an investment allowance of £100 and his actual tax liability would be reduced to £1600. Unlike special depreciation allowances, these investment allowances would be allowed only in the year of the investment.

II

The impact of special depreciation allowances and investment allowances on investment will be analysed, first, for a single act of investment and then for a series of investments.

A single act of investment

With a single act of investment, the taxable income of a farmer for the first five years after the investment is made is reduced below what it would have been, had normal depreciation rates[6] been applied. With unchanged tax rates, the reduction in taxable income leads to lower tax payments by the farmer. Therefore, the net returns after tax from the investment in the first five years are increased above what they would have been, and the returns of subsequent years are reduced, had normal depreciation rates only been applied. The increase in returns from investment in the first five years encourages investment by making it easier for particular assets to meet the pay-off criterion – the criterion that an asset should 'pay for itself' over a period considerably shorter than its effective working life. Furthermore, the supply of funds available for investment is increased in the first five years by the reduction in tax payments. Because his residual income is increased by the operation of special depreciation allowances in the first five years, the farmer will be in a position to invest more. In addition, his ability to borrow will have been increased. But in subsequent years the farmer's tax payments will be increased and his liquidity reduced.

If the farmer has a constant marginal tax rate (that is, farmers with incomes above £16 000 and companies engaged in primary production), special depreciation allowances further encourage investment by raising expected rates of return after tax above what they would have been, had normal depreciation rates only been applied. The total amount of tax payable over the life of the asset is not affected by special depreciation allowances but expected returns after tax are concentrated in the earlier years as a result of special depreciation allowances. However, if the marginal tax rate is progressive, special depreciation allowances could reduce the expected rates of return after tax. Total returns after tax are reduced by the progressive marginal tax rates, but since the expected returns of the first five years are increased and those of subsequent years are reduced, expected rates of return could still be higher than with normal depreciation rates.[7] If the expected rates of return are reduced by the operation of special depreciation allowances, investment by farmers may be reduced, in which case special depreciation allowances will not serve their purpose of encouraging investment.

The investment allowance will always make it easier to meet the pay-off criterion, will always increase funds available for investment (which will never have to be repaid), and will always raise the expected rate of return after tax on a project.

Series of investments

However, it is more realistic to analyse the effects of these schemes on a series of investments over time, because farmers do not engage in just the one act of investment. The effect of special depreciation allowances on the current level of investment then depends not only on the size of the allowances themselves, and on the marginal tax rate, but also on how long the scheme has been operating, and on the shape of the previous stream of investment. Where the amount of investment is constant each year and the farm has been in existence for a number of years, the introduction of a special depreciation allowances scheme will reduce the taxable incomes of farmers for a transition period. The transition period is equal to the lengths of the lives[8] of the assets concerned, that is, it is a period of ten to fifteen years for most assets. The differences between taxable incomes, and therefore the annual tax remissions due to the operation of special depreciation allowances, will increase up to the fifth year; and then decline until the end of the transition period. The size of the remissions depends upon the marginal tax rate and the amount of investment. After the end of the transition period, taxable incomes with either special or normal depreciation allowances will be the same and the tax remissions then will be zero.

With special depreciation allowances there will always be tax remissions when the stream of investment is increasing. These tax remissions will apply to the increased rate of investment only. They will be increasingly offset, as time goes on, by the increasing tax payments due to the absence of normal depreciation allowances on the increasing stock of assets which have been held for more than five years. With both constant and increasing investment, the tax remissions of earlier years will not have to be repaid. However, if the stream of investment declines, the tax remissions of former years will be repaid. In this case, special depreciation allowances are a negative incentive to maintain investment. None of these effects is present with investment allowances, because they relate to current investment only, are independent of the marginal tax rate, and of the previous size and rate of change of investment, and do not alter normal depreciation charges.

When investment is maintained at a constant rate, special depreciation allowances involve no cost to the government after the close of the transition period; when investment declines they recoup part of the revenue losses of previous years; when the rate of investment is increasing, the government is giving tax remissions on the additional investment. The sizes of these tax remissions depend upon the levels of the incomes of the farmers making the additional investment. Regardless of the shape of the investment stream, investment allowances will always involve a loss of taxation revenue to the government. However, the loss of revenue to the government in the current years is a minor consideration. The relevant consideration is the total effect which these allowances have on the economy, and if investment allowances are more effective at promoting investment, they are the better measure.

Special depreciation allowances can be criticised on grounds of equity. Considering, first, the case of the first five years of a single act of investment: because the marginal rate of tax on incomes is progressive, high-income farmers receive, through the operation of special depreciation allowances, larger absolute and proportional tax remissions than do low-income farmers. The following example illustrates this point. Consider two farmers, one with a taxable income of £10 000 (farmer A), the other with a taxable income of £1000 (farmer B), both incomes reckoned after allowance for normal depreciation of (say) 15 per cent, but before allowance for the additional special depreciation of 5 per cent. Each buys an asset for £2000 at the beginning of the taxation year. The effect of the tax remissions due to special depreciation allowances on the cost of the investment for the two farmers is shown in Table 6.1.

Because of the progressive marginal tax rate, farmer A is able to finance 15 per cent of the cost of the asset, and farmer B can finance 5 per cent only, through tax remissions. Clearly in this case the operation of special depreciation allowances is regressive on low-income farmers.

Table 6.1 *Effect of special depreciation allowances on cost of investment*

	Farmer A	Farmer B
(1) Taxable income before special depreciation allowance	£10 000	£1000
(2) Cost of asset	£2000	£2000
(3) Special depreciation allowance (5% of (2))	£100	£100
(4) Taxable income after special depreciation allowance ((1)–(3))	£9 900	£900
(5) Marginal tax rate (1958–59)	12/1 in £	3/10 in £
(6) Tax remission ((5) × (3))	£60/8/4	£19/3/4
(7) Tax remission as per cent of asset in year of acquisition ((6)/(3))	3%	1%
(8) Total tax remission over five years (5 × (6))	£302/1/8	£95/16/8
(9) Tax remission as per cent. of cost of asset ((8)/(2))	15%	5%

Note: The averaging procedure for low-income farmers has been disregarded.

When the entire life of a single act of investment is considered, and where the marginal tax rate is progressive, the farmer will repay more than the initial tax remission. The treatment of farmers on different incomes within this range of rising marginal tax rates is then not inequitable. However, those farmers with incomes of £16 000 or more, who have constant marginal tax rates, receive a more favourable treatment than the former class and this is inequitable. Finally, if investment is constant or increasing, high-income farmers gain more, proportionately, from special depreciation allowances than do low-income farmers, which again is inequitable. To be equitable, the same benefit should be given to all farmers for the same amount of investment irrespective of their incomes. There is no justification for discriminating among farmers on the basis of their incomes, nor is there any justification for giving a greater proportionate benefit to high-income farmers. Investment allowances do not conflict with the principle of equity within farming.

Finally investment allowances have certain other advantages. They are administratively simple to operate; they are flexible because they have no repercussion on depreciation charges in subsequent years – as do special depreciation allowances – and therefore can be easily changed from year to year. If it is desired to encourage expenditure on certain types of investment projects, differential rates of investment allowances can be given. Because assets have different effective lives a uniform rate of investment allowance might encourage investment in short-term assets at the expense of investment in long-term assets.

III

Differential income tax rates for farmers as a means of encouraging investment

Professor Campbell has suggested the use of differential income tax rates as a means of encouraging investment. This scheme would reduce income tax rates on farmers, thereby leaving them with higher disposable incomes.[9] As the marginal propensity to invest is less than one,[10] all of these tax remissions will not be used for investment. The tax remissions associated with the investment allowances are dependent upon the investment being done. Therefore, for a given amount of tax remission, the investment allowances scheme would be much more effective. Differential income tax rates cannot be used to encourage different types of investment within farming. Finally, equity considerations between farming and non-farming militate against the use of a differential income tax, and, in addition, it is still inequitable within farming.

IV

Special depreciation allowances, investment allowances and the efficiency of resource use within farming

Which scheme is more likely to improve the efficiency of resource use within farming, that is to say, which scheme will more nearly equate rates of profit at the margin of investment by different farmers? This question has no clear-cut answer. If farmers had access to unlimited supplies of funds at the market rate of interest, and if there were no progressive income tax system, then investment by all farmers would be carried to the point where the marginal rate of profit was equal to the borrowing rate of interest. Progressive marginal tax rates on incomes make a given investment project appear more profitable *after* tax to low-income farmers than to high-income farmers. If investment is carried to the point where rates of profit *after* tax are the same for all farmers, rates of profit *before* tax must be higher for the high-income farmer. Hence the scale of investment of high-income farmers must be less than that required for the most efficient use of resources within farming. However, this is a direct consequence of society's desire for a greater income equality brought about through the use of a progressive income tax system. There is always this conflict between equity considerations and resource allocation under a progressive income tax system, and this has to be accepted.

Moreover, supplies of funds to farmers are not unlimited (this is one of the reasons why the government introduced special depreciation allowances), and investment by low-income farmers is more likely to be curtailed by lack of funds than investment by high-income farmers. This will reduce – and could even reverse – the differential between marginal rates of profit *before* tax on investments made by high- and low-income farmers. If it is the case that the marginal rates of profit *before* tax of low-income farmers are less than the corresponding rates of high-income farmers, special depreciation allowances, which give greater benefit to high-income farmers, will tend to narrow the differential, thereby improving the efficiency of resource use within farming. Investment allowances, by giving the same benefit to both types of farmers, will tend to leave the situation unchanged. If, because of shortages of funds for low-income farmers, their marginal rates of profit *before* tax are greater than the corresponding rates for high-income farmers, the effect of special depreciation allowances will be to widen the differential. Investment allowances again leave the situation unchanged. No evidence is available to indicate which is the more likely case. The conclusion must be that special depreciation allowances could either improve or worsen the efficiency of resource use within farming, and that investment allowances will leave the situation unchanged.

Conclusion

On grounds of both equity and effectiveness, the investment allowances scheme advocated here would be preferable to both the existing scheme of special depreciation allowances and to differential income tax rates for farmers. No definite conclusion can be drawn as to which method would be preferable on grounds of efficiency of resource use within farming.

Notes

1. See Sir John Crawford, 'Australian Trade Policy: Comment and Question', *Australian Journal of Agricultural Economics,* vol. 3, no. 1, July 1959, 1–10.
2. See Keith O, Campbell, 'Some Reflections on Agricultural Investment', *The Australian Journal of Agricultural Economics,* vol. 2, no. 2, December 1958, 98–99; H. W. Arndt and Burgess Cameron, 'An Australian Consumption Function', *The Economic Record,* vol. XXXIII, no. 64, April 1957, 108–115.
3. See, for example, F. H. Gruen, 'Capital formation in Australian Agriculture', *Proceedings of the Conference of Agricultural Economists,* Sydney, February 1957, 107; R. A. Pearse, 'An Empirical Micro-Study of Some Factors Influencing Farm Net Investment', *The Economic Record,* vol. XXXI, no. 61, November 1955, 271; Keith O. Campbell, *op. cit.,* 102, F. G. Jarrett and D. H. Penny, *An Economic Survey of the Reclaimed Area of the Lower Murray* (Adelaide: Griffin Press, 1960).
4. See D. B. Williams, *Economic and Technical Problems of Australia's Rural Industries* (Melbourne University Press, 1957), 70.
5. That is, any expenditure on assets 'used during the year of income wholly and exclusively for the purposes of agricultural or pastoral pursuits', except motor cars (Commonwealth of Australia, *Income Tax and Social Services Contribution Act, 1936–1959* (Canberra: Commonwealth Government Printer), Section 57AA).

6. Normal depreciation rates generally are less than 20%. For example, the rate on tractors was 10% (reducing-balance or prime cost); on buildings and structural improvements, 3% or 2%.
7. The expected rate of return is defined as that rate of discount which makes the present value of the expected annual returns (in this case, net of tax), on a project equal to its current supply price.

   Let q = expected annual return when normal depreciation allowances are given.

   i = change in expected annual returns due to operation of special depreciation allowances, i.e. the difference in tax payments under the two schemes.

   r = expected rate of return with normal depreciation allowances.

   R = expected rate of return with special depreciation allowances.

   C = current supply price of asset.

   Subscripts refer to relevant years. All returns are net of tax.

   Consider a project of expected life $i(i > 5)$. With constant marginal tax rates and (i) with normal depreciation allowances,

$$C = \frac{q_1}{(1+r)} + \ldots + \frac{q_5}{(1+r)^5} + \ldots + \frac{q_i}{(1+r)^i}$$

   (ii) with special depreciation allowances

$$C = \frac{q_1 + t_1}{(1+R)} + \ldots + \frac{q_5 + t_5}{(1+R)^5} + \ldots + \frac{q_i - t_i}{(1+R)^i}$$

$$\sum_{n=1}^{n=5} t_n = \sum_{m=6}^{m=i} t_m$$

   Obviously $R > r$

   However, with a progressive marginal tax rate,

$$\sum_{n=1}^{n=5} t_n < \sum_{m=6}^{m=i} t_m, \text{ so that } R \gtrless r.$$

8. As decided by the Tax authorities.
9. Keith O. Campbell, *op. cit.*, 102–3.
10. F. H. Gruen, *op. cit.*, 107.

7
Taxation and Business Surplus*

with J. W. Bennett

In this note it is presumed that the aim of investment decisions is the achievement of the most desired spread of consumption over time, and that the maximisation of periodic profits is only a means of achieving this aim. It is further presumed that the allocation of resources is to be determined by the free operation of the price mechanism unless there are specific reasons for interfering with this allocation. In the light of these presumptions it is proposed to examine the present tax base of accounting profit and a proposed tax base of 'economic income'. 'Economic income' is defined as revenues less current opportunity costs. This can be contrasted with accounting profit which is revenues less historical costs. In practice economic income can be calculated by making several adjustments to accounting profit. It would be necessary to calculate depreciation allowances by the annuity method described below, and to adjust for those items recorded in the prices of past accounting periods. The latter consists of revaluing depreciation allowances (as defined) in terms of the current replacement costs of fixed assets, and of revaluing the 'Costs of Goods Sold' in current terms to remove the stock appreciation element from accounting profits.

The assessment of taxation requires that businesspeople calculate returns from operations for discrete periods of time. This process is known as the matching procedure, and gives rise to the distinction between

* Originally published in the *Economic Record*, vol. 36, 1960, 425–8. The authors are indebted to the members of the Departments of Economics and Commerce of the University of Adelaide for their comments on this note.

revenue and capital items, and to the problem of averaging capital payments for factors of production. With the existing taxation legislation the original outlays on such capital items are allowed as deductions either by a simple averaging process (straight-line depreciation), or by allowing a constant proportion of the original outlay less amounts previously written off (reducing-balance depreciation). In both cases the total of the amounts deducted cannot be greater than the original money outlay. To maximise profits businesspeople make decisions concerning alternative investment projects and the relative proportions in which factors of production are to be combined. This requires comparisons of revenues and costs[1] which, in the economic sense, depend upon both the amount and the timing of the relevant receipts and outlays. For example, the average annual cost of a capital asset involving an outlay of £1000 with an effective life of 10 years, is not £100 per annum as with straight-line depreciation, but rather one of a series of annuities, the present value of which is equal to £1000. With a marginal cost of capital of 5 per cent the annual cost would be £129.5.[2] This is the cost of capital which a rational businessman would consider when comparing alternative projects and choosing the most desirable combinations of factors of production. *In this case the total of the amounts deducted is greater than the original money outlay and, therefore, the amounts at present allowed for taxation purposes.* This difference seriously distorts the allocation of resources.

It is clear that taxation reduces profitability relative to pre-tax situations. If investment is to be based upon comparisons of relative pre-tax costs, and as businessmen make decisions on the basis of post-tax data, it is necessary that the relative costs of the factors of production should not be distorted by the imposition of taxation. The existing taxation legislation, because it under-estimates the cost of capital, gives rise to the adoption of more labour-intensive techniques than the desired allocation of resources would require. The annuity method of assessing depreciation allowances for taxation purposes would obviate this distortion as the relative costs of the various factors of production would then be unaffected by taxation payments.

In the absence of taxation the total cost of an investment project to a businessman can be written as:

$$C + L\,a_{\overline{n}|i} \qquad (1)$$

where C = the money outlay on the capital asset at time O;
L = the annual payments for labour and raw materials; and

$a_{\overline{n}|i} = \frac{1-(1+i)^{-n}}{i}$

where i = the marginal cost of capital.
n = the effective life of the capital asset in years.

With the existing taxation legislation the cost can be written as:

$$C - \frac{tC}{n} a_{\overline{n}|i} + L\,a_{\overline{n}|i} - tL\,a_{\overline{n}|i}$$

where t = the marginal tax rate.
That is, assuming a positive taxable income in each year, the present values of the costs of capital, labour and raw materials are reduced by the present values of taxation deductions subsequently allowed, multiplied by the marginal rate of tax. This expression reduces to:

$$C\left(1 - \frac{t}{n} a_{\overline{n}|i}\right) + L\,a_{\overline{n}|i}(1-t) \qquad (2)$$

The *relative costs* of capital, labour and raw materials in equation (2) differ from those in equation (1), except in the trivial cases of $n = 1$ or $i = $ O. However, with the proposed annuity method, the cost can be written as:

$$C - \frac{tC}{a_{\overline{n}|i}} . a_{\overline{n}|i} + L\,a_{\overline{n}|i} - tL\,a_{\overline{n}|i}$$

This reduces to $(1-t)(C + L\,a_{\overline{n}|i})$ (3)
(In this case the depreciation allowances x are derived from the expression $C = x\,a_{\overline{n}|i}$, and not $x = \frac{C}{n}$ as above.)[3] The relative costs in equation (3) are identical with those in equation (1) as they are both multiplied by the common factor $(1 - t)$, that is, the choice between capital, labour and raw materials is unaffected by the imposition of taxation.

It will be apparent that the marginal cost of capital (i) will differ as between firms. The relevant marginal cost of capital will vary according to the circumstances in which the firm is placed and indeed may be the borrowing or lending rate of interest, or the rate of return on the project which is marginal to the firm.[4] If taxation is not to distort the allocation of resources, the rate of interest used in the calculation of depreciation allowances for tax purposes must be equal to the marginal cost of capital to the firm concerned. Clearly this is impracticable, and it would therefore be necessary to use a uniform rate of interest as, for example, the current rate of interest on bank overdrafts. This is likely to be the minimum cost of capital to the firm. To the extent that it is less than the actual marginal cost of capital a distortion would remain, but it would be less than the distortion existing with the present taxation legislation which makes no allowance at all for the time factor, that is, it implies a marginal cost of capital of zero.

With the existing tax base of accounting profit, depreciation allowances suffer from a further limitation in that they reflect historical costs rather than the current opportunity costs relevant to the measurement of profitability for current decision-making purposes. This is also true of the 'Costs of Goods Sold'. To overcome these limitations, depreciation allowances and 'Costs of Goods Sold' must be based upon current replacement costs. This requires the two additional adjustments to accounting profit referred to in the first paragraph above. The calculation of these adjustments arising from changes in the costs of asset replacement have been set out by Professors Mathews and Grant.[5]

It has been argued that economic income is the relevant concept of periodic profit for the purpose of assessing taxation. To the extent that business people aim to maximise economic income the above analysis is fully applicable. If, however, businesspeople are not rational, and aim at the maximisation of a concept of profit which is inconsistent with the maximisation of economic income, for example, accounting profit, the suggested change in the tax base can still be justified on two grounds. First, if a distortion exists because of irrational behaviour on the part of businesspeople, then it is worsened by the existing taxation legislation. Secondly, in so far as businesspeople are influenced by the concept of surplus used by the taxation authorities, the adoption of economic income as the tax base could lead directly to a more efficient allocation of resources.

Notes

1. By 'costs' is meant the current opportunity costs of the factors of production concerned.
2. It is clear that interest *as such* should not be allowed as a deduction for taxation purposes.
3. It has been assumed that conventional depreciation allowances are assessed on the straight-line basis.
4. There is currently a controversy as to which rate of return is relevant in different situations. See, for example, J. Hirshleifer, 'On the Theory of Optimal Investment Decision', *Journal of Political Economy*, vol. LXVI, no. 4 (August 1958), 329–52; Martin J. Bailey, 'Formal Criteria for Investment Decisions', *Journal of Political Economy*, vol. LXVII, no. 5 (October 1959), 476–88.
5. See Russell Mathews and John McB. Grant, *Inflation and Company Finance* (Sydney: Law Book Co. of Australasia, 1958), chapter II.

Postscript 1999

I reprint this silly paper in order to show what fools we can be if we mix up two conflicting approaches to economic analysis and policy.

8

Investment and Initial Allowances as Fiscal Devices*

The aim of this paper is to analyse the use of investment and initial allowances as fiscal devices for encouraging investment, and to appraise their relative effectiveness. Initial allowances have been given in the United Kingdom since 1946; investment allowances have been given for selected industries and assets for various periods, for example, 1954–56, and from 1959 on.[1] By contrast, initial allowances have not been given in Australia since 1951 (with the exception of special depreciation allowances for primary producers), and investment allowances have never been used.[2] It will be shown that investment allowances (in the form suggested by Mr Barton and the present writer)[3] are more effective than initial allowances in stimulating investment.

The paper is in four sections. In section I, the characteristics of each type of allowance are briefly discussed and their various policy uses are outlined. The mode of operation of the allowances and their impact on investment streams are analysed in sections II and III. The relative advantages of the two schemes are assessed in section IV.

I

Initial allowances are a form of accelerated depreciation which can be defined as any scheme whereby the depreciation allowances granted on fixed assets for taxation purposes are initially at a greater rate, or are

---

* Originally published in *The Australian Accountant*, September 1962, 473–77. The writer is indebted to Dr. R. F. Henderson, of Corpus Christi College, Cambridge, and to members of the Departments of Economics and Commerce in the University of Adelaide, for their comments on drafts of this paper.

received in a shorter time, than normal statutory depreciation allowances. Thus, in the United Kingdom between 20 and 40 per cent of the cost of an asset (depending upon the type of asset) could be written off in the year of purchase; in Australia, the special depreciation allowances for primary producers enable certain assets to be written off in five equal installments of 20 per cent each. With initial allowances proper, an allowance reckoned as a percentage of the cost of the asset, as well as the normal depreciation allowance, is given in the year of acquisition. The depreciation allowances of subsequent years are reduced (if the reducing balance method is used), so that the original cost (less scrap value) is written off by the end of its life. If the straight-line method is used, the balance of the original cost is written off over a shorter number of years. The Australian special depreciation allowance is therefore an accelerated straight-line allowance.

Investment allowances are a straight-out investment subsidy.[4] An investment allowance plus the normal depreciation allowance is given in the year of acquisition, but the normal depreciation allowances of subsequent years are not reduced, or written off, over a shorter period. That is to say, the total amount allowed to be written off for taxation purposes exceeds the original cost (less scrap value) of an asset by the amount of the investment allowance. The investment allowance recommended by Mr Barton and the present writer is of the following form: depreciation allowances for taxation purposes should be normal statutory allowances (preferably calculated by the annuity method and appropriately adjusted for price changes).[5] Taxable income would then be estimated using these, and taxation would be assessed on the resulting income. An allowance equal to a given percentage of the investment carried out by the taxpayer over the financial year concerned would be subtracted from the assessed taxation to give the actual taxation payable.

II

Initial and investment allowances are means by which governments can specifically encourage either investment in aggregate or in particular industries or assets. Governments may wish to encourage investment either for employment-creating purposes or in order to increase the rate of economic growth by raising productivity through the use of more capital-intensive methods of production. With the latter aim, a case can be made for shifting the burden of taxation away from investors as a class on to other classes in the community, for example, consumers, so that aggregate investment can be increased. If, however, governments wish to re-deploy the resources already in the investment goods industries by a judicious combination of tax rates and investment or initial allowances for particular industries or assets, there may be no need to change either the distribution of the aggregate burden of taxation as between investors and consumers, or the aggregate amount of resources used for the production of investment goods.

Initial and investment allowances affect both the inducement to invest, that is, the demand for capital assets, and the means to invest, that is, the supply of funds available to finance investment. Investment decisions can be rationalised by assuming that businesspeople decide on investment projects by comparing the present values of the expected gross cash surpluses (after taxation) of the projects with the present values of the outlays required on the projects, using the cost of capital to the firm as the relevant rate of discount. Initial allowances do not change either the total taxation payments or the total cash surpluses over the whole life of an asset (assuming, for the moment, constant marginal tax rates and one act of investment), but they do increase the cash surplus of the first year of operation and reduce those of the latter years. This increases the present value of the expected cash surpluses. By reducing the taxation payable in the first year of operation and by leaving unchanged the cash surpluses of the remaining years, investment allowances of the United Kingdom type clearly raise the present value of the cash surpluses; so, also, do the investment allowances recommended by Mr Barton and the present writer. For these reasons the inducement to invest will be increased, since some projects that were previously thought to be unprofitable will now be judged profitable. As a result investment by firms and aggregate investment will increase.

An alternative approach to the impact of these allowances on the inducement to invest is to consider the risks associated with investment and the greater uncertainty about the distant as compared with the near future, which are important factors affecting the demand by businessmen for fixed assets. Businessmen often allow for them by use of the 'pay-off' or 'pay-back' period – the criterion that an asset should 'pay for itself' over a period considerably shorter than its effective working life. (The 'pay-back' period is said to be between two and five years for most items of plant and machinery.)[6] For the purchase of an asset to be considered worthwhile, the expected cash surpluses must amount to at least its original cost by the end of the 'pay-back' period. By reducing the taxation payments on the cash surpluses attributed to the earlier years, initial and investment allowances make it easier for some assets, previously marginal, to meet the 'pay-back' criterion. This also would increase individual and aggregate investment.

While it is unexceptional to analyse the effect of these measures on the demand for investment goods by taking one act of investment in isolation, this procedure is open to two objections as far as the supply of funds is concerned. First, the pattern of the tax remissions associated with initial allowances (but not investment allowances, assuming that no changes in tax rates occur) depends on the shape of the preceding stream of investment. Secondly, in considering their effect on the supply of funds, it must be remembered that both the normal depreciation allowances received on past investment and the tax rates in force are likely to differ from those which would have applied, had no initial allowances been given. [In the case of investment allowances, tax rates (but not depreciation allowances) are likely to differ as between the two situations.] The purpose of section III is to analyse the impact on the supply of funds of initial and investment allowances, assuming increasing, constant and decreasing streams of investment, and that the rates of taxation, initial or investment allowance remain unchanged.

III

If investment in a firm is increasing, the introduction and continuation of a scheme of initial allowances leads to a remission of taxation, that is to say, the firm pays less tax than it would have done had it received normal depreciation allowances only. The tax remissions are much greater proportionately in the earlier years after the start of the scheme. In the earlier years, the tax remissions due to initial allowances are not offset by the increased tax payments due to lower (than normal) 'wear and tear' allowances (or no allowances at all), on investments of previous years. However, provided that investment continues to increase, some tax remissions will always be received. With investment allowances, these offsets are absent, and the tax remissions received per unit of investment remain the same, regardless of how long the scheme has been operating.

If a firm invests a constant amount each year, under a system of initial allowances it will receive tax remissions during what may be called the transition period following the introduction of the scheme. The transition period may be very long, for example, 30 years in the case of assets of expected lives of 30 years.[7] Eventually, however, the firm will pay the same amount of taxation regardless of whether it receives accelerated or normal depreciation allowances. With investment allowances, a tax remission is always received. With either scheme, the tax remissions of the transition period will never have to be repaid. Only when a firm invests a decreasing amount each year (or makes one investment) will the tax remissions of the earlier years have to be followed by repayments in later years – and then only in the case of initial allowances.

The appropriate measure of the additional funds made available by initial and investment allowances is the difference between actual taxation payable and that which would have been payable had only normal depreciation allowances been given. To make estimates of these amounts it is necessary to estimate, first, what the taxable incomes of the taxpayers concerned would have been had no initial or investment allowances been given, and, secondly, what tax rates would have been in force in this 'otherwise' situation. If this could be done, it would be found that fast-growing businesses would benefit significantly from these allowances, even if (as is probable) higher tax rates were in force.

IV

Investment allowances are superior to initial allowances,[8] first, because the tax remissions associated with them are independent of the previous stream of investment and do not affect the taxation payments of subsequent years. Secondly, when the marginal tax rates of taxpayers are different, as, for example, in the case of primary producers, initial allowances (and special depreciation allowances) clearly help the high-income farmer more than the low-income farmer. Quite apart from equity considerations these allowances are designed to encourage investment, and should be related to the amount of investment undertaken rather than to the income of the taxpayer concerned. Many high-income farmers form themselves into companies for tax purposes. However, provided that their flat rates of tax are greater than the marginal tax rates of low-income farmers, the above criticism still applies.

When there is a progressive marginal tax rate, there is always the possibility that initial and special depreciation allowances will actually reduce investment. By increasing the taxable incomes of the later years of operation of an asset, so that a higher marginal tax rate than that associated with the tax remissions of the earlier years could be operative, the expected cash surpluses of these later years may be so reduced that present value of all the cash surpluses will be reduced also. Unless there are specific reasons for encouraging investment by high-income taxpayers (or discouraging it should the second alternative be generally true) the investment allowance which is related to the amount of investment undertaken is clearly to be preferred. (These strictures therefore apply to the United Kingdom investment allowance also.) Thirdly, investment allowances are administratively simple to operate, so that they can be easily changed from year to year.

If the overall level of investment is to be encouraged, the appropriate policy is to give investment allowances generally and to shift the distribution of taxation away from investors to other classes in the economy in order to maintain overall balance. If the allocation of resources is to be affected investment allowances could be given to those sectors that it is desired to encourage, and tax rates could be changed appropriately to maintain balance. Differential rates of investment allowance would have to be given in both these cases, because a uniform rate would encourage investment in short-term assets at the expense of investment in long-term assets. Finally, before investment allowances can be regarded as the appropriate policy measure, it has to be shown that investment rather than, say, the particular industries concerned need encouragement. Otherwise general tax remissions are to be preferred since they do not affect the relative prices of the factors of production and so the choice of techniques. In Australia, the present tax base of accounting profit favours labour-intensive techniques.[9] Granting investment allowances may therefore partially redress the balance.

Notes

Since this paper was submitted for publication, the Prime Minister has announced a 20% investment allowance on new plant in manufacturing industry. Broadly, the plant eligible for the allowance is all new machinery and equipment delivered to manufacturing premises on or after 7 February 1962, and which is used within the premises to produce manufacturing goods. The allowance is equivalent to an allowance of the form recommended in this paper of between 7% and 8% for public companies and 5% and 7% for private companies. (Public companies pay 7/- in the £ on taxable incomes up to £5000 and 8/- on incomes in excess of £5000; the corresponding figures for private companies are 5/- and 7/- respectively.) Unless there are specific reasons for giving special encouragement to investment by public companies in manufacturing industry, a flat rate allowance would have been preferable.

1. For comprehensive accounts of the initial and investment allowance schemes used by various countries, see Sidney Davidson, 'Depreciation, Income Taxes and Growth', *Accounting Research*, July 1957, 44–9, and D. P. Barritt, 'Accelerated' Depreciation Allowances and Industrial Investment', *Journal of Industrial Economics*, October 1959, 80–98.
2. This may partly explain the lack of discussion among Australian economists of the impact and relative effectiveness of these allowances.
3. See A. D. Barton and G. C. Harcourt, 'Investment Allowances for Primary Producers', *Australian Journal of Agricultural Economics*, December 1959, 12–18, Chapter 6 of this volume.
4. In a sense, initial allowances are also investment subsidies, since it is possible, for rates of under 100%, to choose a rate of initial allowance which will have an effect on the demand for investment assets equivalent to that of any given, rate of investment allowance. (See J. Black, 'Investment Allowances, Initial Allowances, and Cheap Loans as Means of Encouraging Investment', *Review of Economic Studies*, October 1959, 46.)
5. See J. W. Bennett and G. C. Harcourt, 'Taxation and Business Surplus', *Economic Record*, August 1960, 426, Chapter 7 of this volume.
6. Richard Goode, 'Accelerated Depreciation Allowances as a Stimulus to Investment', *Quarterly Journal of Economics*, May 1955, 195.
7. For a discussion of the transition period associated with special depreciation allowances, see A. D. Barton and G. C. Harcourt, *op. cit.*, 14–15, Chapter 6 this volume.
8. Unless only fast-growing firms are to be encouraged.
9. See J. W. Bennett and G. C. Harcourt, *op. cit.*, 426–7, chapter 7 this volume.

9

Investment-Decision Criteria, Investment Incentives and the Choice of Technique*

Introduction

Postwar economic policy in the United Kingdom and other advanced capitalist economies has been increasingly concerned with the level and rate of increase of labour productivity, both at the national level and at industry and firm levels. One aspect of this concern has been successive attempts by governments to encourage investment expenditure through fiscal incentives; for example, initial allowances were introduced in the United Kingdom in 1946, investment allowances were introduced in 1954, they were combined in 1959 and they were replaced by cash investment grants in 1966. Over the same period there have been various attempts to encourage the finance of investment by internal funds, the latest of which is the corporation tax (1966), an avowed object of which is to lower dividend pay-out ratios and so, it is hoped, encourage internally financed investment expenditure.

The United Kingdom Government has also attempted to 'educate' businesspeople by encouraging them to adopt certain 'correct' rules of investment appraisal. In particular, the use of *Discounted Cash Flow* (DCF) *procedures* of investment appraisal has been advocated strongly, and the widespread use of 'rules of thumb', such as the pay-off period

---

* Originally published in the *Economic Journal*, vol. 78, 1968, 77–95. The writer is grateful to D. M. Nuti, Graham Pyatt, W. B. Reddaway, R. E. Rowthorn and G. Whittington for helpful comments, to M. Panić and Marion Clarke and her assistants for carrying out the preliminary calculations, to H. T. Burley for programming the main calculations for TITAN and to Professor M. V. Wilkes, Mathematical Laboratory, University of Cambridge, for the use of TITAN.

criterion, or variants of the accounting rate of profit, has been criticised.[1]

The link between the level and rate of increase of productivity, on the one hand, and investment expenditure in an economy, an industry or a firm, on the other, is obviously a complicated one,[2] and only one small part of the process is discussed in this essay, namely, the choice from the current 'best-practice' techniques available of the technique with which to produce a *given* level of output per year. It is clear that the *more* capital-intensive (as measured both by the investment – labour ratio and by the investment – output ratio) is the technique chosen, the greater, *other things being equal,* will be the ensuing rise in labour productivity. Presumably, therefore, the various fiscal devices introduced in the postwar period and the recent encouragement of the use of DCF procedures were meant, as one of their aims, to result in the choice of *more* capital-intensive techniques than otherwise would have been the case, that is to say, to result in 'deepening' investment expenditure.

The aims of this essay are three: first, to attempt to order the *relative* capital-intensities which result from the use of various investment-decision rules in a situation characterised by a common technology, given expectations about changes in product prices and money wages, and no taxation or investment incentives;[3] secondly, to analyse the impact of the introduction of taxation and, then, two alternative investment incentive schemes on the choice of technique. The object here is to see whether taxation changes either the capital-intensities or the ordering of the techniques chosen by the rules and whether investment incentives, when associated with particular rules, do in fact lead to more 'deepening' investment than otherwise would have occurred. The third aim is to discuss the implications of past and present United Kingdom tax systems for the choice of technique, as these systems have special features which are not included in the simple systems.

The three investment-decision rules discussed are (1) *the present-value rule* – choose the technique with the highest present value; (2) *the pay-off period criterion* – here defined as choosing the technique which gives the highest expected net receipts over the pay-off period, subject to the constraint that the expected net receipts are at least equal to the investment expenditures associated with the technique (this is *not* the same as choosing the technique with the shortest pay-off period);

(3) *the accounting rate of profit rule* – choose the project with the highest expected accounting rate of profit. The three fiscal systems are: (1) a proportional tax; (2) this tax combined with a simple initial allowance scheme; and (3) this tax combined with a simple investment allowance scheme. The United Kingdom tax systems considered are: (1) the old profits tax and standard rate of income tax combined with investment and initial allowances, and (2) the new corporation tax and cash investment grants.[4]

The essay is in five sections. In section I the technology, expectations and basic assumptions are set out, the various tax systems are briefly described, and the concepts and notation used are defined. In section II the analysis of the relative capital-intensities resulting from the application of the three rules in the *pre-tax* situation is set out. In section III the impact of the three simple tax systems on the choice of technique is analysed. In section IV the results which arise from the special features of the two United Kingdom systems are presented. The main conclusions of the article are gathered together in section V.

I

The basic technology

Suppose that there are a number of ways of producing a given stream of output per year, characterised by decreasing labour requirements per year as current investment expenditures increase. As the techniques become more capital-intensive, however, the saving in labour is assumed to become less. The labour requirements per year of each technique and the level of output per year are assumed to remain the same for the entire *engineering* life of the equipment associated with each technique (which is assumed to be *considerably* greater than its economic life). Maintenance and raw material costs are ignored.[5] If investment expenditure (K) is plotted on the horizontal axis, and labour requirements per year (l) on the vertical axis, the curve, ll (the *ex ante* production function) is obtained (see Figure 9.1). K_1, K_2 and K_3, are the investment expenditures associated with three 'best-practice' techniques of producing a given level of output (x) and l_1, l_2 and l_3 are their respective labour requirements.

Expectations

Perhaps the most simple, plausible expectations are that the price of the product will rise (for simplicity, at a constant rate per year, g) and that costs will rise at a faster rate than price, mainly because money wages, on average, can be expected to rise at a rate per year (G) which reflects both the rise in the general level of prices *and* the rise in overall productivity. The expected economic life of the equipment associated with a given technique is assumed to be given by the point where the expected net receipts (in this instance sales receipts *less* wage costs) first become zero (but on this, see the opening para. of section V below).

The expected annual sales receipts and the expected labour costs of techniques 1, 2 and 3 of Figure 9.1 are shown in Figure 9.2, together with their expected economic lives, n_1, n_2 and n_3. Length of life in years (n) is measured on the horizontal axis, annual sales receipts (Q) and

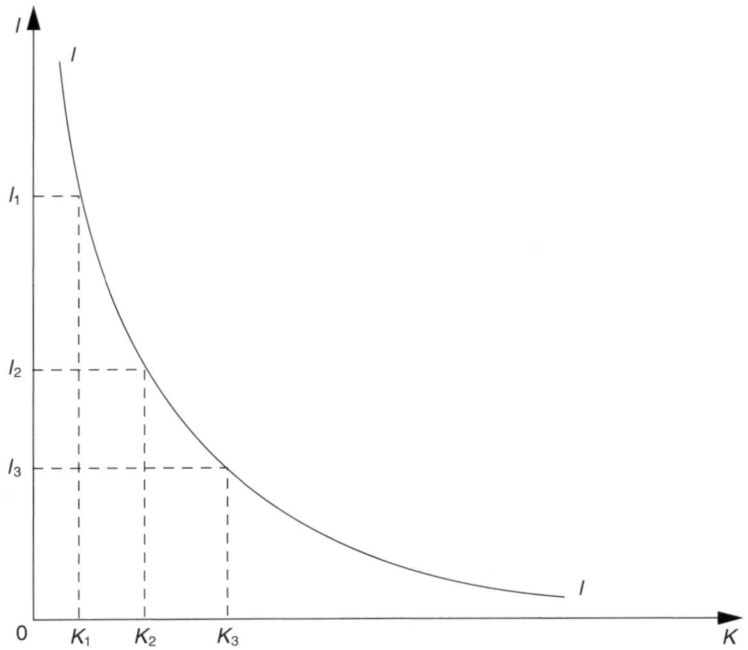

Figure 9.1

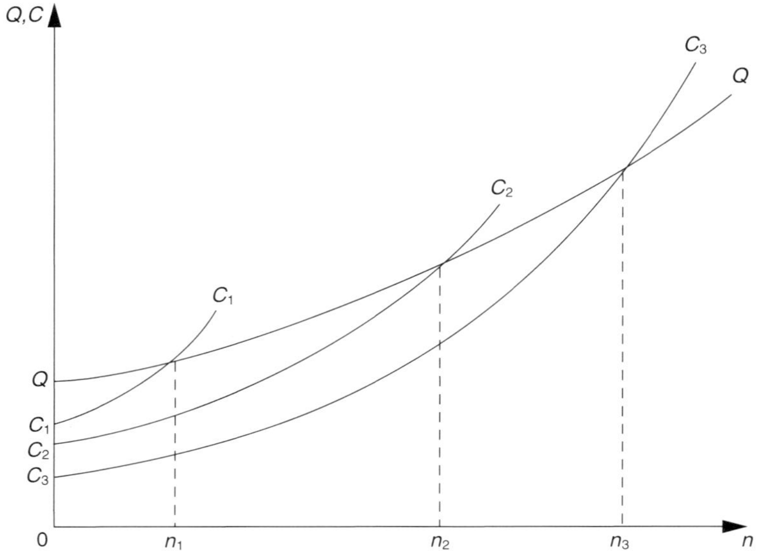

Figure 9.2

labour costs (C) on the vertical axis. The curve QQ shows annual sales receipts, and the curves C_1C_1, C_2C_2 and C_3C_3 show the annual labour costs of techniques 1, 2 and 3 respectively. The level of sales receipts at the end of year i ($i = 1, \ldots n$) are: $Q_i = p_o x(1+g)^i$ where p_o = the price of the product at the beginning of year 1, and x = output per year. Labour costs of technique $j(j = 1, \ldots m)$ at the end of year i are: $C_i^j = w_o l_j (1+G)^i$, where w_o = money wage at the beginning of year 1, and l_j = annual labour requirement of technique j. The totals of the expected annual net receipts (q) are the areas between QQ and the respective CC curves. It can be seen that with the present assumptions, capital-intensity and economic length of life are positively related.

Investment-decision rules (in their pre-tax form)

Investment-decision rule 1 (the *present value* (V) *rule*) states:

$$\text{Choose } K_j \text{ such that } V^j = \sum_{i=1}^{n} \frac{(Q_t - C_i^j)}{(1+R)^t} - K_j = max \qquad (1.1)$$

where R is the rate of interest used as the discount factor.[6]

Investment-decision rule 2 (the *pay-off period criterion*) states:

$$\text{Choose } K_j \text{ such that } \sum_{i=1}^{b} (Q_i - C_i^j) = max$$

$$\text{subject to } \sum_{i=1}^{b} (Q_i - C_i j) \geq K_j \tag{1.2}$$

where b is the pay-off period, measured in years.

Investment-decision rule 3 (the *accounting rate of profit* (P) *rule*) states:

$$\text{Choose } K_j \text{ such that } P^j = \frac{\sum_{i=1}^{n} (Q_i - C_i^j) - K_j}{nK_j} = max \tag{1.3}$$

The simple tax and investment incentive schemes

The simple tax and alternative investment incentive schemes are now described.

(1) The tax system (tax system A.1)

Annual company profits, net of 'wear and tear' allowances, are assumed to be taxed at a rate of t%. The rate of 'wear and tear' allowance is $d(=\frac{3}{2\bar{n}})$, where $\bar{n}$ is the length of life of equipment for tax purposes and is assumed to be the *same* for all the machines associated with the current 'best-practice' techniques for producing a particular product.

(2) The accelerated depreciation allowance scheme (tax system A.2)

An initial allowance of i% is given in the year of purchase, together with the 'wear and tear' allowance, so that $K(1 - i - d)$ is left to be written off at a rate of d per year for the remaining $(\bar{n} - 1)$ years. Taxation is again at a rate of t%.

(3) The investment allowance scheme (tax system A.3)

An investment allowance of I% is given in the year of purchase, as well as the 'wear and tear' allowance. $K(1 + I)$ is therefore written off for tax purposes over $\bar{n}$ years. The rate of taxation is t%.

The three investment-decision rules can all be restated to include the impact of the tax and other provisions on the expected net receipts. For example, under tax system A.1 rule 1 becomes:

Choose K_j such that

$$V_j = \left\{\sum_{i=1}^{n} \frac{(1 - t)(Q_i - C_i^j)}{(1 + r_i)^i}\right\} + \left\{\sum_{i=1}^{n} \frac{tdK_j(1 - d)^{i-1}}{(1 + r_i)^i}\right\} - K_j = max$$

where $r_t = R(1 - t)$.

The first term is the present value of the expected net receipts adjusted for tax payable on them; the second term is the present value of the tax saved by the receipt of 'wear and tear' allowances. The rate of interest used as a discount factor is measured *net* of tax. (As *post-tax* amounts are being discounted, it seems reasonable to use a *post-tax* rate of interest as the discount factor.) The expressions corresponding to the other rules can be similarly adjusted, both for taxation and for the appropriate investment incentives.

The two United Kingdom tax systems

(1) The old profits tax and standard rate of income tax combined with investment and initial allowances (tax system B.1)

Prior to 1966, expenditure on new plant and machinery by manufacturing firms outside the development districts (the discussion will be confined to these firms) carried with it for tax purposes an investment allowance (I) of 30% and an initial allowance (i) of 10%. These two allowances, together with the normal statutory 'wear and tear' allowances (d), were deductable from taxable income (supposing sufficient profits to be earned by the business as a whole, but not necessarily by the new investment itself), though the actual tax remissions were not received until, on average, eighteen months later. The total 'wear and tear' allowances of subsequent years were reduced by the amount of the initial (but not the investment) allowance. Taxable profits of companies bore a profits tax ($\bar{p}$) of 15% and the standard rate of income tax (s) of 8s. 3d. in the £. This system is a combination of tax systems A.2 and A.3 above.

(2) The new corporation tax combined with cash investment grants (tax system B.2)

Under the new system a cash grant (G_2) of 20% (temporarily raised to 25% for the fiscal year 1967–68) of the purchase price is given, and the investment and initial allowances, but not the 'wear and tear' allowances, are withdrawn. The latter, however, apply only to the *balance* of the purchase price after subtracting the cash investment grant. The cash grant eventually will be received six months after the date of purchase and is not dependent upon a profit being earned. Taxable profits now bear a corporation tax at a rate (c) of 40%, and income tax payable by shareholders depends upon the proportion of post-tax profits (net of depreciation) which is distributed, that is, on the pay-out ratio (α).[8]

Again, the three rules can be restated to take account of the tax and other provisions. For reasons of space, they are not shown here (the expressions for the present-value rule are in paras. 1.4. to 1.8 of 'Cash Investment Grants, Corporation Tax and Pay-out Ratios,' see note 4). Finally, it could be noted that it is sometimes claimed that rule 3 is applied in its *pre-tax* form, in which case expression (1.3) is applicable.[9]

Now suppose that a businessperson decides the technique in which to invest on the basis of one of the rules described in this section. The questions with which the next sections are concerned are: Can the resulting techniques be ordered according to their *relative* capital-intensities? And does the introduction of taxation and investment incentives into the analysis change the capital-intensities and their ordering?[10]

II

Investment-decision rules and relative capital-intensities in the pre-tax situation

Essentially, the questions asked in this section are: what are the values of the slope of the *ex ante* production function at the points corresponding to the techniques chosen by each rule, and can they be unambiguously ordered? These values are found, for rules 1 and 3, by obtaining the first-order conditions for a maximum present value and a maximum accounting rate of profit respectively, and expressing them in terms of the slope of the production function, $\frac{\delta l}{\delta K}$. The corresponding value for the pay-off period criterion is obtained by a different method (see Rule 2 below).

Rule 1

This rule may be written as:

$$V_j = p_0 \, x B - \omega_0 \, l_j A - K_j = max \tag{2.1}$$

where

$$A = \frac{(1+G)\left\{\left(\frac{1+G}{1+R}\right)^n - 1\right\}}{G-R}, \quad B = \frac{(1+g)\left\{\left(\frac{1+g}{1+R}\right)^n - 1\right\}}{g-R}$$

and $R > G > g$, by assumption. (For moderate rates of increase of prices and money wages, this seems a reasonable assumption.)

To find the first-order condition for (2.1) to be a maximum, partially differentiate (2.1) with respect to K and put the resulting expression equal to zero to obtain:

$$-\frac{\delta l}{\delta K} = \frac{1}{\omega_0 A - \frac{\delta n}{\delta l}\left(p_0\, x\, \frac{\delta B}{\delta n} - \omega_0 l\, \frac{\delta A}{\delta n}\right)} \tag{2.2}$$

Rule 2

This criterion requires that:

$$p_0\, x B' - w_0\, l_j A' = max, \text{ subject to } p_0\, x B' - w_0 l_j A' \geq K_j,$$

where

$$A' = \frac{(1+G)\{(1+G)^b - 1\}}{G} \quad \text{and} \quad B' = \frac{(1+g)\{(1+g)^b - 1\}}{g}.$$

Write the constraint as the equality:

$$l = \frac{p_0\, x B'}{\omega_0 A'} - \frac{K}{\omega_0 A'} \tag{2.3}$$

Equation (2.3) is a straight line (*LL* in Figure 9.3) with a slope of $\left(-\frac{1}{w_0 A'}\right)$ and an intercept on the vertical axis of $\frac{p_0 x B'}{w_0 A'}$. The curve, *ll*, of Figure 9.1 is also shown in Figure 9.3. Provided some labour and some investment expenditure are needed to produce a given level of output, *LL* will either intersect *ll* at points such as P_1 and P_2 (where the constraint is satisfied) or will be tangential to *ll* at a point such as P_3 (or will not cut *ll* at all, in which case no technique will satisfy the criterion). At P_2 the pay-off period criterion is satisfied (because net receipts for the pay-off period are the highest possible, given that the constraint must be met) and the technique associated with an investment expenditure of K_2 is chosen.

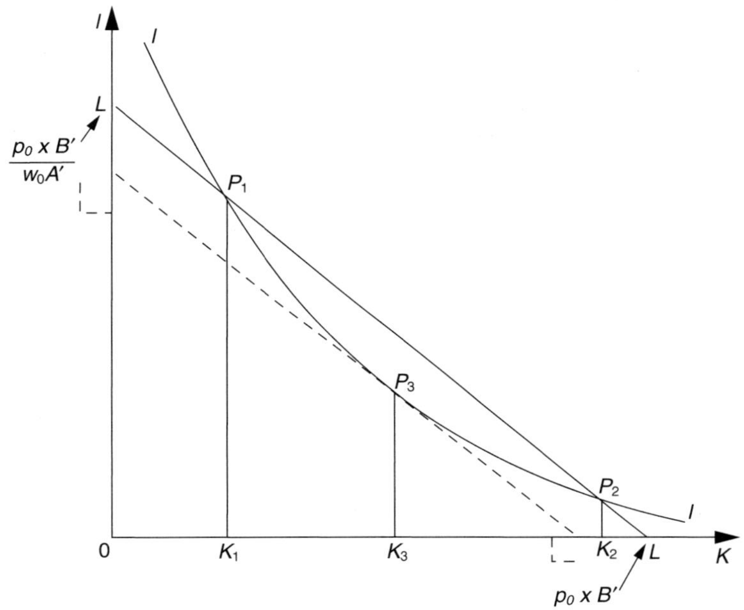

Figure 9.3

At P_2, $-\frac{\delta l}{\delta K} < \frac{1}{w_0A'}$ because ll cuts LL from below. $\left(\text{The other possibility is the tangency solution at } P_3 \text{ and there, } -\frac{\delta l}{\delta K} = \frac{1}{w_0A'}\right)$ Therefore,

$$-\frac{\delta l}{\delta K} \leq \frac{1}{w_0A'} \qquad (2.4)$$

Now compare equation (2.2) with (2.4) and suppose, initially, that $n = b$ for all techniques. Equation (2.2) therefore becomes:

$$-\frac{\delta l}{\delta K} = \frac{1}{w_0A''} \qquad (2.5)$$

where

$$A'' = \frac{(1+G)\left\{\left(\frac{1+G}{1+R}\right)^b - 1\right\}}{G-R}$$

Because $A'' < A'$, it is obvious that (2.5) > (2.4).

In equation (2.2), $\left(p_0 x \frac{\delta B}{\delta n} - w_0 l \frac{\delta A}{\delta n}\right)$ may be $\lesseqgtr 0$. If it ≤ 0, (2.2) > (2.4), for a wide range of values of n;[12] that is to say, over this range, which is greater, the greater is the value of R, the present-value criterion results in a *less*-capital-intensive technique being chosen. If $\left(p_0 x \frac{\delta B}{\delta n} - w_0 l \frac{\delta A}{\delta n}\right) > 0$ (which is more likely to happen at *low* values of n) it does not necessarily follow that (2.2) < (2.4), especially as $w_0 A < w_0 A'$, for given values of n, and $\frac{1}{w_0 A'}$ is the upper value of the inequality, $-\frac{\delta l}{\delta K} \leq \frac{l}{w_0 A'}$. Thus, it seems reasonable to conclude that, given the present assumptions, the pay-off-period criterion often results in the choice of a *more* capital-intensive technique than does the present-value rule, and that this is more likely to occur, given the value of the pay-off period, the higher is the rate of interest used as the discount factor and the shorter is the economic length of life of the equipment concerned. If $b = 4–5$ years, $R = 15–20\%$, $G = 4–6\%$, and $n = 10–15$ years are taken as realistic orders of magnitude, 'back-of-an-envelope' calculations show that the result is widely applicable.

Rule 3

This rule may be written as:

$$P^j = \frac{1}{nK}\{p_0\, x B''' - w_0 l_j A''' - K_j\} = max \qquad (2.6)$$

where

$$A''' = \frac{(1+G)\{(1+G)^n - 1\}}{G} \quad \text{and} \quad B''' = \frac{(1+g)\{(1+g)^n - 1\}}{g}$$

A rough idea of the relative capital-intensity which results from this rule, as compared, first, with the pay-off period criterion can be obtained as follows. In Figure 9.4,

$$\pi_j \left\{ = \frac{\sum_{i-1}^{b} (Q_i - C_i^j)}{bK_j} \right\}$$

is plotted on the vertical axis and K on the horizontal axis. The values of π_j are the average expected gross rates of profit for the pay-off period

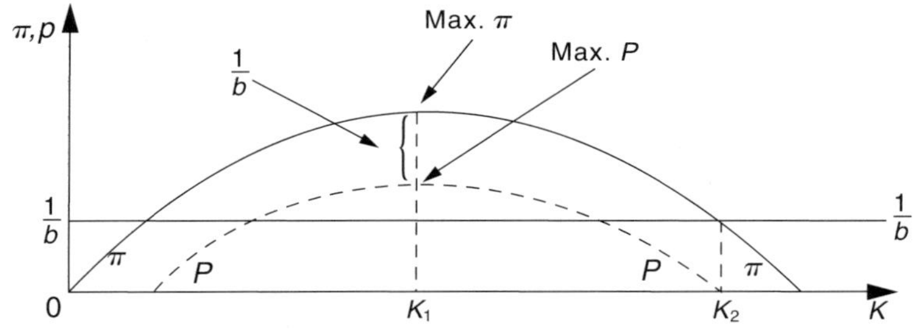

Figure 9.4

of each technique – the *inverses* of the number of years that it takes to 'repay' the respective investment outlays. Because the undiscounted net receipts of the techniques are bounded by the pay-off period and because labour requirements decline at a decreasing rate as K increases, π will rise to a maximum and then decline as K increases, giving the curve $\pi\pi$ in Figure 9.4. If rule 2 were an instruction to choose the technique with the *lowest* pay-off period the technique associated with an expenditure of K_1 would be chosen. However, it is possible both to increase expected gross profits *and* to satisfy the pay-off period criterion by choosing the technique associated with an expenditure of K_2; at which value $\pi = \frac{1}{b}$, the inverse of the pay-off period. With this technique, $\sum_{t-1}^{b}(Q_i - C_i^j) = K_j$, and is also maximised.

Now suppose that annual *net* profits (P) are averaged for a period equal to the pay-off period, and that depreciation is reckoned as $\frac{K}{b}$ per year. If P^j is plotted against K (see the curve PP in Figure 9.4) it will reach a maximum at the *same* investment expenditure (K_1) as π. Therefore, with these assumptions, rule 3 results in a *less* capital-intensive technique being chosen than that resulting from rule 2.

If, now, the assumption that $n = b$ is dropped, the maximum of the curve PP may well occur at a value of K which is closer to K_2; but it does seem that there will be a considerable number of cases where this rule results in a *less* capital-intensive technique being chosen.

What can be said of the ordering of rule 3 in relation to rule 1? To answer this, consider the first-order condition for a maximum P^j. It is:

$$-\frac{\delta l}{\delta K} = \left\{\frac{p_0 x B''' - \omega_0 l A'''}{K}\right\} \left\{\frac{1}{\omega_0 A''' - \frac{K}{n}\frac{\delta n}{\delta l} - \frac{\delta n}{\delta l}\{p_0 x(\frac{\delta B'''}{\delta n} - \frac{B'''}{n}) - \omega_0 l(\frac{\delta A'''}{\delta n} - \frac{A'''}{n})\}}\right\} \quad (2.7)$$

Comparing equation (2.7) with (2.2), and ignoring the last two terms of the denominator of (2.7) and the last term of the denominator of (2.2), the ordering turns on whether the effect of $\left\{\frac{p_0 x B''' - w_0 l A'''}{K}\right\} > 1$, which tends to make (2.7) > (2.2), outweighs, or is outweighed, by the effect of $w_0 A''' > w_0 A$, which tends to make (2.7) < (2.2). Therefore, while both rule 1 and rule 3 often result in *less* capital-intensive techniques being chosen than those resulting from rule 2, the techniques corresponding to rules 1 and 3 cannot themselves be ordered.[13]

The results of this section are summarised in Figure 9.5. $-\frac{\delta l}{\delta K}$ is plotted on the vertical axis and n on the horizontal axis. Because n increases, and $-\frac{\delta l}{\delta K}$ decreases, as K increases, a downward-sloping curve such as *DD* (shown as a straight line for simplicity) is obtained. $-\frac{\delta l}{\delta K}$ is also a function of n in the expressions for the first-order conditions for a maximum of rules 1 and 3 (see equations (2.2) and (2.7), and of b in the inequality condition of rule 2 (see (2.4)). These expressions are shown in Figure 9.5 by the curves *EE* (rule 1), *FF* (which is a horizontal straight line, the height of which is determined by the values of b, w_0 and G) (rule 2) and *GG* (rule 3). The economic lengths of life of the techniques chosen by the rules are those associated with the points where *EE, FF* and *GG* cut *DD*.

The positive relationship between K and n is the line *HH,* in the bottom half of Figure 9.5, and the investment expenditures associated with the choices which result from each rule are shown on the vertical axis. (As shown in Figure 9.5, rule 1 results in the choice of a less capital-intensive technique than rule 3; but this ordering need not

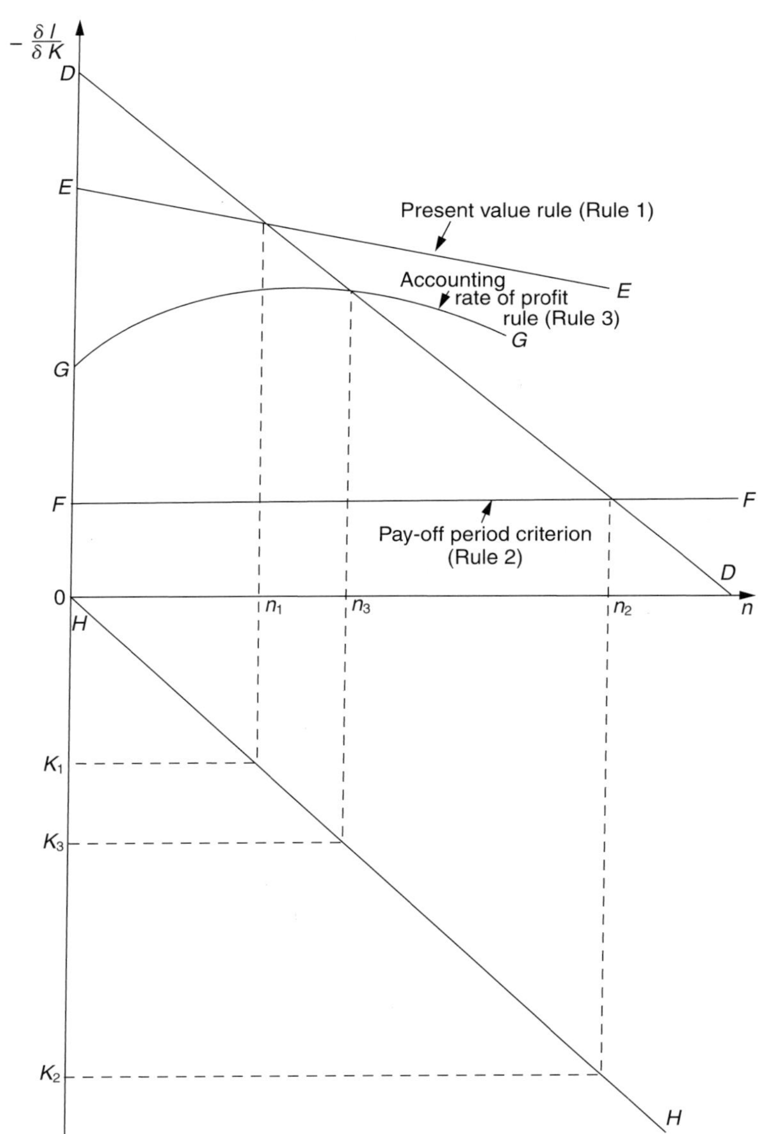

$-\frac{\delta I}{\delta K}$
D
E
Present value rule (Rule 1)
E
Accounting rate of profit rule (Rule 3)
G
G
F
F
Pay-off period criterion (Rule 2)
D
0
n_1
n_3
n_2
n
H
K_1
K_3
K_2
H
K

Figure 9.5

occur.) The significant result at this stage is that the pay-off period criterion often results in the choice of the *most* capital-intensive technique of the three rules examined (of four rules, if the internal rate of return is also considered, see note 6 above).

The next section discusses whether taxation and investment incentives change the relative orderings resulting from the three rules, and whether investment incentives do, in fact, lead to 'deepening' investment expenditure. It could be noticed in passing that if factor and product prices and the inputs per unit of output of each technique are assumed to be independent of the scale of operation of the individual firm, the results of this and the following sections relate to the choice of the capital intensity of a *unit* of output. In this case $x = 1$ in the expressions and l and k should be interpreted as the labour requirements and investment expenditure, respectively, of a unit of output.

III

The expressions for $-\frac{\delta l}{\delta K}$ in the *post-tax* situations (which, for reasons of space, are not shown here) are basically similar to those of the *pre-tax* situation, except they have additional terms which contain the rates of taxation, investment incentives and other allowances. In some instances the direction of the change in capital-intensity when taxation and investment incentives are taken into account is clear from the expressions themselves. But in others it was necessary, first, to place orders of magnitude on the values of the appropriate variables. The values were: $t = 0.25, 0.50$; $i, l = 0.10, 0.20, 0.30$; $d = 0.25, 0.20, 0.15$ (implying $n = 6$, 8 and 10 years, respectively); $G = 0.03, 0.06, 0.09, 0.12$; $R = 0.10, 0.25, 0.50$; $b = 2, 3, 4$ and 5 years; and $n = 6, 8, 10, 12, 15$ and 20 years.

The main results of the analysis of the new expressions are:

(1) The orderings of the capital-intensities resulting from each rule in the pre-tax situation probably still hold in the *post-tax* situation, though, in some instances, the range of values of n within which rule 1 results in the choice of a *less* capital-intensive technique than rule 2 is narrowed.

(2) Taxation *by itself* results in the choice of *less* capital-intensive techniques if rules 1 and 2 are used, but has no impact if rule 3 is

used. These results reflect the fact that, relatively, the tax savings associated with the receipt of 'wear and tear' allowances are greater, the *less* capital-intensive is the technique concerned (either because their discounted value is relatively greater (rule 1) or because a greater proportion of their total is included in the pay-off period (rule 2)). The technique chosen by rule 3 is not affected by a proportional tax, as it affects the sizes but not the order of the rates of profit.

(3) Investment incentives do result in more 'deepening' than otherwise would have occurred if rules 1 and 2 are used. Their impact more than offsets the counteracting effect of taxation on the choice of techniques, if rule 1 is used, but not if rule 2 is used. However, if rule 3 is used, accelerated depreciation has no effect, and investment allowances have a 'perverse' effect in the sense that *less* capital-intensive techniques than otherwise would be the case are chosen. This reflects the fact that, relatively, the impact of the tax saving associated with a given rate of investment allowance on the rate of profit is greater, the *less* capital-intensive is the technique concerned. As the accounting rate of profit rule is said to be widely used in the United Kingdom, this 'perverse' effect of its use in association with investment allowances is not without interest.

(4) For *given* values of l and i, and with the use of rules 1 and 2, investment allowances result in more deepening than do initial allowances. However, there are values of i greater than l which reverse the orderings associated with $l \geq i$.

IV

In this section, the choice of technique under the two United Kingdom tax systems is briefly considered. Tax system B.1 is, in effect, a combination of tax systems A.2 and A.3. Tax system B.2 includes the additional complication that the amount of income tax payable by shareholders and thus, the *post-tax* net receipts of given investment projects, depend upon the size of the pay-out ratio adopted.

The expressions for $-\frac{\delta l}{\delta K}$ for these tax systems are again not shown; they are similar to those of the *pre-tax* situation, but include extra terms which are analogous to those of the simple tax systems. The following orders of magnitude were placed on the rates of taxation and investment incentives, and so on. For reasons explained elsewhere, the values of the fiscal rates were: $\bar{p} = 0.15$; $s = 0.4125$; $c = 0.40$; $l = 0.30$; $i = 0.10$; $G_2 = 0.20$; and $d = 0.25, 0.20, 0.15$ (implying $\bar{n} = 6, 8$ and 10 years respectively).[14] $G = 0.03, 0.06, 0.09, 0.12$; $R = 0.10, 0.25, 0.50$; $b = 2, 3, 4$ and 5 years, and $\alpha = 0, \frac{2}{5}, \frac{3}{5}, \frac{2}{3}$[15] and 1 were used also.

1. Comparisons with the pre-tax situation

Comparing the techniques which result from the use of each rule under the two tax systems with those of the *pre-tax* situation, it is found that the use of rule 1 results in a 'natural' outcome under both tax systems, rule 2 probably results in a 'natural' outcome under tax system B.1 but not under tax system B.2, and rule 3 results in a 'perverse' outcome under both systems. ('Natural' and 'perverse' mean that more (less) 'deepening' than otherwise would be the case occurs.)

2. 'Orderings' under the two tax systems

Under the old tax system there seems to be no reason to change the finding that the most capital-intensive technique is likely to be associated with rule 2; but there now seems a greater chance that rule 1 may result in the choice of a *more* capital-intensive technique than rule 3. Under the present tax system, it appears that, except in the case of a *small pre-tax* rate of interest (<5%) or the *combination* of a high pay-out ratio with higher *pre-tax* rates of interest, the pay-off period criterion still results in the choice of the *most* capital-intensive technique of those chosen by the three rules.

3. Comparison between the tax system for common rules

The final set of comparisons relates to the relative orderings, as between the two tax systems, of the capital-intensities chosen by a given rule. This is the most interesting set of comparisons, because it throws some light on the impact of the recent (1966) changes to a corporation tax and cash investment grants on the choice of techniques. Too much should not be made of the results, however, because they are the outcome of a 'partial' analysis. While the values of the tax rates used are appropriate for an 'otherwise situation' comparison, it may well be that the prices of capital goods and the rates of increase of product prices and money wages would have been different as between the two situations.

If the techniques resulting from use of the present-value rule are compared it is found that the technique chosen under tax system B.2 is *less* capital-intensive than that chosen under tax system B.1. Similarly, the use of the pay-off period criterion almost certainly results in a *less*-capital-intensive technique being chosen under tax system B.2. (The use of rule 2 under tax system B.1 usually resulted in the choice of a more capital-intensive technique relative to the *pre-tax* situation (depending upon the value of b in relation to $\bar{n}$, namely, that $b \leq \bar{n}/2$), while the opposite result occurred under tax system B.2).[16]

Finally, if the capital-intensities resulting from the use of rule 3 are compared it is found that, except for very low pay-out ratios (for the orders of magnitude examined, less than approximately 23%), *more*-capital-intensive techniques are chosen under the present tax system (B.2). Therefore there arises the possibility of a paradoxical result, if the corporation tax results in the adoption of very low α's, or if firms already have low α's, or if the income tax payable by shareholders is ignored by managers when investment decisions are made (which is formally equivalent to assuming a pay-out ratio of zero).

V

Before setting out the main conclusions of this article, some of the limitations of the analysis are discussed. The first limitation is that the analysis consists, essentially, of comparisons between different situations, where only the variables associated with the particular fiscal system in force are allowed to change. It may well be, though, that the changes in factor and product prices as between the 'otherwise situations' would be so important in practice that the results of the comparisons in this article could not be applied to situations of actual change. The second limitation is that *higher* investment expenditures may not in fact be associated with *lower* labour inputs over the entire life of the equipment involved. The greater is the investment expenditure, the more complex is the equipment likely to be, and therefore the greater may be its maintenance costs (and, thus, indirect labour input) in its later years. This point has been guarded against to some extent by supposing that economic lives are considerably shorter than engineering lives. Thirdly, the expected economic length of life *may* be less than that determined by the point where expected quasi-rents first become zero, if the expected rate of technical progress is taken into account by businesspeople in a more sophisticated way than is assumed in this essay, or if they operate in an imperfectly competitive situation. However, these considerations do not affect the *ordering* of techniques by length of life, which is the relevant factor for the present analysis. Moreover, this effect increases the possibility that the pay-off period criterion will result in the choice of the *most* capital-intensive technique of three rules considered. Fourthly, the comparisons between the tax systems are not applicable if businesspeople ignore taxation provisions when making investment decisions.

The fifth limitation is that the relative capital-intensities which result from the use of the various rules have been discussed in the context of a situation in which the *level of expected output* is assumed to be given. If, instead, the level of *investment expenditure* is assumed to be given it can be shown that the pay-off period criterion and, perhaps, the present-value rule result in the choice of *less*-capital-intensive techniques than those indicated by the present analysis. Therefore, if businesspeople are in the latter situation, or if they see the problem of the choice of techniques as one of allocating a given amount of investment funds rather than as one of deciding the capital-intensity to be used to produce a given level (or unit) of output, the orderings associated with the three rules *may* differ from those suggested here.[17]

Bearing in mind the above limitations, the conclusions of the article are:

Conclusions which apply to all tax systems and to the pre-tax situation

(1) In both the *pre-tax* and *post-tax* situations it appears that the use of the *pay-off period criterion* often results in the choice of a *more* capital-intensive technique than does the *present-value rule*, or the *accounting rate of profit rule*.

(2) Taxation *by itself* results in the choice of *less* capital-intensive techniques than in the *pre-tax* situation if the *present-value rule* or the *pay-off period criterion* is used, but has no impact if the *accounting rate of profit rule* is used.

(3) Investment incentives result in more deepening than otherwise would have occurred if the *present-value rule* or *pay-off period criterion* is used. Moreover, if the former rule is used their effect more than offsets the impact of taxation on the choice of

techniques. However, if the *accounting rate of profit rule* is used either they have no effect (accelerated depreciation) or a 'perverse' effect (investment allowances) in the sense that *less* capital-intensive techniques than otherwise would be the case are chosen.

(4) For *given* values of the rates of investment incentives, investment allowances result in more deepening than initial allowances if the *present-value rule* or the *pay-off period criterion* is used.

(5) In general, it is not possible to order the *relative* capital-intensities which result from the use of the *present-value rule* and the *accounting rate of profit rule*. However, under all tax systems that include investment incentives there is a greater chance than in the *pre-tax* situation that the *present-value rule* will result in the choice of a *more* capital-intensive technique than that which results from the *accounting rate of profit rule*.

Conclusions which apply specifically to the United Kingdom tax systems

(1) The use of the *accounting rate of profit rule* under both United Kingdom tax systems results in 'perverse' movement in the sense that *less* capital-intensive techniques are chosen than would have been in the *pre-tax* situation. This is also true of the use of the *pay-off period criterion* under the present tax system of a corporation tax and cash investment grants, but probably not of its use under the previous tax system, or of the use of the *present-value rule* under either tax system.

(2) If the *present-value-rule* is used the change from the old tax system of profits tax and the standard rate of income tax combined with investment and initial allowances to the present tax system results in the choice of *less* capital-intensive techniques than otherwise would have occurred.

(3) If the *pay-off period criterion* is used the change from the old tax system to the present tax system will almost certainly result in the choice of *less* capital-intensive techniques than otherwise would have occurred.

(4) The *accounting rate of profit rule* will result in the choice of *more* capital-intensive techniques under the present tax system than would have occurred under the old tax system, *unless* pay-out ratios are very low, or are reduced to very low levels, or the income

tax payable by shareholders is ignored by businesspeople when making investment decisions.

(5) If at the time when the corporation tax and cash investment grants were introduced a firm changed from using the *pay-off period criterion* to using a DCF procedure it may well choose *less* capital-intensive techniques than otherwise would have been the case. A change from the *accounting rate of profit rule* to the *present-value rule* under the same circumstances, however, *may* result in more 'deepening' investment than otherwise would have occurred.

Appendix

(a) Simplifying assumption about the operation of the British tax systems

(1) The cash investment grants are received immediately, initial and investment allowances at the end of the first year of operation.
(2) Reducing-balance 'wear and tear' allowances are used, at the three official rates of 25, 20 and 15%, implying lives for tax purposes ($\bar{n}$) of 6, 8 and 10 years respectively $\left(d = \frac{3}{2\bar{n}}\right)$.
(3) Sufficient profits are assumed to be made in the business to allow the investment and initial allowances to be claimed immediately.
(4) Profits tax and income tax apply to the *same* year's taxable income.
(5) The rates of interest (r) used as the discount factors for the present-value calculations are assumed to be *net* of tax (p. 126). Under tax system B.1 ($p + s$ with I and i), $r_1 = R(1 - p - s)$; under tax system B.2 (c with G_2), $r_2 = R(1 - c - \alpha s\,(1 - c))$, where the subscripts refer to the tax systems concerned.

(b) Notation

Q_i = expected annual sales receipts in year i, ($i = 1, \ldots n$);
C_i^j = expected annual labour costs in year i of technique j, ($j = 1, \ldots m$);
q_i = expected annual net receipts in year i;
p = product price;
w = money wage;
g = rate of increase of product price;
G = rate of increase of money wage;

x = annual output;
l_j = annual labour requirement of technique j;
K_j = investment expenditure associated with technique j;
r_t, r_i = *post-tax* rate of interest (i = 1,2);
R = *pre-tax* rate of interest;
ρ = internal rate of return;
V^j = present value of investment project using technique j;
P^j = accounting rate of profit of investment project using technique j;
n = economic length of life in years;
$\bar{n}$ = length of life for tax purposes in years;
b = length of pay-off period in years;
t = rate of tax in simple tax systems;
$\bar{p}$ = rate of profits tax;
s = standard rate of income tax;
c = rate of corporation tax;
I = rate of investment allowance;
i = rate of initial allowance;
G_2 = rate of cash investment grant;
d = rate of reducing-balance 'wear and tear' allowance ($d = \frac{3}{2\bar{n}}$);
α = pay-out ratio;

subscripts 1, 2 refer to the respective United Kingdom tax systems.

Notes

1. See, for example, National Economic Development Council, *Investment Appraisal* (London: HMSO, 1965).
2. The best analysis of this link at the industry and firm levels is the late W. E. G. Salter's pioneering work, *Productivity and Technical Change* (Cambridge: Cambridge University Press, 1960).
3. This topic has been analysed more fully by the writer in 'Investment-decision Criteria, Capital-intensity and the Choice of Techniques' a paper presented at the IEA Conference on *Planning and Markets: Modern Trends in Various Economic Systems* (Nice, August–September 1966) (subsequently published in J. T. Dunlop and N. P. Federenko (eds), *Planning and Markets: Modern Trends in Various Economic Systems* (New York: McGraw Hill, 1969), 190–216.
4. The impact of the change to the corporation tax and cash investment grants from the previous system, and from one which included corporation tax and retained investment and initial allowances, on the present values of given investment projects has been analysed by the writer in 'Cash Investment Grants, Corporation Tax and Pay-Out Ratios', *Bulletin of the Oxford University Institute of Economics and Statistics*, August 1966, 163–79, and February 1967, 87–93.

5. The significance of these assumptions is discussed further in section V (first para.) below. Sometimes it is convenient to assume that the inputs per unit of output associated with each technique are *independent* of the scale of operations (see the concluding remarks to section II below). The influence of raw-material costs on the choice of technique is discussed on pp. 211–12 of 'Investment-decision Criteria, Capital-intensity and the Choice of Techniques'. With the exception of the accounting rate of profit rule, where their effect is indeterminate, they result in the choice of *less* capital-intensive techniques than otherwise would be the case.
6. Another DCF procedure which is often recommended is the *internal rate of return rule:*

   Choose K_j such that ρ in the expression

   $$\sum_{i=1}^{n} \frac{(Q_i - C_i^j)}{(1+p)^i} - K_j = 0$$

   is a *maximum*, where ρ is the internal rate of return.

   It is shown on pp. 201–2 of 'Investment-decision Criteria, Capital Intensity and the Choice of Techniques' that (with the present assumptions) this rule *always* results in the choice of a *less* capital-intensive technique than that resulting from the *present value rule*, which is used as the representative of DCF procedures in the present analysis.
7. This one of many possible variants of the accounting rate of profit, see note 13 below.
8. A number of simplifying assumptions concerning the operation of the two tax systems are in the Appendix to this chapter; they are discussed in detail in para. 1.1. of 'Cash Investment Grants, Corporation Tax and Pay-out Ratios', see note 4.
9. See *Report of the Committee on Turnover Taxation,* Cmnd 2300, 1964, para. 282.
10. The notation used in the article is in the Appendix.
11. The writer is indebted to R. E. Rowthorn for this proof.
12. If $(p_0\, x \frac{\delta B}{\delta n} - w_0 l \frac{\delta A}{\delta n}) \leq 0$ (which is more likely, the *greater* is the value of n), and because $\frac{\delta n}{\delta l} < 0$, $-\frac{\delta n}{\delta l}(p_0\, x \frac{\delta B}{\delta n} - w_0 l \frac{\delta A}{\delta n}) \leq 0$. It therefore is an offset (or, at least, not an addition) to $w_0 A$, which, however, becomes greater as n increases, so that the value of $-\frac{\delta l}{\delta K}$ which satisfies equation (2.2) *decreases* with n.
13. Two other measures of the accounting rate of profit which are widely used in practice are: (i) expected net profit of the *first* year as a proportion of the initial outlay, and (ii) expected net profit as a proportion of the average amount of capital employed, itself arbitrarily measured as, say, $\frac{K}{2}$ (see note 7 above). The first-order condition for (i) to be a maximum is:

   $$-\frac{\delta l}{\delta K} = \left[\frac{p_0\, x - \omega_0 l}{K}\right]\left[\frac{1}{\omega_0 - \frac{K}{n}\frac{\delta n}{\delta l}}\right] \tag{2.6a}$$

   Equation (2.7) is the corresponding condition for (ii) to be a maximum. (2.6a) > (2.7) and, for a wide range of values of n, (2.2) and (2.4) also. It follows that this variant of the accounting rate of profit rule *certainly* results in the choice of a *less* capital-intensive technique than those resulting from the other two variants and, often, from the other two rules as well.

14. See para. 2.1 of 'Cash Investment Grants, Corporation Tax and Pay-out Ratios' see note 4 above. They are believed to be the appropriate rates for comparisons of 'otherwise situations'.
15. If α, $\approx \frac{2}{3}$, r_2 $(= R(1 - c - \alpha s(1 - c)) = r_l = R(1 - \bar{p} - s))$.
16. If the values of b relative to $\bar{n}$ are such that *more*-capital-intensive techniques are chosen by rule 2 under B.1 than in the *pre-tax* situation (namely, $b \geq \bar{n}/2$) the use of rule 2 still results in the choice of a *less* capital-intensive technique under the present tax system than under the old, if the pay-out ratio is greater than the following values:

b \ $\bar{n}$	6	8	10
4	$\frac{2}{6}$	$\frac{2}{4}$	0
5	$\frac{2}{3}$	$\frac{3}{5}$	$\frac{3}{5}$

17. For a detailed discussion of this limitation see 'Investment-decision Criteria, Capital-intensity and the Choice of Techniques' p. 215, n. 31.

Part IV

Accounting Conventions and Policy

10

The Quantitative Effect of Basing Company Taxation on Replacement Costs*

The differences between company profits reckoned as revenues less historical costs, and company profits reckoned as revenues less replacement costs, have been considerable in many of the postwar years, mainly because of the neglect of stock appreciation and the inadequate allowance by historical cost depreciation allowances for durable capital consumption in the former reckoning.[1] In consequence, many writers have been led to call for reforms both in accounting procedures and in the methods of estimating company profits for taxation purposes.[2] Generally, the accounting profession has not been in favour of any of the suggested schemes that attempt to replace historical cost accounting by replacement cost accounting (for example, the use of L.I.F.O. (last in, first out) methods for stock valuation and the adjustment of historical cost depreciation allowances by indices of the prices of fixed assets), nor did the Millard Tucker Committee or the Royal Commission on the Taxation of Profits and Income suggest reforms incorporating such principles. The granting of initial allowances (and, later, investment allowances) for expenditure on plant and machinery did, in effect, compensate for (sometimes more than compensate for) the inadequate allowance by historical cost depreciation allowances for durable capital consumption;[3] but this result was a byproduct of their main purpose, which was to encourage investment expenditure, and, moreover, the result depended upon companies spending the same or an increasing amount on durable assets in future years.[4]

---

* I want to repair a shameful omission of over 40 years standing by recording my thanks to Gordon Fisher for his very helpful comments on a draft of this essay.

It is not proposed to advocate either historical cost or replacement cost accounting principles here or to debate the desirability or otherwise of using profits reckoned as revenues minus replacement costs as the measure of profits for taxation. The purpose of this article is to estimate what would have been the quantitative effects of changing the tax base to such a measure of profit in 1950 and 1951, the two postwar years when stock appreciation was greatest:[5] specifically, to estimate the size of additional company taxes that would have had to be raised in order to bring in the same revenue from the changed tax base, and the changes in the incidence of company taxation, because of the reform, on companies in various United Kingdom manufacturing industries.

The article is in four sections. Section I sets out the assumptions that are used in the subsequent analysis. Section II contains estimates of the new rates of taxation that would have been levied. Section III sets out the conditions under which a company, after the reform, paid more tax, the same tax or less tax than previously. Estimates of the values of these conditions for 1950 and 1951 are shown. Section IV contains an analysis of the changes in the incidence of company taxation on companies in various manufacturing industries that would have occurred in 1950 and 1951.

I

The estimates of the effects of a reform in the tax base are for 1950 and 1951 only; the greatest stock appreciation of the postwar period occurred in these years, so these are estimates of the *maximum* changes in tax rates and incidence that could have occurred. It is assumed that the reform in the tax base would not have altered the aggregate amount of revenue that the government intended to raise from company taxation; and that the companies would have distributed the same amount of dividends, despite the reform in the tax base. The first assumption, that the reform in the tax base would not have altered the aggregate amount of revenue that the government intended to raise from company taxation, is reasonable, provided that the required increase in tax rates are not too great.[6] The important decision that the government has to make is the amount of revenue that it wishes to raise from each particular source; then it can decide the appropriate rates of taxation.[7] The second assumption, that companies would have distributed the same *amount* of dividends rather than the more plausible assumption that the companies would have distributed the same *proportion* of their (now lower) profits, is used because dividend restraint was in operation in these years and it is probable that companies on the whole did not distribute as much as they would have in the absence of this restraint.

Though initial allowances plus annual statutory depreciation allowances were greater than durable capital consumption, they were not greater than capital consumption and stock appreciation combined; so aggregate taxable company profits in 1950 and 1951 were considerably greater than they would have been, had there been this reform in the tax base.[8] Therefore, income and profits tax at the rates current in 1950 and 1951 would not have brought in as much revenue as before. It is assumed that the government imposed a supplementary tax on taxable profits (as reckoned after the reform) at a rate which would bring in an amount equal to the amount by which the yields of the other two taxes on the new tax base fell short of the total amount of company tax the government wished to raise. The method of estimating these rates is shown in the next section.

II

The assumptions are that the total amounts of company taxation and dividends and the rates of income and profits tax remain unchanged, but that the tax base is changed to profits reckoned as revenues less replacement costs. Therefore, the rate of supplementary tax is the difference between total taxation and the combined yields of the income and profits taxes from the new tax base, divided by that base.

The standard rate of income tax was 9 s. 6 d. in the pound in 1950 and 1951; the profits tax was 30 per cent in 1950 and 50 per cent in 1951 on distributed profits and 10 per cent in both years on undistributed profits.[9] Estimates of the aggregate profits of United Kingdom companies less stock appreciation and durable capital consumption in 1950 and 1951 were prepared (see Table 10.1).

Taxable profits, after the assumed reform, would have been 15 per cent. less than the actual taxable profits of both 1950 and 1951.[10]

Gross dividends – that is, dividends before payment of income tax – are shown in Table 10.2 Using these gross dividends, the estimates of taxable profits given above, and the income and profits tax rates of

1950 and 1951, the combined yields from these two taxes following the reform were estimated (see Table 10.2). The differences between these yields and the actual tax paid (also shown in Table 10.2) are the amounts that would have had to be raised by the supplementary tax;

Table 10.1 *Aggregate taxable company profits before and after the assumed reform in the tax base, 1950 and 1951*

	1950 (£m)	*1951* (£m)
Gross trading profit of companies operating in the United Kingdom	2131	2489
Non-trading profit	363	391
Total Profits	2494	2880
Less capital consumption	329	376
Less stock appreciation	440	465
'True' Profits	1725	2039
Less interest payments	31	36
Taxable Profits after reform	1694	2003
Taxable Profits before reform	1989	2352
(Total profits *less* annual statutory and initial depreciation allowances, and *less* interest.)		

Source: *National Income and Expenditure*, 1957, tables 26, 47, 57, p. 71.

Table 10.2 *Estimates of supplementary tax, 1950–51*

		1950	1951
(1) Taxable profits after reform	£m	1694	2003
(2) Gross dividends	£m	597	641
(3) Yield from income tax (1) × 0.475	£m	805	951
(4) Yield from profits tax $(2) \times \frac{0.1575\ (1950)}{0.2625\ (1951)} + (1\text{–}2) \times 0.0525$	£m	152	240
(5) Total yield from income and profits taxes (3) + (4)	£m	957	1191
(6) Total tax raised before reform	£m	1103	1433
(7) SUPPLEMENTARY TAX	£m	146	242
(8) RATE OF SUPPLEMENTARY TAX	percentage	9	12

Source: *National Income and Expenditure*, 1957, tables 26, 47, 57; S. J. Prais, 'The Measure of Income for Shareholders and for Taxation', *Accounting Research*, vol. 6, no. 3, 1955, p. 200.

the rates of supplementary tax are those amounts divided by company profits less capital consumption and stock appreciation. The rates of supplementary tax would have been 9 per cent in 1950 and 12 per cent in 1951 (Table 10.2); both rates are lower than the rates of the Excess Profits Levy introduced in 1952 and 1953.[11,12]

III

In section II the aggregate changes in the rates of taxation made by the reform in the tax base were discussed. The purpose of this and the succeeding section of the article is to discuss the implications of the reform for tax payments by individual companies (and by the companies in particular industries).

First, individual companies. What are the formal conditions under which a company would pay more, the same or less tax than before? What conditions are most favourable to it paying less?

The conditions are deduced for two models, one assuming that the company distributes the same amount of dividends after the reform as it did before, the other assuming that it distributes the same *proportion* of a (now lower) profit.

Let Taxable profit	$= Y$
Tax	$= T$
Gross dividends (dividends before income tax)	$= G$
Undistributed profit $(Y - G)$	$= U$
Standard rate of income tax	$= S$
Rate of profits tax on distributed profit	$= P$
Rate of profits tax on undistributed profit	$= P$
Rate of supplementary tax	$= e$
Subscript$_1$ indicates before reform	
Subscript$_2$ indicates after reform	

First model

Assumptions: $Y_1 > Y_2$, $G_1 = G_2$, S, P, p = constants.
Aim: To find the conditions under which $T_1 \lesseqgtr T_2$

$$T_1 = SY_1 + PG + pU_1$$
$$T_2 = SY_2 + PG_2 + pU_2 + eY_2$$

$$T_1 - T_2 = (SY_1 - SY_2) + (PG_1 - PG_2) + (pU_1 - pU_2) - eY_2$$
$$= S(Y_1 - Y_2) + p(U_1 - U_2) - eY_2 \text{ (as } G_1 = G_2\text{, the second term cancels out).}$$

$$\text{Now } U_1 = Y_1 - G_1$$
$$\text{and } U_2 = Y_2 - G_2 = Y_2 - G_1 \text{ as } G_1 = G_2$$
$$\therefore U_1 - U_2 = Y_1 - G_1 - (Y_2 - G_1) = Y_1 - Y_2$$
$$\therefore T_1 - T_2 = S(Y_1 - Y_2) + p(Y_1 - Y_2) - eY_2$$
$$= (S + p)(Y_1 - Y_2) - eY_2$$

$$\text{that is, } T_1 < T_2 \text{ if } (S + p)(Y_1 - Y_2) < eY_2$$
$$T_1 = T_2 \text{ if } (S + p)(Y_1 - Y_2) = eY_2$$
$$T_1 > T_2 \text{ if } (S + p)(Y_1 - Y_2) > eY_2$$

The corresponding conditions for the **second model** (where $G_1 > G_2 = \frac{Y_2}{Y_1} G_1$) are:

$$T_1 < T_2 \text{ if } M < eY_2$$
$$T_1 = T_2 \text{ if } M = eY_2$$
$$T_1 > T_2 \text{ if } M > eY_2$$

where $M = \left\{1 - \frac{Y_2}{Y_1}\right\} \{Y_1 (S + p) + G_1 (P - p)\}$[13]

Whether a company would pay more, the same or less taxation than before depends directly on the rates of income and profits tax, the difference between taxable profits before and after reform, and inversely upon the rate of supplementary tax and the level of taxable profits after the reform.[14]

The conditions most favourable to a company paying less tax than previously are moderate stock appreciation and increases in the prices of durable assets for the economy as a whole, combined with severe stock appreciation and increases in the prices of durable assets for the company itself. In these circumstances the difference between taxable profits before and after reform will be large, and the level of taxable profits after reform and the rate of supplementary tax will be small – that is to say, the left-hand side of the third inequality will be large, the right-hand side will be small, so that T_1 will be very much greater than T_2. Conversely, severe stock appreciation and increases in the prices of durable assets generally, combined with moderate stock appreciation and increases in the prices of durable assets (or, worse still, stock *depreciation* and price falls) for the particular company, would lead to considerably heavier tax payments than previously.

What are the sizes of the differences between taxable profits before and after the reform which at the tax rates of 1950 and 1951 would cause a company to pay the same, or more or less tax than before? And, assuming that annual statutory and initial depreciation allowances combined were equivalent to durable capital consumption, so that the difference between taxable profits can be regarded as due to stock appreciation only, what levels of stock appreciation do these differences imply for 1950 and 1951?

The answers to these questions are shown in Table 10.3. The calculations are made on the assumptions that the company distributed the same amount of dividends as previously and that the amount of tax paid before the reform was 55 per cent of taxable profits in 1950 and 61 per cent of taxable profits in 1951. These proportions are those that were in fact borne in these years by aggregate tax payments in relation to aggregate taxable company profits. To have paid the same amount of tax after the reform as before, the difference between the taxable profits of a company before reform and after reform had to be 17 per cent in 1950 and 23 per cent in 1951 (implying stock appreciation equivalent to 17 per cent of taxable profits after reform in 1950 and 23 per cent in 1951).[15]

For all reasonable values of the difference in taxable profits (where taxable profits *after* reform are less than taxable profits before reform) the changes in taxation payment are surprisingly small. A difference of 10 per cent implied an *increased* payment of 6 per cent in 1950 and 10 per cent in 1951; a difference of 25 per cent implied a *decreased* payment of 6 per cent in 1950 and 2 per cent in 1951. Even with a difference of 50 per cent (which implies a very severe amount of stock appreciation, at least double the amounts for all companies in those years), the decreases in payments would have been only 21 per cent in 1950 and 16 per cent in 1951. On the other hand, increased tax payments would have been very heavy; thus a company with no stock appreciation would have paid 16 per cent more tax in 1950 and 20 per cent more in 1951; and even a moderate amount of stock *depreciation* – for example, 10 per cent of new taxable profits – would have led to increased tax payments of 29 per cent in 1950 and 32 per cent in 1951. Stock depreciation of 50 per cent would have more than doubled tax payments in both years.

Table 10.3 *Change in the tax payments, implied stock appreciation levels at the tax rates of 1950 and 1951 (all columns show percentages)*

	1950			1951		
$\frac{Y_1 - Y_2}{Y_2}$ (1)	$\frac{T_1 - T_2}{Y_2}$ (2)	$\frac{T_1 - T_2}{T_1}$ (3)	Stock appreciation as percentage of Y_2 (4)	$\frac{T_1 - T_2}{Y_2}$ (2)	$\frac{T_1 - T_2}{T_1}$ (3)	Stock appreciation as percentage of Y_2 (4)
–50	–35.4	–128.7	–50	–38.4	–125.9	–50
–35	–27.5	–76.8	–35	–30.5	–76.8	–35
–20	–19.6	–44.5	–20	–22.6	–46.3	–20
–10	–14.3	–28.9	–10	–17.3	–31.5	–10
–5	–11.6	–22.2	–5	–14.6	–25.2	–5
0	–9.0	–16.4	0	–12.0	–19.7	0
5	–6.4	–11.1	5	–9.4	–14.7	5
10	–3.7	–6.1	10	–6.7	–10.0	10
15	–1.1	–1.7	15	–4.1	–5.8	15
17	–	–	17	–3.0	–4.2	17
20	1.6	2.4	20	–1.4	–1.9	20
23	3.1	4.6	23	–	–	23
25	4.2	6.1	25	1.2	1.6	25
35	9.5	12.8	35	6.5	7.9	35
50	17.4	21.1	50	14.4	15.7	50

Y = taxable profits
T = tax

Subscript 1 indicates before reform
Subscript 2 indicates after reform

Column (2) calculated by letting $Y_2 = 100$, $Y_1 - Y_2$ = the values in column (1), substituting these values in $T_1 - T_2 = (S + p)(Y_1 - 100) - e\,100$ and solving for $T_1 - T_2$. Column (3) calculated by dividing columns (2) by 0.55 $\{100 + (Y_1 - 100)\}$ in 1950 and by 0.61 $\{100 + (Y_1 - 100)\}$ in 1951. Column (3) shows the change in tax payments (as a percentage of actual tax payments) that would result if the differences between taxable profits were the values shown in column (1).

IV

Suppose taxable profits had been reckoned on the new base in 1950 and 1951: what companies would have been favoured by the reform (would have paid less tax) and what companies would have paid more tax? An exact answer cannot be given as there are no available figures for the stock appreciation and capital consumption of companies in individual industries. But by using the techniques of the previous section, the amounts of stock appreciation implied by assuming that the companies paid the same amount of tax after the reform can be estimated.[16] An examination of these amounts in conjunction with the investment in stocks by companies in 1950 and 1951, and in the light of what is known of each industry, then shows whether they are reasonable amounts, or too large, or too small. If they are too large, the inference is that the companies concerned would have paid more tax than before as a result of the reform; if too small, that they would have paid less.

The companies examined were the quoted public companies in the following United Kingdom manufacturing industries: chemicals and allied trades, iron, steel and non-ferrous metals, shipbuilding and non-electrical engineering, electrical engineering and engineering goods, vehicles, other metal goods, cotton, wool, other textiles, clothing and footwear, food, drink, tobacco, paper and printing, and other manufacturing industries.[17] First the actual taxable profits of these companies in 1950 and 1951 were estimated;[18] next the taxable profits after the reform on which the companies would have paid the same aggregate amount of tax were estimated, by dividing the actual taxable profits of 1950 by 117 and that of 1951 by 123.[19] The differences between the two estimates of taxable profits were expressed as percentages of the increases in the value of the stocks of the companies in 1950 and 1951, giving estimates of the amounts of stock appreciation that would have been necessary if the companies were to have paid the same amount of tax as previously. These estimates were examined to see if they could be considered reasonable, or too large, or too small. If too large, it was assumed that the companies in that industry would have paid more tax than previously. On this basis, the companies in each industry were classified as probable or possible gainers or losers from the assumed reform in the tax base (see Table 10.4).

Table 10.4 *Possible and probable gainers and losers from the assumed reform in the tax base, 1950 and 1951 (quoted public companies in 15 manufacturing industries in the UK)*

	1950		1951	
Industry	Implied stock appreciation $(Y_1 - Y_2)^a$ / increase in value of stocks (1) percentage	*G* = gainer *Gp* = probable gainer *L* = loser (2)	Implied stock appreciation $(Y_1 - Y_2)^a$ / increase in value of stocks (1) percentage	*G* = gainer *Gp* = probable gainer *L* = loser (2)
1. Chemicals and allied trades	54	L	20	G
2. Iron, steel, non-ferous metals	73	L	118	L
3. Shipbuilding and non-electrical engineering	260	L	47	L
4. Electrical engineering and engineering goods	76	L	22	G
5. Vehicles	128	L	32	Gp
6. Other metal goods	86	L	45	L
7. Cotton	44	L	38	L
8. Wool	11	G	–	L
9. Other textiles	47	L	40	Gp
10. Clothing and footwear	37	Gp	18	G
11. Food	36	Gp	22	G
12. Drink	80	L	50	L
13. Tobacco	21	G	26	G
14. Paper and printing	70	L	33	Gp
15. Other manufacturing	23	G	16	G

[a] *Y* = taxable profits. Subscript 1 indicates before reform; subscript 2 indicates after reform.
Sources: *Company Income and Finance, 1949–1953: 96th and 97th Reports of the Commissioners of Her Majesty's Inland Revenue* (years ending 31 March 1953, and 1954).
See Appendix I for the derivation of column (1).

Had their taxable profits been reckoned as revenues less replacement costs in 1950, the wool, tobacco and other manufacturing companies would certainly have paid less tax and the clothing and footwear companies and food companies probably would have paid less. The chemical, iron and steel, shipbuilding, electrical engineering, vehicles, other metal goods, cotton, other textiles, drink, and paper and printing companies would have paid more tax. In 1951 the companies in the chemical, electrical engineering, clothing, food, tobacco and other manufacturing industries would certainly have paid less tax and the companies in the vehicles, other textiles and paper and printing probably would have paid less. The companies in the iron and steel, shipbuilding, other metal, cotton, wool and drink industries would have paid more.

There are three factors which could explain why the companies in ten manufacturing industries in 1950 and in six manufacturing industries in 1951 would have paid more tax in those years (would have been losers), had the reform been in operation. The first factor is that the losers may have experienced relatively less stock appreciation (as a percentage of their taxable profits before the reform) than did all companies. In these circumstances the differences between the losers' taxable profits before the reform and their taxable profits after the reform would be such that the decrease in tax because of the lower tax *base* after the reform would be less than the increase in tax because of the higher tax rates[20] after the reform – on balance the losers would have paid more tax.

The second factor is that the losers may have spent proportionately more than all companies on durable assets. In these circumstances the initial allowances received because of this expenditure would so narrow the differences between their taxable profits before and after reform that again the decrease in tax because of the lower tax base would be less than the increase in tax because of the higher tax rates. The third factor is that the secular rise in the prices of the durable assets of the losers may have been less than that of all companies. In these circumstances the differences between profits reckoned as revenues less historical costs and profits reckoned as revenues less replacement costs (*ceteris paribus*)[21] would be proportionately less than those of all companies.

The factors which could explain why the companies in five manufacturing industries in 1950 and in nine manufacturing industries in 1951 would have paid less tax (would have been gainers) are the converse of the above three. The companies in these industries may have experienced relatively greater stock appreciation (as a percentage of their taxable profits before reform) than did all companies; they may have spent relatively less on durable assets; and the secular rise in the prices of their durable assets may have been greater than the rises in the prices of the durable assets of all companies.

Some very rough tests (which are described in Appendix II) suggest that the first factor, the stock appreciation experienced by the losers and the gainers, is the most *general* explanation of why the losers would have paid more tax, and the gainers would have paid less, than previously. With rapidly expanding industries – for example, chemicals and allied trades and vehicles – the second factor, relatively greater expenditure on durable assets, is important also.

In view of the importance placed in 1950 and 1951 on the development of the basic and export industries of the United Kingdom, it is interesting to note that the tax reform would not have been favourable in 1950 to these very industries (with the exception of the textile industries). This conclusion is not so true of 1951, for in that year companies in three important industries – chemicals, electrical engineering and vehicles – would have been either probable gainers or possible gainers. However, as has been shown above, unless their stock appreciation was very severe, the decrease in their tax payments would not have been very significant. Similarly, increases in tax payments were also unlikely to have been severe, unless the companies concerned had experienced stock *depreciation* while the remainder of the economy experienced stock appreciation.[22] And if this is true of the years when stock appreciation was greatest, it is even more true of years when it was not so great. Thus a reform of the tax base to include what from the economist's viewpoint is a more logical measure of profits was unlikely in those years to have altered significantly the incidence of company taxation on the companies in different industries. In reaching this conclusion it must be remembered that the initial allowances of 1950 and 1951 had reduced by about half[23] the differences between profits reckoned as revenues less historical costs and profits reckoned as revenues less replacement costs.

Summary and conclusions

This article has examined the quantitative effects of a reform to make the measure of taxable company profits the difference between revenues and replacement costs instead of the difference between revenues and historical costs. The two bases were compared for the years 1950 and 1951, the years with the greatest amounts of stock appreciation since the war. It was found that this reform would have made necessary the introduction of a 9 per cent supplementary tax in 1950, and a 12 per cent supplementary tax in 1951 if the same amount of revenue were to have been raised in those years. Whether a company would pay more tax, the same tax or less tax after the reform depended upon the difference between its taxable profits before and after the reform, the level of taxable profits after the reform, and the rates of income, profits and supplementary tax. The conditions most favourable to a company paying less tax were for it to have considerable stock appreciation and increases in the prices of its durable assets, and for the economy to have mild stock appreciation and inflation generally, so that the rate of supplementary tax would be small. To have paid the same amount of tax after the reform as before, the difference between the taxable profits of a company before and after reform had to be 17 per cent in 1950 and 23 per cent in 1951.

Had the reform been in operation in 1950 and 1951, the companies in five manufacturing industries in 1950 and in nine manufacturing industries in 1951 would have paid less tax than previously. The companies in ten manufacturing industries in 1950 and in six manufacturing industries in 1951 would have paid more tax than previously.

Three factors explain why the companies in particular manufacturing industries would have been gainers or losers in those years from the assumed reform. These factors were the stock appreciation of the companies, their expenditure on durable assets and the secular rises in the prices of their durable assets. Probably the most *general* explanation was their stock appreciation. Expenditure on durable assets was important for companies in rapidly expanding industries.

Had the reform been in operation in 1950 and 1951, many of those companies most important to the prosperity of the economy, that is, companies in the basic and export industries, would probably have been adversely affected – they would have had to pay more tax; but it is unlikely that these additional payments would have been very significant.

Whatever may have been the theoretical desirability of such a reform, its practical effects on the incidence of taxation between different industries were unlikely to have been significant in 1950 and 1951. And what is true of those years is even truer of years with milder price changes. This is not to deny that, when considered in relation to profits reckoned as revenues less replacement costs, the incidence of company taxation generally is too great; but to suggest that if this is so, *rates* of taxation are more in need of reform than the tax base itself.*

Appendix I

Industry	1950				1951			
	Y_1	Y_2 $\left(=\frac{Y_1}{117}\right)$	S	$\frac{Y_1-Y_2}{S}$	Y_1	Y_2 $\left(=\frac{Y_1}{123}\right)$	S	$\frac{Y_1-Y_2}{S}$
	£m	£m	£m	Percentage	£m	£m	£m	Percentage
Chemicals	97	83	26	54	119	97	106	20
Iron and steel	73	62	15	73	107	85	17	118
Shipbuilding	91	78	5	260	111	90	46	47
Electrical engin	67	57	13	76	85	69	74	22
Vehicles	65	56	7	128	74	60	44	32
Other metals	39	33	7	86	55	45	22	45
Cotton	49	42	16	44	61	50	29	38
Wool	23	20	26	11	16	13	–	–
Other textiles	64	55	19	47	75	61	35	40
Clothing	18	15	8	37	16	13	17	18
Food	37	32	14	36	43	35	37	22
Drink	57	49	10	80	66	54	24	50
Tobacco	32	27	24	21	36	29	27	26
Paper	49	42	10	70	83	67	48	33
Other	40	34	26	23	44	36	51	16

Y_1 = actual taxable profits;
Y_2 = taxable profits after reform on which companies would have paid the same amount of tax; and
S = increase in the value of stocks.

Appendix II

The first factor was the stock appreciation experienced by the companies. A rough measure of whether the companies in a particular industry experienced more or less stock appreciation (as a percentage of their taxable profits before reform) than did all companies is a comparison of the ratios:

* I now think this last conclusion is a *non sequitur*.

$$\frac{S_1/Y_1}{S_0/Y_0} \quad \text{and} \quad \frac{S'_1/Y'_1}{S'_0/Y'_0}$$

where S = the increase in the value of stocks;
Y = taxable profits before reform;
Subscripts$_{0,1}$ indicate years$_{0,1}$;
S, Y without primes indicate the companies concerned; and
S, Y with primes indicate all companies.

If $$\frac{S_1/Y_1}{S_0/Y_0} \lesseqgtr \frac{S'_1/Y'_1}{S'_0/Y'_0}$$

the stock appreciation experienced by the companies concerned probably was less than, equal to or greater than that for all companies. These ratios were calculated for the companies in the fifteen manufacturing industries and compared with the corresponding ratio for all companies. If the companies in a particular industry were losers/gainers and their ratio was less/greater than that of all companies, the first factor was regarded as part of the explanation of why they were losers/gainers.

The second factor was the expenditure on durable assets. A rough measure of whether the companies in a particular industry spent relatively more or less than all companies on durable assets is a comparison of the ratios:

$$\frac{i}{I} \quad \text{and} \quad \frac{y}{Y}$$

where i = expenditure on durable assets; y = profits reckoned as revenues less historical costs; and small letters indicate the companies concerned; and capital letters indicate all companies.

If $\frac{i}{I} \lesseqgtr \frac{y}{Y}$ the companies probably spent more than, the same amount, or less than all companies on durable assets. These ratios were calculated for the companies in the fifteen industries and for all companies. If the companies in a particular industry were losers/gainers and i/I was $>y/Y$ (losers), $<y/Y$ (gainers), the second factor was regarded as part of the explanation of why they were losers/gainers.

The third factor was the secular rise in the prices of durable assets. This is the hardest factor to isolate from the available statistics because its effect can be outweighed by other factors. For example, if in the past the stock of durable assets of a company has grown faster than that of all companies, *ceteris paribus* the average age of its assets will be less than that of all companies. If there has been a secular rise in the prices of durable assets the *increase* in the replacement value of the average asset in its stock will be less than the increase for all companies. But its annual depreciation allowances on historical costs will be relatively greater than those of all companies. If replacement cost depreciation is measured by multiplying the annual historical cost depreciation allowances by the ratio $\frac{p_c}{p_a}$ where p is the price index of durable assets, and subscripts c, a indicate the current year and the year of acquisition respectively, then the higher multiplicand may outweigh the effect of a lower multiplier – that is, the third factor may be an explanation but its effect can be outweighed. Only if the rate of growth and the expected life times of the durable assets of the company and the profitability of the company are the same as those of all companies, can the effect of a lower secular rise in the prices of durable assets definitely be isolated. For then both the multiplicand and the multiplier will be less: the multiplicand, because the historical costs of the assets and therefore the annual historical cost depreciation allowances are less; the multiplier, because the rise in prices of durable assets and therefore the ratio $\frac{p_c}{p_a}$ are less.

A very rough measure of whether the secular rises in the prices of durable assets of the companies in a particular industry were less than or greater than those of all companies is a comparison of the ratios:

d/p and D/P

where d = historical cost depreciation allowances; p = profits reckoned as revenues less historical costs; and small letters indicate the companies concerned; and capital letters indicate all companies.

If the companies in a particular industry were losers/gainers and $d/p \leq D/P$(losers) $\geq D/P$ (gainers), the third factor was regarded as part of the explanation of why they were losers/gainers. If $d/p > D/P$ (losers) or $< D/P$ (gainers), the third factor might or might not have been part of the explanation.

	Losers				Gainers		
1950	1st factor	2nd factor	3rd factor	1950	1st factor	2nd factor	3rd factor
Chemicals	yes	yes	*indef.	Wool	yes	yes	indef.
Iron and steel	yes	yes	indef.	Clothing	no	yes	indef.
Shipbuilding	yes	no	indef.	Food	no	no	yes
Elect. engin.	no	no	indef.	Tobacco	yes	yes	indef.
Vehicles	yes	yes	indef.	Others	yes	indef.	yes
Other metals	yes	yes	yes				
Cotton	yes	no	yes				
Other textiles	yes	no	indef.				
Drink	yes	yes	yes				
Paper	no	no	yes				
1951				1951			
Iron and steel	yes	yes	indef.	Chemicals	yes	no	indef.
Shipbuilding	no	yes	indef.	Elect.engin.	yes	indef.	yes
Other metals	no	indef.	yes	Vehicles	yes	no	yes
Cotton	yes	no	yes	Other textiles	no	yes	indef.
Wool	yes	indef.	yes	Clothing	yes	yes	indef.
Drink	no	yes	yes	Food	yes	no	indef.
				Tobacco	no	yes	indef.
				Paper	yes	yes	indef.
				Others	yes	indef.	yes

* indef. = indefinite. This factor may or may not have been part of the explanation.

Standards (ratios, etc.) for all companies			
		1950	1951
$\frac{S'_1/Y'_1}{S'_0/Y_0}$		2.6	1.8
I	£m	628	631
Y	£m	2020	2388
D/P	percentage	12	11

Sources: National Income and Expenditure, 1957, tables 26, 47, 57, p. 71; *Company Income and Finance, 1949–53*, pp. 26–54.

Notes

1.

	1948 £m	1949 £m	1950 £m	1951 £m
Gross trading profit of companies operating in United Kingdom *plus* non-trading profit *less* annual statutory allowances for depreciation (but not initial allowances)	1924	1966	2247	2626
Gross company profits *less* stock appreciation and capital consumption	1637	1719	1725	2039

Source: *National Income and Expenditure*, 1957, tables 26, 47, 57 p. 71.

2. For a discussion of the first subject and a bibliography of recent writings on it, see A. R. Prest, 'Replacement Cost Depreciation', *Accounting Research*, vol. 1, no. 4, July 1950, 385–402. For a discussion of the reform in the methods of estimating company profits for taxation purposes, see Peter Wiles, 'Corporate Taxation based on Replacement Costs', *Accounting Research*, vol. 2, no. 1, January 1951, 77–82. For a discussion of the treatment of depreciation by the taxation authorities of various countries see Sydney Davidson, 'Depreciation, Income Taxes and Growth', *Accounting Research*, vol. 8, no. 3, June 1957, p. 191–205.

3.

		1948	1949	1950	1951	1952	1953	1954	1955	1956
Annual statutory allowances for depreciation[a]	£m	208	220	247	254	287	303	357	435	486
Initial allowances[b]	£m	95	185	227	238	111	104	156[d]	181[d]	208[d]
Total	£m	303	405	474	492	398	407	513	616	694
Capital consumption[c]	£m	295	297	329	376	416	455	499	567	615

[a] [b] *National Income and Expenditure*, 1957, p. 71.

[c] *National Income and Expenditure*, 1957, table 57.

[d] includes investment allowances:

While capital consumption was greater than the statutory allowances for depreciation every year, it was less than these allowances *plus* initial allowances every year except 1952 and 1953 – in the economy at large, but not necessarily for every company.

4. No doubt the clamour by businesspeople and financial journalists for some allowance in the estimates of taxable profits for the war and postwar rises in the prices of durable assets did influence the government's decision to grant initial allowances and, in particular, to increase them to 40% in 1949.

5.

	1950	1951
Stock appreciation (£ million)	440	465
As percentage of company profits *less* stock appreciation and capital consumption	26	23

Source: *National Income and Expenditure*, 1957, tables 26, 47.

6. It is shown below that the increase in rates that would have been needed was relatively small.
7. See J. McB. Grant and R. L. Mathews, 'Accounting Conventions, Pricing Policies and the Trade Cycle', *Accounting Research*, vol. 8, no. 2, April 1957, 158–9.
8.

	1950	1951
	£m	£m
(1) Stock appreciation and durable capital consumption	769	841
(2) Annual statutory allowances and initial allowances	474	492
(3) Difference	295	349
(4) Taxable profit before reform[a]	1989	2352
(5) Taxable profit after reform[b]	1694	2003
(6) Difference	295	349

[a] Company profits *less* statutory allowances and initial allowances and interest payments.

[b] Company profits *less* stock appreciation, capital consumption and interest payments.

Source: *National Income and Expenditure*, 1957, tables 26, 47, 57, page 71.

9. Profits tax was a deductible expense for tax purposes in 1950 and 1951. A device suggested by Dr S. J. Prais (see S. J. Prais, 'The Measure of Income for Shareholders and for Taxation', *Accounting Research*, vol. 6, no. 3, 1955, p. 187–201, particularly Appendix B, p. 200) was used to avoid making this deduction in the calculations of the income and profits tax yields. It consists of charging profits tax on taxable profit at lower rates than the published ones, rates which are equivalent to charging the published rates on taxable profits *less* profits tax.
10. It will be seen that the initial allowances granted in 1950 and 1951 had, in conjunction with the annual statutory depreciation allowances, already gone a long way towards closing the gap between profits reckoned as revenues less historical costs and taxable profits as reckoned after the assumed reform. Had there been no initial allowances in these years, taxable profits after the reform would have been 22 per cent less in 1950 and 21 per cent. less in 1951. (These figures were calculated from the ratio $\frac{Y_1 - Y_2}{Y_1}$ where Y_1 is taxable profits before reform plus initial allowances less the *difference* between the statutory depreciation allowances that would have been received had no initial allowances been given, and actual statutory depreciation allowances; Y_2 is taxable profits after reform.)

11. The rates of the Excess Profits Levy were 15 per cent on taxable profits or 30 per cent on excess profits, whichever was lower.
12. Had the companies distributed the same *proportion* of their (lower) profits, the rates of supplementary tax would have been 10 per cent in 1950 and 14 per cent in 1951.
13. These are not the *only* conditions, but those most relevant for an economist. The only general conditions are $T_1 \lesseqgtr T_2$ if $(S + p)(Y_1 - Y_2) - e\,Y_2 \lesseqgtr 0$ (first model) and if $M - e\,Y_2 \lesseqgtr 0$ (second model). These can be expressed as different inequalities from those shown in the text.
14. In the second model, the amount of gross dividends and the ratio of taxable profits after reform to taxable profits before reform are relevant also. Only the first model will be used in this article as its assumption that $G_1 = G_2$ is the appropriate one for 1950 and 1951. The first model is a special case of the (more general) second model.
15. That is to say, it is assumed that the annual statutory and initial depreciation allowances granted the company in 1950 and 1951 were equal to its durable capital consumption. As was shown above, this assumption is unlikely to be true unless the company spent very little on durable assets in those years. Thus the differences between taxable profits underestimate the amount of stock appreciation implied by the assumption that the company paid the same amount of taxation as previously.
16. It was pointed out in footnote 15 that by this assumption the actual amount of stock appreciation is probably underestimated.
17. The information on these companies is taken from *Company Income and Finance, 1949–53*, National Institute of Economic and Social Research, London, 1957.
18. Actual taxable profits were taken as gross trading profits before depreciation allowances by the companies, plus income from other sources, less interest on long-term loan capital and depreciation allowances, including initial allowances, granted by the Board of Inland Revenue. The first three figures are given in *Company Income and Finance, 1949–53*. The last figure was estimated as follows. The reports of the Board of Inland Revenue gave the ratios of depreciation allowances to gross trading profits for each industry and it was assumed that these ratios were the same for all the companies of that industry. Depreciation allowances granted by the Board of Inland Revenue to the companies were estimated by multiplying their gross trading profit by these proportions. The figures for trading profits in the reports of the Board were exclusive of profits tax, while those of the companies included profits tax. It was possible to estimate the amounts of profits tax for the industries from the ratios of profits tax to turnover given for each industry in the appendices to the reports; the ratios of depreciation allowances to trading profits were adjusted for these amounts of profits tax.
19. As shown above, to have paid the same amount of tax after reform, the difference between the taxable profits of companies before reform and after reform had to be 17 per cent in 1950 and 23 per cent in 1951.

20. The imposition of a supplementary tax together with unchanged rates of income and profits tax is equivalent to a higher tax rate.
21. The other things which have to be equal include the age structure and expected lifetimes of the durable assets, and the profitability of the losers and all companies (see Appendix II).
22. Thus the wool companies would have paid considerably more taxation in 1951, for raw wool prices tumbled in that year, when stock appreciation was greatest for the economy generally.
23.

	1950 £m	1951 £m
Difference between taxable profits and taxable profits after reform	239	249
Difference between taxable profits, had no initial allowances, been given, and taxable profits after reform	481	527

11

Incomes Policy and the Measurement of Profits*

Recently, some old problems have been discussed in the new context of an incomes policy.[1] The old problems are two. Should company incomes be measured by accounting profits – revenues less historical costs – or by current incomes – revenues less current costs? Secondly, is profitability better measured by the ratio of accounting profits to the historical-cost book value of assets or by the ratio of current income to the current-cost book value of assets? It has been argued that investment allowances have served to close the shortfall between historical-cost depreciation allowances and current-cost capital consumption as far as the taxable incomes of companies are concerned, but that this shortfall (and the amount of investment allowances received) are ignored in many published accounts. Profits in these accounts are therefore overstated in periods of creeping inflation, with the consequence that the ratio of accounting profits, thus overstated, to the historical-cost value of assets (which is less than their current costs) leads to an overly favourable view of the profitability of companies. Mr Taylor has recommended that investment allowances should be shown in published accounts, together with the fire insurance values of fixed assets, so that more sober and realistic estimates of profits and the rate of return may be made. These adjustments, presumably, will make it easier to persuade wage-earners to accept an incomes policy, especially that part of it which requires wage restraint.

---

* Originally published in *The Banker's Magazine*, December, 1964, 361–4.

The purpose of this essay is twofold; first, to point out that the aggregate taxable incomes of companies in most years since 1953 – and especially since 1954 when investment allowances were first introduced – have been *less* than their total current incomes. It is true that an incomes policy is concerned with the pre-tax distribution of income, because price-making decisions are related to the incomes earned in the production process, not to the post-tax distribution of these incomes between wage-earners and profit-earners. But in order to persuade wage-earners to accept an incomes policy, it is at least arguable that the post-tax distribution of income is the relevant comparison to make. Using this criterion, there does not seem to be any evidence that profit-receivers have been discriminated against by the present tax system, especially as there is not as yet a capital-gains tax in this country. Reference to post-tax figures may not therefore encourage a policy of wage restraint. Secondly, while the adjustments which have been suggested for obtaining a better measure of the rate of return can be applauded, it will be shown that the measure still contains serious biases which make it unsuitable for use in the context of an incomes policy.

In Table 11.1, total allowances, both investment and other, to companies by the taxation authorities are compared with the total of stock appreciation and current-cost capital consumption for the period 1953–63. It is surprising that stock appreciation has not been mentioned in this discussion because in the aggregate it has often been greater than the shortfall of historical-cost depreciation allowances *vis-à-vis* current-cost capital consumption. And for many companies, for example, woollen and worsted manufacturers, where stocks are a large proportion of their total assets, it must be far more important. As well as the shortfall of historical-cost depreciation allowances, stock appreciation should also be subtracted from accounting profits in order to obtain current income. Stock appreciation is the rise in the value of a given volume of stocks; as these are needed to maintain existing levels of activity, increases in their value cannot be regarded as part of current income. It can be seen that with the exception of 1954 and 1955, total allowances exceeded stock appreciation and current-cost capital consumption combined; in the later years of the period (from 1958 on) the allowances were considerably greater, in fact, by an annual average of £466 m.[2] The implication of these figures is that the aggregate taxable incomes of United Kingdom companies were less

Table 11.1 *UK companies, 1953–63 (m)*

	1953	1954	1955	1956	1957	1958	1959	1960	1961	1962	1963
Initial and investment allowances	104	157	205	227	269	347	399	476	524	547	608
Other allowances	303	364	420	500	569	625	677	737	838	902	1166
(1) Total	407	521	625	727	838	972	1076	1213	1362	1449	1774
Current-cost capital consumption	429	459	516	579	632	672	695	733	795	847	894
Stock appreciation	–44	53	119	159	140	–18	65	90	115	97	164
(2) Total	385	512	635	738	772	654	760	823	910	944	1058
(1)–(2)	22	9	–10	–11	56	318	316	490	452	505	716

Source: *National Income and Expenditure*, 1964, tables 65, 73; p. 104.

than their aggregate *current* incomes over this period (by between 11 and 21 per cent in the last six years of the period).[3] It cannot be concluded from this that their post-tax incomes were more than they otherwise would have been (tax rates would have been different, probably lower, had the allowances not been given). But it can be said that as far as the tax base is concerned, there is no evidence that profit-earners have been discriminated against (especially as it is not generally agreed that current income is the appropriate measure of profits for tax purposes). A comparison of post-tax profits and wages therefore might not lead wage-earners to view favourably a policy of wage restraint.

The adjustments to the measure of the rate of return which have been suggested are meant to deal with the impact of inflation on the usual measure of profitability – the ratio of accounting profits to the historical-cost value of assets (which is referred to below as the accounting rate of profit). In an inflationary situation it would be preferable to adjust accounting profits directly for stock appreciation and the shortfall of historical-cost depreciation allowances, rather than subtract investment allowances (spread over the lifetimes of the assets) as such. Various methods of calculating stock appreciation, capital consumption and the current-cost value of assets have been suggested and these will not be gone into here.[4] But, whatever adjustments are made, they have no impact on other, rarely discussed, defects of the measure, defects which, moreover, are unrelated to the problems created by inflation. These are now outlined.

Assume that there is no inflation and consider a business which has a balanced stock of like machines.[5] Suppose that the expected rate of return on each of these machines is 20 per cent. (The expected rate of return is defined in the usual way as that rate of discount which makes the expected net receipts – revenues less wages, raw material and maintenance costs – associated with each machine equal to the current price of the machine.) If straight-line depreciation is used; if the expected net receipts are constant from year to year; and if they are actually achieved; it can be shown that the longer are the lives of the machines the closer (after a certain critical age) is the accounting rate of profit to a value of 40 per cent, that is, to *twice* the correct rate. Moreover, it is always greater than 20 per cent no matter what are the lives of the machines. Values of accounting rates of profit for balanced stocks of machines with different working lives and patterns of net receipts are shown in Table 11.2. It can be seen that when the life of

Table 11.2 *Accounting rates of profit for balanced stocks of machines (expected rate of return of 20 per cent)*

Pattern of net receipts	*Length of working life (years)* 5	10	20	30
Constant each year (a)	26.9	27.7	31.1	33.5
Falling (b)	24.4	21.4	16.4	12.5

(a) Values calculated from:

$$R = \frac{2}{n}\left\{\frac{nr}{1-(1/1+r)^n} - 1\right\}$$

where R = accounting rate of profit;
n = working life;
r = expected rate of return.

(b) Values calculated from:

$$R = \frac{2}{n}\left\{\frac{(1-b^n)(1+r-b)}{(1-b)(1+(b/1+r)^n)} - 1\right\}$$

where $b = 0.9$, i.e., any year's net receipt is 90 per cent of the previous year's.

machines is 10 years, and net receipts are constant each year, the accounting rate of profit is 27.7 per cent; when the working life is 30 years, it is 33.5 per cent. If the net receipts were to decline by a certain amount each year, the measure would approach a value of 0 per cent, the longer were the lives of the machines. For example, if any year's net receipts are 90 per cent of the previous year's, and if the working life of the machines is 10 years, the accounting rate of profit is 21.4 per cent; if the working life is 30 years, it is 12.5 per cent (see Table 11.2).

Suppose that two companies, A and B, have the same expected rates of profit, but that the machines of A are longer-lived than those of B. Then A will appear to have a realised rate of profit greater than that of B (if the net receipts of both are constant from year to year) and less than that of B (if they decline by a certain amount from year to year). Moreover, it can be shown that if the net receipts of both were constant each year, but A used reducing-balance depreciation, and B straight-line depreciation, the accounting rate of profit of A would approach the correct value, the longer-lived were its machines, but that of B would approach twice the correct value.[6]

The moral of this story is that to relate an incomes policy to accounting rates of profit, no matter how well-intentioned are the adjustments made to them in the process, is to relate it to a very misleading measure indeed, one much more so than the corresponding figures for wages. Any policy of wage restraint that is based on an appeal to such calculations is built on shaky foundations. It would be understandable, therefore, if wage-earners as a group were not impressed by arguments – or exhortations – which rested on them.

Notes

1. See, for example, Basil Taylor, 'A Note of Profits versus Wage Restraint', *Westminster Bank Review*, May 1964, 30–33.
2. Since 1960, aggregate historical-cost depreciation allowances have been greater than current-cost capital consumption. This is due to the following factors. The depreciation allowances given by the Inland Revenue are assessed on a reducing-balance basis, while those in the estimates of current-cost capital consumption are on a straight-line basis adjusted by an inflation factor. If a capital stock is growing, historical-cost reducing-balance allowances exceed straight-line ones. Evidently the rate of growth of the stock of fixed assets in the company sector has been great enough to offset, through the reducing-balance effect, the effects of the mild rates of inflation of recent years.
3.

		1958	1959	1960	1961	1962	1963
Difference between taxable income (a) and current income (b) as per cent of current income	%	12	11	14	14	15	21

(a) Company income arising in the United Kingdom, less interest payments, initial, investment and other allowances.

(b) Company income arising in the United Kingdom, less interest payments, stock appreciation and current-cost capital consumption.

The astonishing figure of 21 per cent in 1963 reflects two changes in the 1963 Budget, both of which are of a once-and-for-all character. The first is the increase in investment allowances on certain assets to 30 per cent; the second is the increase in rates of 'wear-and-tear' allowances on plant and machinery to 15, 20 and 25 per cent, and on industrial buildings to 4 per cent. In the development areas up to 100 per cent write-offs are allowed in the first year.

4. For an excellent discussion of them, see Russell Mathews and J. McB. Grant, *Inflation and Company Finance* (Sydney; Law Book Company of Australiasia, 1958).
5. Assume that all machines have the same expected working life. Then a balanced stock is one in which there is an equal number of machines of every age in existence.
6. These propositions are discussed in greater detail in the present writer's paper, 'The Accountant in a Golden Age', *Oxford Economic Papers*, vol. 17, 1965, 66–80.

12
The Measurement of the Rate of Profit and the Bonus Scheme for Managers in the Soviet Union*

In a recent article Mr Merrett discussed some of the implications of linking money bonuses for managers to the rate of profit in Soviet industry.[1] The purpose of this note is to comment on some further implications of the bonus scheme which arise from the measure of the rate of profit used in the Soviet Union. It is shown that managers in charge of enterprises which use particular types of machines are favourably treated by the bonus scheme and that *if* the sizes of expected bonuses influence the choice of investment projects, the measure of the rate of profit has an arbitrary impact on these decisions. The note concludes with a discussion of the relation between the bonus scheme and the criterion of choice of technique put forward by Professor Meek.[2]

According to Merrett, 'profitability is equal to price less average variable cost multiplied by output, and expressed as a percentage of total fixed and working capital'.[3] Working capital and fixed costs are ignored in what follows; depreciation is assumed to be reckoned on the straight-line basis (this is the method used in the Soviet Union);[4] the fact that the lengths of life implied by the depreciation rates allowed in the Soviet Union are too great is ignored; and the under-pricing of capital goods in the Soviet Union is ignored also (but on this, see

---

* Originally published in *Oxford Economic Papers* vol. 18, 1966, 58–63. The writer is grateful to Esra Bennathan, C. J. Bliss, M. H. Dobb, James A. Mirrlees, R. E. Rowthorn, Aubrey Silberston, Ajit Singh and R. H. Wallace for helpful discussions, to Francis Seton for his comments on an earlier draft and for suggesting the analysis of paragraphs 7 and 11, and to Miss Marion Clarke for carrying out the calculations.

below, paragraphs 7 and 11). The rate of profit is then seen to be the accountant's measure of the rate of profit: the ratio of annual accounting profit to the book value of the assets in the enterprises concerned. Merrett shows that the bonuses paid to managers can be calculated (approximately) from the following expression:

$$B = 0.075\sqrt{p}.K = 0.075\sqrt{(PK)} \tag{1}$$

where B = bonus; P = accounting profit; K = book value of capital; $p = P/K$ = the rate of profit.[5]

It can be shown that the accountant's measure of the rate of profit is a faulty measure of the *ex ante* rate of profit even under 'golden age' conditions where uncertainty is absent, expectations are fulfilled, and the rate of profit has an unambiguous meaning.[6] In particular, if a balanced stock of 'one-hoss shays' (that is constant annual expected quasi-rents associated with each machine) is considered, p approaches a value which is twice the *ex ante* internal rate of return (r), the longer-lived are the machines in the stock; moreover, under any circumstances, p is always greater than r. If the expected quasi-rents decline exponentially from year to year, p approaches a value of zero, the longer-lived are the machines.[7] These results are obviously relevant in the present context, since the size of the bonus is a function of p, not of r, the internal rate of return of the project concerned. It is not assumed that there is anything sacrosanct about the internal rate of return, which is used merely because it is a simple and well-known index of 'equivalence'. The present value of investment projects could just as easily be used and the main points of this note would remain unaffected.

In this note, the sizes of bonuses and rates of bonus per unit of capital associated with balanced stocks of machines which have the same supply prices but different expected lives, internal rates of return, and patterns of expected quasi-rents, are examined. Each machine is assumed to have a supply price (S) of £1000. The lengths of life examined are: $n = 5, 10, 15, 20, 30$ years; the internal rates of return are: $r = 10, 16, 25$ per cent. The first pattern of quasi-rents (q) is that of constant q's, $q'_1 = q'_2 = \ldots = q'_n$; the second is that of declining. q's, $q''_i = bq''_{i-1}$ ($i = 2, \ldots, n$, $b = 0.9$). In the 'one-hoss shay' case,

$$q'_i = \frac{rS}{1 - (1/1{+}r)^n} \tag{2}$$

Table 12.1 *Values of* q'_i, q''_1; B_1, B_2; B_1/K *and* B_2/K

	n = 5		n = 10		n = 15		n = 20		n = 30	
r	q'_i (£)	q''_1 (£)	q'_i (£)	q''_1 (£)	q'_i (£)	q''_i (£)	q'_i (£)	q''_1 (£)	q'_i (£)	q''_1 (£)
10	264	316	163	231	132	210	118	204	106	201
16	305	362	207	282	179	266	169	262	162	260
25	372	434	280	364	259	353	253	351	250	350
	B_1 (£)	B_2 (£)	B_2 (£)	B_1(£)	B_1 (£)	B_2(£)	B_1 (£)	B_2 (£)	B_1 (£)	B_2 (£)
10	67	64	133	119	203	168	276	211	429	279
16	86	82	168	154	267	217	365	270	570	355
25	110	105	225	196	349	276	478	342	741	445
	B_1/K (%)	B_2/K (%)	B_1/K (%)	B_2/K (%)	B_1/K (%)	B_2/K (%)	B_1/K (%)	B_2/K (%)	B_1/K (%)	B_2/K (%)
10	2.7	2.6	2.7	2.4	2.7	2.2	2.8	2.1	2.9	1.9
16	3.4	3.3	3.4	3.1	3.6	2.9	3.7	2.7	3.8	2.4
25	4.4	4.2	4.5	3.9	4.7	3.7	4.8	3.4	4.9	3.0

S = £1000; n = 5, 10, 15, 20, 30 years; r = 10, 16, 25 per cent; b = 0.9.

In the second case,

$$q''_1 = \frac{(1+r-b)S}{1-(b/1+r)^n} \qquad (3)^8$$

The values of q'_i and q''_1 for various values of n and r for $S = £1000$, are shown in Table 12.1.

The annual accounting profit associated with a balanced stock of like machines is: $P = Q - S$, where $Q = \sum_{i=1}^{n} q_i$. The book value of capital is: $K = \frac{1}{2}nS$[9]. Substituting these expression in equation (1),

$$B = \frac{3}{40\sqrt{2}}\sqrt{\{(Q-S)(nS)\}} \qquad (4)$$

is obtained. In the 'one-hoss shay' case,

$$B_1 = \frac{3}{40\sqrt{2}}\sqrt{\{(nq'_i - S)(nS)\}} \qquad (5)$$

in case 2,

$$B_2 = \frac{3}{40\sqrt{2}}\sqrt{\left\{\left[q''_1\left(\frac{1-b^n}{1-b}\right) - S\right][nS]\right\}} \qquad (6)$$

The values of B_1 and B_2, and B_1/K and B_2/K, are shown in Table 12.1.

It can be seen that if machines are 'one-hoss shays', managers in charge of longer-lived machines get greater benefits, in relation to the capital invested, from the bonus scheme. Thus, if machines last five years, the value of B_1/K is between 2.7 and 4.4 per cent, depending on the value of r; if they last 30 years, B_1/K is between 2.9 and 4.9 per cent. If, however, machines are of the second type, managers in charge of shorter-lived machines are favoured. With $r = 16$ per cent, $B_2/K = 3.3$ per cent for $n = 5$ years and 2.7 per cent for $n = 20$ years. Moreover, if the values of n and r are the same for two enterprises, managers in charge of case 1 machines are favoured relative to those in charge of case 2 machines. With $r = 16$ per cent and $n = 20$ years, $B_1 = £365$, $B_2 = £270$, $B_1/K = 3.7$ per cent, and $B_2/K = 2.7$ per cent. Can any welfare theorist, either side of the Iron Curtain, say why this should be so?

The prices of capital goods are systematically underpriced in the Soviet Union. Suppose that the 'correct' prices of the machines in Table 12.1 all exceed $S = £1000$ by the same amount. Then, it can be shown that the longer-lived are 'one-hoss shays' with the same initial r, the higher are their 'correct' r's (though obviously they are always less than the initial value). Furthermore, the 'correct' r of a 'one-hoss shay' is always greater than that of a case 2 machine with the same n and initial r. Therefore, paying greater benefits to managers in charge of long-lived 'one-hoss shays', or 'one-hoss shays' with the same n and initial r as case 2 machines, may be partially justified by these new results. On the other hand, the 'correct' r's of case 2 machines with the same initial r are greater, the longer are their lives; so favouring managers in charge of shorter-lived case 2 machines appears to be even 'worse' than before.

Now suppose that the prospective sizes of bonuses to managers influence investment decisions, especially the choice of projects. As major investment decisions in the Soviet Union are taken above the enterprise level, managers cannot directly decide the choice of technique. It is believed, however, that the blueprints eventually sanctioned are often powerfully influenced by proposals originating from the enterprise level. Moreover, managers have considerable say as to the current input–output mix and the way in which existing equipment is used and maintained. These decisions may be influenced by the bonus scheme and they, in their turn, may influence those who are directly responsible for investment decisions. Such considerations no doubt underlie discussions of the link between the Liberman proposals and investment decisions, including that of Merrett, and the following arguments proceed on the basis of them.

The first point to notice is that, in general, there is no way in which the present value to managers of bonuses associated with particular projects can be calculated. The value of a bonus is a function of the annual average accounting rate of profit. It is impossible to isolate, as it were, the contribution of marginal investment projects to future annual averages. However, if n, r and S are assumed to be the same for two projects, and if managers have a high rate of time discount, they may well favour projects with high accounting profits in the early years, that is those with the $b^{i-1}q''_i$ streams of Table 12.1 rather than those with constant q'_i's. Capital will be increased by the same amount each year, but the profits of case 2 projects will be greater in the earlier years than those of case 1 projects. For example, with $n = 15$ years and $r = 16$ per cent, $q''_i > q'_i$ for the first four years.

On the other hand, if managers have either low rates of time discount or none at all, they will tend to favour 'one-hoss shays', because, for given S, n and r, $Q' > Q''$, that is the total undiscounted quasi-rents (and profits) of a 'one-hoss shay' are greater than those of a case 2 project. Moreover, regardless of their rate of time discount, they will tend to favour investment in shorter-lived machines with the same pattern of quasi-rents and r, because, as a glance at Table 12.1 shows, the q_i's of the shorter-lived machines exceed those of the longer-lived ones. Mr Merrett might like to justify these implications of the effect of p on the size of bonuses and investment decisions, because they also follow from his suggested rule that bonus payments be based on the level of profits.[10]

If, now, account is taken again of the underpricing of capital goods, and if managers have high rates of time discount, the bonus scheme encourages them to choose 'wrongly', that is to choose machines with the lower 'correct' r's. If managers have low rates of time discount or none at all, the bonus scheme tends to make them choose projects with the higher 'correct' r's. Finally, the preference for shorter-lived projects noted in the previous paragraph is seen to be a preference for projects with lower 'correct' r's, regardless of the pattern of quasi-rents of the machines concerned.

Professor Meek has argued that if two mutually exclusive ways of producing a commodity are compared, the technique with the lower total annual costs is the socially 'correct' one to choose.[11] Consider two projects A and B, both 'one-hoss shays' with the same n and producing the same amount per year of a given commodity. Let the total annual costs of A be greater than those of B, and $q_b/q_a (= Q_b/Q_a) < S_b/S_a$. Then, on the Meek criterion, project B should be chosen. It will now be shown that the bonus scheme will always give a greater rate of bonus per unit of capital to managers in charge of a balanced stock of the 'wrong' machines, that is A machines, and that there is a considerable chance that these managers will also receive larger total bonuses as well.

Let $Q_b = \alpha Q_a$, where $\alpha > 1$, and $S_b = \beta S_a$, where $\beta > 1$. Then

$$\frac{Q_b}{Q_a}(= \alpha) < \frac{S_b}{S_a}(= \beta), \quad \text{i.e. } \alpha < \beta.$$

$$\text{Now} \qquad P_a = \frac{2[Q_a - S_a]}{nS_a} \quad \text{and} \quad p_b = \frac{2[\alpha Q_a - \beta_a]}{n\beta Sa}$$

It is clear that $p_a > p_b$, that is that the rate of profit on a balanced stock of A machines is greater than that on a balanced stock of B machines. It follows that the rate of bonus per unit of capital is also greater on the stock of A machines.

The conditions for $B_a \lesseqgtr B_b$ are now established. From (4),

$$B = \frac{3}{40\sqrt{2}}\sqrt{\{(Q-S)(nS)\}}$$

Therefore $B_a \gtreqless B_b$ if

$(Q_a - S_a)(nS_a) \gtreqless (Q_b - S_b)(nS_b)$,

that is, if $(1-\beta^2)/(1-\alpha\beta) \gtreqless Q_a/S_a$.

In general, there is no reason why the top inequality should not be satisfied in some cases, in which cases, $B_a > B_b$.

Notes

1. Stephen Merrett, 'Capital, Profit and Bonus in Soviet Industry', *Economica*, Nov. 1964, 401–7.
2. Ronald L. Meek, 'Ideal and Reality in the Choice between Alternative Techniques' *Oxford Economic Papers*, Nov. 1964, 333–54.
3. Stephen Merrett, *op. cit.*, 401–2.
4. Herbert S. Levine, 'Comment' on Robert W. Campbell, 'Soviet Accounting and Economic Decisions', in G. Grossman (ed.), *Value and Plan* (Berkeley: University of California Press, 1960), 96–97.
5. Stephen Merrett, *op. cit.*, 401–2. The writer is indebted to Mr D. M. Nuti for pointing out the misplacement of the decimal point in Merrett's original formulation, which does not, however, affect the subsequent argument.
6. G. C. Harcourt, 'The Accountant in a Golden Age', *Oxford Economic Papers*, Mar. 1965, 60–80.
7. *Ibid.*, 71–2.
8. $S = \sum_{i=1}^{n} \frac{q_i}{(1+r)^i}$. In the 'one-hoss shay' case, $S = q_i' \left[\frac{\{1-(1/1+r)^n\}}{r}\right]$, so that

   $$q_i' = \frac{rS}{1-(1/1+r)^n}$$

   Similarly, it can be shown that $q_1'' = \frac{(1+r-b)S}{1-(b/1+r)^n}$.
9. Harcourt, *op. cit.*, 70–1. For simplicity it is assumed that there is only one machine in each age group.
10. Stephen Merrett, *op. cit.*, 407.
11. Ronald L. Meek, *op. cit.*, 335.

Part V

Package Deals

13
The Social Consequences of Inflation*

Explanations of inflation: why is it so?

Following Keynes's analysis in *The General Theory* of the causes of prolonged recessions, economists (including Keynes himself in *How to Pay for the War*) have adapted his analysis in order to tackle the puzzle of inflation. Just as recessions were seen to result from the inability of a decentralised capitalist economy automatically to provide sufficient overall demands with which to absorb the total supplies of goods and services that would be forthcoming *if* the potential workforces and existing stocks of capital goods were fully employed at each point in time, so inflation was seen to be due to an excess of total demands in real terms over available supplies of goods and service *when* the potential workforces and existing stocks of capital goods *were* fully employed. The resulting 'inflationary gap', the tendency for planned investment expenditure to exceed full employment saving, generated tendencies for stocks of goods to be run down, queues to form, order books to lengthen and prices to rise. (The exact mixture of these ingredients depended upon the nature of the market structures of the economy concerned.)

The theory did not predict the *rate* at which prices rose, only that they would tend to rise. It did suggest that rising prices themselves could cure an inflationary situation *only* if their impact on planned real expenditures was to reduce them. Unlike the market for a single good, where an initial imbalance between demand and supply may be removed by a rise in the price of the good, an imbalance between total

* Originally published in the *Australian Accountant*, October 1974, 520–8.

demands and supplies is not necessarily removed by rises in the general price level. For the other side of overall rising prices is rising money incomes of the same amount (abstracting from overseas transactions and the government for the moment), so that the capacity to buy at the higher price levels is not impaired in real terms. (In the market for an individual good, it is reasonable to suppose that the incomes of its purchasers are in the main independent of those of its suppliers, a supposition that is patently false for the economy as a whole.) It *might* be that, in an inflationary situation, there would be a tendency for prices to rise faster than money-wages. Real income then would be redistributed by the inflationary process from a class which tends to spend much of its income, both on average and at the margin (the wage-earners), to one which does not (the profit-receivers), so that the overall level of planned spending in real terms on consumption goods could be reduced. If, also, the level of planned investment in real terms is not raised by the inflationary situation, there may be a level of prices overall that would be consistent with 'full employment without inflation'. But there is no guarantee that this will be achieved – money-wages may not, for example, continue to lag behind prices – and, in any event, as it is the fall in the level of planned spending that is the key, it may be better consciously to bring this about rather than to depend on (and wait for) 'automatic' market forces to do so. Especially is this so in an open economy trading with the rest of the world; in this case the general price level that is consistent with full employment without inflation at home may be associated with a level of demand for imports which *vis-à-vis* export earnings and desired borrowing from, or lending abroad may imply serious balance of payments difficulties. Implicit in this discussion is the assumption of a flexible money supply. Otherwise, rising prices may have such an impact on rates of interest through the rise in the demand for money that expenditures in real terms are sooner or later choked off by higher rates of interest and the accompanying lower supplies of funds.

Also implicit in the preceding discussion is an assumption about the nature of the markets for individual commodities and productive services, namely, that they are competitive ones in which each individual, whether supplying or demanding a good or a service, is a price-taker. That is to say, prices are set by the automatic market forces and individuals lack discretionary power over the prices that they receive or pay for products and services. Clearly this is an unreal assumption to make about most markets in the manufacturing sectors of the economy (where, typically, administered pricing rules in oligopolistic settings) and, possibly, even in most sections of primary production as well. Moreover, most segments of the labour market are now unionised, at least to some extent; money-wage levels therefore are not the outcome of automatic market forces but of bargaining processes which reflect relative bargaining strengths and social, historical, institutional and conventional processes.

The above factors imply that over quite a large range of fluctuations in overall activity, the general price level may be independent of the *actual* level of activity (and changes in it). (In the simple Keynesian model discussed above, the general price level (up to full employment) reflected the outcome of the intersections of individual demand and supply relationships, that is to say, their positions relative to one another and their elasticities and shifts over time.) In the present case we are arguing that the *same* level of activity *over time* may continue to be associated with a rising general level of prices, as autonomous rises in (say) money-wages, or profit margins by price-makers using their discretionary power, or the prices of imported goods used as inputs into the domestic production process, feed through to the overall price level in the now familiar process of cost-push inflation. Because business-people and wage-earners have come to believe that governments are committed to the maintenance of full employment, or, at least, high levels of activity, price-makers are not deterred either from seeking higher monetary awards and/or passing on *in full* autonomous rises in costs. The resulting higher money incomes tend to provide, together with sustained levels of autonomous expenditures (because of confident expectations about sustained activity levels), sufficient demands in real terms to maintain existing levels of activity. (We continue to assume a flexible money supply with which to support at the higher price levels and at least unchanged real rates of interest, the same level of activity.) In an open economy, with a fixed exchange rate, there are limits to the rate of increase which are dictated by movements in the prices of our exports and imports. But, given that inflation has tended to be a worldwide phenomenon for a considerable period of time, it is clear that cost-push inflation could be a self-sustaining process also for a considerable period of time. (Notice that this analysis is consistent with the 'Keynesian Revolution', at least as seen by the original Keynesians. Thus, Joan Robinson

> summarised [the 'Keynesian Revolution'] in the propositions that the rate of saving is governed by the rate of investment, that the level of prices is governed by the level of money-wage rates, and [that] the level of interest rates is governed by the supply and demand of money. (Introduction to Michal Kalecki, *Studies in the Theory of Business Cycles 1933–39*, Blackwell, Oxford 1969, viii–ix)

Both 'demand-pull' (as the orthodox 'Keynesian' theory is dubbed) and 'cost-push' elements obviously are present in the inflationary process that we are experiencing at the moment. Even when taken together, though, they are inadequate as a complete explanation. (I hasten to add that economists generally, unlike some politicians, are perplexed by the modern inflations and that no completely satisfactory explanation, widely accepted, has yet been formulated.) Underlying both theories is an assumption, based upon the experience of the nineteenth and first third of the twentieth century, that while price levels may fluctuate over time, the long-run trend through the cycles is at a pretty constant level; that is, that there is no obvious tendency for price levels either to go up or down over long stretches of time. This view in turn reflects those periods of capitalism where there was considerably more flexibility *in both directions* in money-wages and prices. That it was not an unreasonable assumption for long periods of historical time may be checked by examining the levels of prices (and also the levels of the money rate of interest) over much of the nineteenth century and in the interwar years.

With the commitment of the capitalist world in the postwar period to high levels of activity and growth, coupled with both the will and the power to attain them (if only by using defence spending as a base), the widely held expectation of a continuing long-run steady level of prices has been, at first gradually, and, recently, rapidly and virtually completely eroded. In its place have come very widely spread expectations of continuously rising price levels. These have carried with them in turn, attempts to compensate for past rises and, indeed, anticipate future ones when individual money-wage bargains are struck, either by arbitration procedures or, directly, by collective bargaining processes. Since individual money-wage bargains (that is, within firms or industries or trades) in a decentralised capitalist economy have also the aims of both protecting established (and hallowed) relativities and enabling wage-earners to share in the trend rise in overall national productivity, there has been in recent years a cumulative tendency for previously established sociological 'norms' as to what constitute reasonable rates of increases in money-wages, acceptable both to wage-earners and employers, to break down. This is a worldwide phenomenon, observable (though with time lags) in the United States, the United Kingdom, Western Europe, Japan and, now, in Australia.

Since there has also been a relative relaxation of 'stop–go' policies, at least in their severity (and excluding the United Kingdom under the second Wilson administration and Australia after the first Snedden budget), the outcome has been accelerating rates of increases in money-wages and, thus, prices, both internally and externally, because of the interlocking of countries through international trade. This has been accompanied by a great increase in the quantity of money in most capitalist countries, emanating from the United States and, in the Australian case, exacerbated (until recently) by a large amount of capital inflow together with the reflation of the economy following the 1971–72 recession. The result, worldwide, has been the discrediting of the Phillips curve relationship – the belief in the existence of a discernible stable trade-off between rates of increase of money-wages and levels of, and rates of change in, unemployment. In the Australian case the prices of our imports and exports also have had an effect on the domestic cost level, both directly and indirectly, insofar as they consist of wage goods and so affect the demands made by wage-earners for increases in money-wages.

As long as we live in a world of relatively fixed exchange rates, it is impossible completely to isolate trading nations from price changes that occur elsewhere in the world. Moreover, there is no guarantee that a floating exchange rate would be any protection. With expectations of accelerating inflation widely held, a floating exchange rate may well prove to be destabilising, either starting or continuing a cumulative process to which there is no foreseeable end. Especially is this so when there are strong cost-push forces at work associated with rising import prices and widely held expectations of a continuing rise in the general level of prices.

I hope that it is obvious from the above sketches that all the elements that have been identified with inflationary situations are recognisable in the present Australian experience. First of all, it is clear that there are excess demand elements present; these are shown not only by rapidly rising prices in various sectors, especially in certain key manufacturing sectors associated with the supplies of intermediate goods from other sectors, but also in the widespread phenomenon of shortages, accompanied by lengthening order books. The shortages themselves are a combination of a sustained boom not only in Australia but in the industrialized world as a whole, so that the usual outlet of extra imported supplies is not available as it would be if Australia were experiencing excess demand on its own. As far as excess demand is concerned, it is not possible to pinpoint any particular segment of expenditure as responsible – it is the inconsistency in the total of planned real expenditures, some autonomous, some induced, in relation to total supplies that is the key.

Second, there are cost-push elements that are associated both with the prices of 'importable' and 'exportable' wage goods and inputs into domestic production and money-wage increases. The latter reflect not only demand-pull forces due to the shortages of labour in general and special skills in particular (which belong, of course, under the first head) but also the responses of discretionary price-makers under conditions of extreme uncertainty coupled with expected price increases so that old-established sociological 'norms' go by the board. The rise in militant union pressures and the accompanying increase in industrial unrest reflect both the anxieties of an inflationary situation and the basic class conflicts over the distribution of income which continuously high levels of activity increasingly have brought to the surface. Imposing excess demand on such a situation invariably runs a capitalist economy into what Joan Robinson has graphically called the 'inflation barrier' – the situation in which trade unions and wage-earners generally fight back via rising money-wages against the attempt by other sectors of the community to use resources, for purposes other than the production of wage goods, in such proportions as to imply an intolerable level of real wages.

There is also a strongly entrenched desire to maintain well-established relativities. Here key sectors – for example, certain sectors of the public service – can be vital in giving the initial autonomous push, with other sectors attempting to achieve a flow-on that maintains their relative positions, if only after a lag. The actual increases in money-wages aimed for and attained are influenced increasingly by the impact of unrevised progressive income tax schedules, set originally with much lower levels of *average* money incomes in mind, on effective levels of take-home pay. Thus larger and larger pre-tax incomes have to be bargained for in order to protect and/or improve, at a constant rate, post-tax real incomes. These factors help to account for the phenomenon of stagflation – sustained or even accelerating rates of increases in prices associated with rising levels of unemployment. There no longer seems to be (if there ever was) any simple stable trade-off between unemployment levels and rates of increase of money-wage rates and thus prices. Therefore, though reducing excess demand may be necessary as a measure of economic control, if excess demand features prominently in an inflationary situation, it is certainly not sufficient to remove inflationary pressures because of the other sets of factors that are independent of expenditure cuts and activity levels, at least over those ranges of activity that are politically possible in modern capitalist economies. Moreover, to get rid of *all* excess demand would require intolerably high levels of unemployment. Finally, the very large expansion in the monetary base, until recently, was also responsible for total spending being brought to a level where accelerating (and absolutely very large) rises in prices, especially in certain key sectors – for example, building and construction – were inevitable.

Consequences for the redistribution of income and wealth: never a lender but a borrower be

Apart from the inefficiencies and shortages that are associated with the inflationary process, the waste of energy that goes into stock-exchange speculation, tax avoidance and fly-by-night schemes designed to make a quick profit for their initiators, there occur major redistributions of real income and wealth holdings for which there is no economic, political or social justification. The most obvious examples are people on fixed money incomes, or in receipt of money incomes, the adjustments to which take place only after very considerable time lags. By squeezing the real purchasing power of these groups – pensioners, teachers, nurses, weakly unionised groups – the community is using them as safety valves which allow more favourably placed groups – businesspeople who can maintain or increase their profit margins, wage-earners who quickly can obtain compensating increases in money-wages – to maintain or increase their own spending in real terms. Within the squeezable groups are those who even if they can adjust their money incomes relatively quickly are nevertheless in occupations where all or most of their recorded incomes come within the tax-person's orbit and are subject to rates of taxation that were designed, as we saw above, for considerably lower levels of average money incomes. The scope for avoidance and evasion is most unequally distributed through the community and, as a general rule, those who can least afford to, get the highest proportion of their earnings caught within the tax-person's net. (I am not arguing against either progressive or high rates of taxation as such but for equal treatment for all those with equal economic power.) At the best of times, there is only rough justice, especially in the Australian case where legal tax avoidance has been designed especially to favour the middle and upper income groups, the cumulative result of 23 years of unchanged perspectives in government taxation policies. But in a severe inflationary situation these built-in dodges are compounded, so adding considerably to social unrest and bitterness.

Another group which is at risk when rates of inflation (in the sense of domestic cost levels) differ as between countries are those whose costs are largely determined at home and whose revenues are determined abroad, principally exporters and importers (where, in the main, in the latter case, it is the other way around). We are all familiar with the phenomenon of the cost–price squeeze in the rural exporting sector whereby, in effect, real income is redistributed from the export sector to workers and manufacturers in the domestic manufacturing sector. (This abstracts from the many current and capital subsidies and other schemes that were devised in order to redistribute income back again through the taxation system and government intervention generally.)

Perhaps the most serious redistributions that occur are not on income account but on capital account. A feature of inflation, especially when it 'hots up' and is expected to get worse, is a flight from liquid assets, especially money, into real goods. If, moreover, interest rates are kept artificially low, in the sense that Reserve Bank interference in the money market does not allow the pattern of rates of interest to attain their 'natural' levels in the market, people attempt to change the composition of their wealth portfolios by increasing their holdings of land, pictures, jewelry and, possibly also, shares, in order to hedge against inflation. What may be prudent and rational for the individual turns out to be anti-social for the community as a whole, for the combined efforts of people to so change their portfolios bring about the very sectional price changes which they individually are at pains either to avoid or to protect themselves against. Appreciation in the prices of real assets creates arbitrary pockets of increased wealth which only very imperfectly, if at all, come within the tax-person's orbit and which basically do not reflect any particular productive contribution to society at all.

In the economy as a whole there is a large-scale redistribution from creditors to debtors. In practice, this often means a redistribution of the money saving of low income-earners and negligible wealth-holders to those whose income and wealth positions are such as to make them creditworthy and therefore able to borrow considerable amounts. No more so than in an inflationary situation is the biblical maxim, 'To him that hath shall be given and from him that hath not even that little which he hath shall be taken away', applicable. These effects are greatly added to if there is simultaneously an attempt by the central government and the Reserve Bank to keep down the levels of money rates of interest so that what little money-returns lenders receive in the form of interest payments are effectively made low or even negative by accelerating rates of increases in prices.

Another aspect of inflation, to which accountants increasingly have addressed themselves in recent years, is the problem of accounting for different rates of price increase of the products which their firms sell, on the one hand, and of the assets that are used in the productive process, on the other. As is well-known, historical-cost accounting procedures are especially deficient in these situations, both for assessing incomes earned and guiding pricing, investment and financing decisions. Moreover, tax rates that are levied on incomes as conventionally measured are designed for a world in which the monetary unit is stable over the long haul, result in very different incidences of taxation on current or economic incomes. Incidentally, it was Keynes and his 'true' followers who always stressed that the monetary unit, the money-wage (in relation to productivity) and therefore the general price level needed to be relatively stable in order to preserve democratic capitalist institutions, of which Keynes was a great defender. Events in recent years all round the capitalist world show how correct his intuition was. The bitterness that is inevitably associated with a class society of competing and often irreconcilable interests is greatly enhanced when the arbitrariness of rewards to different groups is greatly increased, not only as between Australia's three broad classes of wage-earners, profit-receivers and exporters, but also within the wage-earning class itself, and as between the young and the old, and the urban and the rural. Bitterness is added to by the uncertainty and anxiety that pervade the everyday actions of the great majority of citizens, combined with an irresistible incentive to dishonest behaviour that is built into lending and borrowing institutions during inflation. By the last point I mean that people take it as a matter of course that it is prudent to borrow in inflationary situations, knowing full well that as contracts are made in terms of money, this inevitably implies robbery by one group from another (unless interest rates are adjusted accordingly). Moreover, both the ability and incentive to make rational decisions about productive investment and employment are greatly reduced in a world in which the basic monetary unit is no longer stable or dependable.

Policy suggestions: what is to be done?

I take it that the usual measures suggested for controlling inflation are well known, as well as their advantages, limitations, deficiencies and difficulties. Thus, in order to tackle excess demand, overall planned expenditure needs to be cut, either directly by reducing government expenditure or indirectly by raising rates of income and indirect taxes, by raising interest rates and/or reducing loans, in order to reduce the private sector's ability to spend. The efficacy of these measures depends upon whether the groups most directly affected believe the measures are permanent or temporary, and on whether the spending functions of the groups are as stable and predictable as orthodox economic theory, designed for other worlds and situations, has assumed. Moreover, the latter set of measures have cost-push consequences that are almost certainly undesirable (witness the reasoning behind Snedden's proposed income tax cuts in the recent election campaign, the validity of which as an anti-inflationary measure rested on these consequences applying). I myself have always opposed the use of cuts (or increases) in government expenditure primarily as demand management tools. The public–private sector split in the use of resources, it seems to me, ought to reflect the basic philosophy of the government in power and the longer-run social and economic developments of the economy, rather than be directed to the shorter-run problems of demand management. True Keynesian theory leads inexorably to a plea for some form of incomes policy emphasising, as it does, the crucial strategic importance of the money-wage rate in determining the stability or instability of capitalist economies. But as Joan Robinson has remarked (she herself has advocated the need for an incomes policy since the mid-1930s), how can one reasonably expect the unions to co-operate in such a policy when they are repeatedly faced, especially in the present speculative and unsettled time, with examples of 'the unpleasant and unacceptable face of capitalism', to quote Mr Heath's immortal phrase? Finally, we have seen in recent years an upsurge of monetarist measures, the guiding star of which is Professor Milton Friedman of Chicago, which take a long (and uncertain) time to work, and the relative impact of which on the price level and activity is still uncertain, even in theory, as presented by the monetarists. We have also seen use of the exchange rate and tariff cuts, courageous measures which hurt sectional interests but seem to have the approval of many academic economists: witness the 130:4 in support of the Labor governments's measures during the recent election campaign.

I want, though, to concentrate on another policy proposal; namely, the suggested reintroduction of automatic quarterly cost-of-living adjustments for all money-wages and pensions, that is, indexation. This has been advocated by both the government and a number of academic economists; for example, Trevor Swan, Eric Russell, Alan Hall, John Nevile, Barry Hughes and (immodestly) me. On the face of it, such a proposal sounds paradoxical, guaranteed, almost certainly, to accelerate the rate of inflation and it has been criticised on just these grounds. (My former colleague, Professor Donald Whitehead of La Trobe, set me up on this one and described the proposal as 'the silliest way to fight inflation': so much for honour amongst thieves.) But I think that good economic sense *can* be made of the proposal though it must be said at the outset that it is as yet a case of 'not proven' and that the proof of the pudding will be in the eating.

The argument in outline (there are, of course, many modifications and qualifications) goes as follows. As we have seen, one factor causing the present rate of inflation is the anxiety associated with widely-held expectations of *continuing* increases in prices. This leads wage-earners to attempt to obtain increases in money-wages that not only restore their real purchasing power but also offer some insurance against its expected erosion in the future. Because, in a mixed capitalist economy such as Australia, money-wage bargains are not made simultaneously across the board but by various groups of wage-earners and employers, either by collective bargaining procedures or before arbitration commissions, it must be expected that each group, quite rightly, will put its own interests first. Yet it is the collective outcome of all the bargains struck which is relevant for the *overall* rate of increase of money-wages, itself an important factor in the overall rate of increase of prices. In order to influence this collective outcome and especially to so reduce the overall rate of increase of money-wages that it is consistent with a single figure rather than the present double-figure rate of increase of prices, it is surely desirable to remove the anxiety that is associated with this erosion of the absolute real income of wage-earners. This the proposed cost-of-living adjustments would do. It might then be hoped that the money-wage bargains which were struck and which, individually, reflect the bargaining power of groups in, and the prosperity of, each industry, would collectively be associated with significantly lower overall rates of increase of money-wages than otherwise would have occurred.

Put succinctly, then, the argument is that the removal of one major source of uncertainty in the general process of setting individual money-wages – namely, that associated with erosion of absolute real income – coupled with widely held expectations of continuing, indeed increasing, price inflation, could lead to an 'otherwise situation' in which the overall increase of money-wages would be substantially lower.

Turning now to details: should indexation be applied to a minimum wage (and the same *absolute* amount added to all) or, at a proportionate rate, to *all*? (The latter would tend to leave relativities unaffected.) My own preference is for the former. I think there is a lot to be said for regarding the wage bundle conceptually as divisible into two segments – 'necessaries' and the wage-earning class's share of the surplus. (This distinction has its roots in classical political economy and has been revived in recent years by Piero Sraffa.) It would be the object of quarterly cost-of-living adjustments to protect the former portion. Relative bargaining strengths, levels of activity and conditions in individual industries and firms should be the factors which (in a capitalist economy with efficiently functioning markets, something we are, of course, far from achieving) determine the latter. This calculation would also provide a guide for the indexation of pensions as well. In an open economy like Australia, some adjustments would need to be made for the impact of overseas prices and there remains the vexed question of what is the appropriate index of prices of wage goods to use. But it does not seem beyond the wit of man both to design one and to get general acceptance from the groups concerned, or, at least, if it is, it suggests that class conflicts have bitten so deep in our society that we should perhaps be thinking of designing a new set of institutions anyway. In order to minimise the impact of seasonal and chance influences on prices, especially of foodstuffs, there would be much to be said for designing an index that incorporates a moving average of prices.

We could note in passing that indexation serves to secure the same objectives as the scheme originally proposed by Professors Weintraub and Wallich (see, for example, Sidney Weintraub, *Keynes and the Monetarists*, Rutgers University Press, New Jersey, 1973, ch. 6) and given some prominence here by Professor Ronald Henderson in his 1971 Joseph Fisher Lecture (*Australian Economic Papers*, June 1972), essentially because much the same true Keynesian analysis has been made, especially concerning the strategic importance of the money – wage level. Both the Weintraub–Wallich and the Henderson schemes are variations on the theme that penal rates of business taxation should be levied on those firms that pay increases in money-wages above certain standard 'norms' set by the authorities with certain upper limits to the rate of increase of prices in mind. The object is to give strong incentives to employers on their side of the bargaining process to keep down the rate of increase of money-wages to levels consistent with relatively low rates of price inflation. All these suggestions are essentially those of people who either through conviction or a sense of realism, at least in the short period, take existing institutions and market structures and social and power groupings as they find them, and attempt to design policies which have reasonable chances of success within these constraints. In practice, they may be disappointed.

The last area that I wish to discuss concerns the protection of people's saving for retirement. I have long advocated a national superannuation scheme whereby, in effect, the productive during *their* active productive lives support the retired or ill or widowed or disabled by current tax provisions (preferably raised by progressive rates), in return for support themselves by the *then* active when they have retired, or become ill, or are otherwise out of action. In a sense, this is what the proposed abolition of the means test implies, and there is much to be said for it if you accept the philosophy that all citizens should have a pension as a right merely by virtue of being citizens and usually because of the contributions that they have made to the revenue during their productive lives. It does mean, of course, giving a bonus to the well-off (who may be so either because of their own efforts, or because of inheritance, or scarcity rents in their earnings while active, or appreciation of the value of their assets) in order to provide for the otherwise destitute. But this may well be a cost worth paying in an affluent society, in order to achieve social benefits by creating a sense of equity and fairness. There would, of course, be room for private superannuation schemes whereby saving could gain people a pension over and above a state one. There would be much to be said for the funds so made available being invested in long-lived development projects, the returns to which would be expected to keep up with any inflationary tendencies.

Finally, I cannot resist putting in a plug for a negative income tax;[1] the break-even point of which would be indexed. This seems to me to be a logical policy measure to be implemented by a government nominally dubbed 'socialist' but which in reality seems more appropriately to have Milton Friedman or even Adam Smith as its patron saint rather than Karl Marx or even, alas, Keir Hardie or Ben Chifley.

Postscript: August 1974

I have left the address as it was originally written in May (and given in August). However, events have moved swiftly over even this short time, so it seems appropriate to add a postscript, especially as three colleagues (Eric Russell, Barry Hughes and Phillip Bentley) and I have become associated, between May and August, with a package-deal set of proposals known as the Adelaide Plan. (The name is rather inept for the principles underlying it, and the measures themselves, broadly conceived, are coming to represent a consensus of opinion amongst non-Treasury economists.) An integral part of the proposals is a variant of indexation, one which stresses proportionality, at least up to quite high income levels, rather than flat-rate adjustments to most incomes (themselves determined by proportionate adjustments for the lowest paid). It is proposed that this scheme be commenced in the early months of the first quarter of 1975 and that the line be held, more or less, on money-wages in the meantime. (This is to allow the recent increases in money-wages and those already in the pipeline, most of which are very large, to feed through into prices by the end of the year.)

Whatever the equity merits of the flat-rate version (in my view, they are considerable), in the present situation of badly ruptured relativities, the effects of introducing such a scheme could be disastrous as an anti-inflation measure. Since the present situation is extraordinarily serious – unchecked, we could be experiencing rates of inflation of the order of 30 per cent per annum or more by the end of 1974 – equity (and efficiency) considerations must take back seats, at least for the time being.

Allied with the indexation scheme are proposals that company profits and the prices of companies' products be controlled through the tax system. It is suggested that (with obvious exceptions for new companies, or those that recently made losses) profits be such as to not exceed the average of the net profit to sales ratio of (say) the last three years. Any excess over this would be taxed away completely, that is, we are proposing a 100 per cent excess profits tax. Also any money-wage increases (measured per hour and including the value of fringe benefits and other factors that add directly to costs) in excess of those allowed by indexation and a mild (say 3 per cent per annum) adjustment for relativities would not be allowable as a cost for tax purposes; their consequent inclusion in *taxable* profits would bear a 100 per cent tax rate also. In this way profit margins per unit would be controlled (larger profits could still be made by selling larger volumes) and there would also be a considerable incentive for businesspeople not to acquiesce in wage payments in excess of the norms established for the emergency period, that is, sweetheart agreements would be out. The accounting profession in their capacity as auditors would be a vital link in this scheme of things. For they would have to certify that the net profit to sales ratios and wage payments had not exceeded the allowable limits. (In this regard, it was most heartening to find at the Whyalla Convention that the accounting profession, as evidenced by the resolution passed by a resounding majority, were favourably disposed towards playing their proposed indispensable role.)

The 3 per cent annum increase allowed for relativities is necessary both because of gross departures from established norms in the recent leap-frog movements in money-wages and also to make sure that trade union officials have worthwhile jobs – indexation by itself is tantamount to voting them out of a job, something neither they nor their union members would wear. In some cases, with really badly out-of-line relativities, the adjustments may have to take a number of years. The self-employed would be subject to a similar system of excess income control, by using the personal income tax system. Promotions, and so on, could be handled by a version of Keynes's deferred pay system whereby excess income over the average increase indicated by indexation plus (mild) adjustments for relativities would be deferred for (say) two years, a modest rate of interest being paid on these amounts in the meantime.

By itself, indexation in this scheme would only serve to stabilise the rate of increase of prices, not to bring it down. (Even the former would, of course, be a major achievement.) To bring it down we must look for 'dampeners' in the cost-of-living index in the form of reduced food prices (at the farm gate), increases in productivity (here the threat of a recession is a real worry as productivity tends to fall or even to become negative with the onset of a recession) and state and Australian government behaviour with regard to charges, direct and indirect taxes. Thus, it is vital that the Australian government puts the state governments in such financial positions that they do *not* have to raise charges or introduce State taxes; indirect and direct tax cuts would also be desirable, if the macroeconomics situation warrants it. Here the recession might be a blessing in disguise, as far as the cost-push elements of the inflation are concerned, for tax cuts would be needed for demand management purposes. Given *very* favourable circumstances, we estimate that inflation rates *could* be down to single figures (high ones, alas) by the first quarter of 1976.

We take the view that the present inflation, whatever its initial causes, is now predominantly wage–price and wage–wage, that is to say, it has a life of its own in terms of these elements. We therefore are opposed to measures which imply a sharp rise in unemployment which is sustained for a considerable period of time, because they are inhumane and inappropriate. We feel that some package deal such as ours, the strands of which are not original but borrowed freely, *could* secure wide community consensus and, conceivably, just might work.

The alternatives are a move towards hyper-inflation (prices rising at 50 per cent annum or more), with all its attendant and undesirable political and social consequences and anxieties, including, as an outside chance, the destruction of our democratic institutions themselves; a wholesale and widespread freeze of wages and prices; or the deliberate creation of unemployment, at least 3 per cent of the workforce, in order to shock the system and break through the expectations barrier. We feel that the last would be the worst of all possible worlds, enough to create a great deal of unnecessary misery and loss of employment and output, not enough to have a significant effect on money-wage increases, unless it is held for an intolerably long time, certainly over a year. We note that up until now (early August) the government has shown every sign of adopting such an evaluation and that its measures to date (in the second half of 1974) are tragically wrong, if our diagnosis is correct. We stress that we are faced with a serious inflationary situation, to which must be added the possibility of a worldwide slump, in which the whole capitalist world is moving in unison, all parts of which faced with inflation and tackling it by reducing demand. Prospects are bleak but we stress that these are the alternatives before us and that our proposals, unpalatable as they may be in the short run, are relatively the least unpalatable of them all.

Notes

1. This concept is due to Milton Friedman. Basically, if a taxpayer's income is less than that at which, at present, no tax is paid, the taxpayer would receive a subsidy (i.e. a negative income tax) equal to some proportion of his negative income for tax purposes. In this way, a floor below which no person's net income could fall is created.

14
Policy and Responses for Australia*

'He who is convinced against his will
Is of the same opinion still.'

I am going to be very old-fashioned in this paper and I make no apologies for this. I shall draw partly on the authority of Giblin (in his Inaugural Lecture of 1930[1]) for my stance; and I am most happy to be joined in it, quite independently, by at least three contemporaries – Harold Levien, Merv Lewis and Jim Perkins.[2] Put succinctly. I want to advocate easier fiscal policy (coupled with offsetting monetary policy) and the support of those of our existing institutions which, hallowed by history and usage, influence those responsible for the setting of *money*-wages and prices. In addition, I shall suggest, drawing on recent American discussions and the general approval of the authors of the McCracken Report,[3] some mild 'carrot and stick' measures that we might consider as back-ups to the influence of our own institutions on the decision-makers in our society. When putting forward these suggestions, I shall try to operate within the constraints imposed by the present Federal government and *its* advisers, try to devise a package that is acceptable to *their* philosophy, and to *their* political and economic outlook. I do this, not because I agree with them – they are in the main repugnant to me – but because I find the present level of unemployment so *unnecessarily* wickedly high as to make unthinkable *either* an emasculated Pontius Pilate act *or* the attitude of let them – the pollies, their advisers *and* the unemployed – stew in their own juice, it can only hurry on the time when the whole system may be overturned.

---

* Originally published in *Economic Papers*, no. 60, December 1978, 61–9.

Why start with Giblin? Because in 1930(!) he wrote of 'three ... major problems, not entirely unrelated, [starting with] the most immediately urgent – the difficulty in meeting our obligations abroad, the loss of income at home and the menace of catastrophic unemployment' (1930: 7). He had not unmodern views on the behaviour of 'the capricious overseas investor ... [who, in one instance, poured] in capital quite out of proportion to [our] economic needs, [in another, withheld] it for motives ... at least very largely psychological, [a] psychology [moreover] which is incalculable and generally irrational, grouping (the investor) at one end of the great family, at the other end of which is the Flemington punter' (1930: 8–9). Giblin stressed the permanent loss of real income from both the decline in overseas capital and the change in the conditions of the export industries. This led him to his famous multiplier calculation in which the only (major) leakage was imports. He forgot saving (but did remember taxes, much smaller then than now), and he came up with an order of magnitude of three. This implied, given his estimate of the multiplicand, 'an addition to unemployment of at least one-sixth of our population' (1930: 11).

To avoid this catastrophe, he called for a real wage cut of 5 per cent so as to maintain the level of activity in the export trades at 'present dimensions' (by restoring much of their otherwise lost real income). They would not expand but import-competing manufacturers would, thus avoiding additional unemployment and confining the loss of real income to the initial impact associated with the cessation of loans and the drop in export proceeds.

Giblin's sympathetic discussion with 'John Smith', that 'good mate, rather touchy on some points of etiquette, but very reasonable when he has cooled down [in whom] when there was real occasion for it, you find courage, helpfulness, self-forgetfulness' (*ibid.*: 25–6), concerning the need for real wage cuts contrasts strongly – and favourably – with the arguments of those politicians, public servants, media pundits – and some academics – who argue for real wage cuts today. Giblin had a modern-style answer to that lot, too; he castigates scathingly those who,

> outside the wage-earner ... hard hit [and] efficiently vocal, are ... out to find the villain of the piece. [They find] someone thumpable who is a small-part-cause of [the] troubles [and take] it out of them

> for the whole account ... [Thus do] wicked unions and agitators [bear] the whole brunt. (*ibid.*, 17–18)

John Smith's answer is also curiously modern (when we adjust for inflation).

> He will say that even if our facts are right, which he does not know, and there is this large shortage of income for the country, that is still no reason why wages should suffer. There are plenty of big incomes in the country to stand the strain, which on our own admission may only last for a couple of years. He can see plenty of signs of big incomes, expensive motor cars, two or three to a family; clothes marked up in the shops at extravagant prices; great hotels crowded with visitors who spend more on food for one day than he spends in a week; expensive looking houses with carefully tended gardens and grounds; thousands of people going off every week to spend hundreds of pounds each sight-seeing in Europe. He sees in the papers the deaths of men leaving millions. He reads of . . . city blocks being bought for fabulous prices. Let these people stand the shortage of income and not put it on the wage-earner, whom he knows by experience to be hard put to make ends meet with a wife and four children. There must be plenty of big incomes in the country. His Union Secretary has told him that there is over £100 m. of income over £500 a year according to the Income Tax returns; and everyone knows that a great deal of income is kept quiet – he reads cases in the paper every week. If the big incomes dropped £50 m., there would still be a great deal left besides the first £500 a year. (*ibid.*: 22–3)

Giblin's reply is modern also: to attack the rich will make the *necessary* saving for capital accumulation impossible. We don't seem to have come *that* far in the 48 years since.

Let me nonetheless come back to the present, to what Okun calls the great stagflation swamp in which we now are stuck.[4] As I lack Okun's facility for creating laws and orders of magnitude – I leave that to the 'practical' men who have preceded me today – I shall confine myself to qualitative analysis, as befits a follower of Joan Robinson. Like their American and European counterparts, our 'makers of monetary and fiscal policy [have] adopted extremely restrictive measures that [have] brought on the most severe recession since the . . . thirties' (Okun, 1978: 8). The Federal government (and Mr Wran) point proudly to what this has done to the rate of inflation – It is now, God save us, in high single figures – but they ignore the fact that the American recession promptly cut *their* inflation rate to about 6 per cent by mid 1975 – and there it remains, at least until very recently, 'despite massive excess supplies of idle people, machines and plants'.

Why? Because 'the nature of price – and wage-making has been transformed in the modern era. We live in a world dominated by cost-oriented prices and equity-oriented wages' (*ibid.*: 7). Except in small segments of our economy (where they adjust only too well) prices do not adjust promptly to equate supply and demand; for most products, prices do not rise faster than standard costs during the boom nor do they rise less rapidly than costs during slumps. For the USA there is a new Okun's law of 8 per cent wages – 6 per cent prices: an irreducible minimum or floor through which it is virtually impossible to push the economy, no matter how Draconian the fiscal and monetary measures imposed. Fiscal and monetary measures put the lid on total money spending on goods and services which then splits between a cut back in production and a slowing of inflation. In the past three years or so in the USA, the split has been most unfavourable to production – to save one point on the basic inflation rate costs more than 5 per cent of the real GNP; 'Idle resources and sacrificed output continue to represent an enormous national extravagance' (*ibid.*: 10).

I trot out these horror stories because we are just at the *beginning* of a situation that the USA has experienced for more than three years. All the signs suggest, as we run up to the Budget, that our Federal government and its advisers have not learnt anything from the American experience. Nor can we plead that the American case is irrelevant because the USA is, for all intents and purposes, a closed economy while we are a small open economy with a severe balance of payments constraint on any plans for reflation. The US economy now is *not* without its balance of payments problems and constraints. I admit to ours, too; but I do not think we should treat them as overriding, about which nothing can be done.

What I think we should do is advance cautiously but steadily, through fiscal policy, in order to affect the level of production and, ultimately, employment. My own preference is for selective government expenditure, for the various reasons outlined by Harold Levien,

(1978: 201–2), and also for social reasons as well. It does not seem to me that we have so mopped up our housing deficiencies, educational deficiencies and the perilous state of much of our transport system, including our roads, that we can afford to forego, through a dogmatic, inflexible commitment to the private sector and private spending in order to allow 'freedom of choice', the use of what would otherwise be idle resources in these areas. Especially is this so when the 'freedom' so often takes the form of the need to titillate jaded middle class appetites into activity through tasteless, often sexist, advertising that plays on our least admirable instincts of lust, envy, greed and pride. Moreover, I think it most important that we direct spending, first, into those areas where it provides work for those groups unemployed in greatest numbers, especially the young and the unskilled young at that.

Moreover, the government spending and/or works that I am recommending should, I believe, have a much lower than average import component, so fending off the balance of payments constraint of a given rise in activity and employment and allowing us to keep in store our eminently sensible decision to borrow in the short run to supplement our foreign exchange reserves rather than make drastic changes in the exchange rate. (Of course, the secondary rounds of the multiplier process would have the usual import component over which there is not the same control, but since the multiplier is under two, we should be able to take that in our stride. An accelerator effect on private investment spending would also have to be considered but, given the present level of excess capacity and the liquidity state of many companies, this may not constitute an immediate problem. And when it *does* start to operate we would hope, through other measures I shall mention, to have an internal cost structure that is more competitive *vis-à-vis* the rest of the world, so that the balance-of-payments constraint will bite less than it would at the present time with a similar level of activity.)

Of course, it is a counsel of perfection in the present circumstances to call for an increase in *government* spending, whether Commonwealth, State or Local. Fraser and Howard, for doctrinal reasons, are dead set against it and their advisers in the Treasury seem to take a delight in backing up the politicians' prejudices. At least, they seem to do it more in glee than in sorrow. In any event, the only policy that has any hope of being accepted by the present government is a call for (further) tax cuts. Jim Perkins has suggested a cut in income tax, coupled with tight monetary measures, so that the resulting increase in the deficit would have to be financed mostly by bond sales, with some accompanying rise in interest rates, themselves still at very low *real* levels at the moment. Merv Lewis made a similar suggestion about two years ago (in the *Financial Review*). He suggested that, first, interest rates would not rise very much anyway, because of the very high saving rate we still are experiencing, so that the danger of 'crowding out' is minimal. (He did point out that this depended upon people generally not being completely obsessed with deficit size fetishism, of the sort which our bogey men in government have been attempting to create over the past three years or so, currently getting hoist with their own petard as their *own* deficit swells drastically above estimates.) Even suggestions of a tax cut may flounder on the government's current obsession with lower interest rates. The Perkins' scheme would need to be coupled with either Stretton – or Henderson – type reforms in the sphere of housing finance (desirable on their own account), in order to protect the lower income groups from the effects of the rise in interest rates.[5]

Personally, I think it would be even better, if we must concentrate on stimulation of the private sector (and I have never understood why government orders to the private sector, for example, the construction industry, is *not* stimulating), to use cuts in sales tax wherever possible. Not only does this stimulate expenditure directly but it also will have indirect effects through the level and rate of change in money-wages and prices as well. We might also consider, as Bob Wallace has suggested to me, that statutory authorities forego rises in their charges for six to twelve months, borrowing, where necessary, in order to cover any short-fall in funds needed to finance any planned expenditure on capital goods over the same period.

What I am banking on is that the stimulus (from whatever quarter) will have its main impact on output and ultimately employment, rather than on prices. The reasons are mainly Okun's (though his, in turn, though he does not acknowledge it, are Kalecki's). There is *some* evidence, based on Ng's work,[6] that Australian businesspeople will respond in this manner. In order to help them to do so I think we should move on two fronts. First, we should continue to support (or start to support) the Arbitration Commission and its indexation procedures in the interests of industrial peace and *money-wage* restraint, together with the new post-tax indexation procedures. Whatever the pros and cons of the past (1974) hike in real wages and its effect on unemployment – I had been reluctantly persuaded by Fred Gruen's work that they had a significant role in the past[7] – it seems to me that further cuts can no longer be defended, nor are they necessary, *if* they ever were.

Thus, I have been privileged to see the draft of an important paper, 'The Lessons of the Cameron Experiment' by Peter Riach and Graham Richards (subsequently published in *Australian Economic Papers*, vol. 18, 1979, 21–35). They point out that the conjunction of a rise in money-wages and *real* wages coinciding is very much the historical exception, as is the association of the real wage rise, the squeeze in profits, and the rise in unemployment. Of course, the present government attributes the last causally to the first. Riach and Richards point out, most persuasively, that the drastic cut in the rate of increase of the money supply, the tariff cut, the considerable *appreciation* of the Australian dollar, the operations of the Prices Justification Tribunal (PJT) and the Trade Practices Act, all of which occurred in the same period, may well have had the effect of making the rise in real wages the consequence and not the cause of unemployment – or, at least, of occurring at the same time as the outcome of the interrelated processes associated with these events. (I am agnostic on the question of real wages of youth. No-one remains young for ever – even I gave up playing Aussie Rules at 47 years of age. If some restraint or even actual cut could be shown to have an impact on the present disgraceful level of youth unemployment, I reluctantly would feel bound to support it.)

I am not adverse, though, to suggesting that we experiment with 'carrot and stick' methods which impinge directly on actual decision-makers. Before I go into details, let me remind you of what Okun has pointed out, what Eric Russell always stressed (and Giblin understood), namely, that it is necessary to move together in step. Isolated movements, for example, money-wage restraint by particular groups, involve very large private sacrifices for piddling public gains; whereas, if we all move together, rather small gestures by anyone of us together imply substantial public benefits for us all. There are two sides to the coin of doing what everybody else is doing in order to protect yourself. 'Ending the discomfort requires a collective decision' (1978: 9).

So how would we put these principles into practice? How would we move towards a series of measures for which there would be some hope of obtaining a consensus? First, we need to state one more general principle. In a capitalist economy the wage bargain must always be made in money terms but it is real wages (incomes), and their maintenance and increase, that we are on about. This requires, in turn, high levels of activity and sustained growth. If, therefore, it can be shown that there are some configurations of money prices and money-wages that are consistent with this, and others that are not, the basis will have been laid down for getting agreement on institutions, the operations of which bear on money-wages and prices. This is what incomes policies are all about and it is also the reason why the traditional instruments of fiscal and monetary policy by themselves are inadequate. As Okun says, '[we] need an anti-inflation program that is not an anti-growth program, and that goes beyond traditional fiscal and monetary measures' (*ibid.*: 12).

Thus Okun (in the company of Heller, Solow, Tobin, Wallich and Weintraub, the last emerging triumphant from a lifetime in the wilderness for being so far ahead of his time) advocates the implementation of voluntary guidelines for money-wages and prices, with tax incentives for surpassing them, tax penalties for exceeding them. They are voluntary in that it is left to the individual decision-makers to decide what to do. The reward for money-wage restraint, that is accepting a money-wage increase that is *less* than the guideline increase, is a tax rebate that sustains take-home pay while the restraint itself serves to reduce the rate of increase of wages as a cost, and, thus, the rate of increase of prices. To induce firms to pass the reductions on, there would be tax remissions for them, too, related to how many percentage points *below* the guideline for prices they achieved. The more widespread is the response to the incentives, the greater will be the *real* value of the concessions to those who receive them – virtue brings its own reward. The stick relates to the granting of money-wage increases above the guideline; it falls both on those that receive *and* those that grant them. This, obviously, would be the most contentious part of the scheme. Without it, however, things are left open-ended, especially when (if) recovery is well on the way and there is a temptation to respond to increased monetary demand by raising margins and prices, and offering (and asking for) higher money-wages, rather than by increasing output and employment.

The authors describe these suggestions as

> complicated and untried schemes ... best design not yet clear ... administrative wrinkles ... to be ironed out. [But] the difficulties are

> trivial compared with the costs of our present impasse – losses of [millions] of dollars of production and of [thousands] of jobs each year that we drag along.[8]

I hope that our politicians, bureaucrats and trade-union members and businesspeople are not that hidebound, that they would not at least consider such schemes. When Ronald Henderson made a similar suggestion in his Joseph Fisher Lecture in 1971 and Braham Dabschek did the same in his 1976 *Australian Economic Review* paper,[9] they were further voices crying in the wilderness; now, so many lost opportunities and ruined lives later, surely it is time that we listened.

I suppose that one big unanswered question is how such schemes could be grafted onto our traditional form of incomes policy, guidelines provided through the Arbitration Commission. Like others who have run an Okun line in an analysis of how the economy works, I have always thought indexation procedures the best way we could institute an *Australian* incomes policy that was acceptable and effective. In the past I have suggested the use of what I dubbed, perhaps unfortunately, a relativities wages fund, whereby those groups who thought they had fallen behind in past years in the wage–wage spiral could argue before the Arbitration Commission for a share in a predetermined amount granted overall, over and above the indexation procedures, in order to restore relativities. The full restoration might well be spread over a number of periods, but the justice of the claim would be established from the beginning. Such procedures would require as well, coordination and cooperation, in particular, agreement as to what *was* a fair structure of relativities, the target to be aimed at and eventually reached.

It seems to me that our industrial-relations institutions are designed to achieve just these sorts of aims, that the Commissioners, the unions and their Counsel, and the employers and their's, would feel at home in attempting to find a consensus on such matters. The role of the Commonwealth government would be to establish the range of above indexation payments that they felt could be lived with in any one year, or shorter period, if they like. The ultimate objective is, of course, to get our money-wage and price levels rising at rates that allow us to remain competitive when the economy is operating at a high level of activity and exhibiting a satisfactory rate of growth. Another major objective would be to move towards a pattern that is consistent with the major restructuring that is required and about which Wolfgang Kasper has spoken earlier.[10] (I realise that the two objectives may not coincide.) Borrowing to support the exchange rate over the transition period, such as we have been doing anyway, is an eminently sensible procedure. The carrot and stick measures I have suggested would be supplementary to these already established methods. They might, for example, persuade those firms and unions with the muscle to take them outside dependence on the indexation procedures to take out their superior position in tax rebates instead of higher than average money-wage and price increases.

Summing up, what I am suggesting for Australia is in accord with the suggestions made by the best Keynesians overseas, Bastards and otherwise – that is why I said I was old-fashioned. Tobin has consistently suggested fiscal and monetary policies as complements to one another, emphasising the sustained, the gradual and the steady as the way to get out of the slump and not into another inflationary impasse. He has stressed as well the complicated inter-relationships of the financial network and activity and warned against the misleading seduction of *simpliste* rules and targets.[11] Sidney Weintraub, drawing on his own brand of 'true' Keynesian analysis, rightly has concentrated on the formation of the price level, as was always implicit and often explicit in much of Keynes's analysis. At the same time he has deplored the use of deflation as the device for containing inflation. If we were not operating within the political constraints imposed by the present government, I would repeat again the need for what Joan Robinson calls 'a real social contract which would satisfy the reasonable demands of the workers for more control over their own work, more security against redundancy, better social services and so forth'. But that, I fear, must await our return to another, better world.

Notes

1. L. F. Giblin, *Australia, 1930: An Inaugural Lecture* (Melbourne: Melbourne University Press, 1930). I am much indebted to Neville Cain for drawing my attention to Giblin's lecture.
2. Harold Levien, 'An Evaluation of Government Economic Policy', *Readings in Economics* (Economic Teachers' Association, 1978), 196–205. M. K. Lewis, 'Why Aren't Taxes Cut?', *Australian Financial Review*, 19 and 20 October, 1976. J. O. N. Perkins, 'Stagflation and the Macroeconomic Policy Mix' Research Paper 67, Department of Economics, University of Melbourne, May 1978. J. O. N. Perkins, 'International Monetary Influences on the Australian Economy', *Economic Papers*, No. 59, Sydney, 1978.

3. '. . . if government are going to adopt a policy of not accommodating high rates of inflation they must be prepared to indicate to those responsible for wage and price determination what kind of behaviour on their part would be consistent with the monetary and fiscal policies the authorities intend to follow', Paul W. McCracken *et al.*, 'Towards Full Employment and Price Stability', *Economic Impact*, 1978/1, 14.
4. A. Okun, 'The Great Stagflation Swamp', *Challenge*, vol. 20, 1978, 6–13.
5. R. F. Henderson, 'Housing Policy and the Poor', *Australian Economic Review*, vol. 1, 1978, 34–9.
6. Y-K. Ng, 'Aggregate Demand, Business Expectation, and Economic Recovery. Without Aggravating Inflation', *Australian Economic Papers*, vol. 16, 19??, 130–40.
7. F. H. Gruen, 'Some Thoughts on Real Wages and Unemployment' in M. R. Fisher, F. H. Gruen, P. J. Sheehan and D. W. Stammer, *Real Wages and Unemployment*, C.A.E.R. Report no. 4, University of N.S.W., 1978, 65–80.
8. From a letter to the *New York Times*, Sunday, 12 March 1978.
9. R. F. Henderson, 'Income Inflation in Australia', *Australian Economic Papers*, vol. 11, 1972, 1–7; B. Dabscheck, 'A Market Based Anti-Inflation Policy', *Australian Economic Review*, 1976/1, 59–64.
10. Wolfgang Kasper, 'Overseas Experience with Unemployment and Job-Creation Policies: Lessons for Australia?' in this issue of *Economic Papers*, 43–58.
11. James Tobin, 'Monetary Policies and the Economy: The Transmission Mechanism', *Southern Economic Journal*, vol. 44, 1978: 421–31.

15
Making Socialism in Your Own Country*

I am delighted to accept the invitation to give the John Curtin Memorial Lecture. When I was a youth in Melbourne I grew up in the heart of Barry Humphries' Land, 24 Faircroft Avenue, Glen Iris, SE6 (as it then was) and my parents, who were loving and kind people, nevertheless were very right-wing, and so people like John Curtin and Ben Chifley, and particularly Dr Evatt, were used as bogeymen to send me to sleep. When I first went to the University of Melbourne I still reflected the views of my parents – but only for the first six months. For during those first six months I found out that not all the world was like 24 Faircroft Avenue. This converted me to socialism. This was in the early 1950s (in fact, it was 1950). In those days we used to worry about two things, well *at least* two things (it is customary in economics these days to use inequalities): what political stance we should take and whether God existed. Having made up my mind on political matters in those first six months principally as a result of the Economic Geography lectures of Molly Bain and Bob Wilson, I settled down for the next three and a half years to decide whether God existed.

Unlike the present generation, I decided that He did. Indeed, I now know that *She* is alive and well, but in those days I was more conventional and so for many years I have been the only Jewish

---

* The Twelth John Curtin Memorial Lecture delivered at the Australian National University, Canberra in August 1982.

The lecture was delivered from notes, then tape-recorded and typed. I have left it much as it came out, except that I have removed some repetitions and made some sentences shorter. I am also much indebted to Terry O'Shaughnessy for his thorough sub-editorial work on the manuscript.

Methodist in Adelaide. I cannot claim to be even that now, because like all declining companies, the Protestant Churches have merged and they now call themselves the Uniting Church. (One of the tragedies of modern Christianity and its Churches is that just when they have become relevant there is nobody in them.) I therefore present myself to you as a very old-fashioned creature, to wit, a Christian socialist who has belonged to the Australian Labor Party when I have lived in Australia and to the British Labour Party when I have lived in Britain and sometimes with an overlap in the sense that I voted in both places at the same time. One of our children was born in Britain and was recorded in both places – so if I could muck up the demography statistics I do not see why I could not follow the old Labor Party adage, especially in Victoria, 'vote early and vote often'.

The talk that I want to give tonight is called 'Making Socialism in Your Own Country', and I want to try to follow at least one maxim of a great socialist and a very fine Australian, Hugh Stretton. John Langmore quoted in his recent paper in the *Journal of Australian Political Economy*[1] a typical Stretton maxim – that the Left 'has to supply simple visions, complicated programmes and competent performance'. I see my role tonight as at least trying to provide some simple visions. Complicated programmes have never been one of my strengths – I grew up in Victoria and played far too long on the back line where the instruction was: 'you go straight, you don't go round, you don't hand ball and you kick long', and therefore to make up a complicated programme is not something that I wish to do, though I shall mention some outlines of programmes. As for competent performance, I tried to follow at dinner tonight my usual adage in all manner of activities: to drink enough to stifle the inhibitions but not to ruin the performance. (Thanks very much, it is always good to have some students around.)

To clear the way for what comes later, which mainly will be about economic theory and economic policy, I first want to take an unequivocal stand on nuclear energy and nuclear weapons. Since it is fashionable in Australia to criticise anyone who does not agree with you as being seditious and a traitor and even other unmentionable things – this is a particularly good ploy followed by the Country Party, or the National Country Party as it is now called – I have been a traitor all my adult life to the National Country Party, except once when I suggested during the Whitlam era that if we did not do something about inflation it might approach 30 per cent per annum, whereupon Mr Anthony quoted me. I want now to quote what a well-known 'Lefty' had to say about nuclear weapons just before he was killed by the IRA, namely, Earl Mountbatten. I think that this may be familiar to some people in the audience, but it may not be familiar to others. For example, I was talking to a reporter from News Limited today – now that Rupert has given up on getting his knighthood, he talks to people like me – and the reporter had not heard of this particular quote. I would like to quote his words to you because as far as I know he has never been regarded as unacceptable by either the CIA or the English equivalent of ASIO. He said:

> I repeat in all sincerity as a military man I can see no use for any nuclear weapons which would not end in escalation, with consequences that no-one can conceive.
>
> And nuclear devastation is not science fiction, it is a matter of fact ... We remember the tens of thousands who were killed instantly [at Hiroshima] or worse still those who suffered a slow painful death from the effects of the burns – we forget that many are still dying horribly from the delayed effects of radiation. To this knowledge must be added the fact that we now have a missile a thousand times as dreadful.

And he added:

> I repeat a thousand times as horrible.
>
> A new World War can hardly fail to involve the all-out use of nuclear weapons. Such a war would not drag on for years. It could all be over in the matter of a day.
>
> And when it was all over, what will the world be like? Our fine great buildings, our homes will exist no more. The thousands of years it took to develop our civilisation will have been in vain. Our works of art will be lost. Radio, television, newspapers, will disappear. There will be no hospitals. No help can be expected for the few mutilated survivors in any town to be sent from a neighbouring town – there will be no neighbouring towns left, no neighbours, there will be no help, there will be no hope.
>
> As a military man who has given more than half a century in active service I say in all sincerity that the nuclear arms race has no

> military purpose. Wars cannot be fought with nuclear weapons. Their existence only adds to our perils because of the illusions which they have generated.
>
> There are powerful voices around the world that still give credence to the old Roman precept – if you desire peace, prepare for war. This is absolute nuclear nonsense and I repeat – it is a disastrous misconception to believe that by increasing the total uncertainty one increases one's own certainty.[2]

So having stated, as any good modern economist would, the necessary condition for discussing our topic tonight, I now move on to sufficient conditions. What I want to do is to relate some recent developments in modern economic theory and economic policy to the thinking that a progressive government would need to make when deciding on its economic policy when it comes into office. I had a sort of go at this when I was serving on the Committee that the Labor Party set up in 1978/79 to find out why it had done so badly in 1975 and 1977, apart from the fact that it had alienated the old, the young, women, the poor, the workers, the businesspeople, the ethnics and the blacks. As part of our work, we wrote Discussion Paper no. 6, which was on economic policy and the future of Australia. When the paper was published we were accorded an editorial in *The Canberra Times* which bore the heading 'An Unreal Proposal'. (I notice that Neil Blewitt is in the audience and he will share my painful remembrance of this fact.) The reason why the editorial writer thought it was an unreal proposal was that towards the end of our paper we mentioned that, possibly, nationalisation was something that ought to be discussed, from which the editorial writer concluded that we had concluded that nationalisation was the cure-all for every possible economic ill of which the modern world could possibly conceive, which was somewhat a distortion of our argument. But I am pleased to be able to report – and I always say this at any lecture or seminar I give in case there are questions afterwards, which I understand there will be, just to let you know who is on my side – as I said, I am glad to be able to report that the very next day the editorial writer was struck down with a painful disease in a private part of his anatomy. This led me to speculate that while in the old days the Lord sent thunderbolts to punish the guilty and innocent alike, these days, His, or should I say, Her, aim is much improved. I leave that story with you when you are phrasing your questions.

It is my contention that since the mid-1970s in the Western world in general and in Australia in particular, we have seen, if not the death, at least the illness in ruling circles of some of the more admirable human virtues; namely, compassion, altruism, charity and tolerance. Their place has been taken by the worship of ruthlessness and selfishness under the guise that in this different environment that they are attempting to create, enterprise and initiative would the better flourish. One of the things that I think a progressive government has to take seriously into account is how do you create institutions in a society like ours – a small open, mixed capitalist economy – in which the more desirable and positive virtues of human nature may be given a go. That is one of the problems which I hope to discuss during the talk. I do not think I will be able to provide necessarily persuasive or simple answers, but it is something to which I think it is very necessary for us to address ourselves.

We could do a lot worse than following what Hugh Stretton said about simple visions and go back to another person who had visions which inspired generations; namely, Bertrand Russell. Bertrand Russell had a vision of:

> the world that we must seek, [a world] in which the creative spirit is alive, in which life is an adventure full of joy and hope based rather upon the impulse to construct than upon the desire to retain what we possess or to seize what is possessed by others. It must be a world in which affection has free play, in which love is purged of the instinct for domination, in which cruelty and envy have been dispelled by happiness and the unfettered development of all the instincts that build up life and fill it with mental delights.

I think that this is an extraordinarily useful starting point for Hugh Stretton's 'simple vision'. Russell added: 'Such a world is possible; it waits only for men to wish to create it.[3]

But when we come down to brass tacks, we start way behind scratch because we have witnessed over at least the last seven years some very disturbing events in our society which may have unfortunate long-run consequences. By this I mean that we have seen an increasing tendency for politicians to make short-run political gains without regard for the long-run consequences that they have for the tacit understandings and arrangements which are necessary in a society like ours in order to make it function effectively, with some hope of bringing about social justice and harmony between the different interest groups in society. I think that some of our leading politicians (it has to be said on both sides of the fence) have been very clever at seeing the short-run moves that they can make for their own political advantage but have not been so clever, indeed sometimes they have been very dense, in working out what the long-run consequences of those particular moves could be. I think that this was given a start by the way in which the Whitlam government was brought down, and it has been continued by events which have occurred since then. We are particularly unfortunate in Australia to have such a short time constitutionally between elections, especially given the complicated nature of economic processes that are at work in our society in these days; but, of course, we have made this a lot worse by insisting on having elections at much shorter intervals than the constitutional requirements stipulate.

In a way it was nice recently to see a letter in the Adelaide *Advertiser* commenting on Des Corcoran's abortive attempt to have an early election. The writer said that Des woke up one night and his wife said to him, 'Des, if you wish to be loved you'll have to have an election first,' and before he had worked out he had not heard aright, he had called one. I say this to the Adelaide people in the audience because if they have lived long enough to know what *The Advertiser* used to be like, they will know that ten years ago you could not have read *that* in its pages. There is a political moral to the story as well.

The point I want to make, however, is that when we think about economic policies, one of the legacies of Keynesianism – not so much Keynes's own writing but of the way in which Keynes has come down into the textbooks – has been, I believe, an excessive preoccupation with the short run. Partly a rather superficial reading of Keynes is to blame for this, partly Keynes himself is to blame for it, but more importantly, I think it is the way in which his message has been disseminated in the textbooks – with one notable exception, I have to say, looking at one of my co-authors in the audience. What I mean is the following: if we look back over the long haul of how political economy developed from the Physiocrats and Adam Smith on, one of the principal concepts that the original writers wrote about (and Marx wrote about them also) was what Smith called the 'centres of gravitation of the system'; namely, those fulcrums or magnets of the system which were brought about by sustained and dominant forces. Adam Smith himself used to distinguish between what he called 'natural prices', which were centres of gravitation, and market prices, which were the actual prices that were observed but which often departed from, in fact *usually* departed from, equality with the natural prices because they were affected by transitory and once-for-all factors like temporary gluts or temporary shortages in harvests. The point about these centres of gravitation was that they were exactly what they are called, centres of gravitation, positions towards which the economy would tend to go, and if there were departures from them, it was believed that there would be forces at work in the economy which would drive the economy back towards these particular positions. When Keynes came to write *The General Theory*, the particular centre of gravitation that he had in mind was one which he said had vanished from the consideration of economists for about a hundred years prior to the time of him writing. He said that if you looked in the writings of economists after the end of the debates between Malthus and Ricardo, you could not find an explicit theory of the level of activity and the level of employment as a whole, that in fact, an account of the forces which determined the level of activity and the level of employment as a whole was missing, and so it was his particular role (he was never a modest man) to provide what had been missing for over a hundred years.

Keynes argued that in a capitalist economy there was a centre of gravitation of employment and output as a whole, that it was not necessarily a full employment one, and therefore there was a case, as we know, for intervention in order to raise the level of output and employment. *The General Theory* revolves around this central idea. In writing it as he did, he laid great stress on the fact that the capital accumulation, the investment expenditure of businesspeople, would not only be one of the most volatile factors in the capitalist economy but also would tend to fluctuate round an average level, its own centre of gravitation, which itself usually was not sufficient to provide full employment for all those wishing to work and for the stock of capital goods in the economy as a whole. Therefore there was a role for intervention at the public level in order to try to do something about this. This has usually descended into the textbooks as being a theoretical argument for using government deficits and government spending, but if we look at what Keynes actually said, he also stressed that it might well be the role of government not so much to spend on its own accord as to try to influence the level and composition of spending by businesspeople on investment goods, because he regarded the way in which we decide on both the level and the composition of our stock of capital goods as not one of the greatest success stories, to put it mildly, of the way in which a capitalist economy functions. Indeed, he has a very entertaining chapter (based no doubt on his own experiences on the stock exchange) describing the irrationalities of using a stock exchange where speculation dominated enterprise as the means to decide how the savings of the community are to be used. He suggested that we should try to get businesspeople to do it right, but if they did not, then perhaps the government itself should think about the socialisation of investment decisions. This is not Lenin, this is not Stalin, it is not even some of our well-known Labor politicians, this is Keynes in 1936. The principal thrust of his book though was that there was a tendency to a deficiency of effective demand in the economy.

The wheel now has come full circle in discussions of economic theory and economic policy due to the influence of, first of all, Milton Friedman, who is the head of what James Tobin calls 'monetarism wave one' or 'mark one', and who has been succeeded by some of his own pupils and followers and colleagues, those whom Tobin calls 'monetarism mark two'[4] and who are known in the trade as 'the rational expectations school' or New Classical Macro-economists! Now Friedman's argument, put very briefly, is that in the long run a capitalist economy *is* self-correcting; or, at least, even if it is not, it self-corrects quicker than if you try to do something about it other than provide institutions which make it behave *as if* it were a competitive economy, and which allow the money supply to advance at a steady rate in order to cater for the growth in productivity. But he said it was an empirical question whether or not this came about. The rational expectations school has taken the argument one step further and has argued that not only is the natural resting place of a capitalist economy one where people are in their preferred positions but, on the whole, these are positions which are reached very quickly indeed. So the best model of our sort of an economy is to suppose that people have voluntarily reached a position which, given the constraints under which they operate, is one in which they find optimal and therefore stabilisation policy (but not policies like cutting minimum wages, or deregulating or increasing information, or retraining or relocating schemes; all these are part of their platform) is likely to do more harm than good because they believe that stabilisation policies are likely to take people away from their preferred positions.

Indeed, we have had a recent article by two members of this school on unemployment in Britain during the interwar years where in a footnote (at least they had the grace to put it in a footnote) they say that because of the level of unemployment benefits in Britain in the interwar years employers did the young of Britain a favour by giving them the sack so that they could take out the dole and that it was a voluntarily position which the unemployed took up.[5]

It is one of the ironies of modern economic theory that in the city of Liverpool in England where unemployment is on average somewhere up near 20 per cent and amongst black youths some extraordinarily higher figure, that the chief proponent of rational expectations in the UK, who stresses that if people are unemployed it is because of voluntary decisions, is the Professor of Economics at the University of Liverpool. All I can say is that it speaks volumes for the legendary tolerance of the British Isles that he has been allowed to lecture without someone coming in and at least throwing a blackboard duster at him. (That happened to me when I was at Melbourne University. I used to teach religious instruction at University High on behalf of the SCM. I threw a blackboard duster at a young man, and when I turned back to the board he threw it back at me. A lesser person would have been rather upset about this but I took both blackboard dusters, I gave one to him, I took the other one myself and I said, 'Now when I count to three, we will fire'. Of course, being young and inexperienced, he threw wildly as soon as 'three' was up – and missed. I, knowing that I had my reputation as a teacher in my hands, took very careful aim and hit him right behind the ear – not a very hard blow, of course, but nevertheless right behind the ear. That would have been a very successful ploy if only I'd been able to observe that the headmaster was watching the lot through the window.) As I say, it says much for the youth of Liverpool that they have not been in to take this professor on.

What comes out of the argument about the natural resting place of a capitalist economy is that there is a dividing line between those who believe something can be done about overall economic performance and those who think that if you do something, you can only make matters worse. Nevertheless, the second group do teach us a very important lesson, one which Maddock and Carter stress, and which is also stressed by another economist who is not favourable to Keynes's way of looking at things (Meltzer), which is that often economic processes take an enormous amount of time to work themselves out. In particular, it is very difficult to turn round habits which have taken a number of periods to form. Therefore, we should not expect miracles from economic policies; rather, we should frame policies which have a long period to run, with which people may become famliar. Indeed, policy should be made explicit so that people do become familiar with what it is that you are trying to do, and then you should hold onto these policies by and large, only making marginal changes as unexpected circumstances occur. Robert Eisner, who has courageously carried on the Keynesian debate against overwhelming odds on the American scene, has argued that if there is, as he believes, this long-run tendency to a lack of effective demand in the capitalist economy, then fiscal policies and monetary policies should not be designed for fine tuning, as it used to be fashionable to call it, but should be designed in such a way that over the long haul they give expansionary help to the level of activity and the rate of growth of the economy. This is a message which I think a progressive government should take to heart and one which I think we on the whole failed to learn in the hectic three years of the Whitlam government.

Now it was true that the Whitlam government was an extraordinarily unlucky government, because when it came in it tried first of all to restructure the economy. At the same time it was faced with the turn around, at the end of the long boom, in levels of activity of major parts of the economy as well as by the oil-price shock and the aftermath of the Vietnam war and its effect on the world money supply. Nevertheless, the essential message which we get from these speculations is one of designing policies which do have sustained effects and which slowly change people's attitudes and habits rather than hoping to bring them about in a twinkling of an eye or, at least, overnight. This is reinforced by the fact that when I said that one of the byproducts of Keynes's message was excessive preoccupation with the short run, there is also another thing which I think is a byproduct of Keynesianism, which we have not completely ground out of our way of thinking about the economy now. We have taken over from Keynes (and from the way in which Chicago economists think about the economy) an inappropriate model of the nature of price formation in our economy.

Keynes himself put into *The General Theory* a very simple Marshallian model of price formation by the impersonal forces of the market, using supply and demand curves, because I think he did not want to fight two revolutions at the same time. He was quite content to let the orthodox have their old-fashioned way of looking at price formation in order that he could tackle the problem of getting rid of massive unemployment. Increasingly, we have become aware that this is a model which will not do for modern capitalist economies – that there are large parts of them where discretion about the prices which you charge for your products and the prices which are charged for the services which people provide are not brought about by the impersonal forces of the market but are to a very considerable extent within the power of the people who are either providing the products or the services. The person who has stressed this in a most thorough way is the late Arthur Okun, who, sadly died far too young at the age fifty-one a couple of years ago. In his last book, *Prices and Quantities*[6] his major preoccupation was with the implications for economic policy of the fact that there are these segments of the economy where considerable discretion holds sway – where there are long-run norms which have been formed and which guide the setting of prices of either products or services. And he has argued, quite rightly, that the byproduct of this is that if you use blunt and crude weapons like contractionary monetary and fiscal policies to try and tackle things like inflation, you are going to have a very considerable impact on the employment of labour and of capital goods but only a very minor and very much spread-out impact on the rates of change of prices and wages. This is a lesson which we are learning only too painfully from the last seven years of the Australian scene, of the British scene, and of the American scene as well. What this left open for us to argue was, I think quite rightly, that we must supplement our conventional fiscal and monetary policies with the appropriate form of prices and incomes policy for the economy under consideration. There will be horses for courses.[7]

I was interested to see that Paddy McGuiness has at last come round to arguing that something like an incomes policy is necessary in the present setting if we are ever to make any progress in moving ourselves out of our present levels of unemployment and sluggish levels of activity. With typical Paddy panache, he has rubbished every incomes and prices policy that has ever been tried before and has put his money, as a good betting man, on the most theoretically logical but practically impossible one, the one that has been advocated by Abba Lerner.

Lerner exploits the notion that you want the monetary value of the gross national product to grow, such that all the growth is in output and none is in prices. You know that particular industries are going to grow faster than the average because they have good prospects and other industries are going to decline and therefore you give people chips which they can buy and sell according to what they believe their output and sales prospects are going to be. If they are believed to be profitable, they will buy them from people who do not believe that their prospects are likely to be profitable, the market will set the price and the end result will be the money gross national product expanding at a rate which provides for full employment. You will not be imposing a controlled prices and incomes policy, you will be using the carrot and stick incentives of market forces and market incentives in order to persuade people to act in a socially desirable way. Now, as I say, whether that is practical or not is a matter that has not yet been tried. There have been variants of these schemes suggested by various American economists including Tobin, Solow, Okun, and especially by Sidney Weintraub and Henry Wallich, whereby you give people incentives not to charge higher prices and not to acquiesce in higher increases in money-wages than are consistent with the overall rate of inflation which you think, given your current exchange rate, will still allow you to be competitive and maintain full employment.

These sorts of ideas ought to get a hearing and ought to be given a chance. It is very heartening to see that the Labor Party, in thinking its way through to the sort of economic policy that it is going to have, has made the restoration of full employment a primary plank, and also, at the same time, has accepted the notion of using an incomes and prices policy to have an effect on the prices and wages which are set by the discretionary sectors of our economy. These are to be coupled with the stimulus of fiscal and monetary policy which is intended to take us steadily but relatively slowly towards a fully employed position. This is a very sensible and realistic stance to take – and a courageous one because it is very difficult for a progressive party ever to talk about using any sort of wage restraint because people, especially wage-earners, understandably, immediately get up in arms about it, and they forget the distinction between money-wages, on the one hand, and real wages, on the other. Whenever I have talked about the need for wage restraint, I have always had in mind money-wage restraint in order that we could run the economy at a level of economic activity and at a rate of growth which allows at least for the maintenance of real wages and preferably and in most circumstances for a steady rate of increase in real wages.

But unless we can do this, the chance of getting back to full employment, particularly when we live in a world where we have contractionary policies being advocated and implemented, is a very remote one indeed. It still is an extraordinarily difficult problem to move out of step with the rest of the world, because when you are a small open economy you have the problem of what are you going to do about the balance of payments? People have addressed themselves to this problem; it is part of the tariff debate, and there are arguments in the community that we should be moving steadily towards reduction in our tariff levels. Interestingly enough, this is not only the province of the 'dries' in the Liberal and National Country Parties. It has been argued recently by a left-wing economist in the last issue of the *Journal of Australian Political Economy*[8] that raising tariffs and imposing import controls are not, on the whole, in the interest of the people they are supposed to help; namely, wage-earning groups who might otherwise be unemployed. It is argued in this recent article that tariffs mainly serve to preserve the profits of the industries which are most protected and at the same time to encourage the installation of machinery and methods of production which affect adversely the employment of labour. My own view has been that one should not go, at least in the short run, and particularly in a period of unemployment, for tariff cuts. What you should do is to sustain your existing level and take a leaf out of the experiences of our near neighbours, who, having kept their tariff structures, went all out for export drives, tailor-made exports for the countries who were to become their partners.

This case has been argued convincingly by Clive Edwards and it seems to me it is a very sensible political economy solution. It is sensible because it signals to Australian businesspeople that they should not waste their efforts and their initiative and their ideas in trying to lobby in Canberra for higher tariffs or higher quotas because they are not going to be forthcoming – you have signalled that you are not going to cut tariffs but you are certainly not going to raise them. Rather what they should be doing (and what businesspeople ought to be given the signal to do) is to go out and find where the most profitable markets are and to construct the products which are most acceptable in those particular markets. That seems to me to be a reasonable political solution, at least at the moment, to the problem of what to do about the tariffs. If in years to come we are successful in getting back to full employment and a reasonable rate of growth, we may be able to consider in a much more favourable climate the long-run advantages of lowering tariffs and diffusing the benefits amongst us as consumers. I mean, the terrible trouble about tariff cuts is that we all benefit marginally as consumers as we bedeck ourselves out in shoes that have come from abroad and so on, and those benefits may give us a marginal jump in our total utility, but this is hardly enough to set against the understandable agony of the people who are thrown out of work in a particular industry in a particular centre. Especially is this so in a country like Australia, where we are the size of the USA but where our centres of industry are spread around and where relocation and retraining is a very considerable job for which we have not set up a completely comprehensive or appropriate set of institutions.

In arguing the case for moving towards not only using fiscal and monetary policy but also an incomes policy which is suitable to our own society, I am glad to be joined by other economists who have long been, as they describe themselves, 'Lib–Lab', in the sense that they like to allow people to have freedom of choice as far as many of the commodities that they buy are concerned but they really have a great hatred of the distribution of property which is thrown up by the unfettered workings of a capitalist society. I have particularly in mind James Meade, who, in his Nobel Prize lecture,[9] suggested that we should use fiscal and monetary policies to affect the rate of growth of the money GNP and money-wages to affect employment, but that the *quid pro quo* for doing this should be a much more comprehensive attack on the distribution of property that is thrown up by the market. I think that the way in which we should attempt to get acceptance of money-wage restraint by wage-earning groups in particular is through the moves that are being made at the moment towards 'the social contract'. The social contract has to include not only comprehensive spending through the public sector on things which are of benefit in particular for low-income groups but also taxes of a form which do have a considerable impact on the distribution of property.

There is, of course, a major difficulty here, for unless the Commonwealth decides to take up the problem of death duties, there is really no way that any particular state government can move – as Mr Cain, admirable though his purpose was, recently found to his cost. He, with the aid of right-thinking unions, has not given a welcome to warships but he has had to scrap a very modest suggestion for the reintroduction of death duties. If he had had James Meade as his adviser, he would not have got away with that at all, because Meade's suggestions (in, for example, his *Intelligent Radical's Guide to Economic Policy*)[10] concerning what you ought to do about gifts, and what you ought to do about property, are extraordinarily radical. Meade rightly makes the point that if you are going to have a just and equitable society, you have to stop accumulation of property in the hands of particular groups and that the way to do that is to make us all start again from scratch after the previous generation has died. I think this is an admirable sentiment; I know it is not one that is particularly popular in the Labor Party at the moment because it is thought to be its death knell, but I think it is one that nevertheless has to be thought about or we will find ourselves in a position where we are not getting the necessary environment and necessary attitudes for consensus policies to be a possibility.

One of the things that I think all people who have thought about policy in an economy such as ours – and here I think especially of my old friend, the late Eric Russell, who always stressed this – is that you do not get effective economic policies accepted in a country like Australia unless you can bring about consensus policies so that people can see not only the sacrifices that they have to make themselves but also the benefits that they are going to get. One of the tragic by-products of the bouts of confrontation policies over the last seven years or so is that we are rapidly drying up those springs of goodwill from which consensus comes. I think that is a very serious thing, and I was comforted – well I was not exactly comforted but in one sense I was – to find that Thomas Balogh in his recent book, *The Irrelevance of Traditional Economics*,[11] argued that, in the UK anyway, they have moved themselves towards such a position that they might well have only one last chance to try and build up again pragmatic, consensus-based policies, such has been the confrontationist nature of the recent experiments with Thatcherism.

I mention these things because I think that people forget how very delicate and shallowly-rooted is the plant of democracy in a country like ours and the UK and that if you go about destroying these tacit understandings, you very quickly get people hankering for a so-called strong leader. I am not saying that we would get a neo-fascist state in Australia, because on the whole I do not believe that we would. (Our cadet corps are far too inefficient to produce the necessary material – after all, I was a cadet lieutenant myself once at the school I went to, and my most celebrated feat was to march the whole of my platoon into a wall because I forgot the order for change direction left.) But I can see that in other circumstances, for example in Italy, it would be possible for the reaction to the breakdown of consensus and the use of the present policies to lead to the emergence of neo-fascist regimes, which would be a detriment to us all.

So, I think that a necessary prerequisite for making a more just and equitable society in a country like Australia is to find some way of getting ourselves back to full employment, and in order to do that we have to use not only the traditional weapons but also we have to build on the institutions that we already have and reestablish an effective prices and incomes policy. I have always advocated that we should use the Arbitration Commission and indexation procedures. I think that it is significant, not because I advocated it, but because the present government and its advisers have thought them not to be effective, that we have seen a concerted effort to downgrade their influence and to move away from using such institutions and depend instead on measures which come directly through the Treasury. Now, those sorts of measures have been described by Balogh very colourfully, but I think with a considerable element of truth, as 'the incomes policy of Karl Marx'. Why the incomes policy of Karl Marx? Well, Balogh says that by deliberately setting out to base the viability of the capitalist system on the maintenance of a large industrial reserve army, monetarists may validate Marx's analysis. I think that there is a tremendous amount of truth in that. Beneath the guise of using contractionary policies, what we have really been seeing is an attempt to redress the change in the balance of power which occurred during the twenty or twenty-five years of virtually sustained full employment and growth whereby power went much more to labour and much less to capital. What we see now is an attempt to swing that around. In the Australian case it has been not only an internal fight between the capitalist class and the wage-earning groups, it also has been an attempt to signal to overseas investors that we now have a quiescent and cowed labour force which makes Australia a good place in which to invest. It also has been a kind of incomes policy. The policy envisaged an average rate of money-wage increases which would give us a price level (and a rate of increase of the price level) which still left us competitive, while at the same time allowing money-wages in the expanding areas to go up in order to attract labour there, this to be counterbalanced by either falling or very slowly increasing money-wages in the depressed or declining industries as a result of the higher levels of unemployment.

I do not think this has been successful, because I do not think this is the way in which the Australian labour market necessarily works. I also do not think it has been successful, because it ignores one of the basic questions which I mentioned at the start of my lecture; namely, that not only one of the most volatile forces at work in the economy but also one which tends to run on average at a level which is not sufficient to maintain full employment, is the level of capital accumulation by private businesspeople. There is nothing like years of sustained failure of sales to dampen what Keynes called the animal spirits of businesspeople. While they may be slowly having an effect on the rate of increase of money-wages, they are simultaneously having a disastrous effect on the confidence and the ability of business people to invest at a rate which not only raises productivity but also gives a level of activity which is a satisfactory one in a capitalist economy.

If we decide that either as a result of what we have done in the past, or for policy reasons, a progressive government ought to have something much more to say about both the rate and the composition of accumulation of capital goods, this immediately brings into focus whether we should put nationalisation back on the agenda. When I go back to my first year at Melbourne University, one of the things that really led me towards thinking about socialism was a description of how oil wells were developed on the Californian oilfields by unfettered private enterprise. The wells were put down so close to one another that they let the gas out and so, much oil which otherwise could have been taken out was lost forever just because the wells were too close together. It seemed to me that this was a very irrational way both to use and to start developing resources which were meant to be used, not only by this generation but by future generations as well. In other words, the horizon for the rational use of oil seemed to me to be much longer than the horizon of any one particular person developing it, and therefore it seemed to me that we ought to develop institutions which allow us to take much longer horizons in planning the development of resources which are vital to the community as a whole, not only the current generation but future generations as well. Now, of course, one of the things that has come out of our experience with nationalised industries is that they also are subject to the whims of politicians, if not to the whims of businesspeople, and that politicians themselves have short-run constraints imposed on them by the distances that they have between elections. Therefore their horizons may often be even shorter than those of the private businesspeople who were thinking about developing the resources, and this is one of the things which has led, I think, to disillusionment with using the public sector and to a movement back to using the market and market signals as the means for developing our resources.

I have to admit at least the partial validity of such an argument, so I now would argue that if we are considering bringing nationalisation back for key industries in our economy, supposing for a moment the constitutional puzzle to be solvable, we would have to do so within a context of at least two major reforms. One is that their managers would have to be given instructions about the time horizon that they were to bear in mind and also about the overall pattern of development of the economy that the government explicitly had set out. The other thing is (and this is an aspect of our experience of the industrial relations of nationalised industries) that there is no point nationalising industries and leaving intact the same hierarchical internal structures as those which traditionally have been used in private enterprise. We now know that the wage-earners become just as browned off with socialised managers as they are with private ones. So if nationalisation is to be put back on the agenda, it will have to be coupled with reforms of the hierarchical structures that are contained within the management structure. I do not pretend to have any profound or wise words on the details, but I do put this forward as a general principle which would have to be considered.

The final major point that I would like to make and which I think interventionists such as myself seriously have to try to think about, has to do with the hierarchical structures of modern civil services. It seems to me that they are such that while we can always ensure that highly intelligent people get to the top in the key decision-making positions, we cannot always be sure that the people who do that also have other desirable characteristics such as altruism and compassion and tolerance. This is not meant to be a criticism of any particular individuals, it is a criticism of the structure of the system; indeed, it is one of the problems of bureaucratic structures, whether they be in the public sector or in the private sector. Therefore, one of the major things which a progressive government will have to look at is how *do* you overcome this puzzle so that when you come in with coherent explicit plans of your own, you can make sure that they are implemented at key points without being frustrated by people who think that they are not necessarily practical or workable – or desirable. This is a major problem and I think it is one of the reasons why there has been considerable disillusionment with the role of the public sector and the revolt against big government, both of which have been features of modern capitalist economies in the last five to ten years. It is a major puzzle and a major problem.

I entitled this lecture 'Making Socialism in Your Own Country' and I am afraid that I have had to spend a lot of time talking about the things that I suppose relatively I know best; that is, about economic theory and economic policy. Nevertheless, I want to say in conclusion that I have tried to keep in mind that vision of a new world which I quoted from Bertrand Russell. While I have at times been disillusioned and distressed about the possibility of bringing about a better society, yet I think that we always have to keep on going, and I do not think that people who call themselves socialists should be ashamed of it; they should not allow 'socialism' to be treated as a dirty word, which is the custom in the media and in the more conservative parts of Australian politics. I personally like to keep in mind – because I think it links onto the vision that Russell put before us – a memory from the days of antiwar protests during the Vietnam war. I remember that we had a march through Adelaide one evening (there is nothing like being an antiwar protestor to get to know your city, particularly the byways and highways when you are trying to get away). This particular march had been busted up, but we had regrouped on the steps of Parliament House. There, we had the long-playing record of Woodstock, itself a quite exceptional happening, noted for some very memorable songs. As the twilight came down in Adelaide, there was a group of women dressed in the long flowing dresses that they wore in those days, dancing to the music of Woodstock in front of the pillars of Parliament House in Adelaide. And I thought as I watched those women dancing that here at least was a generation who would not accept the tired old jingoistic statements that we have been brought up on, who would really believe in making a better and more noble and greater world than we ourselves had experienced. Well, I suppose that was at the beginning of the 1970s when people still had hope, and I suppose after the reaction and the outburst of jingoism in the UK during the recent Falklands War, for example, we might, perhaps, discount some of our hopes for the future. Nevertheless, I take comfort in at least two things. One is that those particular people are still around, they have kept their ideals and have tried to implement them in practice. Second, the Archbishop of Canterbury preached at the end of the Falklands war one of few really Christian sermons – for which he was bucketed in no uncertain terms by both the British Prime Minister and the Tory politicians and Tory press. Well, that is as it should be – Archbishops of Canterbury ought to be bucketted by such groups – I mean the terrible thing is that they have not been more often. Yet all he did was to say that war was a confession of failure and that in the aftermath of war we should remember the parents, the spouses and the friends of all the soldiers on both sides who had fallen. I thought that was a pretty sensible and inspiring thing to say, and indeed I wrote him a letter which said in part that I would be proud to live in a country which had him as the spiritual leader. Joan thinks that MI5 will open it and that when Mrs Thatcher comes to renew my 12-months work-permit this time next year I may well be asked to leave. If I am, I can see at least two Vice-Chancellors[12] in the audience and since I am the risk-taker while I am away, I hope that there at least will be a job of picking up leaves round the ANU campus for me to take on.

Thank you very much.

Notes

1. John Langmore, 'An Economic Strategy for a Labor Government', *Journal of Australian Political Economy*, nos. 12–13 (June 1982), 37.
2. As quoted by Joan Robinson in her splendid 1981 Tanner Lectures 'The Arms Race', in Sterling M. McMurrin (ed.), *The Tanner Lectures on Human Values*, III, 1982 (University of Utah Press, Cambridge University Press, 1982).
3. Bertrand Russell, *Roads to Freedom: Anarchism and Syndicalism* (London: Allen & Unwin, 1919), 210, quoted in Noam Chomsky, *Problems of Knowledge and Freedom*, The Russell Lectures, 1971 (London: Fontana, 1972), 10–11.

4. Rodney Maddock and Michael Carter recently immortalised them, fortunately and unfortunately – I mean, fortunately for Maddock and Carter and unfortunately for the others – in their recent paper 'A Child's Guide to Rational Expectations', *Journal of Economic Literature*, vol. XX (March 1982), 39–51.
5. Daniel K. Benjamin and Levis A. Kochin, 'Unemployment and Unemployment Benefits in Twentieth-Century Britain: A Reply to Our Critics', *Journal of Political Economy*, vol. 90, no. 4 (April 1982), 412–13.
6. Arthur M. Okun, *Prices and Quantities: A Macroeconomic Analysis* (Oxford: Basil Blackwell, 1981).
7. I do not need to explain to an Australian audience what a horse for a course is, but I have had terrible trouble with Italian audiences on this, because they are not as keen on horses as we are, or on the races. I nearly was lynched once when interpreting this phrase, because I was explaining how at Randwick the horses went round one way and at Flemington they went round the other way, and I got them mixed up. You know, I had Randwick going round the wrong way and Flemington going round the wrong way. There were some Australians in the audience, and I was lucky to escape with my life. So I'm not so willing to say which way they go round; I will just say that you have to use horses for courses policies for the various economies with which you are dealing.
8. David Peetz, 'Protection and the Labor Movement', *Journal of Australian Political Economy*, no. 12/13 (June 1982).
9. James Meade, 'The Meaning of "Internal Balance"', *Economic Journal*, vol. 88 (September 1978), 423–35.
10. James Meade, *The Intelligent Radical's Guide to Economic Policy: The Mixed Economy* (London: Allen & Unwin, 1975).
11. Thomas Balogh, *The Irrelevance of Conventional Economics* (London: Weidenfeld & Nicolson, 1982).
12. There were in fact three!

16
Markets, Madness and a Middle Way*

This essay is based on the Second Donald Horne Address which I gave in Melbourne in February 1992, just before the Australian Prime Minister 'insulted' the Queen, declared Australia a potential Republic, and did a U-turn on economic policy. I leave it to others to discern the nature of cause and effect.

I belong to the generation of Australians who, on the whole, did not join the Communist Party (CP) but who did join the Australian Labor Party (ALP) – and the Student Christian Movement! Some of my best friends, though, the people I most admire (who were/are ten or more years older than me) were passionate idealists, who *did* join the CP, only eventually to be bitterly disillusioned by Hungary in 1956 and then Khrushchev's revelations concerning the Stalin era. So when the momentous events of the late 1980s occurred in Eastern Europe, I was sickened by the ridiculous euphoria, the nauseating complacency, and self-satisfaction which emerged in conservative quarters in Western societies. For while I had *never* been an admirer of the authoritarian, cruel, inefficient and often corrupt regimes that were toppled, yet, by the same token, it could not be said that the performance of the economies of the

---

* Originally published in *The Cambridge Review*, February 1993, 40–5.

In writing the Address I have been very greatly helped and encouraged by comments from Keith Abbott, Paul Aiello, Willy Brown, Ha-Joon Chang, Ian DuQuesnay, Peter Groenewegen, Joan Harcourt, Tim Harcourt, Wendy Harcourt, Alan Hughes, Barry Hughes, Prue Kerr, John Langmore, Gavin Mackenzie, Bruce McFarlane, Peter Nolan, Steve Pratten, Ken Rivett, Bob Rowthorn, Claudio Sardoni, Ajit Singh, Hugh Stretton, Tim Stretton and David Vines. Of course, I alone am responsible for the views expressed.

democratic capitalist West over the last twenty years or so was (or is) anything to write home about either. To have destroyed full employment as a goal (let alone the norm it had become), to have greatly increased the inequality of the distribution of income and of property, to have created an underclass and destroyed the dignity, self-respect and hope of large numbers of their citizens, to have substituted ridiculous rewards for paper shuffling for just rewards for making real and useful things, are hardly achievements of which any society could be proud. Although Peter Nolan reminds me that the standards of living of many of those *in work* in most of these economies over this period *did* rise at a healthy rate, I may add that this was partly due to unacceptable redistributions, to eating the seed-corn of future generations and, in the case of the UK, to squandering the benefits of North Sea oil.

How are we to understand this experience? Much may be traced to an uncritical acceptance of the dominance and the alleged superiority of 'getting back to the magic of the market'. However, the choice is not between purely command or centrally planned economies, on the one hand, and free market systems, on the other. Rather, there is a vital place for a middle way which may contribute to the discussion concerning the creation of just and equitable societies, the ultimate aim of those of us who remain democratic socialists. In this discussion we shall need to be guided by people with warm hearts and cool heads, with fertile minds that are not hidebound by dogma or received theory and who are aware of the importance of sociological attitudes and characteristics, of historical events, and of inherited institutions in the creation of explanations and policies. Here, I have in mind my Australian mentors, the late Eric Russell and Hugh Stretton and, outside Australia, Noam Chomsky, John Kenneth Galbraith and, alas, all now dead, Maurice Dobb, Nicholas Kaldor, Michal Kalecki, Joan Robinson, Piero Sraffa and, of course, John Maynard Keynes. For 'markets' are not 'magic', not simple, not monoliths, and history plays its own role in how we understand them.

Adam Smith is frequently invoked as the patron saint of competitive markets, often by people who have never read *The Wealth of Nations* (*WN*) and have never heard of *The Theory of Moral Sentiments* (*TMS*). Yet Smith himself regarded the *TMS* as complementary to and the equal of the *WN*. Smith believed in a natural order of morality; that '... man was endowed with the moral sentiments which [made] society possible' (Joan Robinson, *Collected Economic Papers* (*CEP*), *V*, 1979,

46–7). The thrust of the argument of the *TMS* is the need to design institutions which allow altruism – 'sympathy' – to prevail. Only then would it be desirable and effective to dismantle the overgrown, overblown bureaucratic regulations and monopolies of the Mercantalist period and allow the instinct of self-interest, guided by the invisible hand, to operate in an environment of vigorous dynamic competition. Such an environment would provide growth and promise a distribution of the product between the main classes of society which, in turn, would be favourable to this growth continuing. Smith approved of the government providing comprehensive and efficient infrastructures for society and a just and efficient taxation system for society's citizens. In his wisdom, Smith recognised that one of the essential conditions for competitive markets to function in a 'socially desirable' manner was that economic and political power should be widely diffused so that consumer and producer, employer and employee, would meet as equals – and pretty powerless equals at that – when products and services were exchanged. This notion has been formalised in modern economic theory in the concept of price-taking as opposed to price-making behaviour. With the latter, persons have some, often a lot of, discretion about the prices they charge for their products and/or services. Smith also had no illusions about what anti-social practices citizens could get up to if they had power, nor about how destructive and alienating free-rein competitive, industrial production of the sort immortalised by Charlie Chaplin in *Modern Times* would be for those unfortunate workers inescapably involved in it.

Leon Walras, another great economist whose name is invoked as an exponent of the virtues of free markets, in fact wanted land and key durable capital goods to be nationalised. He tried to show that by using competitive markets for all remaining economic activities, there could be brought about a socially desirable and *sustainable* general equilibrium of purchases, sales *and* distribution of income and property. So at least two of the patron saints of 'magical markets' turn out to be closet Bolshies!

Moreover, modern theory has gone on to lay down very stringent conditions which have to be satisfied before it can be claimed, even in theory, that the market outcome is socially desirable. Of course, it must be said immediately – and this is the core of the argument of the serious pro-marketeers – that it is a *non sequitur* to go from establishing that there may be, in the fashionable jargon, market failures immediately to claiming that therefore government intervention will make things better. It may well be that, in an imperfect world, the market failure outcome is nevertheless the best we can hope for, especially if a huge weight is put on the absolute desirability of individual freedom. This is the philosophical position of that most profound proponent of modern liberal thought, the late Friedrich Hayek. With this proviso, let us now look at the commonsense meaning of some of the conditions which have to be met in order for markets to do their thing.

The first is that actual prices of products should be a true measure both of *social* costs of the resources used to create them and of the satisfaction which their use is expected to bring to their purchasers. That is why Smithian price-takers are needed. Producers can then match their costs to externally given standards which simultaneously signal to purchasers the terms on which they can expect to achieve satisfaction. This requires that prices, most of the time, should be such that what is voluntarily demanded is equal to what is voluntarily supplied. This in turn requires that flows of purchases and flows of supplies in markets should dominate the setting of prices. Inventories, though important for smooth production and sales, nevertheless need to play a subsidiary role in the determination of actual prices. Moreover, if current prices are *not* achieving this match, they must directly or indirectly give out signals which encourage measures to be taken which will quickly achieve such a match, often a very tall order indeed in many important markets.

In fact, this brings out the big difference between vigorous free marketeers and the sceptics. The former think of individual markets, or even whole economic systems, as wolf packs running along smoothly. If, per chance, one or more wolves get ahead or fall behind, forces come quickly into play which return them to the pack. The latter group argue that if the breakaways get ahead, or fall behind, the forces which come into play are much more likely to allow them to get further and further ahead (or fall further and further behind), at least for long stretches of time. Belief in the efficacy and equity of markets as institutions is fundamentally affected by which scenario is believed to be true of the 'real world', as we economists lovingly like to call that which many non-economists may feel we have never experienced. It also has to be supposed that prices act solely as rationing devices. That is to say, nothing else may be deduced from the price of a good or service about its qualities other than its relative scarcity or abundance. Modern work suggests that the demand and supply of labour services, and of credit, do not set up prices with this required characteristic.

If demands are dominated, not by expected satisfaction but by guesses about what prices may be in the future, so that a large element of speculation is present in the formation of prices; and if supplies are offered not in response to perceived costs but in anticipation of future movements of prices (or of other people's expected anticipations of such movements); *then* the ensuing prices which are set may bear no systematic or reliable relationship to the real economic factors of the regular economic activity which prices ought to reflect. And all this is independent of whether power is diffused equally on both sides of the market, or whether it is concentrated in the hands of either buyers, or sellers, or both.

To sum up the argument thus far: if we want markets to work well, we must beware of situations where stocks dominate flows; speculation dominates enterprise or real economic factors; power is not evenly diffused; prices give out complex signals; and processes are cumulative rather than quickly equilibrating.

What then of plans, their virtues and limitations? By plans, I have in mind conscious direction – usually from the centre, often in great detail and sometimes dominated by quantities alone – of much of the economic life of a nation. Here we must distinguish between the intensity and comprehensiveness of planning that *may* be suitable for developing countries, on the one hand, and more advanced countries with different histories, on the other. I include in the first category the alternative scenarios that could have been played out in Poland, Hungary and so on after the Second World War if genuinely democratic socialist governments had been in charge rather than the, often externally imposed, authoritarian Stalinist regimes of fact. We may lay down some very general propositions which are relevant for both sets of societies, before we discuss where, on a whole spectrum of choices, it may be best for a particular society to be.

The first proposition is that the overall workings of economies are *not* just the sum of their parts but may have independent lives of their own, and often unsatisfactory ones at that. It follows that even if market solutions are best for some of the individual parts in isolation, there is still a case for conscious guidance and direction of the broad compositions and levels of overall activity. Thus, had Kalecki's ideas on planning been accepted in Poland when he returned there in the

1950s, we would have seen a society where overall consumption levels per person could have risen gently year by year – there would have been jam today rather than in a forever-postponed tomorrow. In addition, much of the detailed components of consumption production would increasingly have been left to small private businesses, with prices set by market forces; even so, a minimum standard of essential social consumption would have been provided through the State with controlled prices set up by turnover taxes on costs. Full employment would have been an overriding aim so that the portion of the workforce which was not engaged in the production of consumption goods and net exports would have been available for the production of capital goods. Here, the State would have given overall guidance, as well as developing rational investment criteria which individual managers of enterprises would have been urged to follow. Another overriding constraint would have been foreign exchange reserves and earnings, so that the composition of output between net exports, consumption, and investment would again have been a result of conscious decisions. The overall growth rate of the economy would have emerged as a consequence of these interrelated decisions and actions. Within such a framework individual citizens would have had considerable freedom of action with regard to both their consumption behaviour and what they chose to work at – the sticks and carrots of the overall plan could have been manipulated so as to secure the appropriate numbers within each relevant group. In this way, Big Brother would not have run people's lives or decided *in detail* what was good for them, yet the overall performance of the society would nevertheless have been subject to continuous conscious direction.

I do not wish to minimise the possibilities for corruption and the emergence of undue privilege, but with properly democratic decision procedures, checks and balances, and with suitable taxes, it should have been possible in principle to have produced a relatively egalitarian and equitable society. Certainly it would have been worth trying – and it still is – rather than creating huge levels of unemployment, great cuts in the living standards of ordinary citizens, and lands safe for spivs alone, as we now see emerging in these countries, and as Mrs Thatcher's Government had ensured in the UK several years beforehand! Some variant on the above scenario would, I suggest, hold out far more hope for many of the Eastern European countries struggling to come to grips with the collapse of their former regimes than the rather mindless rush for 'free' markets that we are in fact witnessing, with prices allowed a free for all, little or no protection or direction, and little attempt systematically to build up infrastructures for both production and distribution, and create appropriate institutions, including the legel framework.

Let me take Australia as an example. At the beginning of the 1980s Australia put two separate bits of lead in its saddle bags, as it were, by deciding to have a freely-floating currency and a deregulated financial system. Australia was not alone in doing this and probably could not avoid doing so. The important thing, then, is to understand the consequences. Australia needed and needs a considerable amount of restructuring of its industries. Its traditional export products have not only faced secularly declining demands over the last decade or so, but, for much of the period, demand has been pushed below trend by shorter-term cyclical demand deficiencies. This is one of the reasons for the horrendous state of its current account at the moment. Australia did not have anything like the cushion of North Sea oil to give it time and breathing space. Not that Britain took advantage of the cushion; much of it was dissipated in a consumption expenditure, import spree by those made richer by Mrs T's income-tax cuts.

To meet the adverse change in its economic position Australia needed to get its domestic cost levels under control, both in the tradeables sector and, as equity and efficiency combined demanded, in the non-tradeables sector as well. One aspect of this was the implementation of the Accord, a splendid example of conscious and cooperative planning which drew on tried and tested institutions created by Australia's past history and by an appeal to cooperation from the main classes in society, not only amongst themselves, but with the Government as well. For this endeavour I think the wage-earning groups of Australia deserve great praise. Certainly the Accord served to reduce inflationary pressures considerably and allowed employment to grow and unemployment to fall from the unacceptable levels of the early 1980s. Moreover, the employment that was created contained a greater proportion of full-time jobs for males than virtually any other OECD country over the same period. In principle, part-time employment must be approved of for its ability to offer variety and expand choice for all citizens; but to raise employment by such opportunities alone is neither balanced, nor socially healthy. For such jobs are likely to be both badly paid and associated with poor working conditions. The Accord also helped to create the potential surplus for the business classes and the governments combined to do their part with private investment and the provision of public infrastructure. That, by and large, this did not occur is not the fault of the Australian wage-earners.

There are a number of reasons why. A freely floating exchange rate system and a deregulated financial system mean that neither the exchange rate nor the pattern of rates of interest and prices of financial and other assets that prevail reflect underlying economic realities or socially desirable levels. First, interest rates as a dominant tool of policy, in the UK John Major's and Norman Lamont's single golf club: Dennis Robertson once said, apropos the bank rate in the UK, that though it had been called a beautiful and delicate instrument, it was in fact a coarse and blunt one, that its effects could be both unpredictable and often undesirable. I argued earlier that markets only work well when flows dominate and speculative activity is relatively absent. Neither of these conditions is satisfied in these two particular sets of markets.

Financial markets *par excellence* are characterised by huge stocks of existing assets relative to new flows, so that the former dominate the prices which are set daily in order to persuade domestic and overseas people voluntarily to hold the existing supplies. This would not matter that much if the bulk of the holders were looking to underlying economic realities, when deciding what to hold. But if we have a position where, as Keynes once put it, 'enterprise becomes the bubble on a whirlpool of speculation [so that] the capital development of a country becomes a by-product of the activities of a casino, the job is likely to be ill-done' (*The General Theory*, 1936: 159). For the patterns of interest rates and prices of financial assets, and the exchange rates which keep overseas holders in particular happy, may well not be the levels which are consistent with the rate of domestic investment spending, both public and private, that may be needed to bring about the desired restructuring and provide the proper level of activity and employment overall, and with which is associated a suitable supply of exports and demand for imports. In fact, hard-nosed financial analysts in the USA have recently rediscovered Keynes's liquidity preference theory of the rate of interest and his conjecture concerning a 'liquidity trap' level of the rate of interest. They claim to have discovered such a level in the USA – and they have praised Keynes for it. Keynes argued that the pattern of interest rates is fundamentally a conventional one, determined by what people, for all sorts of reasons, think are appropriate or at least sustainable patterns and levels. Yet for the economy to be able to function satisfactorily, such levels may, in fact, be quite 'wrong'.

Implicit in the case for a floating exchange rate was not only a relatively minor and beneficial role for speculative activity but also an inference that there *was* a stable sustainable long-term exchange rate out there waiting to be found. This supposed that countries in their international relationships with each other were akin to the wolf pack which moved steadily along in unison, with any laggards or accelerators quickly induced to return to the fold. But if the other analogy is the correct one, a floating exchange-rate system combined with a deregulated financial market provides a speculator's delight and a policy-maker's and a serious industrialist's nightmare.

There is another, rather neglected, aspect of the 'freeing' of financial markets in the 1980s, not only in Australia but worldwide. In earlier decades, and in the last century, spending by capitalists was ultimately limited by their access to finance and spending by wage-and salary-earners by their incomes. The observed fluctuations in output and employment over the cycle thus originated in spending by capitalists on investment goods because ease of finance and optimism of long-term expectations, and tightness of finance and pessimism of expectations, tended to move in tandem. By contrast, because the spending of the other groups was limited by income and because changes in income affected saving as well as consumption, consumption spending tended to be a much more stable and predictable component of total national spending. This traditional feature of capitalism has now been all but swept away by the deregulation of financial markets and the consequent huge expansion of credit facilities for all. The greatly increased amplitude of fluctuations in spending, and the increased length of slumps, are its consequence. So, ironically, a byproduct of the attempt to enhance the freedom of action of all citizens by allowing through credit facilities a closer match of lifetime needs and lifetime resources than the pattern of income receipts alone makes possible, has been to accentuate the inherent cyclical fluctuations of capitalist economies which formerly were due to the spending behaviour of the capitalist class alone. For now the economic activities of our citizens, our enterprises, and our country are vitally affected by their respective debt to income ratios, and by changes in them, as well as by the incomes themselves.

Associated with this emphasis on the effects of wealth to income ratios and their changes, is the distortion of the uses to which fundamental commodities may be put. The housing market illustrates this. What guided it was the desire for shelter with security, so that the purchase of these services was a long-term, serious matter for both the householders and the providers of them. One of the byproducts of deregulated financial services and the huge flows of short-term funds in and out of Australia has been that land and houses have often come to be regarded as commodities suitable for speculation in, with hunches backed up by borrowing, and dependence on rising markets lasting long enough to allow the shrewd speculator to get in and out. Prices have come no longer to reflect the provision of shelter services but rather the feverish activity of speculators trying to anticipate what the average person thinks will happen – and beat them to it. The same phenomenon may be seen in the over-provision of the services of office blocks in Australia's major cities in which resources that would have been more usefully allocated to other investment activity have gone instead into over-provision of office space. This is a financial disaster for lender and borrower alike; it is also a disaster for the medium-term future of these inner cities which face the prospect of becoming the commercial deserts so familiar in many US cities and towns. Similar phenomena may be witnessed in the spate of takeover raids and mergers for quick gains (and huge losses) which has characterised much of the so-called entrepreneurial activity of the 1980s.

In the old days, when we were allowed to talk about Marx and even admit that, however utopian the old buffer may have been about what a socialist society would and should be like, he certainly understood capitalism very well indeed, we used also to talk about how finance and industrial capital needed to advance in tandem in order for the system to work tolerably well. If one came to dominate the other, and especially if finance capital were to get on top, the ingredients of crisis were readily sown. (Ha-Joon Chang reminds me that in some successful developing countries, for example, South Korea or Taiwan, industrial capital led and finance capital was often owned and always heavily controlled by the State.) It is this phenomenon that we have been witnessing, not only in Australia but in much of the rest of the world, including the conditions which the IMF and the World Bank have been laying down in developing countries. I often think that banks and other financial intermediaries, in their eagerness to respond to the vigorous winds of competition, forget a number of simple but profound truths that came to us from Alfred Marshall in particular. It was he who emphasised in economic theory the important distinction between the short period and the long period. Those whose job it is to advance or withdraw credit need especially to have this distinction at the forefront of their minds. It should have a sobering effect on the tendency, otherwise, for them too often to be swept away by bouts of cumulative optimism and even recklessness in their lending at particular times, and, perhaps even more disastrously, to suffer bouts of cumulative and increasing pessimism and depression at others, so that they needlessly dry up the flow of lending just when it may be most needed.

The Marshallian distinction which is relevant here is that the appraiser of a potential borrower should give much more stress to long-term viability than to very immediate positions, especially with regard to current cash flow. If medium to long-term prospects are encouraging, then any immediate difficulties should be taken on board and seen through by creditors. Now, obviously, this has to be an overall principle – no one creditor can be expected or able to flow against the tide – but if it were to be articulated by for example, Australia's central bank and by the government loudly, clearly and frequently, the financial sector would be given a very clear and sensible lead. No doubt I shall be told that this is already well known and is acted upon. All I can say is that the evidence from Australia and other economies does not completely persuade me that it is not worthwhile stating the principle again.

Another consequence of an undue concentration on the provision of services of financial capital is that reward structures and returns tend to get seriously out of line with their counterparts in industry and the public services, a classic case of perfectly reasonable private self-interest and response *not* leading to desirable social outcomes. Part of the reason for the failure adequately to restructure through sustained investment expenditure must surely be due to the irresistible signals which led many of the most energetic and best workers to work, and risk-takers to operate, in the financial sector.

I have often referred in my writings to the difficulty of designing hierarchies in bureaucracies which ensure that persons with more attributes than just high intelligence and great ambition emerge in key decision-making positions. And I am well aware of the need to think through how to provide effective safeguards against corruption and crime in key parts of both the private and public sectors as a result of the damaging episodes that have been revealed in public life in recent years.

But as there have been many other voices willing and able to expound those themes, I want instead to sound a few warnings. There are some activities and aspects of life where markets, accounting and business procedures are appropriate and others where they are not. A universal application of them can have disastrous consequences. I always remember one of my earliest teachers saying that sometimes a lack of efficiency, in a business sense, may be the necessary price to pay for a selfless uncorrupt public service. And I often think that the zeal with which means have been designed to bring accountability and efficiency into higher education, for example, to flush out the inevitable minority of those who, when left to their own self-discipline, do not properly fulfill their obligations, may be in great danger of destroying the very environment that is necessary for first-class creative teaching and research to occur in the first place. This is a particular example of a general tendency which could be applied equally to the attitude shown, both in Australia and the UK, to recipients of unemployment and other social service payments in periods, moreover, when contractionary unemployment producing policies have been deliberately used to 'tackle' inflation. As a counter-weight, may I in passing applaud the imaginative idea of a graduate tax to help finance tertiary education? The scheme reflects a sympathetic awareness of different social attitudes to borrowing. It removes, at one stroke, what otherwise would have been 'barriers to entry' to those we would most like to have access to tertiary education.

An undue dependence on markets for organising all activities may have unexpected consequences which are not necessarily desirable. The gist of this has recently been put very well by the American economist, Samuel Bowles. He quotes James Buchanan's description of a purchase of fruit at 'a roadside stand outside Blacksburg'. Neither of the persons concerned had any particular interest in the well-being of the other but they 'were able to ... transact exchanges efficiently because both parties agree on the property rights relevant to them'. This creates, says Bowles, 'a psychological environment of anonymity, indifference to others, mobility, lack of commitment, autonomy'. He concludes: 'We learn to function in these environments, and in so doing become someone we might not have become in a different setting' (*Challenge*, July/August 1991: 13). I found this described succinctly my impressions of the profound changes that have occurred in the UK, the USA and Australia over the past fiften years or so.

Commentators, the capitalist world over, are belatedly rediscovering the virtues of fiscal policy, both for its effects on longer-term developments, including equitable distributions of income and property, and its impact on short-term activity and employment. Writing in, of all places, *The New Republic* (23–30 December 1991: 20–21), Paul Krugman has made some 'modest proposals' for the USA. He cited the appalling deficiencies in education, housing, medical care and transport facilities, deficiencies that nevertheless could be removed by the still richest country in the world if only its leaders and citizens had the public and private will to do so.

One of the crucial lessons that the Monetarists taught us is that the economy should not be viewed as a mechanical tap which can be turned on and off at will. Rather, we need always to have in mind the need to create a relatively stable and dependable environment in which those 'animal spirits' of our business people (which cannot be bottled, as Trevor Swan once put it), may be nurtured and enhanced and the longer-term persistent and dominant forces at work in healthy, competitive (in the right place) societies may be given a chance to work themselves out effectively. This is what I think Keynes meant in his posthumously published paper in the *Economic Journal* in 1946. In it he quoted from his last speech to the House of Lords: 'Here is an attempt to use what we have learnt from modern experience and modern analysis, not to defeat, but to implement the wisdom of Adam Smith' (*CW*, Vol. XXVII, 1980: 445). (Keynes literally killed himself in his efforts to get the UK through the war *and* create appropriate international institutions for the postwar world.)

One awful consequence of the policies of the late 1970s and 1980s has been to create not only haves and have nots but also a third category of have-lots (though, as we have recently seen, this may not be a permanent feature of the position of any one member of this group). It does not constitute the politics and economics of envy, nor a desire inevitably to cut down tall poppies, to be scandalised by the ostentatious display of great wealth and the ruthless use of power by a

Robert Maxwell. Not that 'pinching the pension fund' for your own use is confined to Maxwell and the UK (though his performance is the most spectacular example of it).

Something must also be said in this context about immigration and attitudes to immigrants. The most horrible potential scenarios are currently threatening to emerge in Europe, for example, as a result of the sustained and intolerably high levels of unemployment in Western Europe and the collapse of the Communist regimes in what used to be the USSR, and in Eastern Europe. The views expressed by Jean-Marie le Pen and his National Front are only strikingly awful examples of very widespread attitudes. It would be a tragedy if any spokespersons of the world's main political parties were to succumb, as their counterparts in France have, to this vile spew or their local equivalents. Obviously, every country has a right to decide, from time to time, the upper limits to its annual intakes of new citizens. Within these limits, and treating the playing of a decent humane role in the worldwide provision of emergency havens for the genuinely oppressed as a separate issue, it seems to me not only morally correct but also advantageous to continue to apply the broad principles of the Immigration Reform Group of the 1960s. These were set out with admirable clarity and decency in a splendid book, *Immigration: Control or Colour Bar?* (Melbourne University Press, 1962), edited by my old teacher, Ken Rivett.

Basically, they require ensuring that no one ethnic group dominates any particular occupation, and that representatives of all groups are spread through the social structure, both with regard to occupations, and suburbs. When I contrasted the limited fare of my Melbourne childhood in the 1930s with the extraordinary range of dishes and wine that are so widely available in Australia today, I could only offer up a prayer, first for Arthur Calwell (the main architect of the immigration policy of the early postwar days) and then for Ken and his fellow reformers. For they gave us the blueprints whereby, coming from *n* different starting places, we could nevertheless combine together in a wonderfully varied community of 'dinky di' Aussies all.

My generation of economists, like the one before it, was rightly inspired to try to create sustained full employment. But it should never have become an end in itself. Now we must try to make it possible for us all to have purposive lives and that requires that we ask what employment possibilities are socially admirable and consistent with being good citizens, not only of our own countries but of the world too. In pursuing these aims, I am sure cooperative pragmatism and give and take have much more to offer than any simple fix emanating from either the market or overall decree.

17
Macroeconomic Policy for Australia in the 1990s*

As I was called a squib for not setting out systematically the detailed ingredients of a middle way in the Donald Horne Address in February 1992,[1] I must try to do better this time. One reason why I 'squibbed' was because I believed (I still do) that a necessary prerequisite was to analyse the implications of important markets – those for labour, property, foreign exchange, financial assets – *not* behaving in a socially optimum manner as the textbooks would have it. Only then would it be possible to think about policies which were designed to deal with the many byproducts of their individual and collective impacts on the working of the Australian economy. Moreover, as I had been away from Australia for nearly ten years, I thought it would have been a bit of a cheek to arrive home giving *detailed* advice as I stepped off the plane, as opposed to raising key issues and identifying real problems in a more general way. I did make *some* specific suggestions in my Horne Address whenever I felt I was competent to do so.

What is appropriate macroeconomic policy for a small open economy on the Pacific Rim which has an enduring and indeed horrendous balance-of-payments problem, reflecting the need to restructure its industries, an extremely serious unemployment problem, including a frightening level of long-term unemployment,[2] and

* Originally published in *Economic and Labour Relations Review*, vol. 4(2), December 1993, 167–75.

I thank but in no way implicate Jonathan Michie, John Nevile, Peter Nolan, Claudio Sardoni, Rod Tyers, John Wells and an anonymous referee for comments on a draft of this chapter.

major pockets of unacceptable levels of poverty in what basically is still an affluent and relatively harmonious society?

Over the last 20 years or so, we have had a bellyful of 'deficit size' fetishism, as though the economic health of a nation could be measured entirely (or even at all) by the *difference* between government expenditure (G) and government revenue (T), regardless of the *sizes* of G and T themselves, or of the state of the economy when it is measured. So let us get away from this obsession once and for all and reinstate our common sense. I would argue that, by and large, what G should be, at Commonwealth, state and local levels, should be determined by *longer-term* aspirations reflecting both the overall philosophies of the democratically elected government in power and, as a corollary of this, well-thought-out and integrated plans for the provision of social and industrial infrastructure, as well as inducements to, and help for, the private sector.

However, as government expenditure impinges on the *immediate* overall activity of the economy too, the implication is that *most* of the adjustment from the government sector needed to fit in with the activity that the private sector is providing must be through T, complemented by appropriate monetary policy. The latter will have to be associated mostly with selective credit rationing – for if Australia continues to have a floating exchange rate, the structure of interest rates will primarily be determined by the overseas trading, and lending and borrowing positions. (Incidentally, as I am writing about appropriate monetary policy, may I refer readers to the passages in the Horne Address (Harcourt, 1992, 10–11: 241–2 above) where I urged the Reserve Bank of Australia to give a lead in encouraging the trading banks to make longer-term assessments of their customers' viability and, if these are favourable, enable them to see through any short-term difficulties? I would now say that the Reserve Bank should insist and *ensure* that they are able to do this.)

This way of looking at G and T brings to the fore some elementary and old-fashioned lessons which nevertheless are often forgotten: to remember that G itself may be divided into (at least) three categories – current expenditure, capital expenditure and transfer payments. The first two have immediate and direct impacts on employment creation. Their longer-term effects differ markedly and so they should be sharply differentiated from one another. The third category only has indirect effects on activity here and now, and in the future. As it entails transfer between citizens, it is only the *net* effect on spending of such transfers that is relevant for activity and employment. (The equity aspects are, of course, most relevant but are outside the rubric of the essay. I also abstract here from the effects of transfer payments between us and overseas where the effects are much more substantial and direct, both immediately and in the future.)

Making a sharp distinction between current and capital expenditure should lead to a rethink about the nature and significance of government deficits and surpluses. Much of government capital expenditure consists of the provision of needed social and industrial infrastructure, the returns to which only come in the medium to distant future and the immediate impacts of which on employment are markedly different (housing, health, education and transport are obvious examples). It really is foolish economics therefore, to expect total *G* always to be covered by total *T*, regardless of where the economy is in the various stages of the trade cycle, or where it is at in its planned development over the medium to longer term. In an ordinary business which is both viable and growing, we would never expect its *entire* outlays, current and capital, always or, indeed, ever to be covered by its *current* receipts. Periodic profits are in fact struck before interest payments on long-term borrowed funds are taken into account and certainly after periodic amortisation reckonings. (Measuring profits gross of interest payments reflects the fact that viability is in some respects independent of the pattern of finance of – at least – capital expenditures.) Why cannot we use this procedure as an analogy for the government sector and examine how *current* revenues measure up against *current* outlays? We should include in the latter imputed interest on the capital associated with the provision of infrastructure (here we depart from private practice) and estimates of the social rate of amortisation of the capital projects.

It still may be that in some circumstances we would wish *T* greatly to exceed this associated estimate of *G*, depending on how the private sector was faring (and on how the government wished it to fare); but at least we would get away from the foolishness of a crude total *G*, total *T* comparison and from crying 'disaster' if there is a shortfall, even when *T* is adjusted to its 'full employment' level. There is, of course, nothing novel or original in these suggestions. They were made, for example, by Keynes in the 1930s and 1940[3] and recently reiterated in 1992 in a United States context by Robert Heilbroner.[4]

The Australian scene is complicated by our Federal set-up, with the possibility that state governments may be of a different political complexion from that of the Federal government. As in any democracy, compromise and give and take will be needed. At least minimum agreement could be obtained on, first, accounting procedures and, secondly, implementation of those expenditures for which the Commonwealth government is responsible but which in practice are implemented at state levels through state institutions.

If budgets are not balanced over the cycle, that is, if total G on average is greater than T, it will be necessary to keep a close eye on the debt to income ratio implied. For if a deficit (on average) were also to imply a *rising* debt to income ratio, we would be building an eventual source of instability into the structure of our economy. If, however, the ratio were to remain constant over time, not least because increasing the debt in the first place indirectly helped to raise income over time at a satisfactory pace, then there does not seem to be any overwhelming reason to worry about G exceeding T. In general, public debt is not a problem in Australia; by OECD standards, the ratio of public debt to GDP is low.

The vast amount of restructuring required almost certainly requires a brake on *total* consumption expenditure. While there is considerable room for redistribution within this total towards the less well-off, nevertheless the bulk of extra production in Australia at the moment ought to go into capital accumulation. This may require a rise in total T, even though, at the moment, there is heavy unemployment which needs to be steadily reduced. As in the United Kingdom, the long-term needs of the economy and the state of the balance of payments imply that we need a 'High Street'-led recovery (as the Brits say) like we need a hole in the head. I realise that constraints on consumption require a further period of real sacrifice by the bulk of the workforce for, unlike the Brits, Australia does not have the equivalent of a cushion of North Sea oil to allow eight to ten years of a fool's paradise to reign. Enterprise bargaining is going to complicate this task even more, for it will tend to make more unequal the pre-tax distribution of income. We will therefore need some carefully crafted revisions of rates of taxation in order to bear down on total consumption expenditure. Moreover, the instability built into the Australian consumption function by the vast extension of credit facilities for all will make the task even harder. But, as our erstwhile millionaire prime minister was prone to say, 'life was not meant to be easy' and it should not be beyond the wit of the Treasury to provide its ministers with a number of ingenious schemes from which the latter may choose, in order to attain the government's desired ends.

Nor would I suggest brakes on consumption for ever. In a mixed economy the ultimate stimulus to accumulation in large measure must be an expectation of a healthy rate of growth of the consumption demands of its citizens. Only then may we be sure that the 'animal spirits' of the decision-makers in the private sector remain vigorous and dynamic.

I have mentioned our horrendous unemployment problem and the overseas balance constraint. I deplore the departure from a commitment to full employment – a departure, moreover, that had the blessing of a number of prominent Australian economists who, in retrospect, ought to be thoroughly ashamed of themselves.[5] However, I do think it is worthwhile remembering that Keynes and his closest colleagues thought that the statistical orders of magnitude of unemployment which would be associated with the *disappearance of involuntary* unemployment due to deficiency of aggregate demand were around 6–8 per cent of the workforce. (By the 1960s, though, there had been a sea-change in attitudes on orders of magnitude by Keynes's disciples. Richard Kahn, for example, thought that Frank Paish was a semi-Fascist for wanting unemployment in the United Kingdom to be over 2.5 per cent when it was currently at 1.75 per cent of the workforce.) There is a moral here: not that we should rest content with these higher orders of magnitude but that, when they do exist, in order to reduce unemployment to more socially acceptable levels, we should rely more on microeconomic policies (which should be occurring anyway) rather than continuing generally to increase G or encourage private spending. The policies would include retraining, relocation (of both capital and labour), and rehousing. Coupled with this understanding is the need to rethink the new moves in the Accord. For one of the essential aims of the Accord was to influence the overall increase of money-wages and therefore the overall cost level, an essential prerequisite for Australia to reach and *then sustain* levels of unemployment which we could reasonably regard as consistent with full employment and continuing growth.

In the move to enterprise bargaining and with the demand for more flexible labour markets, I fear we are in danger of losing sight of the benefits of some long-established Australian institutions for the overall working of the economy, and also of forgetting the fundamental lessons bequeathed to us by two of our greatest Australian political economists, the late Eric Russell and the late Wilfred Salter. The economic analysis underlying the demand for more flexible and competitive labour markets does tend to treat the demand for and supply of labour as though they were akin to the demand for and supply of peanuts. In particular, it assumes that the demand and the supply curves of particular sorts of labour, and even of labour in general, may be regarded as independent of one another. But modern theory and applied research alike suggest that this is a very dubious assumption indeed. For the productivity of labour may often depend upon the wage (and other conditions of work) of the labour force concerned. Therefore, in so far as the demand for labour depends upon its anticipated productivity, there is a whole family of demand curves, each member of which corresponds to a specific wage level. Moreover, the concept of a supply curve of labour is undermined, for the *quality* of the supply of labour services will vary with the wage postulated to be paid; so that what is measured on the horizontal axis can no longer be regarded as different quantities of a *homogeneous* flow. At best, therefore, we are faced with the possibilities of multiple equilibria and it is not obvious which of them in fact will be established – or, even more daunting, which ought to be. Indeed, the analysis, strictly speaking, becomes incoherent and so is certainly not a satisfactory guide for policy.

Nor is this all. Let me rehearse the main policy conclusions of Salter's 1960 classic, *Productivity and Technical Change*:[6]

> Salter draws three important and topical policy implications . . . The first is that government economic policy should be directed towards creating a flexible economy which enables an easy transference of resources from declining, high cost and price industries to expanding, low cost and price ones. The second is that wages policy should be national in scope rather than related to the circumstances of particular industries. Relating earnings to the 'capacity to pay' of particular industries tends to bolster declining industries and hamper expanding, progressive ones. It delays the introduction of new techniques and has a harmful effect on overall economic growth. Third, a high rate of gross investment is necessary to allow the structure of production to change quickly and, given the structure of demand, to increase the output and productivity of those industries where technical advances are most rapid. (*The Social Science Imperialists*, 1982, 136)

Russell (allied with Salter until the latter's tragically early death in 1964) fought a lonely but ultimately successful battle to have established the principle that money-wage levels should be adjusted through the Arbitration Commission so as to reflect changes in prices *and* effective productivity. Not only is this consistent with equity, with the traditional Australian sense of fair play, it is also the appropriate macroeconomic policy to follow. Most importantly, it allows, *ceteris paribus*, the accumulation processes, which Salter analysed so incisively, to have their maximum impact on the growth in productivity, both in individual industries and overall. The early years of the Accord enshrined this excellent principle. As I said in the Horne Address (Harcourt, 1992, 7–8: 238–9 above), it was not the wage-earners but the Australian capitalists who failed to play their part, to wit, to 'Accumulate, accumulate, that is Moses and the prophets' (and also, so as to keep John Hewson and his constituency happy, the profits as well).

Another aspect of restructuring associated more with microeconomic policy and the role of government should be the provision of government help via information services and back-up generally to exporters (and entrepreneurs involved in import replacement) to help them find and then secure niche markets. This is an obvious lesson which Australia could learn from those newly-industrialised countries (NICs) which gave businesspeople their heads but backed them up in the national interest as well. A byproduct of being successful in this regard may be a reversal of the trend whereby the 'brightest and the best' were attracted to services and finance sectors by the grossly distorted signals which were given out in the 1980s. Another lesson from the NICs is that we should leave tariff levels where they are, at least in the medium term.

We need also to think of measures which will eliminate harmful speculation in finance and property markets so that prices and rewards there may more fully and fruitfully reflect useful economic activity. In this way present and past savings will be gathered together in a more socially useful way.[7] On the side of real investment the government should take the lead in designing investment incentives which persuade business people to invest in those areas which, overall, the government has decided most need to be developed. Provided these areas are defined broadly enough, the chances of corruption will be lessened, yet neither the government nor its public servants will be able to dodge the responsibility for giving leadership in what should be a partnership between the public and private sectors.

Australia must not accept unemployment close to 10 per cent as an appropriate 'natural' rate of unemployment (a non-existent concept anyway, if ever there was one, within the analytical approach taken in this chapter). A greater rate of capital accumulation and appropriate macroeconomic policies, as spelled out in this chapter, can enable a substantial reduction in unemployment over the next five years without a blow-out in the foreign debt or a rapid resurgence of inflation.

Notes

1. *Markets, Madness and a Middle Way: The Second Annual Donald Home Address*, National Centre for Australian Studies, Monash University, Melbourne, 1992, a shorter version appeared in *The Cambridge Review*, February 1993, 40–5, Chapter 16, this volume.
2. In May 1993, 366 000 had been unemployed for more than one year.
3. Donald Moggridge tells me that Keynes was the author of Chapter xxix. 'The Reform of the National Accounts', in the Report of the Liberal Industrial Inquiry, *Britain's Industrial Future* (The 'Yellow Book'), Ernest Benn Ltd, 1928, where this matter is discussed in detail. The most clear-cut argument by Keynes on this matter is in his Memorandum, 'National Debt Inquiry: The Concept of a Capital Budget', *CW*, Vol. XXVII, 1980, 406–13. I am indebted to Bradley Bateman for this reference. Robert Skidelsky has drawn my attention to note 2 on p. 348 of *CW*, Vol. IX, 1933 [1972], 'The Means to Prosperity'. There, Keynes wrote: 'I strongly support ... the suggestion ... that the next budget should be divided into two parts, one of which shall include those items of expenditure which it would be proper to treat as loan expenditure in present circumstances.'
4. Robert Heilbroner, 'The Deficit: A Way Out', *New York Review of Books*, vol. XXXIX (19), 19 November 1992, 11–12.
5. I vaguely remember being summoned by a well-known professor of economics some time in the 1970s to a highly secret meeting of about ten or so Australian professors of economics at the University of Melbourne. There we were urged to 'educate' the public to accept higher levels of unemployment than had been the feature of the postwar world. I remember that only I and one other person present were scandalised by the request; in retrospect I bitterly regret not 'spilling the beans' about it all at the time. Now that I am, I cannot remember exactly when it occurred or who was there!
6. Immodestly, this is taken from the review article I wrote of Salter's book, which was published in the *Economic Record* of September 1962 and reprinted in *The Social Science Imperialists* (Routledge & Kegan Paul) in 1982.
7. See Chapter 18 of this volume for an elaboration of this theme.

18

A 'Modest Proposal' for Taming Speculators and Putting the World on Course to Prosperity*

Following the Horne Address and its sequel on macroeconomic policy for Australia in the 1990s [Chapters 16 and 17 this volume], I wrote a jokey paper with a serious intent for the undergraduate Marshall Society journal at Cambridge, my plan to 'save' the world. In this essay I go over some of the arguments in these three papers, and expand them into a discussion of possible policies for the United Kingdom and Europe in particular, though I continue to argue for the need to take a world perspective and to call for international institutions and cooperation.

Initially, I divided the world and its problems into three broad groups: (1) the developed industrial nations; (2) the former, so-called 'socialist' countries of Eastern Europe and what was USSR; and (3) the developing countries. I said I realised that this was far too crude a classification but that it would do for the purposes I then had in mind. Now I want to add a fourth and fifth group: (4) the rapidly growing NICs on the Pacific Rim – Singapore, Malaysia, Taiwan, South Korea, Thailand, Hong Kong and Indonesia (to a lesser extent); and (5) China,

---

* Originally published in *Economic and Political Weekly*, vol. xxix (28), 17 September 1994, 2490–92.

While many of the specific policy prospects discussed here have been suggested by others such as Ruth Kelly and James Tobin, perhaps I may claim some novelty for the entire package deal of interrelated measures which follows. I thank without implication Philip Arestis, Ha-Joon Chang, Ruth Kelly, Peter Nolan, Nevile Norman, Ajit Singh, Beth Webster, the participants of the Queens' Seminar, Lent Term 1994 and of the Post-Keynesian graduate students workshop in the Lent Term 1994 for their interest and comments.

which *is* following a middle way, freeing up some markets and industries to capitalist influences and creating some capitalist institutions, for example, stock exchanges, while attempting to maintain a tight authoritarian grip on social and political life. As a broad generalisation and relative to the first three groups, the internal problems of groups 4 and 5 are under control and their impact on the first three groups is broadly that of an expansionary injection. [This essay was written in the early 1990s and I was not alone then in *not* foreseing the coming crises!] So I shall continue to concentrate on the first three, for they have, again relatively, the most pressing problems.

The principal economic problem of the first group is sustained mass unemployment with which is associated the need for many of them to restructure in order to solve persistent balance of payments problems; of the second, the need to get through transitions to more market-orientated economies without complete social, political and economic disintegration; of the third, the need to provide necessary infrastructure for development, capital goods for their industries and to find outlets for their exports at steady prices in order to create jobs and raise living standards.

Before setting out what should be done, let me briefly remind readers of the 'vision' of the nature of economic processes that forms the backdrop to the policy proposals that follow. As we argued previously [Chapter 16, this volume], there are two alternative 'visions' in economics: one likens markets, or even whole economic systems, to a wolf-pack running along smoothly. If, perchance, one or more wolves get ahead or fall behind, forces immediately come into play which quickly return them to the pack. In the other 'vision', the forces which come into play when the breakaways get ahead or fall behind are much more likely to allow them to get even further ahead (or fall further and further behind), at least for long stretches of time. The latter 'vision' underlies the following analysis.

Let me also recapitulate what I wrote previously [Chapter 16, this volume] about the nature of markets, their workings and the conditions necessary for them to be beneficial rather than socially harmful. Modern theory has laid down very stringent conditions which have to be satisfied before it can be claimed, even in theory, that the market outcome is socially desirable. (I repeat that it is a *non sequitur* to go from establishing that there may be, in the fashionable jargon, market failures, immediately to claiming that therefore government intervention will make things better.) The first condition is that actual prices of products should be a true measure both of the social costs of the resources used to create them and of the satisfaction which their use is expected to bring to their purchasers. That is why price-takers are needed. Producers can then match their costs to externally given standards which simultaneously signal to purchasers the terms on which they can expect to achieve satisfaction. This requires that prices, most of the time, should be such that what is voluntarily demanded is equal to what is voluntarily supplied. This is turn requires that flows of purchases and flows of supplies in markets should dominate the setting of prices. Inventories or stocks, though important for smooth production and sales, nevertheless need to play a subsidiary role in the determination of actual prices. Moreover, if current prices are not achieving this match, they must directly or indirectly give out signals which encourage measures to be taken which will quickly achieve such a match, often a very tall order indeed in many important markets. It also has to be supposed that prices act solely as rationing devices. That is to say, nothing else may be deduced from the price of a good or service about its qualities other than its relative scarcity or abundance. Modern work suggests – perhaps I should have written 'has rediscovered' – that the demand and supply of labour services, and of credit, do not set up prices with this required characteristic.

If demands are dominated, not by expected satisfaction but by guesses about what prices may be in the future, so that a large element of speculation is present in the formation of prices, and if supplies are offered, not in response to perceived costs but in anticipation of future movements of prices, or of other people's expected anticipations of such movements, then the ensuing prices which are set may bear no systematic or reliable relationship to the real economic factors of the regular economic activity which, it is argued, prices ought to reflect. And all this is independent of whether power is diffused equally on both sides of the market, or whether it is concentrated in the hands of either buyers, or sellers, or both.

Let me now add a little more on speculation and its effects. The traditional case for speculation was that it reduced the amplitude of fluctuations in prices and helped markets to reach their equilibrium levels more quickly than otherwise would have been the case. But if, as we mentioned, markets behave like the second wolf pack analogy, we have to deal with cumulative movements, either virtuous or vile, rather than supposing there to be an equilibrium 'out there' to be found. We have already mentioned that a number of important markets are dominated by speculative forces: for example, the market for foreign exchange and the stockmarket, in both of which recent technical progress has reduced the short *period* to a length of historical time which is probably even shorter than the corresponding length of Marshall's market *day*. The housing market, too, has tended to be dominated by people who are speculators rather than genuine purchasers of long-term housing services; or, at least, the two often conflicting purposes may be combined in the one purchaser, egged on by estate agents and the suppliers of finance.

Now all these phenomena are spread, if not worldwide, at least over most of the developed world, so we need to think about international agreements with which to tackle their effects. Rather than attempting to reintroduce controls, for example, on international capital flows, which both the ideological climate and recent technological advances make unrealistic, there is a lot to be said for getting agreements on some 'Pigovian' carrot-and-stick measures: that is to say, while not directly stopping anyone from doing anything, yet indirectly giving them incentives radically to change their behaviour.

Let us take the foreign exchange markets as an example. If we want exchange rates to reflect real economic forces – trading prospects, real investment opportunities – we need greatly to reduce speculation and thereby its effects on the determination of exchange rates in both the short and longer terms. For neither in the short term nor on average over longer periods do exchange rates at the moment reflect these economic activities. This is especially so if we accept that there is no underlying set of long-term equilibrium exchange rates, reflecting a long-term equilibrium of an interrelated system, but, rather, changing structures which reflect the appreciation and depreciation of individual rates because of the underlying differences in the growth rates of productivity and national products. As I shall argue later, these processes should be tackled by having a fixed exchange rate system with which are associated agreed rules for periodic changes if other measures for attaining internal and external balance in individual countries are not working.

A simple way of tackling speculation and its effects is through the taxation systems of the various countries. The taxation authorities would require that the turnovers of the foreign exchange dealers who pay tax in their countries be classified into three broad categories: foreign exchange bought and sold for purposes of trade (and consumption, for example, tourism[1]) and for long-term investment either in securities or directly. (In so far as the traders were concerned with the sale or purchase of commodities, spot or future, a case would have to be made by the taxpayers that these were to help production, or that they were legitimate sales, rather than for speculation.) This would leave a residual third category which would be mainly accounted for by speculative activities. Then the proportions of each category in total turnovers would be used to assess the total taxation paid on the profits of the dealers. There would be a much higher rate for the third category than for the first two, so that the larger was the amount of speculation which was financed by foreign exchange purchases or sales, the greater would be the taxation on the profits of the dealers.

Similarly, the purchasers or sellers for whom the dealers were acting would have their business or private incomes taxed at different rates according to the categories into which their transactions fitted. For companies, a higher rate of taxation would be levied in relation to their speculative purchases or sales. For individuals, a surtax on their income tax would be levied, according to the extent of their speculative activities.

Exactly the same sorts of schemes could be used to curb speculation on the stock exchange and in the housing market. The taxation authorities would tax dividends at lower and lower rates, the longer shares were held. The rates of capital gains tax, similarly, would be lower, the greater was the length of time between purchase and sale. The taxes placed on stockbrokers would vary according to the proportions in their turnovers which were accounted for by quick sales and purchases of the same shares – the other side of the coin of the measures outlined above. For the housing market, purchase taxes would be varied according to the number of times the taxpayer had bought and sold a house. Exemptions from higher rates would be granted if it could be shown that the sales and purchases were for legitimate economic and social reasons: labour mobility (that is, persons changing jobs and localities), a larger house for an expanding family or for elderly 'reles' to come to live/die in, and so on. Similarly, the transactions of real estate agents or solicitors would be monitored and they would pay higher taxes according to the proportions of *their* turnovers which were associated with speculative transactions, as opposed to the economically and socially acceptable ones identified above. All these schemes need to be implemented in individual countries to stop nationals going 'offshore' and so escaping taxes.

Let me conclude by setting out briefly some broad measures with which to tackle the problems we identified for the first three groups. For the first group, we need a set of coordinated measures, both fiscal and monetary, macro and micro, which together will bring about gentle but sustained expansion. These should emanate from the EC countries in cooperation with the United States and Japan and, to a lesser extent perhaps, the Antipodes. Included in the set of measures would be not only the more short-term measures of lower rates of interest, investment subsidies,[2] possibly tax cuts (much more debatable for those countries with restructuring problems), but also longer-term institutional changes as well. For example, as we argued earlier [Chapter 16, this volume], it would be most desirable for central banks to encourage trading banks to take medium- to long-term views on the viability of their customers' business and/or projects and, if these are favourable, to back up the banks in seeing through any short-term problems of their customers.

At the same time, the advanced countries should give a lead in creating institutions which have aims which are similar to those of Bretton Woods, especially the set of proposals that Keynes argued for. Especially do we need measures which make both deficit and surplus countries react to their situations in such a way as to allow employment to be sustained and growth to continue, individually and collectively. That is to say, we need to have reestablished a regime of reasonably stable exchange rates, but with the well-understood and accepted proviso that coordinated changes may need to occur from time to time, that nothing needs to be carved in stone for ever (except the well-known relationships between marginals and averages). If the taxation measures in regard to speculation were instituted internationally, establishing 'Bretton Woods in spirit' would be more feasible.[3]

The second group – the former so-called 'socialist' countries – will eventually hope to make all manner of goods and services that will be able to compete successfully in the markets of the developed and developing countries. At the moment, though, they have idle people and idle capacity even in the activities they are able to handle, mostly in the heavy industries which are a legacy of their 'Stalinist' pasts. Many parts of the developing world, by contrast, lack basic capital goods for both needed infrastructure and industry and agriculture, as well as the wherewithal with which to pay for them. The World Bank needs to be revamped, and its activities vastly extended so that it can be one of the main channels whereby purchasing power is provided for these countries to buy this equipment, principally, in the first instance anyway, from the former 'socialist' countries that have the people and the capacity to provide it. This will help to give the latter economies the required breathing space to develop their needed, longer-term, restructuring.

The role of economists at the World Bank (whose comparative advantage is surely in microeconomics) should be to vet individual schemes put forward by governments and industries in the developing countries. A prerequisite for these processes to be able to start up through World Bank grants is first to wipe out, preferably completely, the current huge indebtedness of many developing countries which is now a deadweight drag on their activities. Such a cancelling of debt will require coordination between the advanced and developing countries in order to make sure that the banking systems of the former are not destabilised – again a role for coordinated central bank actions in these countries.

If the first group are successful in getting their act together, the sustained expansion in their production and incomes will spill over into world markets so as to put a floor under the prices of, and increase the demand for, the export products of the developing countries. This, in turn, will do much to help them to help themselves with their own development. However, it will also be necessary to guard against overshooting – prices spiralling upwards, for example; so we need to turn attention again to some form of buffer stock scheme, perhaps like those proposed by Keynes and, in the postwar years, by Richard Kahn; see, for example, Gabriel Palma, 'Kahn on Buffer Stocks', *Cambridge Journal of Economics*, vol. 18, February 1994: 117–27.

Finally, to guard against the reemergence of inflationary pressures in the developed world, alongside the proposed coordination of fiscal and monetary policies and microeconomic reforms, incomes policies should be developed which are allied with trade-offs through their public sectors. These should be package deals which are suited to the institutions, history and sociological characteristics of the countries concerned. It is to be hoped that these may reverse the trend towards the euphemistically named 'flexible labour markets', which, quite apart from the social harm they cause, are also economically inefficient. As we saw earlier [Chapter 17, this volume, 251–3], money-wage movements which broadly reflect changes in effective productivity *plus* the general price level are beneficial to overall growth, as Wilfred Salter argued many years ago. For such a policy favours technologically advanced, growing industries and discourages those whose time has not only come but has gone.

I hope it may be seen that all this hangs together and that it is underlaid implicitly by theoretical structures which emanate from Keynes, Kalecki, Kaldor, Myrdal and Joan Robinson.[4] Were it to come to pass, the economies of the world could enter a virtuous upward spiral of sustained expansion and development.

Notes

1. Ha-Joon Chang reminds me that, if this is not to become a loophole, some upper limit on purchases will be needed.
2. On the side of real investment, governments should take the lead in designing investment incentives which persuade businesspeople to invest in those areas which, overall, governments have decided most need to be developed. Provided these areas are defined broadly enough, the chances of corruption would be lessened, yet neither governments nor their civil servants would be able to dodge the responsibility for giving leadership in what should be partnerships between public and private sectors.
3. Paul Davidson has developed some imaginative scenarios which give detailed content to the policies outlined above: see, for example, '*The General Theory* in an Open Economy Context', in G. C. Harcourt and P. A. Riach (eds), *A 'Second Edition' of The General Theory*, Vol. 2 (London: Routledge, 1997), 102–30.
4. Though urged to do so by Nevile Norman, I have deliberately not gone into much detail on any one proposal. I thought it better to set out an overview which could be easily absorbed and so let others, if persuaded, provide detailed recommendations for each part. For the same reason, I have also not included orders of magnitude of, for example, the huge rise in the turnover of business on the foreign exchanges in recent decades which reflects the increasing dominance of speculative movements.

19

Pay Policy, Accumulation and Productivity*

We live in an increasingly competitive environment, nationally and internationally, both with regard to industrial and commercial capital and to financial capital. One consequence of attempts to cope with this situation has been the emergence of sustained mass unemployment in the advanced capitalist economies. Yet inflation still remains stubbornly persistent in most countries and there has also been a decline in the rate of growth of productivity in some of them. We have witnessed, as well, instability in major markets – those for foreign exchange, labour, property and financial assets – and great variability in the rate of accumulation around unsatisfactory average levels in many industries and in economies as wholes.

In this essay I want to examine the interrelationships between these phenomena in order to try to reveal their causes and to suggest in broad outline some policy proposals through which to tackle their unacceptable

* Originally published in *Economic and Labour Relations Review*, vol. 8, 1997, 78–89.

The article is a revised version of a chapter in Jonathan Michie and John Grieve Smith (eds), *Employment and Economic Performance: Jobs, Inflation and Growth* (Oxford: Oxford University Press, 1997). I am most grateful to, but in no way implicate, Willy Brown, Andrew Glyn, John Grieve Smith, Bryan Hopkin, John King, Peter Kriesler, John Nevile, Brian Reddaway, Bob Rowthorn and John Wells for their comments on a draft of the chapter/article. I would also like to thank, with the same proviso, the participants in the Post Keynesian Economics Study Group (February 1996), in the conference of the volume in Robinson College (May 1996) and in the seminar series of the University of New South Wales (March 1997) for their comments. I also thank the editors of the book and Oxford University Press for allowing me to publish this revised version in *ELRR*.

effects. Though in writing it I had the UK most in mind, the analysis, I hope, does apply to the workings of advanced capitalist economies, and especially to Australia. Indeed, the discussion is crucially relevant for current debate in Australia. The move from a centralised wage system to enterprise bargaining has important implications which are related to the main theme of the essay. The cures suggested are part of a larger scheme of interrelated policies which I have outlined elsewhere, see Harcourt (1995), chapters 1–3 [Chapter 16, 17 and 18, this volume] and Grieve Smith, *et al.* (1996).

Antecedents and obligations

I start by setting out antecedents and obligations. I only met the late Wilf Salter a few times but, as it happens, I had something to do with virtually everything he wrote. In particular, I wrote the review article of his classic, *Productivity and Technical Change* (1960) for the *Economic Record*, Harcourt (1962; 1982, chapter 9). His work on productivity and technical change was the major inspiration for several of my papers in the 1960s and 1970s. So when I started to think about themes for the present essay, I naturally returned to his 1960 book and its splendid sequel which is buried in a 1965 IEA volume edited by Austin Robinson. I came away from the 1960 book refreshed by his crystal-clear analysis of the relationship between demand, prices and investment in new techniques at the margins of the existing stocks of capital goods. I was also struck anew by the crucial relevance of his major policy conclusions and by how just about all current policies in most capitalist countries, and especially in this benighted country (the UK, not yet Australia, though there are strong pressures to move it in that direction) are in effect the exact opposite of what Salter proposed. In particular, the current fetish for what are euphemistically called flexible labour markets and for their supposed roles in setting real wages and allocating labour, itself cruelly and unnecessarily vastly underemployed, flies in the face of common sense, good economic analysis and policy recommendations, that is to say, of analysis of the sort which masters such as Wilf Salter consistently supplied.

Other sources of inspirations for the chapter are, first, Michal Kalecki's 1943 classic 'Political Aspects of Full Employment', especially the crucial distinction which he made there between the political economy of *attaining* full employment, on the one hand, and of *sustaining* it, on the other. The distinction is central to the argument of the present chapter. Secondly, and this is a sad one, because it came so soon after the death of James Meade just before Christmas 1995, is the 1957 Meade–Russell paper which is a classic in the Australian literature. Meade wrote it with my other Australian mentor, the late Eric Russell, who was my closest friend at Adelaide. Any understanding of how the Australian economy works must start from this paper, but the analysis is not confined to my native land. It concerns the process of income distribution between capitalists and wage-earners in a small open economy in which the principal exports are from the primary sector and are subject to price fluctuations on world markets, see Harcourt (1977; 1982, chapter 21; Chapter 3 this volume) for an account of the origins and contents of the paper.

Building on this paper both Eric and Wilf gave sage advice to the then Australian Council of Trade Unions (ACTU) advocate, Bob Hawke, for the late 1950s Basic Wage Case concerning the principles which should guide the setting by the Arbitration Commission of the Basic Wage and, in effect, the rate of increase of the average money-wage in Australia as a whole. Salter provided the statistical data, conceptual analysis and argument, Russell, the theoretical argument and statement of principles.[1] Between them they not only greatly influenced the setting of the Basic Wage through the 1950s and 1960s but they also sowed the seeds for the principles behind the various Accords which were crucial planks of the policy of the Hawke–Keating Australian Labor Party (ALP) government of 1983–96. The fact that the Accords were relatively successful for a number of years, both in reducing inflation and in being associated with rising employment, no doubt makes me more sanguine about the feasibility and effectiveness of incomes policies than many UK economists and commentators. (John King (27 March 1997) pointed out to me, though, that they were less successful in offsetting the rise in the inequality of incomes.)

There is, finally, James Meade's last book (1995), published only a few months before he died, *Full Employment Regained?*

Wage levels and accumulation

Having set out inspirations, antecedents and aims, I now outline the arguments and in a general way, the package deal of policies which follow from the political and economic analysis. Basically, the aim is to provide a set of policies which allow sustained full employment with agreeable rates of inflation and more satisfactory rates of growth of GDP and productivity. A necessary corollary of achieving these is to raise the overall level of accumulation.

We may start by reminding ourselves of Salter's analysis. The problem he set himself to explain was why, in situations in which technical progress is steadily occurring, old machines of an inferior vintage are to be found operating alongside new best-practice techniques in most industries, a problem which was never clearly stated nor satisfactorily solved either in classical analysis (including Marx) or by neoclassical analysis, and especially not by Marshall. In fact, we may read into both sources that in the final long-period position,[2] if it were ever reached, we would only find operating machines incorporating current best-practice techniques. The capital–labour and capital–output ratios associated with these machines would have been determined by the expected movements in long-period prices and wages at the beginning of the analysis (and period). The state of knowledge – the capital-labour and capital-output ratios of the array of best-practice techniques – is summed up conveniently in terms of either a family of isoquants or, if there are constant returns to scale, a unique isoquant of various associations of inputs per unit of output.

Salter's crucial contribution was to show that if we suppose that technical progress in each industry is steady but discrete (and if, for the moment, we abstract from the effects of the cycle), investment in the current best-practice techniques chosen in the existing situation will, in competitive conditions, be pushed to the point where the prices established for the output which these machines and the accumulated vintages from past bursts of accumulation help to produce allow only the normal rate of profit to be received on the best-practice techniques. That is to say, *total* long-period costs including normal profits are just covered by the prices set and sales receipts received. The sales receipts associated with the outputs of previous vintages which are still operating and contributing to the current supply only have to cover their existing *variable* costs in order to remain operating – 'Bygones are bygones'. Of course, all but the marginal vintages will do better than this. Machines are retired and, sometimes, scrapped only when their quasi-rents are less than zero. In this way the benefits of technical progress are embodied in the stocks of capital goods and passed on to consumers in lower prices, yet some older vintages are able to exist side by side with the new improved ones.

Both at the level of each industry and, even more, at the level of the economy as a whole, the levels and rates of increase of wages are crucial to the process. (Wage movements may legitimately be regarded as exogenous at the level of the firm or even of the industry in many cases, but are obviously endogenously determined at the level of the economy as a whole.) They are among the principal determinants of variable costs, both directly and indirectly, and therefore of which machines remain in operation and of how far investment in new machines may go before prices reach levels where only normal profits are received so that accumulation comes temporarily to a halt: temporarily, because technical progress is a continuing process so that new sets of best-practice techniques become available over time and the accumulation and retiring/scrapping processes start up anew. (Of course, this is an artificial way of putting it, first, because individual industries are not synchronised by time and period so that, *overall*, accumulation and embodiment are continuous; and, secondly, because we have made the simplifying assumption that technical advances occur at discrete intervals in order to make the analysis of output, accumulation and price-setting tractable. We have also concentrated on the volume of accumulation determined by wage movements, keeping at the back of our heads the effect of relative prices on the choice of the best-practice techniques, see Harcourt (1968; 1982, chapter 11; Chapter 9, this volume), and Harcourt and Kenyon (1976; 1982, chapter 8).

The analysis is essentially Marshallian in spirit but overcomes the vagueness and misleading inferences of Marshall's own long-period analysis (but see Dennis Robertson's (1956) defence of the master, that there were two concepts of the long period in Marshall, one abstract, theoretical, the other more attuned to real life. John Nevile has also proved that it is, as ever, 'all in Marshall' by referring me to footnote 1 on p. 352 of the 8th edn (Papermac) of the *Principles*). Moreover, Salter (1960: 90–3) shows that if we have imperfectly competitive or even oligopolistic market structures, much the same processes tend to occur though the forces driving decision-makers to install and retire may be neither as strong nor as persistent as in the competitive situation. This view was first set out by Marx though not as explicitly or as convincingly. Salter considers either profit-maximisation or strategic behaviour in the non-perfectly competitive situations. We consider later the implications of some of the mark-up theories which link the profit margin and price setting to investment requirements.[3]

Policy conclusions

For the purposes of the present essay, it is the systemic implications of these industry processes which are most relevant (Salter extended his analysis to the system as a whole in Salter (1965). From what we have argued so far, if we are interested in overall growth of output as a whole and of output per head,[4] the most favourable conditions for achieving high rates of growth in both is that declining industries and expanding industries do so quickly. For this to occur, the last thing we want is a flexible labour market for its proponents tell us that the money-wages of labour should reflect the respective levels and rates of change of productivity in their particular industries (or even firms, as stressed by the proponents of enterprise bargaining on all sides of the political fence in Australia).[5] But this means money-wages *for the same sorts of labour* will be low and the rates of increase low in the declining industries, so that they linger on, their existing vintages still profitable to keep operating, *ceteris paribus*. By contrast, the industries that should be expanding rapidly have the required accumulation process held back by high money-wages based on the capacity to pay! The outcome is certainly a lower level of productivity in the economy overall and probably a lower rate of increase of productivity overall, than would be the situation if the levels and advances of money-wages were to follow the more efficient and equitable course for which we argue below.[6]

In brief, the guiding principle should be that money-wages are adjusted for changes in the cost of living and effective productivity – the overall change in productivity adjusted for any permanent change in the terms of trade. Thus Salter (1960: 153–4) drew these basic policy conclusions from his analysis which may be summarised as follows:

(a) Government economic policy should be directed towards creating a flexible economy which enables an easy transference of resources from declining, high cost and price industries to expanding, low cost and price ones.
(b) Wages policy should be national in scope rather than related to the circumstances of particular industries. Relating earnings to the

'capacity to pay' of particular industries tends to bolster declining industries and hamper expanding, progressive ones. It delays the introduction of new techniques and has a harmful effect on overall economic growth.

(c) A high rate of gross investment is necessary to allow the structure of production to change quickly and, given the structure of demand, increase the output and productivity of those industries where technical advances are most rapid.

In Salter's book the level and rate of growth of aggregate demand were external to each industry. But when discussing pay policy and full employment, this cannot remain so. It is here that Kalecki's distinction, mentioned above, becomes vitally relevant. While business-people are happy (or at least, used to be!) for some government activity to be taken to lift an economy out of a deep slump which has reduced their profits and dimmed their animal spirits, they are not at all happy with the social and political conditions which emerge when full employment is reached and then sustained, despite the obvious advantage which high demand brings them. The sack ceases to be effective as a regulator of work effort and wage changes, since the balance of political, social and economic power tends increasingly to pass from capital to labour. Yet if animal spirits are to be revived and maintained, the maintenance of something akin to sustained full employment is necessary – witness, for example, the experience of the Golden Age of Capitalism. But unless continual and persistent action is taken about pay policy, the situation will be increasingly threatened by cumulative inflationary pressures associated especially with the setting of money-wages. For though real wages are an ultimate determinant of the standard of living and increases in it, in a monetary production economy, that is our world as we know it, the wage bargain may only be made in monetary terms, as Keynes taught us long ago.

So we must be able to implement an incomes policy, despite the fact that each employer would like to be free of the inconvenience which the policy brings to him or her. The policy must include as one of its features, increases which are consistent with the control of inflationary pressures, as determined by our international situation, yet which also allow the great potential benefits of the Salter processes to be realised in the growth of productivity associated with operating at full employment output levels. Such a position will, of course, be favourable for the support of the animal spirits necessary to allow the accumulation processes identified by Salter to be implemented. All this coming together will reward the economic communities for agreeing to money income restraints, so allowing everyone to share fairly and fully in the rising prosperity – a virtuous, cumulative, reinforcing process will have been created.

Practical problems

An obvious implication of Salter's analysis is that the guiding principle of wage setting should be that, *ceteris paribus*, money-wages change by amounts dictated by changes in the cost of living and overall productivity. This guiding principle is just, as well as efficient. At the level of the economy as a whole capital and labour are complements and so jointly contribute to the rise in overall productivity. It is just, therefore, that all citizens should share in the benefits that flow from this. Including the change in the cost of living insures people who are unable to protect themselves against a decline in their real incomes from sustained inflation, thus removing a major cause of anxiety and insecurity and, incidentally, making it easier for people generally to agree to money-income restraint in an overall package policy deal.[7] This deal nevertheless will not be easy to secure because it has to pay some heed to past ruptures of established relativities, the need to match job opportunities with some (limited) financial incentives and the need to have a floor to the level of money-wages (and other incomes) in a minimum wage, for reasons which are related to the efficiency-wage hypothesis.[8]

As to the main guideline, while it may be *relatively* easy to get agreement on what constitutes the cost-of-living index and its increases – certainly that is something which trade union, employer and government representatives could profitably get together on – a real problem of principle may arise in the measurement of effective productivity changes in a world dominated by floating exchange rates. Why? Because with floating exchange rates and deregulated financial markets, we have a classic case of markets where stocks dominate flows and speculative influences dominate real economic factors in the setting of both day-to-day market prices and the average of prices over the medium to longer term. This state of affairs is compounded when we take into consideration that in a dynamic world economy in which the Salter processes are of very unequal strength as between different countries and regions, the notion that there exists an underlying set of stable long-period equilibrium exchange rates, only awaiting to be found by market forces, is, to say the least, problematic.

It follows that the idea of effective productivity – domestic productivity adjusted for changes in the terms of trade – is an elusive concept in theory and certainly in practice as far as agreed upon estimation is concerned. Yet some rough agreement, some compromise, would need to be found between interested groups. No doubt the institutions set up to tackle the problem of ruptured relativities could also be expected to make reviews and periodic adjustments for the effects of revisions of estimates of effective productivity as well. Clearly this requires people of good will – are there any left? – but all consensus and sensible and, ultimately, efficient policy making requires this anyway.[9]

We mentioned earlier that Salter processes are at their most effective when competitive market structures, or something akin to them, may be assumed to be present. But much effort has been devoted in Post-Keynesian circles (and others, of course) to describing non-competitive (or imperfectly competitive) market structures and their implications for pricing and the investment decision. Ball (1964), Eichner (1976), Wood (1975), Harcourt and Kenyon (1976; 1982, chapter 8), Coutts, Godley and Nordhaus (1978) and Kaldor (1986) are obvious examples. Much of this work is microeconomic in character and the systemic effects have at best only been sketched. Nevertheless, there are some disquieting aspects that need to be thought about.[10] Before doing so, let me conjecture that with the increase in international competitiveness of the last two decades, both in goods and in services, especially financial services, the world economy *may* be closer to the competitive model, albeit a ruthless jungle red in tooth and claw, than it was when the writings referred to above were first developed. If so, our minds may be put more at ease on that score anyway.

The most disquieting microeconomic result is an implication of the work which I did with Peter Kenyon. There, we argued that prices in oligopolistic industries characterised by large price-leaders are set by profit margins designed to raise the internal funds needed to finance investment and that there was a process of mutual determination involved. It follows that margins would be greater the greater was the investment that was planned, *ceteris paribus*. But investment would be less, the higher were the margins and therefore the prices set, because this would allow older vintages to remain in operation that much longer, thereby reducing the shortfall in expected output which new investment would be needed to cater for. In microeconomic terms at least this is a drawback on accumulation, productivity growth and attaining and sustaining full employment. Moreover, the higher price levels, *ceteris paribus*, may make the control of inflation more difficult. I am not sure that these arguments go through at the level of the system as a whole, but at the very least, they need to be explored.

There may also be another source of inflationary bias involved in non-competitive situations. Firms with below average increases in productivity will have rising costs which may be passed on in prices in order to avoid bankruptcy. Those with above average increases may nevertheless not allow the consequent lower than average rise in costs to be fully reflected in prices because they wish to retain profits for extra investment. Overall therefore, the price level will tend to rise. How important this tendency is depends on how fast demand for particular commodities is growing, and on the feedback effects of this on the system's behaviour.[11] Another limitation is that, because services have risen in importance, we need a comprehensive analysis of Salter processes in service industries.

Concluding remarks

Let me conclude: by relating the nature of Salter processes to their policy implications for incomes policy we have identified interrelationships which promise a virtuous, cumulative performance of higher growth and higher employment, a performance which has some possibility of being sustained, if reasonable skill is shown over macroeconomic policies (notably demand management). For the policy measures promise to create an environment where animal spirits may be more consistently robust, even dynamic, and the resulting potential rise in the standard of living rewards the community for acquiescing in a policy of money-income restraint. I do not wish to over stress the cosy side of the story. There are deep-seated structural problems present in many advanced industrialised countries, not least the UK and Australia, so that bottlenecks and balance-of-payment constraints are only too real and often bite. Moreover, while it may be possible to create favourable climates for businesspeople there is no guarantee that they will necessarily do their thing or do it properly – this was certainly the experience of Australia during many years of the Accords when the level and composition of investment were far from what was needed. It may be that governments can give some general pointers by the use of broadly based investment-incentive schemes, as I suggest in Harcourt (1995: 38, n. 3; Chapter 18, n. 2, this volume). But whatever misgivings we may have,[12] what is proposed is surely more efficient and more just than the present hotchpotch of non-policy and one-sided attacks on the standard of living and employment opportunities of wage-earners.[13]

Notes

1. Eric subsequently published his principal arguments for such a policy for Australia in *Australian Economic Papers* in 1965 (Russell, 1965).
2. It is an equilibrium of long-period supply and demand in the neoclassical case.
3. Brian Reddaway has pointed out to me that both Salter and I are 'assuming away' a host of problems which spring from the presence of imperfect competition, especially the implications of non-homogeneous commodities. I do rather feebly try to tackle this later in the essay. He added that 'uncertainty is largely responsible for non-investment and retention of old models'. I can only respond by saying that if the analysis of this chapter is correct and if the package deal of policies proposed were to be implemented, the environment so created might well reduce the effects of uncertainty and allow higher rates of accumulation to occur.
4. Not only are they desirable in themselves, they are also the necessary prerequisite for obtaining and sustaining full employment and of having some chance of implementing an incomes policy which is consistent with an overall rate of inflation that maintains the competitiveness of the economies concerned.
5. Bryan Hopkin has challenged me to quote chapter and verse for this. It does seem to me to be the implications of the arguments currently in the public domain for the virtues of flexible labour markets and enterprise bargaining.
6. Bryan Hopkin has pointed out a potential *non sequitur* here: it is low productivity industries which should go, high productivity ones which should grow and they are not necessarily synonymous with declining and expanding industries respectively. Salter does obliquely cover himself on this point, see Salter (1960: 153).
7. The confident tone of this argument probably reflects Australian experience where we have had many periods in which cost-of-living adjustments have been an integral part of national wage cases and/or automatic. Bryan Hopkin is deeply sceptical, calling the proposals the 'principle of hope over experience' in the light of UK experiments in the postwar period; but he is in favour of incomes policy in principle.

8. Willy Brown has pointed out that there are serious social problems for some regions as well, in that even if there were to be full employment, children may have to move from regions dominated by declining industries in which their parents were initially employed. This could be offset, to some extent anyway, by encouraging investment in new industries to go to the regions containing these communities.
9. John Wells has kindly pointed out to me that *Economic Trends* carries estimates of the terms of trade by quarters from 1970 on and has drawn my attention to an annual series of UK GDP per capita in real terms adjusted for the terms of trade from 1950 on. Bryan Hopkin reckons I have overemphasised the difficulties (this reflects the fierce debates on this issue in Australia in the 1960s) and that some rough approximation could well be agreed to. In Australia, we could start by revisiting the work of Russell and Salter.
10. At this point Brian Reddaway made a typically down-to-earth comment: 'The fact that commodities are not homogeneous and have varying amounts of services attached to them is particularly awkward for the would-be producers of elegant analysis.'
11. I am indebted to Peter Kriesler for this argument.
12. Andrew Glyn has drawn my attention to Rudolf Meidner's 1993 paper on 'Why did the Swedish Model Fail?' The economic analysis is similar to that of this essay and some salutary lessons from history are documented; but see Rowthorn (1992) and Stegman (1987), the conclusions of which made me more optimistic about the possible success of the policies proposed in this essay.
13. John King (27 March 1997) feels there is 'a significant flaw in the argument: the pressures for increasing wage inequality are so powerful that even centralised wage determination ... proved unable to overcome them [so that my] argument is stronger as a statement of principle than as a practical proposal'. Still, you have to try.

References

Ball, R. J. (1964) *Inflation and the Theory of Money* (London: Allen & Unwin).

Coutts, K., W. Godley and W. Nordhaus (1978) *Industrial Pricing in the United Kingdom*, DAE Monograph 26 (Cambridge: Cambridge University Press).

Eichner, A. S. (1976) *The Megacorp and Oligopoly* (Cambridge: Cambridge University Press).

Grieve Smith, J. *et al.* (1996) 'Full Employment Without Inflation: A Strategy for Pay', Cambridge, mimeo.

Harcourt, G. C. (1962) 'Review Article of W. E. G. Salter, *Productivity and Technical Change* (1960)' *Economic Record*, vol. 38, 388–94, reprinted in Harcourt (1982), 129–37.

— (1968) 'Investment-Decision Criteria, Investment Incentives and the Choice of Technique', *Economic Journal*, vol. 78, 77–95, reprinted in Harcourt (1982), 146–67; Chapter 9, this volume.

— (1977) 'Eric Russell, 1921–77: A Great Australian Political Economist', the

1977 Newcastle Lecture in Political Economy, reprinted in Harcourt (1982) 331–45; Chapter 3, this volume.
— (1982) *The Social Science Imperialists. Selected Essays*, edited by P. Kerr (London: Routledge & Kegan Paul).
— (1995) *Capitalism, Socialism and Post-Keynesianism. Selected Essays of G. C. Harcourt* (Aldershot, Hants.: Edward Elgar).
— and Peter Kenyon (1976) 'Pricing and the Investment Decision', *Kyklos*, vol. 29, 449–77, reprinted in Harcourt (1982) 104–26.
Kaldor, N. (1986) *Economics without Equilibrium: The Okun Memorial Lectures at Yale University* (Cardiff, University College: Cardiff Press).
Kalecki, M. (1943) 'Political Aspects of Full Employment', *Political Quarterly*, reprinted in Kalecki (1971) 138–45.
— (1971) *Selected Essays on the Dynamics of the Capitalist Economy 1933–1970* (Cambridge: Cambridge University Press).
Marshall, A. (1969) *Principles of Economics. An Introductory Volume*, 8th edn (Papermac) (London: Macmillan).
Meade, J. E. (1995) *Full Employment Regained? An Agathotopian Dream*, DAE Occasional Paper no. 61 (Cambridge: Cambridge University Press).
— and E. A. Russell (1957) 'Wage Rates, the Cost of Living and the Balance of Payments', *Economic Record*, vol. 33, 23–8.
Meidner, R. (1993) 'Why did the Swedish Model Fail?', in R. Miliband and L. Panitch (eds), *op. cit.*, 211–28.
Michie, J. and J. Grieve Smith (eds) (1997) *Employment and Economic Performance: Jobs, Inflation and Growth* (Oxford: Oxford University Press).
Miliband, R. and L. Panitch (eds) (1993) *Real Problems False Solutions. Socialist Register 1993* (London: Merlin Press).
Pekkarinen, J., M. Pohjola and B. Rowthorn (eds) (1992) *Social Corporatism. A Superior Economic System?* (Oxford: Clarendon Press).
Robertson, D. H. (1956) *Economic Commentaries* (London: Staples Press).
Robinson, E. A. G. (ed.) (1965) *Problems in Economic Development. Proceedings of a Conference held by the International Economic Association* (London: Macmillan).
Rowthorn, B. (1992) 'Corporatism and Labour Market Performance', in J. Pekkarinen, M. Pohjola and B. Rowthorn, *op. cit.*, 82–131.
Russell, E. A. (1965) 'Wages Policy in Australia', *Australian Economic Papers*, vol. 4, 1–26.
Salter, W. E. G. (1960) *Productivity and Technical Change* (Cambridge: Cambridge University Press), 2nd edn with addendum by W. B. Reddaway, 1966.
— (1965) 'Productivity Growth and Accumulation as Historical Processes', in E. A. G. Robinson, *op. cit.*, 266–91.
Stegman, T. (1987) 'Incomes Policy: Some Issues', in T. Stegman *et al. op. cit.*, 1–24.
—, K. Schott, P. Robson and G. Scott (eds) (1987) *The Future of Income Policies in Australia*, CAER Paper no. 24, Sydney, University of New South Wales.
Wood, A. (1975) *A Theory of Profits* (Cambridge: Cambridge University Press).

Part VI

General Essays

20
The Payment of Prisoners*

At the present time, prisoners in all gaols in Australia are paid at very low rates (well under 4/- a day). These rates of pay make it virtually impossible for any but long-sentence-men to accumulate a sizable fund to take with them on release. As released men are not eligible for unemployment benefits until a fortnight after their release (they can register after a week but do not receive a *week's* pay until a fortnight is up) unless they have a job to go to, or get a job almost immediately, *and* unless they are paid in advance, they may be forced into crime again. Good resolutions made in prison, and attempts at rehabilitation by prison and welfare officers, will then be thwarted by their material needs in that vital first fortnight.

Furthermore, because of these low rates of pay, it is impossible for prisoners to contribute towards the upkeep of their families while they are waiting for trial and serving their sentences. As a result, their families often suffer great material hardship as well as the social hardships associated with the shame of the husband's and bread-winner's imprisonment, the break-up of the family unit which occurs, and possibly the ostracism of relatives, friends and neighbours. Many marriages are unable to stand these financial and social strains, and the broken marriages which result make the job of rehabilitating prisoners even more difficult.

---

* Originally published in the *Australian Quarterly*, December 1961, 86–89. I was at the time Secretary of the Howard League for Penal Reform (S.A. Branch).

I must apologise for the sexist tone, there were in fact few women prisoners in South Australian prisons at that time.

The main arguments for proper remuneration are: as an incentive for more economically productive work; to give the prisoner a sense of his own continued dignity as a person, and to mitigate any sense of social enmity; to enable prisoners to meet financial charges such as aid to dependents, savings for when he leaves prison, legal compensation for his crime (where applicable), and payment for amenities, board and lodging whilst in prison. The prevention of financial indebtedness and distress would clearly assist in reducing the return to crime, the infection of criminality in a prisoner's family, and the infliction of suffering on a prisoner's innocent dependants. The object of this essay is to outline a scheme whereby the financial problems of prisoners on release and of their families while they are in prison could be solved with a minimum addition to the burden of the taxpayer. The solution of prisoners' financial problems should clear the way for the more fundamental task of making prisoners useful and accepted members of society.

Briefly, the proposed scheme is that prisoners should be employed in the production of commodities which are sold, competitively, on the open market. From the proceeds of these sales, prisoners could be paid the standard award wages for the jobs performed. A certain portion of their wages could be earmarked for the upkeep of their families, and for the prisoners themselves, and income taxation would be subtracted in the same way as is done for free wage-earners. The remainder would serve to meet both the immediate needs of the prisoners in gaol, that is, cigarettes, books and so on, and to build up a fund for them on their release. A small proportion of their earnings might also be earmarked for a general state fund for compensating victims of crime.[1] Paying the award wage rather than (say) the basic wage recognises the principle that similar work should receive similar pay, no matter where it is done. It might be argued that paying award wages in effect modifies sentences. The *time* that is spent in gaol should be regarded as the punitive aspect of sentences, so that what is done there can be regarded as the reformative aspect. However, if this argument is not accepted, longer sentences would be a worthwhile price to pay for the reformative aspects of the scheme advocated here.

The prison authorities should be able to predict with reasonable accuracy the number of prisoners serving each length of sentence. It should therefore be possible to select commodities, the manufacture of which would be suitable for a work force of this nature. As far as long-term men are concerned, the commodities selected should be such as to train them for a job when they come out, if this is at all possible. Shorter-term men will at least be fully employed each day, which should contribute towards their rehabilitation.

The commodities chosen should be reasonably homogeneous regardless of where they are produced. Many farm products fit into this category. Another possibility would be to manufacture commodities that are much the same as those of a large number of producers, so that the impact of prison production on the sales of any one firm would be negligible. Shirts and bread products are good examples. The prices of these commodities should be determined competitively so that the additions to the total supply coming from prison production would form only a small part of the total production. Prison authorities could thus leave the problem of price-setting to the market. Moreover, the output of these commodities in prison could be geared to the available prison labour force without the worry of having to cut prices to sell additional amounts. Finally, prisoners could make novelties (such as the wicker work of blind institutes), which would compete with all other commodities for the consumer's pound. The production of the above three groups of commodities by prisoners would constitute no threat either to the employment of free labour or to the profits of other producers. In a period of full employment, and with the *total* prison population such a small proportion of the workforces concerned, there is nothing in the argument that 'cheap' prison labour is a threat to employment or profits. In any case it would no longer be 'cheap'. The policy of full employment, to which all our political parties are pledged, should therefore minimize the traditional objections by trade unions and businesspeople to the sale of prison products on the open market. It makes me angry and sad to read this in 1999!

The relatively high level of unemployment being experienced at the moment raises the question whether prisoners should receive higher rates of pay than the unemployed receive in weekly relief. As a long-run aim, it is to be hoped that both groups will receive higher rates of pay, if only because of the hardships suffered by their families. In the short run, there is no reason to delay getting rid of one social injustice because another (albeit more serious) exists.

There remains the problem of paying the prisoners who cook, launder, tailor and so on for the prison population itself (one American Report suggests that only 12.5 per cent of the total prison population *need* fall into this category, though actual percentages are often very much greater).[2] These men should be paid award rates for the type of work performed. Perhaps a proportion of these payments could be met from any surplus of sales proceeds of the prison factories over their wage and raw material payments.

At present, most prison products are used by other government departments, so that the recommendations of this essay would require fresh thoughts on the products which prisons should manufacture. However, it is intended to sell the products of the new minimum security training farm at Cadell in South Australia, and, as a long range plan, there do not seem to be any insurmountable obstacles to the introduction of products for sale into maximum security prisons as well.

This essay is an outline only of the proposed scheme. Obviously there would be problems associated with the choice of products which would meet the requirements above and, at the same time, make possible the training of men for suitable occupations when they come out of gaol. Furthermore, the prison workforce is likely to be much less efficient than that outside, not only because of the turnover associated with different lengths of sentence but also because of 'the low working-ability of the average prison population'.[3] This may make it difficult to earn a surplus from the sale of the products over their wage and raw materials costs. As a partial offset, paying prisoners award wages may well increase their productivity. It would probably be necessary to extend the working hours of prisoners to a full 40 hours a week (this in itself would be a very good thing). There is the problem of financing the original outlay on capital equipment for the factories. Probably, as an interim measure, it would be necessary to use most of the traditional prison trades, provided that the sales receipts from these products could cover the immediate costs associated with their production. Over the long term, new prisons would be financed either by taxation or from loans, and when built, could include the capital equipment needed for the products involved.

It cannot be guaranteed that the proposed scheme would entail no additional cost to the taxpayer. But these costs have to be seen in the whole social context. Since recidivism (and the infection of criminality in prisoners' families) would be reduced, there would be entries to be made on the credit side as well as the debit side of the taxpayer's balance sheet, and it might even be that in the long run the taxpayer would gain. And this consideration, of course, leaves aside any non-financial social benefits. Finally, it should be noted that schemes such as the one advocated here have been proposed or tried in other countries.

Notes

1. See *The Economist*, 17 September 1960, 1065.
2. See Max Grünhut, *Penal Reform – A Comparative Study* (Oxford: Oxford University Press, 1948), 200.
3. Max Grünhut, *op. cit.*, 223.

21
Notes on the Social Limits to Growth*

These notes are intended to pose more questions than they provide answers to. They are prompted by an important book, the *Social Limits to Growth*, published by a lifelong socialist, Fred Hirsch (1977) the year before he died; and they draw on three stimulating and challenging reviews of Hirsch's work: the first by Robin Matthews (1977); the second by Anthony Clunies Ross (1977) in a review article of Hirsch's book and Hugh Stretton's (1976) *Capitalism, Socialism and the Environment*; and the third by Don Lamberton (1977). As I have said, Hirsch was always a socialist; moreover, he knew an incredible amount about the detailed workings of the financial institutions of modern capitalist economies. I believe that his views should be accorded respect and that they are of great relevance to those of us who are thinking about the nature of economic growth and the role it has to play in the transition to a more just and equitable society.

Hirsch himself poses three main questions (1977: 1):

1. 'Why has economic advance become and remained so compelling a goal to all of us as individuals, even though it yields – he asserts, then argues – disappointing fruits when most . . . achieve it?' He calls this the *paradox of affluence*.
2. 'Why [are we so concerned] . . . with the division of the pie . . . when it is clear that the great majority of people can raise their living

* Originally published in *Economic Forum*, Summer 1981, 1–8. This paper was presented at the Conference of Labor Economists, Brisbane, Australia, May 1978.

standards only through production of a larger pie?' That is, why do we suffer from *distributional compulsion*?

3. 'Why [have we witnessed in] the twentieth century an increasingly predominant trend toward *collective* provision and state regulation in economic areas . . . when *individual* freedom of action is especially extolled, [indeed] given unprecedented rein in noneconomic areas – aesthetic and sexual standards, [for example]?' (The emphases are mine.) This is the phenomenon of *reluctant collectivism*.

Hirsch's basic answer depends on his classification of goods into *material goods* and *positional goods*. Access to material goods is a function of *real* income, so that both for society as a whole, and for individuals, growth may be expected to bring greater quantities of them. With positional goods, however, access is a function of *relative income*, and general growth does not necessarily, or even usually, increase their availability, not least because many of them are in fixed supply. In a sense, Hirsch's distinction is related to the Ricardian distinction between 'commodities, the value of which is determined by scarcity alone' and those 'commodities only as can be increased in quantity by the exertion of human industry'. Ricardo, of course, thought that in maturing capitalism the latter would dominate the former, at least until the stationary state was reached. Hirsch is examining the consequences in modern economies of the former tending to reach parity with the latter.

In Hirsch's view material goods are those which serve to satisfy our biological needs. We leave aside for the moment the question whether this is a tenable definition. Since there are limits to these biological needs, growth increasingly must satisfy them and so expenditure on positional goods figures more and more prominently in our individual expenditure patterns, and in national expenditure as a whole. This implies in turn that to an increasing extent the goods that people want cannot be provided – 'delivered by growth'. Positional goods are 'like places in a race. Only one person can come first. More efficient methods of running will not increase the number who can get first prizes' (Clunies Ross, 1977: 180). More prosaically, supply is limited, the rise in demand paradoxically both raises the price *and* diminishes the ultimate satisfactions. What I get, you must miss out on because there is only a limited stock of what we both want. Examples are leadership of a (once great?) political party; general manager of the largest company; 1890s bluestone houses in Adelaide;

accessibility and seclusion – what was country for me as a child in Victoria is now an inner Melbourne suburb.

The most serious example, as far as this self-defeating process is involved, relates, in my opinion, to education and educational qualifications. It is serious because it leads to frustration and disillusionment, and these in turn may lead to the destruction of valuable institutions and to undesirable uses (or non-uses) of the community's resources. While educational qualifications may open the door to a higher income as well as to a more satisfying occupation and lifestyle for any one person, provided that they are available to them alone, *all* attempting to attain educational qualifications means often only that the qualifications demanded for access to the limited supply of such jobs are raised. Educational qualifications are then a sifting device rather than ends in themselves.

These are just specific examples of a general proposition: the standing on tip-toe paradox. The trouble is that the market system does not give the correct signals to warn us that if we *all* attempt to stand on tip-toes, *none* of us will be better off. Externalities, far from being an exception in a world of mainly material goods, become the rule in a world increasingly dominated by positional goods:

> the benefits ... claimed for the competitive system are ... reduced, even by its own standards ... [To] an increasing extent the goods that people want are not capable of being delivered by growth ... concealed by national accounting definitions, which too often count means as ends. (Matthews, 1977: 574)

Hence the distributional compulsion and the reluctant collectivism, because of increasing market failures inevitably associated with the very nature of positional goods.

Because we are reluctant to adopt, and begrudging about, collectivism, and quickly disillusioned with it – witness the backlash to the Whitlam years, modest and timid though much of the programme was, now so successfully exploited by Fraser[1] – a new source of instability may be diagnosed in our society. Its source goes back a long way. Redistribution and collectivism are responses to aspects of the process of growth which bring in their train disillusionment and dissension. We have glorified self-interest, made capitalism institutionalised selfishness, as Milton Friedman proudly tells us, drawing on the socially beneficial byproducts of Adam Smith's 'invisible hand' for justification. (Joan Robinson (1978: 62), however, has recently reminded us that in Smith's day the invisible hand related to the case against protection. Now, though, it has been generalised to much wider applications than that.) What the champions of vulgar Smithism forget to tell us is that Smith was also the author of *The Theory of Moral Sentiments*, in which it is argued that there are altruistic, compassionate and tolerant attributes in human beings which also can be harnessed by suitable institutions. It is the neglect of these, and of the provision of appropriate institutions to accommodate and foster them, together with the fostering of greedy and selfish outlooks, institutions and behaviour, which is the new source of instability that the spread of externalities brings to the fore. Capitalism may have been saved from itself so far, not so much because of the beneficial nature of the invisible hand, nor the predominance of material goods in its earlier stages, itself a debatable hypothesis, but because of the hangover of the moral presuppositions and constraints of a pre-capitalist age.

> Adam Smith believed in a natural order of morality, [that man] was endowed with the moral sentiments which would make society possible ... [The] second part of his doctrine ... has succeeded in undermining those sentiments to a very considerable extent ... putting in their places the doctrine that the pursuit of profit is a substitute for morality (Robinson, 1978: 64). As Matthews says (1977: 576), Smith never intended that 'the model of man is and ought to be that of a gangster'.

Hirsch himself sums it up (1977: 12): 'the principle of self-interest is incomplete as a social organizing device' – who controls the controllers? Why expect them to act other than in accordance with *their* self-interest? In another context, the (so-called) failure of Keynesianism is placed at the door of Keynes's belief that public servants, in particular, and indirectly the politicians that they advise, would operate within the constraints imposed by 'the presuppositions of Harvey Road':[2] that the fundamental political and economic policy decisions would continue to be always made by a small group of enlightened and rational people who had the interests of society as a *whole* continually before them. Such a belief, it is argued, is completely at variance with the true nature of the sources of power and decision-making in our society. Kalecki's political trade cycle is much closer to the mark as a description of the operation of modern-day capitalism. Again, Australian experience in recent years offers confirmation of these fears.

Thus it is becoming increasingly apparent that the hierarchical and promotional structures of modern bureaucracies are not designed to ensure that altruistic and disinterested (as well as intelligent) people necessarily will emerge in key positions. There is little doubt that intelligence will win out but, too often, it is accompanied by ruthlessness and coldness, a lack of compassion which is not necessarily compensated for by great ambition and drive. All this was borne in on me when I read, a couple of years ago, a series of profiles of the heads of the main public service departments in Australia. On the whole it was not pleasant reading. Yet the people themselves are not entirely to be blamed; it is the system within which they have to operate, especially interdepartmental jealousies and rivalries, together with the often random or irrelevant allocations of their political chiefs to each ministry, which are to be held mainly responsible. It is not surprising, therefore, that we have witnessed in recent years a reaction against, indeed abhorrence of, 'Big Government'. Those of us who nevertheless remain interventionists will have to come to grips with this phenomenon.

One of Hirsch's conclusions is that if we are to restore stability to our social life, we are going to need to reestablish Adam Smith's moral sentiments (with a dash of the presuppositions of Harvey Road – for all). We need to establish 'a consensus on certain aspects of social ethics and on the proper distribution of income and wealth'. Since the process of growth turns us inevitably towards distributional compulsion and reluctant collectivism, this should be accompanied by explicit discussion and explanation of why it is so. Redistribution and collectivism have been unsatisfactory policies just because, as Matthews says, we suffer from 'the illusion that the privileges of the haves could be maintained *and* made available to the have-nots' (1977: 578).

Another aspect of Hirsch's thesis which Clunies Ross homes in on is the increasing commercialisation of the provision of services which detracts from the very satisfactions they are meant to bring. Hirsch himself illustrates this by bought sex. 'Orgasm as a consumer's right rather rules it out as an ethereal experience' (Clunies Ross, 1997: 101). More generally,

> [as] cash income becomes increasingly dominant in governing consumption activities and attainment of social and economic position, so it must increasingly dominate productive activities ... [Growing] more dependent on money for our life and leisure, we ... grow more dependent on money earnings ... the internal logic in the process of ... commercialization. (*ibid.*, 104)

Nor is this phenomenon confined to the private sector. We have already referred to the disappointments and frustrations associated with educational expenditure. The same point may be made about highway expenditures. These, too, are examples of the central issues of Hirsch's book, the 'adding-up problem: what individuals want and what individually they can get, society cannot get; and society has to find some means for determining how the difference should be reconciled' (1977: 106). It is the

> competitive system [that] produces an excessive and increasing *bias* towards *commercialization*, conducting the business of life by means of self-interested one-off transactions at arm's length [instead of] on the basis of friendship and mutual trust. (Matthews 1977: 576).

What then are we to do? The first point to make is that the concept of biological needs is *not* a viable one, if it is meant in a strict sense. Even for such basic needs as food, clothing and shelter there are historical and social determinants involved so that the material/positional distinction is blurred. Second, it is *not* obvious that satiation of desire for material goods has been reached, only that with the existing distribution of incomes and property it may often be thought necessary to titillate jaded middle-class appetites to raise demand for them. There is, therefore, still a strong case on both humanitarian and Keynesian effective-demand grounds for a more egalitarian structure to our income distribution and, especially, to the distribution of wealth. This argument shades over into the positional one as well, in that if it is, for example, non-pecuniary attributes which make many occupations attractive, there is no need to have the positive correlation between attractive jobs and real incomes that is characteristic of our income distributions today. Clunies Ross thinks straight away of university teachers in this regard. Hugh Stretton has consistently argued for an income range which does not exceed 3:1. Hirsch's book adds further good reasons. A cut in monetary rewards would reduce the 'total demands for such jobs by shedding potential applicants for whom the pay advantage is dominant' (1977: 183). For example, universities are now paying for their greed of the 1960s when the going was good. The public then was both excited about and favourable towards education as an end in itself. University staff took advantage of this climate more to secure large incomes than to ensure that they created conditions whereby creative and productive scholarship would be ensured. Due to the, probably necessary, phenomena of tenure, their huge salary bills are now akin to fixed costs, and for many of the tenured staff, their salaries bear a close resemblance to sinecures. This means that younger scholars, research facilities, study-leave schemes and the students themselves have to bear the painful brunt of the major restructuring and retrenchment which is occurring at the moment, all over the world. Yet, if tenured scholars were altruistic enough to forgo increases in their real incomes, for say a five-year period, it would be possible to create a sustained number of new positions for their younger colleagues, which would be beneficial not only for them but also for students in particular (who would continue to be taught, at least in part, by the brightest and the best, those still on the frontiers) and for scholarship in general. Externalities are nowhere more to be found than in great educational institutions – benefits and costs which rarely can be caught or counted by penny-pinching bureaucrats and antagonistic politicians, trying merely to balance the books of our educational institutions.

Another, rather nebulous, conclusion is that we should always explain what it is that we are doing, and why, and what the costs (and benefits) will be for particular groups and for society as a whole. In the light of the experience of the Whitlam years this *should* be a lesson that is easily absorbed. We need to devise means whereby people are encouraged to act 'as if' they were altruistic:

> [People] must recognize [for example] that they ought to pay their taxes, because although it would be in their interest not to, it would [even more] not be in their interest to have a system in which no one did. (Matthews, 1977: 577)

Matthews points out that getting such a moral code accepted has great practical difficulties associated with it. Obviously, it would be impossible to precede every major proposed economic change by a discussion of the 'general-equilibrium analysis of what would happen if everyone acted on the same principles'! So we must settle instead for some rules of thumb; but they in practice too often turn out to be silly.

What are the practical implications of all this for democratic socialist parties such as the Australian Labor Party, both in opposition and in power? The first is that we now have a compelling new set of arguments with which to attack the back-to-the-market, get-out-of-the public-sector attitudes of the current conservative government. Second, social democrats as well as democratic socialists may reaffirm their belief in an egalitarian distribution of income and wealth and in the need to take measures to secure them. Third, and in the long run the most important, it establishes the need for thoroughgoing discussions of major economic and social changes before they are enacted. In particular, people always need to be made aware of the costs and benefits involved, especially when the former are often concentrated and local, while the latter are widely diffused, but nonetheless real and important for that. In saying this I am not meaning to overlook either Hirsch's own warnings nor Don Lamberton's, that information is both very costly and, while partly positional in character, is mainly an *intermediate good*, 'a necessary social cost', so that the 'information sector may grow while the product dwindles' (Lamberton, 1977: 66).

Notes

1. Gough Whitlam, Leader of the Australian Labor Party, was Prime Minister of Australia from 1972 to 1975; Macolm Fraser, Leader of the coalition of the Liberal and Country Parties, was Prime Minister from 1975 to 1983.
2. *See* Buchanan, Burton and Wagner (1978).

References

Buchanan, J. M., J. Burton & R. E. Wagner (1978) *The Consequences of Mr Keynes* (London: Institute of Economic Affairs).

Clunies Ross, A. (1977) 'Review of *Social Limits to Growth*', *Journal of Economic Studies*, November 4.

Hirsch, F. (1977) *Social Limits to Growth* (London and Henley: Routledge & Kegan Paul).

Lamberton, D. (1977) 'Review of *Social Limits to Growth*', *Economic Analysis and Policy*, March.

Matthews, R. C. O. (1977) 'Review of *Social Limits to Growth*', *Economic Journal*, September, 574–8.
Robinson, J. (1978) 'Morality and Economics', *Challenge*, March/April, 62–4.
Stretton, H. (1976) *Capitalism, Socialism and the Environment* (Cambridge: Cambridge University Press).

22
University Ideals and the Market*

I

Friends and Fellow Wyverns, it is one of the greatest pleasures as well as one of the greatest privileges of my life to be asked to give this lecture. We managed to get here a little early, surprise, surprise, for anyone who knows the Harcourt family. So Joan and I took Tim and Jo to see where we were married. The Chapel seems to have become larger (or we have become smaller) since that happened. I was delighted that Joe [Isaac] was to introduce me, for Joe was my first mentor in Queen's, and was always extraordinarily kind to me. Indeed, I don't know how he put up with the number of knocks on his door when I kept coming to bug him about various things in economic theory and personal problems when I decided that I was going to leave Miss Hoy's boys and girls and try to be an academic economist instead of a schoolteacher. I have always admired Joe as an economist, but even more as a man. He was a role model to students at Melbourne and Monash, and later when he was on the Arbitration Commission. It is, therefore, an enormous pleasure and privilege to be introduced by him.

---

* The Third Sir Halford Cook Lecture given on 15 September 1995 at Queen's College, Melbourne.

This essay is the transcript of the lecture which was given in September 1995, only slightly tidied up. I am most grateful to Louise Elliot and Owen Parnaby for providing the transcript and to the Master, Fellows and students of Queen's and to the Friends of the Library for asking me to give the lecture. May I also thank Louise Elliot, Ian Manning and Owen Parnaby for their helpful suggestions on presentation of the lecture in printed form?

I am also delighted to know that my old billiards sparring partner whom I never ever beat, Norm Young, is here. Not a day passed in Queen's but that we had at least one game of billiards. It was a divine one for he was training for the ministry at the time. That no doubt is why he had strength on his side and always won. I am delighted as well to see a lot of old friends amongst the economics profession and pollies. I am especially pleased to see Brian Howe here. I don't know whether we ever actually played together in Darling Road Methodists which was an offshoot of the Queen's footy team. While I am talking of such matters I must draw attention to one glaring omission in Owen Parnaby's marvellous history of the College. I actually brought the Queen's cricket team out of the wilderness in 1953 as a non-playing Captain (I didn't make too many runs) to win the Premiership. I noted that he has a photo of the 1964 winning premiership side, but I thought that, in an otherwise perfect work of scholarship, it was a terrible omission not to have a photo of the 1953 side as well.

We have had a roll call of Queen's economists; to that I would like to add Ian Castles, who was a student of mine in Queen's, and who has recently retired as the Commonwealth Statistician. He was a most important public servant. Also Keith Hancook was an outpatient at Queen's and he still twigs me about the fact that in my first year of tutoring (I was still an honours student), I insisted that I and he and the other students wear gowns. Everyone knows that I did not wear a suit for 20 years; I actually had to get the one I have on tonight because I was going to Wendy's wedding, so I've worn it tonight along with this tie which some of you will recognise as an old style Queen's tie which I have not worn for 40 years. Richard will appreciate that that is good saving.[1]

Joe also mentioned some of the other economists. It is a very impressive list. The person who is the most professional economist that Queen's (and Australia) has ever produced is Murray Kemp. Murray is professional in everything he does. When he first came to Cambridge in the 1950s I arranged for him to open the innings with me for King's. When I was scoring faster than him he succeeded in running me out. He claims this was because of my slowness; I claim he was showing a wee bit of competition. As I said the list of economists is a distinguished one, not least because it includes Ross William's wife Lynne who nearly killed me when she took me running at Macquarie University at an economists conference.

II

What I want to talk about tonight is 'University Ideals and the Market'. I was interviewed on the ABC today and after I had talked on LO, I went to do an interview for the regional stations. The interviewer was a very enthusiastic former Monash student who had done economics and he mentioned how excited he had been at hearing a lecture by a very old and frail white-haired woman, Joan Robinson he thought her name was, while he was student. I said 'Look, mate, she was then the age I am now, and I can hear you now telling someone that you met this bald-headed old git who staggered into the studio to record a chat on your show'.

When I came here three years ago to give the Horne Address on Markets, Madness and a Middle Way (1992; Chapter 16 of this volume), it turned out to be an opportune time because the republican debate was just starting and Keating was about to do a mild U-turn (or, in his case, a non-U turn) in economic policy. Now I note there is a big debate going on about what is happening in universities because my old pal, Mal Logan, has had a lot of interviews, profiles and editorials on his ten glorious years at Monash. I did not know that would happen when I decided I would talk on university ideals and the market. Perhaps it is a happy time to make some points about this topic anyway?

As my next door neighbour (suburb, anyway) Barry Humphries used to say, 'Call me old fashioned but . . .': I do want to make what you may consider some conservative and possibly reactionary remarks about the nature of universities and at least the need for some caution before we go overboard completely on applying the market as an institution to the running of universities. I am very glad to talk about this in Queen's because I owe more to Queen's as an institution than to any other institution I have ever been associated with. It was an absolute watershed in my life, a complete opening up of all the potential possibilities of intellectual, philosophical and, as it turned out, political and religious life to me; and all this was overwhelming because of the extraordinary atmosphere which was then to be found in Queen's and which is documented so movingly and accurately by Owen Parnaby in his History. I was glad to see that Owen picked out the admirable positive qualities of Raynor Johnson who was the Master in my time, because it squared exactly with the inspiration I received from him;

though some sad things happened afterwards, I do think that, like Keynes, when you put all things into the balance, 'Sam' Johnson was a good man, and a wonderful Master who created through his benign non-interference an atmosphere where rather immature, often private-school boys, could develop into mature, sensible and thoughtful people. I owe a tremendous amount to Queen's for that, to the fact that Queen's reflected what universities should be about. We played hard, we worked hard and we had lots of time, as awakening individuals, to talk about the verities, the puzzles and problems of the human condition.

All this was aided and abetted by having the theological school on site. Owen Parnaby mentions that in Queen's the theological students were a most substantial part of the intellectual life of the college because they happened to be pretty bright (at least the top cohort were), as well as there being a lot of them. And it was extraordinarily helpful to those of us in the 1950s who were interested in politics and religion to have those first-rate minds to guide us and lead us on. In addition, of course, we also had Normie Lade, who was one of the Professors in the Theological School, a kind, good man, who was very supportive of all those young people, the surrogates for the children he and his wife never had. He loved all the people who were here and was always a very receptive person. I certainly found him a great influence, help and support. That is one of the major things that comes out of collegiate parts of universities.

I know that outside of Oxbridge it is economically impossible to set universities up in a collegiate way because it is a relatively huge use of resources, very expensive, and while you need it for people coming down from the country to go to universities (and even that need is getting less with the spread of universities) it is not possible to reproduce the Oxbridge model completely now that we have taken the very important step of increasing the proportion in the relative cohorts of those that are able to go to university. We must not lose sight of the great advantages of people having time at this crucial stage in the life of young people to get together and to be able to talk about the things that worry them as well as have a lot of fun. This is going to be reinforced now that we have the wonderful development of people of mature age coming back for further education, people who have parented their children and then decided that they want to return and/or add to what they have already learnt. It is most important that we keep that sort of atmosphere.

III

I think that a lot of those ideals are under threat from the too naive adoption of accounting and so-called business methods for the management of universities in order to cut costs and strive for efficiency. I want to set out why I think this is so. In universities the main stick as opposed to carrot is self-discipline. It cannot be otherwise. University teachers and researchers have to make themselves do their jobs. That inevitably means that you are going to have a longer tail of free-riders and slackers than you have in other organisations. You have to devise some ways of minimising this, but you must not be so keen to cut off the tail (which is still a small minority in my experience of universities) that you destroy the environment where research and teaching really flourish among those people who are in universities because that is what they want to do. They want to crack intellectual problems, jump intellectual hurdles and take the students over them with them. (In the case of Neville Norman it is a high jump, but the rest of us go over hurdles, we haven't his energy or ability.)[2]

In the attempt to drive out people who are not pulling their weight, you can destroy the environment which brings out the very best work. That could be an absolute tragedy, not only for the people concerned, but also for the university, the community and humanity in general. People do need an environment where they feel they can get on with tackling difficult problems without feeling that they are all the time being measured, reported on, assessed, having to fill in forms, and so on. Accountability is obviously necessary, but it can be carried to extremes in order to get rid of *all* the people who are not pulling their weight. It is rather like the Tories in the UK who, having used mass unemployment to try and control inflation, then rush round talking about people ripping off other people through unemployment benefits, and devising schemes so that they can flush out everybody. This puts a stigma on all the unemployed, most of whom are unemployed through no fault of their own, but principally through government policy. It is one of the most wicked and immoral things I know of, deliberately using unemployment to control inflation and then attacking the unemployed. What I am really arguing for is some sense of proportion in devising checks and balances when bringing in accountability. Otherwise for short-term gains you are going to ruin the contributions that otherwise would be made in the long run, contributions that would be of lasting value.

IV

One of the things under discussion now is tenure. There are only two compelling arguments for tenure. One is that it allows people to speak out fearlessly on important social issues without the suffering the fate of whistle-blowers in, for example, the National Health Service in the UK. With the introduction of free market-style managers, if you blow a whistle you are out before you can say 'Joan Robinson'. The first argument for tenure is to allow people to follow arguments where they lead and to speak out if they feel that they must. I have to say, from my own experiences, that is not always honoured by the great majority. During the anti-Vietnam War movement to which Joe referred you could count the number of staff who were actually involved on the fingers of about two hands. I don't think that destroys the principle, it is just a pity that people didn't live up to what is implied.

The other reason is more academic. The results of fundamental research cannot be predicted before hand, that is, what you are going to find and what the value of it, if anything, is going to be. If you could do that, it wouldn't be fundamental because it would already be known. There are many examples of people with tenure who have made fundamental contributions but have taken a long time to do so. On 3LO today I quoted two Australian examples: one is a Professor of History at Adelaide, Trevor Wilson (who I found out from Owen was one of his students at Auckland). He spent over ten years writing what is recognised as possibly the best, certainly one of the best, books ever written on the First World War. That would not be possible in a situation of short-term contracts and specified detailed accounts of what the grant was for. The other example is a labour historian also in Adelaide, Tom Sheridan, who has produced two marvellous books on Labour History, one on the Amalgamated Engineering Union and the other on the Arbitration Commission (Court) and industrial relations generally in the Chifley years. They took a long time to write because they were extraordinarily thoroughly researched. Tom worked away at them and when they come out they were recognised as definitive. The other examples I gave were from Cambridge. One was Max Perutz who received the

Nobel Prize for his discoveries on haemoglobin. It took him nearly 20 years to crack the problem that was to win him the Nobel Prize. One of my own mentors and friends, the economist Piero Sraffa, was kicked out of Italy by Mussolini and lived the rest of his life in Cambridge. He took about 35 years to write his *magnum opus* of 99 pages. He also produced the great editions of Ricardo's works and correspondence. Embryonic Sraffas, or Wilsons or Sheridans or Perutzs coming up now just would not get their chances, so we must remember that one of the costs of getting rid of tenure and having short-term contracts and grants is to nip in the bud people like them. This does not mean that receiving tenure should be a piece of cake. It has to be earned by peer review, publication, teaching and pulling your weight in your department. It is not something to be given lightly, but we should think very carefully, nevertheless, before getting to a stage where we make it a general rule that we don't have it.

That leads me on to something else which is nevertheless related, the nature of finance of higher education, and what we do if we have to depend increasingly on outside funds. In principle this may be desirable. The great American universities have always done it, and some of the continental universities are financed to some extent like this. The Ancient Universities are also like this because they were the robber brigands in early times and they have built up their endowments. (Trinity College, Cambridge is second only to the Queen in wealth.) There is nothing wrong with this in principle, but I do make an appeal that when this is done that the givers of funds are just – givers. They can put their names on the funds, but the actual decision about how the research will be done should be made by the people doing the research and their peer assessors. Again, when you are appointing someone to, say, a chair endowed from industry, commerce, or finance, by all means give great credit to the altruism and generosity of the givers but as far as the appointments are concerned they should be a purely academic decision, otherwise you get a creeping erosion of academic freedom, which – whatever the short-term gains may be – is ruinous in the long term. I say this because there is a move afoot to go outside much more. Mal Logan has been a pioneer in this, and also another member of this college, the outgoing Vice-Chancellor of Melbourne University with whom I think I slightly overlapped in Queen's. I throw all this out as a warning that we ought to be careful.

V

As the universities expand and bring in increasing numbers in the cohorts that can come, what about the nature of teaching and research? One of the great strengths of Melbourne University in my time as an undergraduate and postgraduate in the Commerce Faculty was that we had pass courses and honours lectures right from the start. People who thought that they would like to know more about their subject could nominate for honours, go to honours lectures and attempt some honours question in the exam. I hope that that sort of idea, though it has an elitist tinge to it, continues, for I think it is a sensible and pragmatic idea. As you get a greater and greater number of people coming into the university sector, so the spread of interests and capabilities of students will get wider and it will be increasingly hard for teachers to make a maximum impact: on the one hand, if you pitch your lectures at the middle, they will be still hard for the people below the mean; on the other hand, the people who are way above the median may find them boring and unchallenging. A good compromise is to have standard courses where you set the standard fare we all need to get, and then to give honours courses, and for the teachers concerned to encourage particularly the shy and unassuming to at least have a go at honours. This is so not least because often those people who think they are honours material are not nearly as good as some of the people who are brighter, because often the brighter students are, the more self-critical they are, and the less they feel they are on top of their subjects. It is the person who just scrapes through who thinks he or she has really got it taped; whereas really bright students agonise because they know how much they don't know. What they don't know is how much they do know, relative to their peers. You therefore need the sorts of teachers who encourage those sorts of people to go on.

That draws me onto this problem of size – Mal is quoted as saying 'big is beautiful', Wilfred Beckerman from Oxford is quoted as saying 'small is stupid' (which was a crack at Schumacher, another Oxford guy, who said 'small is beautiful'). Sure 'big' may be beautiful, but it has not been conclusively proved that there are increasing returns to bigness in university education. Even if there are, as Mal likes to think, should we use the American model (he was very much impressed by the University of Wisconsin which has a much greater number of students than we could have in, say, the Australian or the UK model until recently)? Even if there are and we do, and there are arguments for this, let us nevertheless make sure that within the units there is enough contact between students and staff to bring out what, after all, a university is about. What a university is about is young people, middle-aged people and old people collectively cracking intellectual nuts together. You can only get that atmosphere if there is easy contact between students and staff. I was appalled to find that at the University of NSW Economics Department they don't have even big tutorials, and they have exams which are almost all true and false. People don't write essays or even paragraphs. I checked up on Melbourne and I was pleased to find that Melbourne is not so dissimilar from when I went through 45 years ago. The tutorials have grown to about 20, whereas I think they were about 12–16 in my day. We must ally big campuses, if we are going to have them, with small units within them so that we do get this personal contact, this critical ability, this support. Otherwise we shall lose what universities are about.

Some faculties are going to remain vocational. When I was young, if you said you were going to the university the neighbours would say, 'that's nice, are you going to be a doctor?' That was the image. Australia, having never had an aristocracy (thank God), had to use the medical profession as a substitute. We are always going to have vocational courses and very fine ones. But we are also going to have courses which are a general education on what it means to be a good student and citizen. Those are very valuable things as well. One of my former colleagues in Cambridge who is mad with the market refers to students as 'clients' or 'customers'. They are not clients, they are fellow-seekers after knowledge and truth. We are cooperating to try to find them. I don't think of universities as production functions – inputs of knowledge, outputs of more knowledge. We should think of them as moulding minds and critical abilities and allowing people to chase arguments, to learn how to follow arguments wherever they lead no matter how unpalatable the conclusions. Joan Robinson's favourite saying of Keynes was 'If someone persuades me that I am wrong, I change my mind. What do you do?' That is an extremely good motto to put above the mantelpiece in any student's study. While there is a case for efficiency and so on, let us not push it too far so that we start thinking of ourselves as selling things to customers who are out there in lectures or tutorials.

VI

Let me say something about appraisal. Again, I think it is an excellent thing that there is feedback about how students react to their lectures and teachers, that there is peer group appraisal, and so on. But let us also try to remember that when you are a student what you may think is the best lecture, or who you think is the best lecturer, may not be your opinion twenty or thirty years on. Being a student is partly a maturing process and as you mature you change your views. Many of the best lecturers I had were the ones who totally challenged you and you came out of the lecture highly stimulated, but not sure that you had really understood it all. You rushed away to re-read the books which it was hoped you had already read before you had gone into the lecture, because the best lecturers pay people the compliment that they have already read the books. They thus try to bring out the significance, the balance, the perspective that lie behind the topics discussed. That is much more important than having everything laid out so that you don't have to read anything. The best sort of lecturers are those that take account of the technical part of the lectures, hand out diagrams and equations, but do not write down every word that is going to be said in the lecture. Help the students by allowing them to follow the argument, but don't present them with a ready made theory which they can digest and then regurgitate at the appropriate time, when they take the exams. That is not education. While we must use student appraisal as part of our accountability, we must not go completely overboard on it as the only way we can get an assessment as to whether people are good teachers or not. Often you will find that students come back years later and say: 'I thought what you were doing at the time was extraordinarily difficult and I didn't get it all, but now I find that, having thought about it, I realise in retrospect that really was a good set of lectures'. When we are devising ways of appraising people, let us not be completely literal about what comes back as feedback from either peers or from the people who are at the moment learning.

The other thing I want to say is that when you build incentives into the system you must not build in incentives which take people away from their three-fold task as university people, researching, teaching, and taking on their fair share of running the faculties and the university. At the moment the brownie points which are given for research are making it very difficult to keep people devoting the amount of time they ought to their teaching and their administration as on the whole there are no brownie points for doing so. Everything is relative, but there is too much emphasis put on adding on entries to your CV at the expense of your other duties. I don't criticise people for responding to these signals, because if they don't they get left behind in the race. That is what competition is about. When people rave on about competition, what they forget is the downside of competition, that failures drop by the wayside and those that succeed get the prizes. That is all very well, but one of the things Marx taught us is that labour is done by human beings; so, when you are using the competitive process to weed out the inadequate, you have to consider the human cost of that and how you pick people up and allow them to start again. Too often all this is forgotten in the drive for efficiency, prestige, publications and so on. Moreover, the drive for publication has an element of short-termism in it because, while it is true we try to make lists of what are the really brownie point journals, nevertheless there is tremendous emphasis on getting something into journals – any journals – especially when you have these periodic research exercises. People try to tot them all up before the date of the assessment; they try to get their publications out before the date of the assessment. This is a ridiculous way to run a university. I hope we will avoid excesses like that.

VII

In the Horne Address I set out the conditions which have to be satisfied before the market can be relied upon to bring about a socially optimum result. One of the conditions is that there should be an equilibrium out there to be found. I am not sure what the notion of an equilibrium in a higher education sector would be. I would have thought that a higher education sector was much more likely to exhibit a cumulative causation process, feeding back on itself and expanding all the time. In that sort of situation there is a lot to be said for the old-fashioned ideals with which we were familiar, and were introduced to so well by Queen's and its traditions, rather than some of the new management schemes that are now being tried. I don't want to appear to be old-fashioned (but I am!); I just want to sound a few warning notes so that the ideals on which this college was founded, which it has fostered in over a hundred years of existence and for which I personally am extraordinarily grateful, may continue in the future. What I witnessed in Queen's were people who presented role models which embraced the ideals I have been talking about. I was very fortunate to meet Ken Inglis who was a Tutor on High Table when I first came to Queen's and he has always been one of my role models. He has never been a careerist; he has always been extraordinarily supportive, he is a great Australian patriot, he writes like an angel, he has enormous integrity; he has been – and is – an unassuming but an extremely important Australian historian. There was a notice of his retirement in the Academy of the Social Sciences *Newsletter*; it said that Ken should be hired to give the response at every retirement dinner because he would produce the ideal model that no one could improve upon. So you 'rent an Inglis' when your retirement time comes. Queen's was just tuppence a dozen with people like Ken, and I would like to see, as we go forward into the very exciting time ahead with this great expansion in higher education, that those sorts of ideals continue.

On the finance of higher education there is a litmus-paper test as to whether you are a true radical or not. I got into awful trouble when I gave another litmus-paper test in the Horne Address. There, I said the test as to whether you were a democrat or not was whether you disapproved of Kerr sacking Whitlam and approved of Don Dunstan sacking the police chief. I really got it in the neck from the right-wing press for this so let's see if I can repeat the performance tonight.

When the argument about student loans was starting just after the Vietnam War was over, there was protest outside Parliament House in Adelaide about student loans. I went down and said:

> I think the litmus-paper test of a radical on this issue is the following: by and large a university education is financed by taking taxes from the poorest people and using them, again by and large, to educate the children of the richest people in order to allow them to go into professions and jobs which have higher than average lifetime incomes. It is the most regressive tax you could imagine if you make the university free for everybody. What you should do is to give grants to people who come from low-income families, then have an intermediate zone in which grants go down and loans come in more and more, and when you get to a certain level you are on your own – either your parents send you, or you work, or you borrow.

Having been the darling of the Left before I said this, I was now booed and hissed. Dr David Tonkin, the Liberal Premier, then came out and said, 'I am going to Canberra next week, I'm going to see my friend Malcolm Fraser and I'm going to say that your grants are lousy and he should not bring in loans, and he should raise grants.' He was cheered to the echo. Australia's experiment in bringing in a graduate tax is a very fine experiment. Three cheers for it, for it is in keeping with Australian democratic mores. I hope that it is extended until eventually we reach a situation where universities are self-financing as far as teaching is concerned. We may still need to use taxes and outside grants for research.

VIII

The only other thing I would like to say is that people ask me 'What are students like today? Are you finding them disappointing?' The answer is: 'Of course not'. Young people are always wonderful, and one of the joys of being a university teacher is that your students never grow old. I don't think I'm growing old either. I still feel like an eighteen-year-old and I find it quite easy to relate to students though increasingly they call me Dr Harcourt instead of Geoff. I regret to say that the young women started to do this before the young men. Students the world over are students. They are wonderful people, but I think they face a more anxious, uncertain and worrying future than we did. I was born at the bottom of the depression – my brother John got there a quarter-hour earlier; he got a kick start (I was a breach birth). My father came in with a bucket and said to my mother 'Which one do you want to keep?' It was the only time she could not make up her mind. We were born when the birthrate was very low and we came to maturity when the baby booms were on and the Murray Commission had occurred, so we had a dream run as university teachers. That is not so now and students are anxious. One of the things that results from this is that they are not as interested in the ideals I have outlined as in making sure that they do reasonably well and get a qualification and a job. There are obvious exceptions to this. It is partly the circumstances of the time that has brought it about. If I had one plea for how students ought to change now (when I think of the students of the 1960s) it is that there be a big uprush again in intellectual curiosity.

I wish that students were once again more intellectually curious about the conceptual bases of their subjects and the criticisms that can be made of them. I understand why they are lacking it. Life is much harder for them than it was for us. Nevertheless it would be better if when you went in to talk to them you felt you had a whole lot of people agreeing, yes, that is what we want to write on. Joan Robinson was reported as saying the following at the end of her last teaching post before she died (it was at Williams in America), she took her favourite student from the semester aside and said, 'Promise me whatever you do, you won't be an economist?' I thought that was sad. I would rather say to my students 'Come on board. There is a fight on, there is a flame to be carried on. Help us do it.' But you can't do that unless they have intellectual curiosity and they won't have intellectual curiosity unless the ideals which this marvellous college carefully nurtured continue, both in colleges like this and in universities generally.

So my wish in honour of Sir Halford Cook, about whom I read in Owen's book and who seemed to me to have many of the right ideas, though I think he was a bit right-wing, is that those sorts of traditions continue in this college and in universities generally. If they do, universities will be able to contribute to keeping Australia as one of the most extraordinary examples of a great multicultural democracy. One of the people associated with this had links with Queen's – my old teacher, Ken Rivett, who was a pioneer immigration reformer. I never cease to be amazed, when I come back to Australia, by what an extraordinary splendid, varied heterogeneous society it is. It would drive a neoclassical economist bananas, because there is not a bit of homogeneity in sight. I am proud to be an Australian patriot and a Cambridge economist. I am the luckiest person who ever existed, I think, because I carry on two great traditions. I owe a lot of this crucially to the years I spent in Queen's with my friends here, not least Norman Young, who not only taught me billiards but gave me the example of what a Christian gentleman can be.

I thank you very much for your patience in coming along on a Friday night when you could have been getting ready for the Finals. To all Wyverns here, I say 'It is great to be back', and to those who are not I offer you a very warm welcome. We used to get a lovely cup of tea and an arrowroot biscuit after Chapel in the old days and, no doubt, even in these impoverished times Queen's might be able to run to a cup of cocoa.

Notes

1. A reference to my cousin, R. D. Harcourt, the theoretical chemist, who is renowned in our family circles for his careful ways.
2. A reference to the well-known Australian economist who, though an Ormond man, came to the lecture.

References

Harcourt, G. C. (1992) 'Markets, Madness and a Middle Way', the Second Annual Donald Horne Address, *Australian Quarterly*, vol. 64, 1–17; Chapter 16 this volume.

Parnaby, O. (1990) *Queen's College, University of Melbourne: A Centenary History* (Carlton: Melbourne University Press).

23
Economic Theory and Economic Policy: Two Views*

I Introduction

I am delighted and honoured to give the Seventh Colin Clark Memorial Lecture. I only met Colin a few times but, of course, as a graduate of both Melbourne and Cambridge I was often referred to his writings and regaled with anecdotes about him. I witnessed the celebrated clash between Colin and Trevor Swan over the history of import controls in Australia at an Annual Meeting of Australian economists; and I was delighted to get a letter from Colin concerning my 1978 Academy Lecture, 'The Social Science Imperialists', in which he enthusiastically approved of the critique I made of Becker's writings on marriage, divorce and extra-marital affairs! We rarely agreed on economic, political or religious matters but I like to think, certainly this is so for me, that this enhanced our affection and respect for each other. So if I talk today about the contributions of Nicky Kaldor and Joe Stiglitz, whose views on theory and policy do not overlap that much with Colin's but whose general approach to political economy and policy-making and whose *raison d'être* for being economists certainly do, perhaps it may be granted that I have chosen an appropriate set of

* Originally published in *Economic Analysis and Policy*, vol. 27, September 1997, 113–30.

In writing the lecture I have drawn on a review which I wrote of Stiglitz (1996) for the *Journal of Institutional and Theoretical Economics* and on a review article of Kaldor (1996) which I wrote for *Economic Systems/JOICE*. I am most grateful to Matthew Gray, Keith Hancock, John McCombie and Tony Thirlwall for their comments on a draft of the lecture.

people, ideas and issues with which to celebrate the life and work of one of Australia's most illustrious adopted sons.

II

Nicky Kaldor was my first PhD supervisor and subsequently a colleague and friend at Cambridge. His writings have always had a major impact on my thinking. He, alas, died nearly 11 years ago. Joe Stiglitz, hurrah, is still very much alive. He has just been made Chief Economist of the World Bank. Prior to this, on leave from Stanford, he was Chairman (I hope that is the proper description) of President Clinton's Council of Economic Advisers. There, as he told us in his superb Alfred Marshall Lectures at Cambridge in 1996, he advised the Clinton administration to implement a package deal of policies which had their fundamental origins in the lessons Stiglitz learnt from the Keynesians, especially Kaldor, at Cambridge, to which university he came as a graduate student from the other Cambridge (MIT) in the early 1960s. Initially he had a room next to me in what is now the Austin Robinson Building and I recall that he seemed to write a paper a week. Certainly his productivity was extraordinary and it has continued to be so. Paul Samuelson and Bob Solow had sent Joe to sit at the feet of Joan Robinson. Joe was eager to learn and was not at all unsympathetic to her views; he was also a radical in a political sense (a dove on the Vietnam War, for example). Unfortunately, Joan stereotyped him as archetypal American neoclassical (what could be worse than that?) and they did not get on at all so that Joe went to Frank Hahn as supervisor. He did, however, get on well with Kaldor and liked his writings, which held Stiglitz in good stead in later years, not least, as I said, when he came to advise Clinton.

In 1990 Stiglitz gave the prestigious Wicksell Lectures, *Whither Socialism?* Subsequently these were made into a book, Stiglitz (1996), which contains one of the most profound internal critiques of mainstream neoclassical economics I have ever read. In addition he spells out the significance of his critique for, first, why the so-called former socialist economies of the USSR and Eastern Europe were destined to fall apart in the late 1980s and, secondly, why the advice which has been given to these countries on the roads they should take to more market-orientated economies is seriously flawed, something which perhaps could not be deduced from the fees paid to those who have given the advice. He also uses his critique of orthodoxy to show the incoherence of the justification offered for some of the more extreme policies followed in the advanced capitalist economies in recent years.

In 1984, two years before he died, Kaldor gave the Raffaele Mattioli Lectures in Italy. They have only now been published as a book by Cambridge University Press as Kaldor died before he had finished preparing them for publication. Two of his biographers subsequently edited the manuscript for publication. Its title is: *Causes of Growth and Stagnation in the World Economy*, Kaldor (1996). In a profound sense the book is Kaldor's last will and testament to our profession. It allowed him to have a final say as an outsider (he was always critical even as an insider) on what is wrong with orthodox mainstream neoclassical economics; to present his own analytical approaches and apply them in an analysis of some of the pressing issues then facing the world economy (they are much the same now); and, finally, to present a package deal of policies with which to tackle them. Fittingly, the critiques, approaches and policies of Kaldor and Stiglitz are not that far apart, a nice irony, I think.

III

Kaldor and Stiglitz take the Arrow–Debreu (AD) model of general equilibrium as representative of the best, or at least the most refined and developed form of modern theory. Stiglitz puts more stress on the two fundamental propositions of welfare economics which flow from it and provide a basis for its application to policy.[1] Kaldor views AD as meant to be a descriptive analysis of the real world, at least ultimately. Stiglitz appears to be at one with him here. I found this strange, because some of its most subtle practitioners do not regard AD as descriptive at all. Rather it is the rigorous setting out of the conditions that have to be satisfied in order that what they regard as Adam Smith's central conjecture – that a set of greedy people let loose in a competitive environment would bring about a sort of social optimum – may be true. Frank Hahn, for example, has often said of this exercise that by setting out the conditions we find why they are unlikely to be met in the real world. This view led him, for example, to a prolonged and courageous critique of the monetarists and the new classical macroeconomists who often argued that their ghastly policy recommendations followed from a procedure which took AD to be descriptive of the real world. Kaldor sees the supporters of AD as arguing that it is supported by scaffolding which when removed would reveal a durable building. He argues that this is misguided, that whenever we attempt to put into the model certain inescapable facts of life of the real world, the whole building comes tumbling down, that it has only stayed up for as long as it has because even more special assumptions and axioms have been used to support it.

The facts of life which he stresses are, first, increasing returns, as set out by Smith in classical times and brought into a more modern age by Kaldor's mentor and teacher, Allyn Young, in his 1928 *Economic Journal* paper. These increasing returns are dynamic, historical, not the static ones (analytically) which so worried Cournot and then Marshall because they were incompatible with competition, in the static sense of many small price-taking agents, being sustained.

Secondly, and, of course, related to the first, Kaldor and Stiglitz argue that the most notable feature of capitalism is that it creates an environment conducive to technical progress, much of which is endogenous, a characteristic of its natural process of development, and that this feature cannot be satisfactorily introduced into the AD model. The latter tries to cater for time by having markets for everything from now to Kingdom Come. But how can we conceive now of markets for the products associated with inventions, let alone innovations, which have not yet occurred? (Stiglitz highlights lack of information and missing markets as the two most damning factors destroying the robustness of the results of the AD model.) Moreover, since the environment of any capitalist economy is argued to be challenging, even threatening, it is hard to reconcile this with the fact that all essential decisions in the AD model are made in period I and then hold for and unfold over the rest of time. As Kaldor (1996: 7) says, 'From period 2 on, life must become very boring!' Stiglitz, too, picks up on this point under the rubric of the economics of information to which he has made significant contributions over the past 20 years and more. (There are over 100 items either due to him alone or joint-authored in the bibliography of Stiglitz, 1996.)

Another critique common to both is that in the real world prices are rarely *only* indexes of relative scarcity. Yet that is what they have exclusively to be if the AD model is satisfactorily to do its thing. This observation is associated with another obvious but significant real-world fact of life – that, with few exceptions and Chicago true believers not withstanding, imperfect and oligopolistic market structures rule, not price-taking, purely competitive behaviour, and it is not possible to treat the former satisfactory, if at all, within the AD framework. Stiglitz has made his mark in the credit-rationing literature in which a willingness to pay a high rate of interest may signal credit risk rather than worthiness, so that well-behaved supply and demand curves for credit become problematic. (Long before Stiglitz wrote, Michal Kalecki had made a similar but in some dimensions more profound point with his work on the principle of increasing risk. Indeed, it is remarkable how many similar crucial ideas Kalecki had before either Kaldor or Stiglitz and how grudgingly late or even non-existent has been the acknowledgment of this.)

Stiglitz is very critical of the limited role for the entrepreneur/manager in the AD model and the virtually non-existent role for the firm. He criticises the dominance which markets exert in the AD model, leaving no place for firms as we know them nor for a satisfactory theory of why they exist and what their roles are, or why team work – cooperation – may be as important as competition for efficient outcomes. Stiglitz has sensible things to say on the roles of teamwork and cooperation in raising productivity, even though he has a rather dim view of human nature (including his own), feeling that we inevitably need incentives (positive and negative) to make us behave in ways that are in any way acceptable, both individually and as groups.

A further corollary of his critique is the destruction of the theoretical basis for market socialism which was thought to arise from the competitive model developed by Lange and Lerner and which seemed at the time (1930s–1940s) to provide a telling answer to the claim by von Mises, Hayek and their followers of the impossibility of socialism. Stiglitz argues that neither Lange–Lerner nor Arrow–Debreu could find a place in their theories for the proper roles of socialist or capitalist managers, that in their system both sets were condemned to mechanical applications of the maximising or minimising under constraints theorems of Samuelson's *Foundations* – clever in one dimension but basically boring, unimaginative, repetitive; indeed, actions which are remarkably like those of many Young Turks in the trade today who, having been similarly equipped, swing the changes on assumptions within this approach but who lack conceptual understanding and the sorts of insights which Stiglitz sets out so well in his pithy and readable prose.

Kaldor has long been associated with the concept of 'stylized facts' – broad empirical generalisations which hold in a rough and ready way, often for long periods of historical time – and he adopts a 'horses-for-courses' approach by creating situation-specific models built up from such observations. He is thus most critical of the abstract axiomatic approach which underlies AD. Stiglitz is less so; he prefers small, often partial models which nevertheless abound in lemmas and theorems founded upon simple axioms. The latter are not that conspicuous in *Whither Socialism*? for he also is blessed with an uncanny ability to explain in simple language what the economic intuitions of his lemmas/theorems are.

While Kaldor concentrates his criticism on the AD model, they have to be seen within the context of his overall view of the principal issues which have preoccupied economists almost from the word go. He divides these into static resource allocation puzzles and the causes and consequences of growth. He argues that a major mistake was made by neoclassical economists when they tried to use the framework they developed for the first set – basically the AD model – to analyse those of the second set. His most fundamental concern about this procedure is well-captured by the title of one of his last books, *Economics without Equilibrium* (1985). This reflects his mature stage when he rejected as flawed the mechanical equilibrium analogy in the analysis of the behaviour of individuals, firms, markets and the economy. In its place he put Myrdal's principle of cumulative causation. As early as 1934 he had clearly stated the basic principles of path-dependent equilibria which capture, to some extent anyway, Myrdal's (and Smith's and Young's) insights.

I usually illustrate the contrasting processes for my students by a wolf-pack analogy. (I should really check whether my zoology is sound.) The first view thinks of economic processes as a wolf-pack running along at a steady pace. If one or more wolves get ahead or fall behind, powerful forces immediately come into play which return them to the pack. The second view argues that the accelerators or laggards are affected by forces which either send them further and further ahead, or cause them to fall further and further behind, at least for long periods of time. The first view embraces existence and stability and the assumption that the factors responsible for existence (and uniqueness) are largely independent of those responsible for stability, so that equilibria await patiently to be found. The second view rejects both the independence and, indeed, the equilibrium concepts themselves.

Another important landmark in Kaldor's intellectual development is his greatest theoretical paper, 'Speculation and Economic Stability' (1939) (his assessment as well as that of shrewd Kaldor watchers, for example, Hahn and Hicks). In it he analysed the behaviour of markets and economic systems in which stocks dominated flows in the determination of prices and the values of other economic variables and speculators' expectations about the expectations of other participants and their behaviour dominated the effects of underlying real economic variables in the determination of supplies and demands. Superimpose these ideas onto systems characterised by cumulative causation, either virtuous or vile, and the workings of the world look very different from those of the harmonious, equilibrating, long-period competitive systems underlying so many modern policy recommendations. There is good evidence that Kaldor's insights illuminate the workings of the foreign exchange markets, stockmarkets and property markets of the advanced capitalist economies of the past 20 years or more. There is not only the fact that speculative transactions have come to dominate the processes for long periods of time, but also that as they overlay a cumulative causation rather than an equilibrating process. they are likely to make fluctuations and instabilities much worse than they otherwise would have been. (Friedman's basic argument for the beneficial effects of speculation in a regime of floating exchange rates, as well as for the economic system itself, depended upon there being unique, stable, long-lasting, long-period equilibria out there to be found.)

Allied with Kaldor's stress on the process of cumulative causation is his analysis of the workings of competitive and non-competitive market structures and his method of looking for 'stylized facts' in need of explanation. In the Mattioli Lectures the 'stylized fact' that stand out most strikingly and in need of explanation – for the inferences of orthodox theory do not, Kaldor argues, predict them – is the extraordinary volatility of the prices of raw materials in recent times, especially of those materials which are argued to provide the real world counterparts of products with the appropriate characteristics to be traded in competitive markets, for example, wheat as foodstuffs, cotton or copper as industrial materials. He refers specifically to the role of dealers ('jobbers'), which is to equate flows of demand and supply by judicious use of price quotes and stock additions or run-downs. He does not think their job well done – 'these are the sectors with the least satisfactory features of capitalist market economies ... prices [go] regularly up and down like a yo-yo, even when the differences between the rates of production and consumption are relatively small' (Kaldor, 1996: 13). The source of instability is how weak a belief there is in a normal price based on 'normal' cost of production. Like Keynes and Arthur Okun, Kaldor always stressed the need for the establishment of 'norms' in order to give stability (if not optimality) to the workings of economic systems, the modern counterpart of the role which natural prices and prices of production respectively played in the classical and Marxian systems and normal prices and quantities played in Marshall's *Principles*.

IV

I mentioned that Kaldor was critical (as Stiglitz is too) of the application of AD to explanations of growth and distribution in capitalist (and now former so-called socialist) economies. Kaldor himself was much influenced by Marx and by Keynes (of *A Treatise on Money*, 1930, as well as by *The General Theory*, 1936). The influence of Marx on Kaldor was not with regard to the theory of value, on which Kaldor was more a pragmatic Marshallian together with his own kind of oligopolistic *cum* price-leadership theory of price, but with regard to Marx of the schemas of reproduction. Marx asked the question: What conditions must be fulfilled period by period, in order that both aggregate demand and aggregate supply, *and their respective compositions*, match? This is not the same thing as proposing a steady-state growth model – rates of growth could vary from period to period yet there still could be conditions which allowed aggregates and their compositions to match, see Sardoni (1981). Marx himself used three sectors (departments) – wage goods, capital goods and luxury goods – and set out the conditions which ensured that each could take in their own and the other sectors' washing. By establishing how special the conditions were, Marx highlighted the distinct possibility of imbalances resulting in instability and even crises in the real world. Kaldor follows the same strategy in these lectures but concentrates not on aggregate demand and supply within a closed capitalist economy, but on balances and sources of imbalance and their consequences as between rural areas and towns, as between primary products and industrial goods (where the former are associated with rural areas, the latter, with towns), extending this dichotomy to international trade and so, painting on a yet more broad canvas, to the growth of the world economy.

These commodity balances and imbalances may be thought of partly as the supply-side aspects of his story, in some ways analagous to Marx's sphere of production. The demand-side of the story emanates from Keynes's *Treatise on Money* and Kalecki's basic model of income distribution and the level of employment. It is more analogous to Marx's sphere of distribution and exchange, with the theory of effective demand made coherent and explicit. Initially, Kaldor (1955–56) used these ideas for his 'Keynesian' macro theory of distribution. This was a long-period theory and he assumed full employment of labour, so that the investment-saving nexus determined the distribution of income rather than the level of income and employment as in *The General Theory*. It is usefully thought of as asking how the *potential* surplus available in the sphere of production, itself the outcome of the conditions of work, past accumulation and the present state of the class war, whereby wage-earners working with existing equipment are able to produce more than their own wage goods, may be realised as an *actual* surplus by the forces of aggregate demand, in particular those parts of it which are exogenous to the production of wage goods. In Kaldor's model (in contrast to the classical and Marxian model), the accumulators get first bite of the cherry, and the residual is then available for the wage-earners, an unrealistically passive lot (until recently anyway).

If we think of a closed economy in which only wage – consumption – goods are produced, even if the wage-earners spend all their wages, wage-good producers as a class will at best cover their variable costs. (In the economy as a whole intermediate purchases of materials net out.) If wage-earners save – a point which Kaldor considers in the light of the rise in institutional saving in recent decades – not even this is so. Therefore, we need production and expenditure from elsewhere to create wages (and other incomes) to be spent on consumption goods and so provide a source for profit over and above wage costs. This insight is contained in the 'fundamental equations' of *A Treatise on Money*; it was spelt out by Kaldor in his writings of the 1950s and early 1960s. Kalecki independently and earlier than Kaldor produced a similar mechanism but without confining himself to either full employment or the long period. Given the level of investment, the productivity of labour in both the consumption goods and investment goods sectors and the mark-ups on costs used by businesspeople, there is a unique level of employment in the consumption goods trades which will allow the production of consumption goods for these wage-earners and for those in the investment goods sector. The economy will tend to settle at this level where there will be just enough profits created to allow saving to match investment. In Kaldor's version, given long-period full employment output, there is a unique distribution of that income which gives a share of saving from it to match the exogenously-given share of investment in income. (Though Kaldor refers continually in the text to saving financing investment, in the discussion of the lectures he makes explicit (on pp. 125–30) the vital importance of the banking system in providing finance to allow investment to occur in the first place, so to create the profits from which the saving may come.)

Kaldor originally used his approach to offer his solution to Harrod's problem. Harrod thought his central contribution was to find the instantaneous rate of growth of accumulation – his warranted rate of growth, g_w – which if implemented would, through the multiplier process, provide enough aggregate demand to match the ensuing aggregate supply so that, *after the event,* decision-makers would find that not only were their investment plans fulfilled, but also the plans themselves were justified by the rise in sales being what had been expected when the plans to enlarge capacity were made.

There was, of course, no reason why this particular value of g_w should coincide with the natural rate of growth, g_n. Kaldor showed that if we feed the value of I/Y_f which allows growth at g_n into his model, Π/Y_f would settle at the level which allows S/Y_f to equal I/Y_f, and so g_w to equal g_n. (I = investment, S = saving, Π = profits, Y_f = long-period, full employment income.) Thus a variable S/Y_f due to variations in the distribution of income does in Kaldor's model what variable K/L and K/Y ratios do in the Swan–Solow model.

Long before he came to give the Mattioli Lectures, though, Kaldor had ceased to be satisfied with these particular arguments. He now thought that the problems of steady growth arose, not from the saving–investment balance, but from the difficulty of keeping the growth of the availability of primary products in line with the growth of the absorptive capacity of the industrial sectors of the world. He argued that in essence, both the Keynesian and the neoclassical growth models were single-sector and so could not handle the basic *complementarity* of an integrated world. The latter required a multi-sector model to do it justice, to tackle the mutual interdependence of different sectors where the development of each depends on and is stimulated by the development of the others.

Kaldor sets out the characteristics of the traditional classification into primary, secondary and tertiary activities. The first are 'land-based' activities; the second are associated with transforming raw materials through long chains of processes in manufacturing industries; and the third sector takes in transport and the distribution of the products of the first two sectors as well as activities such as medical, educational and so on – services rendered by persons and not (primarily) through material products. Once a surplus emerges in agriculture or manufacturing, 'the engine of growth' may take off and provide major advances in human knowledge which are reflected in new products and industries and in transformed and enlarged preferences. Its productivity increases with the size of the market – a unique characteristic. It is, Kaldor stresses, hard to disentangle the prior changes in techniques which induce increased demand by making products relatively cheaper from the changes which occur because of the rising demand itself. Services use up an increasing proportion of resources but are characterised by low increases in productivity because their typical market structure results in excess capacity. With the exception of agriculture, imperfect or monopolistic competition are universal and this has far-reaching consequences for the mode of operation of markets. Prices are set by sellers not by market-making middlemen. Owing to economies of scale in manufacturing we tend to have 'competition amongst the few'; in the tertiary sector the strength of demand in the economy influences the number of companies which are viable by raising or lowering 'break-even' points.

V

Kaldor uses a simple two-sector model of agriculture and industry in order to bring 'to light aspects of the economic problems that tend to be neglected both in micro- and macro-economics' (Kaldor, 1996: 41). There is dual interpendence between the sectors, each being a market for the other's product and a supplier of the means necessary for the other's production. The industrial sector needs material inputs as its means of production and wage-goods – food – for its employees; the primary sector depends on the industrial sector for capital goods. Technical progress is 'land-saving' in agriculture. There is assumed to be a stream of innovations, the adoption of which requires additional investment for their realisation. The agricultural sector produces 'corn', industry, 'steel' (capital goods). Kaldor assumes a community with surplus labour, most of which is attached to agriculture, so that industry may hire workers in unlimited numbers at a wage in 'corn' sufficiently above real earnings in agriculture to induce whatever migration is required.

Both sectors accumulate capital by saving part of current income. In agriculture, saving requires a decision to refrain from consuming part of 'corn' output. The 'corn' thus released is sold on the market in exchange for the capital goods which the introduction of new accumulation requires. Its rate of accumulation is therefore determined by the amount of corn saved and the rate of exchange – terms of trade – between corn and steel. In industry, investment comes first, creating the profits from which saving then comes. Steel producers accumulate capital by retaining a proportion of their current output in order to expand their own capacity and sell the remainder on the market. Their costs consist of the payment of wages (fixed in corn) so that the total amount of corn sold by agriculture determines total employment. If steel output per worker is given, the total output of steel is given irrespective of the price of steel. Its minimum price is wl (where w is the wage in terms of corn and l is the labour requirement per unit of steel), below which no steel is produced. At prices above wl we have a relationship between the degree to which price exceeds costs and the proportion of steel reinvested, with the resulting profits being just sufficient to provide the saving to match the investment undertaken.

Kaldor has a neat diagram (1996: 44) which has the price of steel in terms of corn (p) on the vertical axis and the associated rate of growth of each sector (g) on the horizontal axis (Figure 23.1). The cheaper the agricultural sector can obtain steel the faster it can grow for a given saving ratio. Because of diminishing returns the g_A curve would shift inwards unless this is offset by 'land-saving' innovations which, *ceteris paribus*, shift it out. The g_I curve slopes upwards because the cheaper is corn, the more labour for making steel can the sector buy and the more of its own output it may invest, and so the faster it may grow.

The price is written as $p = wl(1 + \pi)$, where π is the mark-up. (The g_I curve shifts when either the real wage or labour productivity, $1/l$,

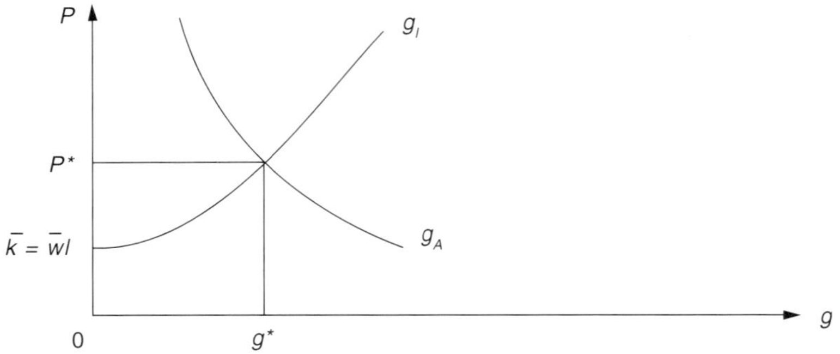

Figure 23.1

changes.) At the point, p^*, g^*, where the two curves intersect, we have rates of growth in both sectors and terms of trade between sectors which allow the supply and demand of agricultural and industrial goods to balance.

In telling the stability stories – convergence on the intersection of the two curves – Kaldor emphasises that the steel producers are quantity adjusters, acting so as to bring the growth in capacity in their sector in line with sales, whereas competition between agricultural producers tends to bring the price of corn in terms of steel to a point where the growth rates are equal and, more fundamentally, demand and supply match.

An important feature of the model is its dependence on the persistence of 'land-saving' innovations which in the model keeps the system growing at a constant rate as long as growth is not hampered by scarcity of labour *in the world as a whole*. Kaldor argues that we are nowhere near such a problem, that unemployment is a growing problem even though, he notes, the rate of growth of world population had passed its peak (when he wrote 13 years ago).

Kaldor then uses his model to illustrate the effects of 'labour-saving' innovations in steel (associated with Verdoorn's Law and the induced rise of the *rate* of growth of productivity in the economy as it grows), and to consider the destabilising effects of the inherent instability of both curves due to, for example, weather, a non-steady rate of technical innovations in both sectors and the different pricing behaviour as between the sectors.

Suppose we bring in money so that corn is sold for money which can be used to buy steel. We consider the effect of a new superior crop which shifts the g_A curve to the right by a 'large' amount. We suppose that the price of corn also falls by a 'large' amount because the market-making middlemen are unwilling to increase their commitments until the price falls to abnormally 'low' levels. Steel producers find their sales restricted by 'effective demand' and emerging surplus capacity unleashes a downward spiral which is both contractionary – investment plans are revised downwards – and deflationary.

If both corn and steel had had the same regime for marketing, this 'absurd' result would not have occurred because the price of one commodity could not have fallen so much as to reduce the producers' purchasing power over the other. The remedy is to reduce the large fluctuations in the prices of primary products by the use of buffer stock schemes, *not* to go back to market-determined prices for manufactures (as the modern world increasingly seems to have done, and to have been told to do so by economists). Buffer-stock schemes actually do what the market-making merchants are supposed to do. Kaldor points out that the great slump of 1929–32 had many of the features of his examples and concludes that: 'In a well-functioning world economy it is the availabilities of primary products which should set the limit to industrialisation – the expansion possibilities of which are limitless, or rather are only limited by demand – and not the other way round' (Kaldor, 1996: 54).

VI

When we come to the 1970s Kaldor discerns another set of causes of deep troubles which he discusses in his fourth lecture on the spatial aspects of the economic problem. He regards primary products as land-based commodities which are geographically spread while industrial activities are concentrated in urban areas, so that exchange between primary products and manufactures is also an exchange between the products of town and country. Industrial producers devote only a part, if any, of their activities to their own consumption. The greatest part is obtained by exchange. Agricultural producers could produce only for their own consumption while industrial producers can operate *only* in a social setting with activities dependent on demand from others through the market, their success or failure depending on the strength of this demand.

A typical Kaldorian generalisation and insight follows: that the world may be divided into relatively rich and relatively poor areas and that this is a matter of relatively recent occurrence, reflecting persistent differences in rates of growth over the past 2–3 centuries. The basic cause is neither differences in resource endowment nor a reward for virtuous thrifty behaviour (as opposed to spendthrift expenditure); rather it results from the process of industrialisation and its 'fall out' in terms of political and educational institutions. Industrial activities are not self-sustaining but depend upon demand for goods coming from outside the industrial sector, the ultimate causal factor which accounts for all other activities. It involves a sort of multiplier process. Industrial activities are concentrated in urban areas because of the growth of marketing activities and the social economies gained by division and subdivision of the making of articles into a number of separate operations (Kaldor (1996: 58) quotes a well-known passage from Allyn Young on this). He also mentions the advantage of having highly specialised workers in close proximity to one another together with small and specialised firms. He cites the Italian industrial districts (Kaldor always knew how to flatter a host) and Marshall's analysis of a similar phenomenon, engulfing the static and dynamic economies of large-scale production and the economies of large production.

The existence of increasing returns makes a great difference to the way markets develop and competition operates. With increasing returns, a rising market share means success, but a falling one – failure. In a growing market a business can never stand still, indeed it must grow if it is to survive (Kaldor, 1996: 64). Kaldor comments that only Marx fully recognised this in the nineteenth century – in neoclassical theory each firm has an optimum size so that the number of firms has to increase when the industry grows. So we move on to success meaning more success, failure meaning more failure – Gunnar Myrdal's 'principle of circular and cumulative causation' (Kaldor, 1996: 66).

Having earlier on (1996: 61) shown the very special circumstances in which free trade benefits all, Kaldor now argues that free trade in the field of manufacturing goods allied with the process of cumulative causation begets a process of polarisation which inhibits growth of such activities in some areas while concentrating them in others. In a nutshell this is what happened during the industrial and transport revolutions of the nineteenth century. He reviews the history of United Kingdom manufactures and their export and the role of tariffs when other countries industrialised. The successful ones were discriminating in their use of tariffs, as were Japan and then the NICs in the postwar period. The Latin American countries made indiscriminate use of them and the resulting costs of their products in terms of primary products made them too expensive to enter world markets successfully.

Thus Kaldor is led to the key role of export-led growth in successful development and to the ultimate constraint imposed by the value of the income elasticity of demand for imports. The balance of payments is seen as the effective constraint on growth, the rate of which will be higher, the greater is the value of the income elasticity of demand for exports and the lower is the value of its import counterpart, see also McCombie and Thirlwall (1994). Kaldor recognises that price elasticities are important for trade in traditional goods like textiles and shoes where the newly developed countries may copy the latest technical advances in other countries and have huge advantages because of the lower price of labour services. Kaldor quotes with approval Hufbauer's classification of 'low-wage' trade and 'technological-lead' trade (Kaldor, 1996: 69). But, in the large picture, it is incomes – quantities – not prices which are the basic clue to the nature of growth processes and the success or otherwise of development.

VII

Kaldor's last lecture is concerned with the policy implications of the current world situation (then the mid 1980s but not that different from the mid-1990s, say his editors). Kaldor starts with a nutshell description of the 'long boom' – 1948–73 – the most rapid, most widespread and most even growth ever recorded,[2] the strength of which was as unexpected as was its end in 1973. He contrasts what actually happened to growth – overall, food, manufactures – and productivity with what turned out to be the pessimistic predictions of even such a wise and seasoned a campaigner as the late Arthur Lewis. After 1973 the falls in rates of growth of developed countries were remarkably uniform and were accompanied by falls in rates of growth of productivity; the latter were blessings in disguise as unemployment rates, instead of being merely disgraceful, would have been catastrophic, for example, in the USA Kaldor argues they would have been over 20 per cent and in Europe three times as high as were actually experienced.

Why did the long boom last so long? Kaldor argues that sustained growth is only possible if the growth in primary products is in line with the requirements of industrial production. This does not imply that they must grow at the *same* rate (though this is an implication of Kaldor's little model. While he says that it is not an essential result I have not been able to see how *in his model* he could get any other, but see Thirlwall (1986).) In the real world, with the exception of oil, primary products grew at considerably lower rates than most of secondary and tertiary production as fabrication, transport and distribution took up a steadily growing proportion of the final price of the average commodity. These differentials were partly due to differences in pricing behaviour which is encapsulated by the effects of technical progress under the rubric of the 'Prebisch Effect' – the benefits are passed on in lower prices in primary products, but are retained as higher wages and profits by the producers of manufactured goods.

Up to the first oil shock in 1973, the terms of trade between primary products and manufactured products remained relatively stable. This was not due to flows but to the handling of surplus stocks by public agencies who first absorbed them at maintained prices, then, from the mid 1960s on, unloaded them via 'soft food loans' combined with enforced acreage restrictions in the developing countries. Raw material and energy flows kept pace with requirements until the end of the 1960s and prices were stabilised by strategic stockpiling. The 'long boom', Kaldor sums up, was due to continuous growth in demand for manufactured goods in all the main industrial countries and the consequent 'important "spill-over effects" on the growth of services in housing and construction, as well as on demand for primary products' (Kaldor, 1996: 76).

As far as the conscious contribution of the USA was concerned, it was not its fiscal policy (except in the Kennedy years) but its stress on institutional arrangements for restoring liberal capitalist systems – steady liberalisation of trade, reduction in tariff barriers, restoration of currency convertability (on current transactions) and generous financial aid from the USA itself and through the Bretton Woods institutions. In the UK, because of Keynes's lasting influence on the state budget, there was a deliberate effort to match overall demand to the expected growth of productive potential – but the policy-makers were too pessimistic about the latter, so that a golden opportunity was probably missed. France with its series of indicative five-year plans achieved a rate of growth of 5 per cent per annum. West Germany, Italy and Japan too were not driven by conscious fiscal policies but by strong rates of growth of their exports, rates of over 10 per cent per annum for nearly 20 years. This enabled Germany to absorb several million Germans expelled from East Germany and then a stream of 'guest workers' (sending them back when blips occurred), while France and Italy had substantial reserves of labour in their agricultural sectors.

Kaldor attributes a primary role to the US dollar as the *de facto* international reserve currency. The USA had unlimited borrowing power and its increasing deficits on 'basic transactions' gave other countries additional reserves. This allowed them to expand without hitting balance of payments constraints. Until 1971 the USA was in deficit almost every year, implying an addition to the demand for goods and services in the world outside. But the seeds of destruction were planted from the very beginning of the era. As countries obtained more and more dollars and the USA's official liabilities came to exceed its gold holdings by several times, countries became increasingly less willing to hold dollars, especially when the deficit assumed large dimensions during the war in Vietnam.

The Bretton Woods agreement collapsed in 1971 but the world economic system still continued to boom. Commodity prices rose as bad harvests in Russia and China and ensuing purchases emptied USA grain reserves for the first time in 40 years. Stocks of non-ferrous metals went down and their prices rose, not least because of speculative activity in commodities because of an assumption of general inflation, following the suspension of the convertability of the US dollar into gold. All these factors were reinforced by the sharp rise in the rate of increase of money-wages in industrialised countries from 1968–69 on, rupturing well-established 'norms' to which the stability of the various economic systems was anchored. Prices of manufactured goods rose at 5 per cent per annum from 1969 on.

The actions of OPEC at the end of 1973 started the era of stagflation. The change in the distribution of the incomes of the world that they implied and the inability of the OPEC countries to spend immediately their rise in incomes resulted in a huge contraction in world income. From 1980 on there was a new wave of recession, mainly confined to Western Europe. Kaldor blames Mrs Thatcher (as she then was) who came on stream (steam?) at much the same time as North Sea oil. Her monetarist policies produced a huge slump in manufacturing output (a fall of 15 per cent); they destroyed much of the UK's industry and required its oil revenues to be used more for paying the unemployed than to allow the required restructuring of the economy through imports of investment goods from other countries who would have bought North Sea oil.

Instead of which monetarism spread in the UK and in the USA – 'the incomes policy of Karl Marx' as Kaldor's contemporary, Thomas Balogh, had it, reversing the shift in economic, social and political power from capital to labour by recreating the reserve army of labour to try to control inflation. In effect, after the failure of monetarism, a failure which was generally acknowledged by the end of the 1980s, there emerged, in Kaldor's view, a complete paralysis of policy-making at the international level, while no one country (with the possible exceptions of USA now and the UK in 1981–82) could go it alone any more.

So Kaldor concludes by outlining the necessary policies for recovery, policies which would need worldwide agreement. First, there would need to be coordinated fiscal actions which used a set of balance-of-payments targets and 'full employment' budgets. (When Kaldor gave the Mattioli Lectures, most 'full employment' budgets were restrictive with government expenditure less than the taxation which would have been raised at the level of full employment, exactly the opposite of what was – is – required.) Kaldor regards trade liberalisation, even though it was a positive influence during the years of expansion, as a serious obstacle to recovery in a period of prolonged stagnation. Groups of countries need to set agreed import to export ratios and coordinate their overall policies if expansionary policies are not to be brought to a halt by balance-of-payments crises. Then there is no reason why full employment should not be restored through expansionary policies, preferably directed by the expansion of state investment in much needed social infrastructure.

Real interest rates should be brought down as fast as possible and as much as possible. (In the past 20 years or more we have had extended periods with real interest rates at levels which Keynes in his wildest dreams would not have thought any even remotely sensible government and central bank could have allowed.) If the USA will not agree to this, Kaldor suggests that European countries impose an interest equalisation tax to make it unattractive for their nationals to hold money in US dollar balances.

The most important requirement is to prevent the volatility of commodity prices. Kaldor would do this by creating buffer-stock schemes directly out of a newly created international currency acceptable to participating governments, just as SDRs were used then to settle claims. SDRs themselves should be issued to an international commodity corporation which would use them to pay for commodity purchases so that the cost of holding stocks would not fall on the taxpayers of such nations but be a 'backing' or 'cover' for a reserve currency convertible into national ones. Kaldor wanted the system to start gradually and when there were low prices and recessions so that it would be desirable and possible to stimulate future production and investment in an environment of stable prices. He would have us start with food grains and non-ferrous metals and gradually extend the net in order to bring in all sorts of commodities.

Like Keynes, Kaldor also seems to leave unresolved (unresolvable?) the chronic tendency for inflation to accelerate under full employment conditions. He attributes this mainly to the process of setting wages by collective bargaining agreements and he identifies three major objectives of wage-earners which are incompatible with one another: a desire to maintain relativities, a desire to have a 'fair' share of any increase in companies' profits and a reluctance to allow any encroachment on achieved standards of living due to unfavourable events which may be external. Because productivity increases at different rates as between industries and as between firms in the same industry, the second objective conflicts with the first so that money-wages tend to grow faster than effective productivity. Successful oligopolists compound this tendency by not cutting prices and by paying wages above normal market rates in order to try to secure good industrial relations for themselves. Kaldor cannot see any way out of this impasse short of a system of continuous consultation between social partners to secure social consensus concerning a 'fair' distribution of income, reasonably full employment and monetary stability. He cites certain periods in the postwar in Austria and West Germany as success stories of this nature.

This is rather a lame way for him to end. I was surprised he did not refer to the work of Wilfred Salter (1960, 1965) and Kalecki (1943) whereby adjusting nominal incomes for effective productivity *plus* prices greatly enhances the chances of economies establishing high productivity scenarios. These in turn offer real gains in return for money incomes restraint, so providing a chance to overcome the basic dilemma that Kalecki discerned in the difference between *getting* to full employment and *sustaining* it, see Harcourt (1997); chapter 19, this volume. I was also surprised that neither Kaldor nor Stiglitz advocated the use of some variant of the Tobin tax in order to dampen down the systemically harmful effects of speculation by Marshallian/Pigovian carrot and stick measures, see Harcourt (1995); chapter 18, this volume.

VIII

Let me close by sketching my suggestions under these two heads.

First, full employment without inflation: I returned to the writings of Salter and Eric Russell and combined their ideas with Kalecki's insight that the political economy of getting to full employment differs fundamentally from that of *sustaining* it. A major policy implication of Salter's 1960 and Russell's 1965 classics was that nominal incomes should be adjusted for effective productivity *plus* prices. Then low productivity, often declining industries would be knocked out quickly and high productivity, potentially expanding industries would be invested in and grow much faster than otherwise. The result would be that we would enter a new regime of a much higher growth of overall productivity. Real incomes would be able to grow at an agreeable (or more agreeable) rate, so offsetting the inflationary pressures associated with the change in the balance of power between employers and employees at sustained full employment. An acceptable *quid pro quo* could be offered in a fully employed economy for sustained money-incomes restraint, a *quid pro quo* which is unlikely, to say the least, to be forthcoming in a regime of flexible labour markets and enterprise bargaining.

I have stated all this *very* baldly – the ifs and buts and qualifications and doubts may be found in Harcourt (1997); chapter 19, this volume.

As to the control of the systemically harmful effects of speculation in those markets, the workings of which are dominated by it, especially the foreign exchange and property markets and the stock exchange, I suggested for the first market a generalisation of the Tobin tax. (I have to confess that I generalised it before I had actually heard and read of it.) Dealers in foreign exchange and those on whose behalf they dealt would have their turnovers classified into three categories for tax purposes: trade, investment and *prima facie*, a third residual category of speculation. The total rate of tax paid would then be determined by a weighted average of the tax rates corresponding to each category, the weights being the relative contributions to total turnovers of the three classifications. The speculation category would entail the imposition of a penal rate, the others, the imposition of more usual rates of taxation. So a Marshallian/Pigovian carrot and stick system would be used to encourage dealers and dealt with to indulge in systemically beneficial activities. The measures would have to be universal in scope to avoid offshore defeats of them – hence Kaldor's argument for the need for international cooperation and institutions to be revived or recreated. (Stiglitz told me that it would be hard to cope with derivatives within these proposals.)

I next suggested variants of this approach for both the stock exchange – people would be rewarded by lower tax rates for holding shares for longer periods (as Keynes suggested in *The General Theory*) – and property transactions would be exempted from penal rates of taxes (on both estate agents and vendors) only if housing purchases and sales could be shown to fall into socially acceptable categories, that is, to be genuine purchases or sales of housing services and not speculative buys or sells.

Well, I suppose you may say that pigs might fly, too. But if ideas akin to these are not floated by economists who have diagnosed systemic faults, we shall be doomed to endure situations of mass unemployment, increasing inequality of incomes and property, and worsening social relationships even in prosperous democratic countries such as Australia. I cannot believe that, with his humane values, Colin Clark would have this occur and I certainly cannot.

Notes

1. The first states that under certain conditions every competitive equilibrium is Pareto efficient – no one may be made better of without someone being made worse off. The second provides the conditions under which any Pareto-efficient allocation of resources may be obtained through market mechanisms, see Stiglitz (1996: 6–8).
2. John McCombie (22 May 1997) reminds me that Nicky may have been too sweeping at this point, that there were substantial disparities in the rates of growth of the advanced economies over this period.

References

Harcourt, G. C. (1995) *Capitalism, Socialism and Post-Keynesianism: Selected Essays of G. C. Harcourt* (Cheltenham, Glos: Edward Elgar), ch. 3; Chapter 18 this volume.

— (1997) 'Economic Policy, Accumulation and Productivity', in J. Michie and J. Grieve Smith *op. cit*; Chapter 19, this volume.
Hufbauer, G. C. (1966) *Synthetic Materials and the Theory of International Trade* (London: Duckworth).
Kaldor, N. (1934) 'A Classificatory Note on the Determinateness of Static Equilibrium', *Review of Economic Studies*, vol. 1, February, 122–36.
— (1939) 'Speculation and Economic Stability', *Review of Economic Studies*, vol. 7, October, 1–27.
— (1955–56) 'Alternative Theories of Distribution', *Review of Economic Studies*, vol. 23, 83–100.
— (1995) *Economics without Equilibrium* (Armonk, New York: M. E. Sharpe).
— (1996) *Causes of Growth and Stagnation in the World Economy* (Cambridge: Cambridge University Press).
Kalecki, M. (1943) 'Political Aspects of Full Employment', *Political Quarterly*, reprinted in Kalecki (1971), *op. cit.*
— (1971) *Selected Essays on the Dynamics of the Capitalist Economy 1933–1970* (Cambridge: Cambridge University Press).
Keynes, J. M. (1930) *A Treatise on Money*, 2 vols (London: Macmillan), C. W., Vols V, VI, 1972.
— (1936) *The General Theory of Employment, Interest and Money* (London: Macmillan), C. W., Vol VII, 1973.
McCombie, J. S. L. and A. P. Thirlwall (1994) *Economic Growth and the Balance of Payments Constraint* (London: Macmillan).
Michie, J. and J. Grieve Smith (eds) (1997) *Employment and Economic Performance: Jobs, Inflation and Growth* (Oxford: Oxford University Press).
Robinson, E. A. G. (ed.) (1965) *Problems in Economic Development* (London: Macmillan).
Russell, E. A. (1965) 'Wages Policy in Australia', *Australian Economic Papers*, vol. 4, 1–26.
Salter, W. E. G. (1960) *Productivity and Technical Change* (Cambridge: Cambridge University Press), 2nd edn, 1966.
— (1965) 'Productivity Growth and Accumulation as Historical Processes', in E. A. G. Robinson (1965), *op. cit.*, 266–91.
Sardoni, C. (1981) 'Multi-Sectoral Models of Balanced Growth and the Marxian Schemes of Expanded Reproduction', *Australian Economic Papers*, vol. 20, 383–97.
Stiglitz, J. E. (1996) *Whither Socialism?* (Cambridge, Mass.: The MIT Press), paperback.
Thirlwall, A. P. (1986) 'A General Model of Growth and Development on Kaldorian Lines', *Oxford Economic Papers*, vol. 38, 199–219.
Young, A. (1928) 'Increasing Returns and Economic Progress,' *Economic Journal*, vol. 38, 527–42.

24
The Vital Contributions of John Cornwall to Economic Theory and Policy: A Tribute from Two Admiring Friends on the Occasion of His 70th Birthday*

with Mehdi Monadjemi (M. M.)

Introduction

I first met John Cornwall in 1963 and M. M. was his doctoral student at Southern Illinois University from 1970 to 1972. John and I were on leave from our respective universities (Tufts and Adelaide) in Cambridge during the latter's most exciting decade of the postwar years. Ken Arrow and Bob Solow were both spending a year there, Solow to give the Alfred Marshall Lectures on two mythical creatures, 'Joan' and 'Nicky' (with only one of the real creatures, Joan, able to attend, as Nicky was in Australia). Frank Hahn and Robin Matthews were writing Hahn and Matthews (1964) and Piero Sraffa's (1960) book had only recently been published. The 'Secret Seminar' was in full flight and the members of the Faculty of Economics and Politics (which included the Department of Applied Economics) read almost like a *Who's Who* in modern economics, young and old. John and I saw a great deal of each other; I found John to be the nearest to an Australian an American was

*Originally published in Mark Setterfield (ed.), *Growth, Employment and Inflation. Essays in Honour of John Cornwall* (Basingstoke, Hants: Macmillan, 1999), 10–23.

ever likely to be! We had endless discussions on economics and other matters. John wrote a comment (entitled 'Wham') on the first draft of Hahn and Matthews's survey of growth theory, and advised me on the two-sector model which I was then developing (Harcourt, 1965), introducing me to the term 'recursive' to describe the method used in it.

M. M. met John at Southern Illinois University in Carbondale in 1970 as a graduate student in a seminar course in advanced macroeconomics. The course was offered in the autumn of 1970, its purpose being to generate ideas for graduate students to pursue in their doctoral dissertations. A dozen students enrolled, all enthusiastic to gain inspiration from the professor of economics newly appointed from Tufts University. Given his distinguished background – Cornwall had been a student of James Duesenberry's and he had published several articles in prestigious economic journals, such as the *American Economic Review*, the *Quarterly Journal of Economics (QJE)* and the *Review of Economics and Statistics* – they felt proud to be his students. John based the course on monetary transmission mechanisms, with particular emphasis placed on the countercyclical behaviour of housing in the United States. His approach was likely a result of his working at that time on Cornwall (1972), or else his observation of the two severe downturns in housing construction in the United States in 1966 and 1969. He introduced us to many leading articles in the area of housing cycles, although it became clear that no previous study had emphasised disintermediation as a prime cause of housing downturns, as did John (see Cornwall, 1972).

Because M. M. was so impressed by John's teaching and research leadership in the seminar course, he enthusiastically enrolled in another of his courses (on economic dynamics and growth) in the winter of 1971. So many students had become aware of Cornwall's reputation by then that the class was three times larger than the previous one. Almost all of the economics graduate students participated. John directed them towards many leading articles in growth theory including Harrod (1959) and Domar (1947), where for full employment of labour and capital to be maintained, output must grow at the warranted rate which, in turn, must equal the natural rate of growth. He also introduced them to several articles by Robert Solow, including Solow (1956, 1957, 1970), and also Denison's (1964) embodied technological growth model. During the semester, he referred to his conversations with Solow and discussed the neglected role of demand in neoclassical growth theories. This objection is still relevant and is still apparent in John's recent writings on growth (see Cornwall, 1970; Cornwall and Cornwall, 1994).

The remainder of this chapter is organised as follows: Cornwall's major intellectual contributions to M. M.'s economic thinking are discussed in the penultimate section, following my discussion of John's contributions to economic theory and policy.

Cornwall's growth schema

When John came to Cambridge in the autumn of 1963, he had more in common with the first generation of Keynesians – Austin and Joan Robinson, Richard Kahn, Nicky Kaldor, Dick Goodwin – than with the more neoclassical (though also Keynesian) economists either encamped or visiting – James Meade, Robin Matthews, Frank Hahn of the locals, Ken Arrow and Bob Solow of the visitors. He had just published his lead article in the *QJE*, 'Three Paths to Full Employment Growth' (1963), and was reading Alexander Lamfalussy's (1961) *Investment and Growth in Mature Economies*. The seeds of the first of his six (to date) great books were being planted (see Cornwall, 1972, 1977, 1983, 1990, 1994; Cornwall and Maclean, 1984).

In those days, Cornwall was an optimistic and enthusiastic Keynesian as far as his theoretical structures were concerned. (Another great influence was his PhD supervisor at Harvard, James Duesenberry, especially the approach which Duesenberry took to growth and cycle theory. To John, Duesenberry 'was the first economist [he] had known who understood the need for economic theory to have explanatory power' (Cornwall, 1992: 98)). He was also vitally interested in the long-term historical episodes of modern capitalist economies, the formation of institutions and their role in the political economy of societies. His polities were left-wing by any standards and remarkably so by those of the USA – he and Arrow were doves on the Vietnam War, for example – whilst the need for conscious intervention by the state in economic life was never a stumbling block for John, either then or now. He was (and remains) a vigorous democrat who hated injustice and underprivilege and who wished to see them eliminated, especially if they arose from needless malfunctionings of the economic system.

John was keenly interested in but also most critical of growth theory, both Keynesian and neoclassical alike. His starting point was a profound critique of Harrod's basic approach, which implied that the warranted and natural rates of growth, g_w and g_n respectively, could be analysed as though their values were independent of each other – as though the factors responsible for one were entirely, or at least overwhelmingly, separate from those responsible for the other. John regarded this as an incorrect extension of the Marshallian distinction between demand and supply and of the factors responsible for them to the analysis of the economy as a whole. How can it be argued that g_n is independent of g_w (and vice versa)? For surely the potential rate of growth of the economy due to the growth of the labour force and of its efficiency due to technical advances (neutral or biased) cannot be regarded as independent of the demand factors subsumed in g_w? The rate of growth of potential productivity is directly dependent on the rate at which new things are embodied by investment in the stock of capital goods (and, now increasingly, in the stock of human capital as well). That is to say, it is dependent on effective demand and the rate of accumulation, the latter either being equal to g_w, or related to it in the sense that the ways in which rates of actual accumulation move depend upon their relationships (and those of planned accumulation) to g_w itself.

So growth in a Keynesian setting has to be seen at the very least as the outcome of the interrelationships of the supply and demand factors underlying g_w and g_n, taking into account the considerable overlap involved, especially in the direction $g_w \rightarrow g_n$, though Cornwall initially stressed the relative strength of $g_n \rightarrow g_w$, in a system of some mutual determination. Hence g_n itself can affect expectations and therefore whether or not actual growth equals g_w. John's approach to the theory of growth was always to proceed from this basic foundation, one which leads immediately to path-dependent processes and the notion of cyclical growth (in the sense of Goodwin) rather than to steady-state growth (separate from the cycle) in the sense of the Keynesians, or the pure neoclassicals or even the neoclassical Keynesians, such as Meade, Solow and Swan.[1]

Another of John's criticisms of conventional growth theory concerned its neglect in any but the most mechanical sense of technical progress. Repeatedly we find him arguing that in the real world, technical advances and demand changes leading to the need for large structural changes in economies are so rapid that models which concentrate on the properties of the ultimate steady-state equilibria on which the model economies converge (if they do) have little relevance. This is because the calendar time required for this convergence process is so much greater than the calendar time necessary for changes in technical knowledge (and their application) and in tastes and demand to occur. The latter are often induced through advertising and other devices. John was also critical of the almost universal use of perfectly competitive microeconomic market structures in growth theory. These points of view made him, on the one hand, as critical of Joan Robinson's and Richard Kahn's Golden Age analysis as of the Solow/Swan model and, on the other, partial to Kaldor who, while he thought of steady growth as a 'stylized fact', was nevertheless always impatient to have his models apply directly to real-world situations. John's approach rejected the strategy of Joan Robinson, Kahn and also Pasinetti of going through the preliminary stage of Golden Age analysis in order to get various key relationships clear and concepts defined in the simplest but also the most abstract setting.

Phases of capitalism

With this theoretical approach, John set about interpreting the various phases of the history of capitalism, using the OECD countries as his laboratory and extending and modifying his basic models as postwar capitalism moved through its 'Golden Age' – the 'long boom', as the Marxists called it – to the unstable 'stagflation' era and now to the most recent phase of relative stagnation (when compared to the mostly remarkable performances of economies during the 'long boom') and inflation rates near or at the 'Golden Age' values. At each stage, Cornwall has identified both the strengths and weaknesses of the economy, distinguishing between transient characteristics and those likely to last. He has also identified the presence of contradictions, whether inherent in the workings of the systems themselves, or resulting from faulty diagnosis by policy-makers or the deliberate designs of the dominant classes in society. John has always robustly, even brutally, called spades spades!

In recent years, Cornwall has become increasingly gloomy about the possibility of implementing sensible and enlightened policies in the advanced capitalist economies whether they act alone or together (which he now sees as necessary if not sufficient if these economies are to overcome their individual and collective problems). The problem is not so much one of diagnosis, though this is a serious problem in its own right, but lack of political courage, wisdom and goodwill in political decision-making centres. John remains faithful to Keynes – to his economic analysis, views on the educational role of economists, and on the role of the state and its public servants, whose motivation may be summed up in Harrod's (1951: 183, 192–3) phrase, 'the presuppositions of Harvey Road'. This last referred to the class of intelligent, well-trained and disinterested persons who analysed situations, gave advice, and were driven by a desire to make their societies more rational, fair and humane rather than to maximise their incomes or status (though the latter often occurred if they were good at their jobs).

Having made coherent and explicit the sources of the strengths and weaknesses of the years of the 'long boom', John turned to the subsequent phases. There he identified at least two major factors at work: first, the increasing dominance of the Keynesians by the monetarists, and then, the new classical macroeconomists, that is to say, the return to dominance of those whom Keynes dubbed the classical economists in the provision of explanation and policy. In particular, this implied a resurgence of the view that a capitalist economy is strongly self-regulating provided only that competitive institutions rule in all its markets and activities – and especially in its labour markets. Large domestic monopolies or oligopolies are but the powerless price-takers of the competitive model when set in the world scene, according to Milton Friedman who, at the same time, would cheerfully smash a labour union whenever he saw one.

Second, John identified as a major issue the implementation of the recommendations of the McCracken Report (1977), the authors of which were mostly pragmatic Keynesians who were turning their attention to the emergence of inflationary pressures. The latter were associated with the profound sociological changes that had taken place over the course of the 'long boom', whereby the balance of political, social and economic power had moved progressively from capital to labour (with the leaders of labour itself becoming the most articulate, educated and confident set in history); the breakdown of the Bretton Woods institutions and 'rules of the game'; the financing of the war in Vietnam in the USA as though the US economy were a peacetime one; and the first oil shock.

Cornwall singled out for detailed criticism the McCracken strategy of a short sharp shock to the system – read: quickly create high levels of unemployment – to rid it once and for all of inflationary expectations, coupled with the belief that the system would then move back to the full employment trend rate of growth of the Golden Age with (early) Golden Age rates of inflation. John could not accept this analysis because he felt that it lacked a proper understanding of the behaviour of the labour market and of the behaviour of businesspeople in general. He attributed much of the successful performance in the early to middle years of the 'long boom' to the behaviour of labour itself. In many of the OECD economies, labour voluntarily imposed self-restraint on money-wage increases. This allowed notions of 'fairness' with regard to increases in real wages and patterns of wage relativities to be met by the underlying growth in productivity, redistributions through taxes and expenditure in the public sector, and full employment itself. (Not all OECD countries were so blessed: John distinguishes two main models, the one described above which he calls 'a social bargain strategy' (Cornwall, 1997: 400), the other 'a market power strategy' (Cornwall, 1997: 399). In the latter, wage settlements are the outcome of a collective bargaining process in which little account is taken of common interest or national goals.)

John also believed that the relatively fixed exchange rate regimes operating in the years of the 'long boom' and especially the controls on capital movements kept speculation in check and allowed any deficits in the balance of payments, themselves not alarmingly large in those countries which experienced them, to be addressed without resort to unduly drastic retrenchment policies.

Institutional change and economic breakdown

The happy conjunction of events and results that characterised the 'Golden Age' unravelled during the next twenty years or so. Well-established norms were ruptured towards the end of the period, labour generally became more militant and strove for maximum gains from the money-wage bargain regardless of the systemic outcome, and disillusionment with 'big government' became increasingly widespread both within and between countries. John analyses what he dubs the systemic 'inflationary bias' which emerged as the 'Golden Age' progressed. This is associated with real wage resistance and the 'fair' pattern of wage relativities, neither of which would be surrendered in the event of an exogenous shock to the system – oil price rises, for example, or secular changes in the terms of trade which necessitate real income adjustments. He feels that attempts to rid the economy of its inflationary tendencies by contracting demand are doomed to failure because whatever short-term success they may have will not be maintained. This is partly (but importantly) because contraction has a negative impact on the rate of accumulation which in turn affects the rate of growth of productivity. When the upturn, either natural or policy-induced, occurs, there is not a high enough rate of growth of productivity to meet the renewed money-wage demands without the resurgence of inflation, especially as wage-earners aim at increases in real wages which embody a catch-up element. Cornwall, like Marx and Keynes, appreciates that the processes at work in capitalism often imply basic contradictions, that the measures taken to get labour and its costs under control (the euphemism is flexible labour markets) adversely affect the 'animal spirits' and so the desire of capitalists to invest. Those in the real world, as opposed to the mathematical models of it, know that reviving 'animal spirits' after a policy-induced shock is an incredibly difficult task to perform quickly, or even at all. This is especially so when financial capital dominates industrial and commercial capital, so that the rewards for risk-taking appear, and often are, much greater and more obvious in the former's sphere than in the latter's. As a result, long-term real investment projects associated with much-needed structural change are increasingly neglected, not least because the brightest (if not necessarily the best) are attracted to the huge rewards from finance capital.

These destabilising elements have been reinforced by other institutional changes, especially the floating of exchange rates and the deregulation of financial markets, together with the huge technical advances which have tended to make at least the financial aspects of the operations of capitalism 'one-world capitalism'. Devaluations are likely to be ineffective, partly because of real wage resistance, partly because of the huge rise in the proportions of total foreign exchange transactions accounted for by speculative transactions. This leads to one-way speculative-induced movements of currencies which greatly affect the domestic cost of living (through increases in the prices of imports, importables and exportables) in the countries concerned. John may be inclined to revise this generalisation a little following the recent British experience. In autumn 1992 the UK was forced to leave the European Exchange Rate Mechanism and, as a consequence, experienced the devaluation which many British Keynesians were advocating. The then Tory government ridiculed their suggestion until it was forced upon them. They then attributed the beneficial results of the devaluation, including the absence of the offsetting reactions which John had predicted, to their own coherent, explicit policy wisdom.[2]

Increasingly, John has been adopting a hysteresis analysis of labour markets, combined with a critique of the usefulness of the concept of the natural rate/NAIRU. He rejects the first variant because he does not accept that the world may be thought of as a competitive Walrasian general equilibrium system in the way in which that fine Marshallian scholar, Milton Friedman, first defined the natural rate, so that the latter was a resting place without any involuntary unemployment present. John is, of course, willing to concede that in any situation-specific episode, there could be a level of statistical unemployment (or indeed levels) at which the forces making for accelerating price rises would be offset by those making prices go in the other direction, resulting in a sustainable constant rate of change of prices.[3] However, he is not willing to admit that such a position has any optimum or necessarily desirable properties – much less, that it would be free of undesirable, unacceptable levels of involuntary unemployment and worsening distributions of income and property. He also criticises those who come some way to meet him by admitting that not all unemployment at the NAIRU is voluntary, only to claim that, nevertheless, it is all classical, associated with 'too high' real wages rather than a lack of effective demand. Indeed, he believes that real wages can never be too high because they are set in the product market (except in the unlikely case where the labour force is governed by one big monopoly union).

Financial disintermediation and the housing cycle

M. M.'s main encounter with John Cornwall was when he agreed to be his dissertation supervisor. It was an honour to be able to write a dissertation under his supervision. The problem of choosing an appropriate topic was quickly resolved when John suggested an empirical study of postwar housing cycles in the United States, using quarterly flow of funds data. He stressed the use of quarterly data because annual data are incapable of showing the turning points of households' portfolio substitution and mortgage flows during short cycles. John strongly supported the idea of housing-led recovery, a view that is now dominant in industrial countries with developed financial sectors.

Many studies in the 1960s (such as Albert, 1962; Guttentag, 1961; Maisel, 1963; Sparks, 1967) attempted to provide theoretical explanations for the postwar housing cycles in the United States. John's explanation departed from these studies, however, by taking account of 'the portfolio adjustments undertaken by the household sector in response to changes in different yield differentials' (Cornwall, 1972: 185) and emphasising the supply of funds and the process of disintermediation as a primary cause of housing cycles (Cornwall, 1972: 173–201). He argued that most of the liabilities of thrift institutions (TIs) (savings and loan associations and mutual savings banks) are held by households. Furthermore, during the 1960s and 1970s, 75 per cent of total residential mortgage flows were, on average, accounted for by TIs. Naturally, any significant change in the liabilities of TIs would produce a substantial change in total mortgage flows and residential construction expenditure. John stressed the process of 'disintermediation' as a major cause of downturns in the housing market. In fact the word 'disintermediation' was introduced in the financial literature during the so-called credit crunch of 1966, when all of the financial intermediaries in the United States experienced an unusual loss of deposits to the capital market. The main cause of disintermediation is a rise in the rates on capital market instruments relative to the rates paid by financial intermediaries on their deposits. This change in the yield differential provides an incentive for households and other depositors at financial intermediaries to reduce or withdraw their funds and place them directly on the market. In the 1960s, the widening of the yield spread between securities and deposits was mainly due to the inflexibility of the rates paid on deposits. This rigidity was in turn due to the long-term nature of the assets held by the intermediaries which caused a slow turnover of their portfolio. At a time when market rates were rising, if these institutions had attempted to increase their deposits and match the increase with an increase in rates on their assets, the higher rates on deposits would have applied to all deposits, whereas the higher rates on assets applied only to newly acquired assets, which were a fraction of total deposits.

At the time, mortgage rates in the United States were fixed for the life of the mortgage. During tight money periods, the yield spread between capital market instruments and deposits widened and the flow of deposits into financial intermediaries declined. This process of disintermediation in turn affects mortgage lending and expenditure on housing. The most severe bout of disintermediation occurred during the unusually tight money period of 1966, when all financial intermediaries experienced a drastic loss of deposits to the capital market. This development forced financial intermediaries to reduce their mortgage lending and was soon followed by a sharp decline in residential construction expenditures. Similar and equally severe developments occurred during 1969. In short, John argued that 'thrift institutions are an important source of construction loans to tract builders. If the flow of funds into these thrift institutions is cut back, as it would be in a process of disintermediation, mortgage lending and housing must be affected, unless other lenders make up for the cutback in mortgage lending by thrift institutions' (Cornwall, 1972: 116).

The title of M. M's dissertation, which involved a theoretical and empirical analysis of housing cycles in the United States during the postwar period, was 'Savings Deposits, Residential Mortgage Credit, and Housing Starts'. Guided by John, the theoretical part of the study emphasised household portfolio adjustments and the consequent effects of these adjustments on mortgage flows and housing expenditure. The empirical analysis employed quarterly flow of funds data, which was relatively new at the time, building an econometric model for TIs' savings deposits and mortgage flows. John also suggested that the dynamic properties of the model would shed some light on the countercyclical behaviour of residential construction during the postwar period.

Most of the studies from the 1960s that attempt to explain the countercyclical behaviour of housing assume that the demand for commercial credit is sensitive to changes in aggregate economic activities, but relatively insensitive to the cost of funds, whereas the demand for mortgage credit is sensitive to the terms of credit but relatively stable with respect to changes in economic activities. Moreover, lenders have a high cross-elasticity of demand for mortgages with respect to bond yields. Based on these assumptions, changes in aggregate economic activities create forces which cause mortgage flows and residential construction to move countercyclically. John remarked

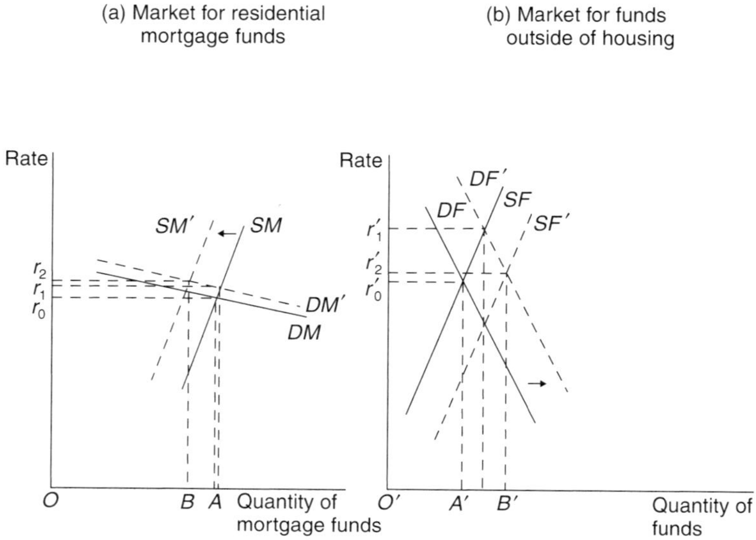

Figure 24.1 The market for residential mortgage and non-housing funds

on the need to provide some form of analytical explanation for the countercyclical behaviour of housing. Figure 24.1, an extract from M. M's dissertation, summarises his response to John's suggestion.

In Figure 24.1, *DM* and *SM* are the demand for and supply of residential mortgage funds and Or_0 and *OA* are the initial equilibrium mortgage rate and quantity of mortgage funds, respectively, *DF* and *SF* are the demand for and supply of non-housing funds and $O'r'_0$ and $O'A'$ are the initial equilibrium bond yield and quantity of funds respectively. As aggregate economic activity increases, *DF* shifts to the right more than *DM*, hence bond yields rise relative to mortgage rates, that is, $r'_0r'_1 > r'_0r_1$. Given lenders' high cross-elasticity of demand for mortgages with respect to bond yields, they shift from mortgages to bonds, hence *SF* shift to *SF'* and *SM* shift to *SM'*, and the supply of mortgage credit declines. This causes the mortgage rate to rise to Or_2 and with a highly elastic demand for mortgage funds, the quantity of mortgages demanded falls, $OB < OA$. On the other hand, the equilibrium quantity of non-housing funds expands, that is, $O'B' > O'A'$. When economic activity decreases, the opposite movements take place and the equilibrium quantity of mortgage funds demanded and supplied increases.

Cornwall (1972: 117–18) argues that

> During the boom, as the demand for loanable funds begins to outstrip the supply, interest rates, especially those on primary securities, begin to rise absolutely and relative to rates paid on fixed-price near monies. This induces the non-financial domestic holders of funds to bypass financial intermediaries, and to place them directly in the capital markets.

Anderson (1964) shows that in the tight money periods of 1953, 1957 and 1959, the inflow of deposits into the Boston mutual savings banks were at their lowest levels, whilst outflows in the form of withdrawals were at their highest levels. A similar type of development was experienced by savings and loan associations when, from 1960 to 1968, their inflow of deposits declined by 1.8 per cent.

M. M's supervisor wanted to see an econometric study of housing cycles emphasising changes in the flow of funds as a source of instability in the housing market. Sparks (1967) comes close to adopting this approach. His study places heavy emphasis on the mortgage market and the flow of savings deposits at the financial intermediaries. Sparks's regression results may be criticised, however, for estimating the supply of mortgage credit without using a mortgage rate in the equation. It is difficult to interpret Sparks's regression as a supply function, because it is neither a reduced form model nor a true supply function which should include a mortgage rate. Sparks's study can also be criticised for using annual data. John encouraged M. M to use quarterly data to explain households' responses to changes in capital market conditions and the effect of such changes on mortgage lending. The response of savings deposits to changes in the market rate of interest is so quick that low-frequency data may fail to indicate these responses.

The main object of M. M's dissertation was to develop an econometric model capable of testing the hypothesis proposed in Cornwall (1972), that fluctuations in residential construction are largely explained by changes in the flow of funds at thrift institutions. The model consisted of an equation for changes in household holdings of savings deposits at the TIs, and a simultaneous equation model for the mortgage market consisting of a demand and a supply function. The statistical results, based on quarterly data from 1953 to 1970, produced a statistically significant coefficient for the yield spread between the savings rate and the corporate bond rate in the equation for savings deposits. Furthermore, simulation experiments indicated that changes in interest rates lead to changes in mortgage flows and housing cycles ahead of cycles in economic activity, and in particular that changes in the yield differential between TIs' deposit rates and corporate bond rates in recession and boom periods are consistent with the countercyclical behaviour of mortgage flows at thrift institutions. In short, M. M's dissertation showed that the salient role played by TIs in conjunction with the inflexibility of savings deposit rates account for the countercyclicality of the housing market – precisely the view that is maintained in Cornwall (1972).

It is interesting that widespread bankruptcy among major mortgage lenders during the early 1980s has been attributed to the substantial disintermediation that occurred during this period. From 1980 to 1986, about 600 out of 4000 TIs failed (Brumhaugh, Carron and Litan, 1989). Brumhaugh and Carron (1987) blame regulatory constraints and the inability of TIs to adapt to rising interest rates for the crises of 1980s, drawing renewed attention to a point first emphasized in Cornwall (1972). It seems that John's perceptive conjectures during the 1960s and 1970s were all too amply confirmed by the experience of the 1980s.

Conclusion

John has always had a fiercely independent mind; he was scornful of the mainstream equilibrium economics which dominated the courses when he first became an economist.[4] As he reveals in his fascinating autobiography in Arestis and Sawyer (1992), he approached economics by reading widely in the originals of his own and other disciplines, ultimately developing an approach that has embraced the dynamic analysis of growth and distribution, historical knowledge and an awareness of how institutions form, change and affect economic processes. To read his books – again, as an independent free spirit, he has resisted the fashionable cringe to the natural scientists' approach of only publishing articles – and see his views evolve as concrete situations change is both a privilege and an inspiration to his friends and admirers, M. M and I amongst them. So happy 70th birthday,

John, and here's to many more birthdays, appropriately interspersed with your enlightening and courageous writings.

Notes

1. It is significant that Solow (1994: 379) has recently stated his agreement with this view (even though those who followed his initial lead have usually missed the point entirely).
2. In a comment on a draft of this essay John wrote: 'What I maintained in the 1990 and 1994 books was that devaluations *accompanied by AD policies aimed at achieving full employment* would fail, because the devaluations would be offset by speculation and real wage resistance. The 1992 devaluation worked because, unlike Mitterand's efforts in the early 1980s, it was not accompanied by strong stimulative AD policies' (emphasis in original).
3. Indeed, he stresses that many such positions may exist at any given point in time. This claim is important because it makes Cornwall's long-run Phillips curve (LRPC) negatively sloping, not vertical. All of the points along this negatively-sloping LRPC involve stable inflation, with the realised outcome depending on aggregate demand and the policies that affect it. The entire structure is then subject to hysteresis effects, as movements along the LRPC can also result in shifts in the position of the LRPC itself.
4. John suggests that his response was based on measured argument rather than scorn, but M. M and I think he combined both!

References

Albert, W. W. (1962) 'Business Cycles, Residential Construction Cycles, and the Mortgage Market', *Journal of Political Economy*, vol. 70, 263–81.

Anderson, P. (1964) 'Mutual Savings Banks and Tight Money', *New England Business Review*, January, 10–11.

Arestis, P. and M. Sawyer (eds) (1992) *A Biographical Dictionary of Dissenting Economists* (Aldershot: Edward Elgar).

Brumhaugh Jr, D. and A. Carron (1987) 'Thrift Industry Crises: Causes and Solutions', *Brookings Papers on Economic Activity*, no. 2, 349–455.

Brumhaugh Jr., D., A. Carron and R. Litan (1989) 'Cleaning up the Depository Institution Mess', *Brookings Papers on Economic Activity*, no. 1, 243–83.

Cornwall, J. (1963) 'Three Paths to Full Employment Growth', *Quarterly Journal of Economics*, vol. 77, 1–25.

— (1970) 'The Role of Demand and Investment in Long-term Growth', *Quarterly Journal of Economics*, vol, 84, 48–69.

— (1972) *Growth and Stability in a Mature Economy* (London: Martin Robertson).

— (1977) *Modern Capitalism: Its Growth and Transformation* (London: Martin Robertson).

— (1983) *The Conditions for Economic Recovery: A Post-Keynesian Analysis* (London: Martin Robertson).

— (1990) *The Theory of Economic Breakdown: An Institutional-Analytical Approach* (Oxford: Basil Blackwell).

— (1992) 'John Cornwall (born 1928)', in P. Arestis and M. Sawyer (eds), *op. cit.*, 97–102.
— (1994) *Economic Breakdown and Recovery: Theory and Policy* (Armonk, NY: M. E. Sharpe).
— (1997) 'Notes on the Trade Cycle and Social Philosophy in a Post-Keynesian World', in G. C. Harcourt and P. A. Riach (eds), *op. cit.*
— and W. Cornwall (1994) 'Growth Theory and Economic Structure', *Economica*, vol. 61, 237–51.
— and W. Maclean (1984) *Economic Recovery for Canada* (Toronto: James Lorimer).
Denison, E. F. (1964) 'The Unimportance of the Embodied Question', *American Economic Review*, vol. 54, 90–4.
Domar, E. D. (1947) 'Expansion and Employment', *American Economic Review*, vol. 37, 34–55.
Guttentag, J. (1961) 'The Short Cycle in Residential Construction, 1946–59', *American Economic Review*, vol. 51, 275–98.
Hahn, F. H. and R. C. O. Matthews (1964) 'The Theory of Economic Growth: A Survey', *Economic Journal*, vol. 74, 779–902.
Harcourt, G. C. (1965) 'A Two-Sector Model of the Distribution of Income and the Level of Employment in the Short Run', *Economic Record*, vol. 41, 103–17.
— and P. A. Riach (eds) (1997) *A 'Second Edition' of The General Theory*, 2 vols (London: Routledge).
Harrod, R. F. (1951) *The Life of John Maynard Keynes* (London: Macmillan).
— (1959) 'Domar and Dynamic Economics', *Economic Journal*, vol. 69, 451–64.
Lamfalussy, A. (1961) *Investment and Growth in Mature Economies*; (New York: Macmillan).
McCracken P., G. Carli and H. Giersch (1977) *Towards Full Employment and Price Stability* (Paris: OECD).
Maisel, S. J. (1963) 'A Theory of Fluctuations in Residential Construction Starts', *American Economic Review*, vol. 53, 359–83.
Monadjemi, M. (1972) 'Savings Deposits, Residential Mortgage Credit, and Housing Starts', unpublished PhD dissertation, Department of Economics, Southern Illinois University.
Pasinetti, L. L. and R. M. Solow (eds) (1994) *Economic Growth and the Structure of Long-Term Development* (London: Macmillan).
Solow, R. M. (1956) 'A Contribution to the Theory of Economic Growth', *Quarterly Journal of Economics*, vol. 70, 65–94.
— (1957) 'Technical Change and the Aggregate Production Function', *Review of Economics and Statistics*, vol. 39, 312–20.
— (1970) *Growth Theory* (Oxford: Oxford University Press).
— (1994) 'Concluding Comments', in L. L. Pasinetti and R. M. Solow (eds), *op. cit.*, 376–9.
Sparks, G. R. (1967) 'An Econometric Analysis of the Role of Financial Intermediaries in Postwar Residential Building Cycles', *Determinants of Investment Behavior* (New York: National Bureau of Economic Research).
Sraffa, P. (1960) *Production of Commodities by Means of Commodities. Prelude to a Critique of Economic Theory* (Cambridge: Cambridge University Press).

Index